Islamic Legal Orthodoxy

Frontispiece. Leiden MS fol. 150a.

The colophon of *Nūr al-ḥaqīqah wa-nawr al-ḥadīqah* ("The Light of Truth and the Blossoms of Paradise"), completed on 12 Dhū 'l-Qa'dah 945/1 April 1539 and dedicated to the Ottoman sultan Suleiman, where the Twelver Shiite jurist Ḥusayn b. 'Abd al-Ṣamad al-'Āmilī (d. 984/1576) signs his name "husayn b. 'Abd al-Ṣamad *al-Shāfi'ī* al-Ḥārithī al-Hamdānī." Reproduced by kind permission of Leiden University Library.

Islamic Legal Orthodoxy

Twelver Shiite Responses to the Sunni Legal System

DEVIN J. STEWART

THE UNIVERSITY OF UTAH PRESS

SALT LAKE CITY

Library of Congress Cataloging-in-Publication Data

Stewart, Devin J.
Islamic legal orthodoxy : Twelver Shiite Responses to the Sunni Legal System / Devin J. Stewart.
p. cm.
ISBN 0-87480-551-1 (alk. paper)
1. Islamic law—History. 2. Sunnites. 3. Shiites. 4. Authority—Religious aspects—Islam—History. I. Title.
LAW
340.5'9'09—dc21 98-16874

For my parents

Contents

Conventions

Transliteration of Arabic is according to the system of the Library of Congress; the *tāʾ marbūṭah* is indicated with an "h." In isolated words, phrases, and book titles, case endings and elisions are not represented, and the definite article is given as "al-," even with sun letters. In connected prose, a closer phonetic transcription is followed.

A number of frequently cited terms are not given in transliterated forms; these include Koran, hadith, Shiite, Imami, and others.

Abbreviations

BRISMES	*Bulletin of the British Society for Middle Eastern Studies*
BSOAS	*Bulletin of the School of Oriental and African Studies*
GAL	Carl Brockelmann, *Geschichte der arabischen Litteratur*
GAS	Fuat Sezgin, *Geschichte des arabischen Schrifttums*
EI^1	*Encyclopaedia of Islam*, 1st ed.
EI^2	*Encyclopaedia of Islam*, new ed.
IJMES	*International Journal of Middle East Studies*
JAOS	*Journal of the AmericanOriental Society*

I

Introduction

The ninth, tenth, and eleventh centuries witnessed the rise and consolidation of the classical Sunni legal *madhhabs*, generally termed "schools of law" in Western scholarship on Islam. As is well known, in this process four *madhhabs*, the Ḥanafī, Mālikī, Shāfiʿī, and Ḥanbalī, came to be accepted as standard, with recognized legal traditions going back, at least in theory, to their eponymous founders, Abū Ḥanīfah, Mālik, al-Shāfiʿī, and Aḥmad b. Ḥanbal, jurists of the eighth and ninth centuries. Other legal traditions that arose during this period, such as the Ẓāhirī and Jarīrī *madhhabs*, were weeded out during this process of consolidation, and had died out by the end of the eleventh century. The consolidation of the *madhhabs* went hand in hand with the jurists' establishment of dominance over Islamic religious discourse and institutions. They made strong arguments for their exclusive religious authority, particularly at the expense of the authority of theologians, hadith experts, and the caliphs. The jurists used the institution of the *madhhab* as a means to establish their exclusivity and theoretical autonomy from outside powers, such as the rulers and the caliphs. In order for a Muslim to attain a position of religious authority and to voice recognized opinions on religious topics, he had to complete a legal education in one of the recognized *madhhabs* and gain acceptance by master jurists as a qualified legal scholar. With the establishment of mosque-hostel (*masjid-khān*) complexes in the tenth century and *madrasahs*, endowed colleges of law, in the eleventh, the jurists established control over Islamic educational institutions, which regularly excluded the natural and philosophical sciences and ensured the law its pride of place among the Islamic sciences.[1]

1. See George Makdisi, *The Rise of Colleges* (Edinburgh: Edinburgh University Press, 1981); idem, *The Rise of Humanism in Classical Islam and the Christian West* (Edinburgh: Edinburgh University Press, 1990), 1–59; Christopher Melchert, "The Formation of the Sunni Schools of Law, Ninth-Tenth Centuries C.E." (Ph.D. diss., University of Pennsylvania, 1992).

Ever since the tenth century, the legal *madhhab* system has dominated religious discourse, particularly in urban settings, throughout the Muslim world. Compromises have been worked out between Sunni jurists and Muslim sovereigns, allowing rulers wide discretionary control over issues of public law, such as taxation, defense, and the maintenance of public order, while the jurists controlled private law, including trade and contracts, marriage and divorce, inheritance, and so on. Signs of the formative influence of the legal *madhhab*s may be seen in many areas of Islamic social, political, and intellectual history, but the features and workings of these thousand-year-old institutions remain poorly understood. Attention to the margins of the system may prove helpful in understanding the *madhhabs*' historical dynamics. The responses of marginal groups to the *madhhab* system reveal the pressures it applied, show how it exerted control, and point out the modifications in behavior it promoted. Particularly important in this regard are the two major sets of religious sects or schools of thought which already existed by the time the *madhhab* system arose: those which had arisen out of differences over the historical imamate/caliphate, the position of leadership of the Muslim community, including the Shiites and the Khārijīs, and those which had arisen out of theological differences, such as the Muʿtazilīs, Ashʿarīs, Karrāmīs, Kullābīs, and so on. It is to the former set of groups that this study turns, and to the Twelver or Imami Shiites in particular.

The oldest historical division within Islam is the split over the leadership of the Muslim community which began less than thirty years after the death of the Prophet in 11/632. As is well known, ʿAlī's reign as the fourth caliph or "successor" of the Prophet, between 35/656 and 40/661, witnessed a fierce civil war during which the community was torn between rival candidates for leadership. ʿAlī's supporters and the historical movement they began would become the Shiites, whose name derives from the (probably derogative) term *Shīʿat ʿAlī,* "ʿAlī's party" or "ʿAlī's supporters." Shiism, in its most basic sense, is the belief that leadership of the Muslim community after the Prophet Muḥammad should be entrusted to ʿAlī and his descendants. Their victorious rivals would become the Sunni majority, and deserters from ʿAlī's cause would become the Khārijīs. The end of the inter-Muslim war with the murder of ʿAlī in 40/661 did not settle the conflict definitively, and the three factions continued to support rival candidates for the position of leadership and battle periodically to oust the usurper and install the rightful caliph. Shiite doctrine projects the existence of Shiism, defined as support for ʿAlī to succeed the Prophet as leader of the Muslim community, back to the Prophet's demise, or even before, and Madelung finds support for this view in the historical record.[2] In any case, the

2. Wilferd Madelung, *The Succession to Muḥammad* (Cambridge: Cambridge University Press, 1997).

existence of Shiism as a coherent movement became clear with the defense of ʿAlī against detractors during his caliphate and probably in the revolt against his predecessor, ʿUthmān, which resulted in ʿAlī's assumption of the office.

Thus were created the three great sectarian divisions in Islam that still exist today. Later sources, influenced by the development of philosophical theology, stress the theories of the imamate which these three factions came to espouse, but at this early time their conflict did not revolve so directly around the nature of the office of caliph or its principles of succession. It was simply an issue of allegiance. Just as one could not convert to Islam in this early period without becoming a client (*mawlā*) formally affiliated with an Arab tribe, one could not be a Muslim without pledging allegiance to the caliph. A well-known hadith states, "Whoever dies without a pledge of allegiance on his neck has died a pagan death" (*man māta wa-laysa fī ʿunuqihi bayʿatun fa-qad māta mītatan jāhilīyah*). The Prophet had established a religious community that was at the same time a political entity, and as the head of the community his religious authority encompassed its devotional, social, and political life. With his demise, the caliphs took over these functions, even though the prophecy itself had ended. The caliphs were undeniably religious authorities—one would be hard-pressed to detect any other religious authorities in the Muslim community at this time, whether theologians or jurists of the sacred law. Crone and Hinds have argued convincingly that the early Sunni caliphate was more like the Shiite imamate than is usually allowed and that the Shiite conception of the imam is the archaic rather than the innovative view.[3] They state that the caliph "was both head of state and ultimate authority on questions of law and doctrine in Islam."[4] They hold that in the first two Islamic centuries the Sunni caliphs voiced claims to religious authority which were de-emphasized in subsequent history. The popular distinction, therefore, between the Sunni caliph (= political leader) and the Shiite imam (= religious leader) is thus untenable, at least for the early period. The terms *imam* or *ṣāḥib hādhā ʾl-amr* were used by both Sunnis and Shiites to designate what was seen as the same office.

The numerous revolts led by descendants of ʿAlī during the Umayyad caliphate (40–132/661–750) and the early Abbasid period, to which al-Ashʿarī

3. Patricia Crone and Martin Hinds, *God's Caliph* (Cambridge: Cambridge University Press, 1986), 1–3. While I agree with the general argument of the work, the authors read entirely too much into the use of the title *khalīfat Allāh*, "the caliph/successor of God." It makes very little difference whether the caliph was called *khalīfat Allāh* or *khalīfat rasul Allāh*, "the successor of the Prophet of God," for both terms represent, or may be used as, a justification of exclusive religious authority on the bearer's part. The term *khalīfat Allāh* was probably either understood as an ellipsis for *khalīfat rasūl Allāh* or used as an emphatic form meaning "the (one and only) caliph!"—a type of usage seen often in later Arabic expressions, such as *ʿaduww Allāh*, "the enemy of God," as a common term for heretic, or *khayl Allāh* "the army of God," which appears in al-Mutanabbī's panegyrics for Sayf al-Dawlah. See Adel Allouche's review of *God's Caliph* in *Muslim World* 79 (1989): 71–74.

4. Crone and Hinds, *God's Caliph*, 2.

devotes one section of his *Maqālāt al-islāmīyīn,* not only expressed political and military aspirations but also involved claims to religious leadership of the community.[5] These revolts included the famous uprising of Ḥusayn, which ended with his martyrdom at Karbalā' in 61/680, the revolt of the "Penitents" in 64–65/683–84, the revolt of Mukhtār al-Thaqafī in 66–67/686–87, and the revolt of Zayd b. 'Alī in 122/740, all in southern Iraq and directed against Umayyad rule. The Shiite role in the establishment of the 'Abbāsid caliphate (132/750) and Caliph al-Ma'mūn's (d. 218/833) nomination in 201/816 of 'Alī al-Riḍā (d. 203/818), the eighth imam of the Twelver Shiites, as his successor to the caliphate also support the idea that sectarian dynamics revolved around the issue of the caliphate as late as the early ninth century. So, too, does the proliferation of subsects among the Shiites, most of which were defined by allegiance to a specific line of imams. The best known are the Zaydī, Ismā'īlī, and Imāmī (later known as Ithnā'asharī or "Twelver") branches, but others, as well as many subdivisions of these three, also existed.

Imami Shiite doctrine of the early centuries of Islam, as it was formulated by the mid-eighth century, held that human society was in need of religious guidance in all ages. This guidance was embodied in an imam, a divinely guided leader entrusted with upholding ritual obligations in the community and endowed with the authority to settle disputes over religious questions.[6] The imam had to be a member of the Prophet's house (*ahl al-bayt*), one of his descendants through 'Alī. The Shiites cited scriptural texts in support of this view, such as the prophetic tradition known as the hadith of the two weighty matters: "I am leaving among you something with which, should you cling to it, you will never go astray: the two weighty matters, the Book of God and my progeny, the People of my House." Another common text is the hadith report, "The People of my House among you are like Noah's Ark; those who embark on it will be saved, and those who stay behind will drown "[7] The believer must know and grant his allegiance to the imam of his time. The imam, according to the Imami Shiites, had to be a living descendant of the Prophet Muḥammad through Fāṭimah, Muḥammad's daughter, and 'Alī b. Abī Ṭālib and had to be chosen through designation (*naṣṣ*) by the previous imam.[8] The theory that the imam was *ma'ṣūm* or divinely protected from sin and error was introduced by Hishām b. al-Ḥakam (d. 179/795–96) in the mid-eighth century.[9] The

5. Abū al-Ḥasan al-Ash'arī, *Maqālāt al-islāmīyīn wa'khtilāf al-muṣallīn,* ed. Helmut Ritter (Wiesbaden: Franz Steiner Verlag, 1963), 75–85.

6. On the Twelver theory of the imamate in general, see Wilferd Madelung, "Imāma," *EI*[2]; al-Sharīf al-Murtaḍā, *al-Shāfī fī al-imāmah,* 4 vols., ed. Sayyid 'Abd al-Zahrā' al-Ḥusaynī al-Khaṭīb (Tehran: Mu'assasat al-Ṣādiq, 1989–90).

7. al-Murtaḍā, *al-Shāfī,* 3: 120.

8. Marshal G. S. Hodgson, "How Did the Shī'a Become Sectarian?" *JAOS* 75 (1955): 1–13.

9. Wilferd Madelung, "Hishām b. al-Ḥakam," "'Iṣma," *EI*[2].

imam was taken to possess religious knowledge through divine inspiration or by transmission from his predecessors. Though he did not transmit divine scripture, he was endowed with the ability to interpret it in an authoritative manner.

The death of the eleventh imam, Ḥasan al-ʿAskarī, in 260/874 without an undisputed heir presented a crisis for the Twelvers that took nearly a century to resolve. Twelver Shiite doctrine came to be that, in 260/874, the alleged young son of Ḥasan al-ʿAskarī had disappeared in the town of Sāmarrāʾ in Iraq and had gone into hiding.[10] For over sixty years following this date, communication with the Hidden Imam was possible through a succession of four men from the Shiite community who served as intermediaries, termed variously *bāb*, "gate," *safīr*, "messenger," or *wakīl*, "representative." These were ʿUthmān b. Saʿīd al-ʿAmrī (d. ?), who moved from Sāmarrāʾ to Baghdad, his son Muḥammad b. ʿUthmān (d. 305/917), Ḥusayn b. Rawḥ al-Nawbakhtī (305–26/917–37), and ʿAlī b. Muḥammad al-Sāmarrī (326–29/937–41). They would take messages to the Hidden Imam from the believers and return with his replies, termed "rescripts" (*tawqīʿāt*). This period became known as *al-ghaybah al-ṣughrā*, "the Lesser Occultation." In 329/941, the last *safīr* died without designating a successor. By the mid-tenth century, with the works of al-Kulaynī (d. 329/941), Ibn Abī Zaynab al-Nuʿmānī (d. 360/971), and Ibn Bābawayh al-Qummī (d. 381/991) influencing doctrine, direct, intentional communication with the twelfth imam was cut off—communication through dreams, visions, or rare personal encounters was still possible—and *al-ghaybah al-kubrā*, "the Greater Occultation," had begun. It was held that God had miraculously prolonged the imam's life, just as He prolonged the lives of biblical figures such as Adam and Noah, and that the imam circulates among the believers, in human form, although one cannot identify him. He will reveal himself before the end of time and inaugurate a reign of peace and justice.[11]

10. For the various dates given for the twelfth imam's birth, see Hossein Modarressi, *Crisis and Consolidation in the Formative Period of Shiʿite Islam* (Princeton: Darwin Press, 1993), 77 n. 123.

11. The course of events and the development of doctrine related to the Occultation did not proceed smoothly, and are much more complicated than later doctrine implies. Jaʿfar, the brother of the eleventh imam, claimed to be the legitimate imam following Ḥasan al-ʿAskarī's death. The functions and succession of the office of *safīr* are not clear. A crisis occurred ca. 890–900 A.D., by which date most of the eleventh imam's close associates had passed away and correspondence with the Hidden Imam through the *safīrs* was cut off. Correspondence was resumed in 918/305 under the supervision of Ḥusayn b. Rawḥ al-Nawbakhtī, but this step served only to create more doubts and divisions among the believers. On the beginning of the Occultation and the establishment of Twelver Shiite doctrine on the issue, see Said Amir Arjomand, "Imam *Absconditus* and the Beginnings of a Theology of Occultation" *JAOS* 117 (1997): 1–12; idem, "The Crisis of the Imamate and the Institution of Occultation in Twelver Shiʿism" *IJMES* 28 (1996): 491–515; Verena Klemm, "Die vier sufarāʾ des Zwölften Imāms," *Die Welt des Orients* 15 (1984): 126–43; Etan Kohlberg, "From Imāmiyya to Ithnā-ʿashariyya," *BSOAS* 39 (1976): 521–34; Modarressi, *Crisis and Consolidation;* Abdulaziz Abdulhussein Sachedina, *Islamic Messianism* (Albany: State University of New York Press, 1981).

SHIITE LAW AND THE IMAMATE

Islamicists have been in agreement that legal and theological differences between Sunnis and Shiites arose after the initial conflicts over the imamate, as a result of doctrine regarding that issue. Goldziher states: "the basic doctrine of Shiite Islam entails, by its very nature, a way of thinking that essentially differs from Sunni thinking on fundamental theological issues as well. The Shiite conception of the nature of the Imams had to have an effect on the formation of their ideas of God, law, and prophecy."[12] The modern Iranian Shiite scholar Muḥammad Ḥusayn Ṭabāṭabā'ī also holds that the essential element of Shiism is the imamate and that legal and other differences are derivative: "*Shī'ah,* which means literally partisan or follower, refers to those who consider the succession to the Prophet—may God's peace and benediction be upon him—to be the special right of the family of the Prophet and who in the field of the Islamic sciences and culture follow the school of the Household of the Prophet."[13] The tendency to view Shiite history and thought as a logical projection or unambiguous derivation of the theory of the imamate has shaped the study of many aspects of Shiite Islam. It has often prevented or impeded the examination of Shiite topics from other angles, despite the tremendous change in the organization of the Shiite community which occurred after the Occultation.

Most discussions of Shiism begin and end, in a logical sense, with the historical origin of Shiism in the struggles over leadership of the Muslim community during 'Alī's caliphate. The approach based on historical origin is a useful mnemonic or pedagogical device but fails to explain many developments in Islamic history other than during the period very close to the original schism. Textbooks treating Islam and Islamic history portray the doctrine of the imamate as defining Twelver Shiism for all time and use conceptions of the imamate to explain aspects of Shiite theology and law that arose long after the political conflicts over the imamate had ceased to be a vital issue. This view is not limited to elementary manuals but is also found in specialized studies on Shiism. Henri Laoust's extensive work on schisms in Islam focuses almost exclusively on the theory of the imamate and the struggles over the caliphate.[14] Despite the large number of sources treating Twelver Shiite law that have become available since the time of such authors as Goldziher and MacDonald, and despite major advances in our understanding of both the Sunni and Shiite legal systems, this tendency persists in general scholarship on Islam.

12. Ignaz Goldziher, *Introduction to Islamic Theology and Law,* trans. Andras Hamori and Ruth Hamori (Princeton: Princeton University Press, 1980), 202–3.

13. Muḥammad Ḥusayn Ṭabāṭabā'ī, *Shi'ite Islam,* trans. Seyyed Hossein Nasr (Albany: State University of New York Press, 1975), 33.

14. Henri Laoust, *Les schismes dans l'islam* (Paris: Payot, 1965).

One feature of this tendency is the projection of the Shiite legal *madhhab* back to the time of Jaʿfar al-Ṣādiq (d. 148/765). Modarressi writes, "By the time of the Abbasid revolution in 132/749, the Shīʿite movement had thus grown into a complete and independent political, legal, and theological school."[15] If the terms "legal school" and "theological school" here are meant to designate entities like the classical Sunni schools of law and traditions of philosophical theological study like that of the Muʿtazilīs, this statement is anachronistic. Neither the classical Sunni legal *madhhab*s nor the Imami *madhhab* can be said to have taken recognizable form as organized institutions for the teaching and transmission of legal scholarship until much later in history. Just as the idea that the formal structure and legal traditions of the Sunni *madhhab*s derives directly from their eponymous founders is untenable, so is the idea that the Imami legal system derives in a logical, automatic fashion from the teachings of Jaʿfar al-Ṣādiq.

A number of scholars link the religious leadership of the imams with that of the modern jurists by stressing the "authoritarian" nature of Shiism as opposed to more "democratic" Sunni Islam. MacDonald holds that the Shiite *mujtahid*s "seem to have in their hands the teaching power which strictly belongs only to the Hidden Imam. They thus represent the principle of authority which is the governing conception of the Shīʿah."[16] Goldziher concurs that whereas Sunni Islam is based on the concept of consensus, Shiite Islam is based on authority, which characterizes both the Imams and the modern Shiite jurists: "Thus if we wish to characterize in brief the essential difference between Sunnī and Shīʿī Islam, we may say that the former is based on the *ijmāʿ* and the latter on the authoritarian principle." He also emphasizes the role of the Imam as the sole recognized interpreter of the law:

> Only the teaching and the will of the infallible Imām, or of his authorized deputy, carry a sure guarantee of truth and justice. Just as in any age the Imām alone is the legitimate political head of the Islamic community, so the Imām alone has the authority to decide questions that have not already been decided at the outset and for all time by received law, and the Imām alone has the authority to interpret and apply the law.[17]

Other recent scholars have repeated this view, contrasting Shiism as a "church of authority" with Sunnism as a "church of consensus."[18] Such statements are taken to characterize Shiism throughout its history.

15. Modarressi, *Crisis and Consolidation*, 4.

16. Duncan B. MacDonald, *Development of Muslim Theology, Jurisprudence and Constitutional Theory* (New York: Charles Scribner's Sons, 1903), 116.

17. Goldziher, *Islamic Theology and Law*, 191.

18. E.g., George Makdisi, "Scholasticism and Humanism in Classical Islam and the Christian West," *JAOS* 109 (1989):175–82, esp. 176; idem, *Rise of Humanism*, 29.

The modern Shiite legal system has been described as a temporary, ad hoc measure that does not appreciably affect the essence of the faith. Coulson describes the system of religious authority within Shiism, emphasizing the issue of the caliphate and its political aspect: "the Shīʿites represented a rigidly authoritarian concept of political power." He then goes on to characterize the entire history of Shiite legal authority as following that system which could have worked only before the Occultation, ignoring developments of over one thousand years of religious and intellectual history. He claims that the Shiites reject reason as a source of the law, a claim belied by the bulk of Shiite legal scholarship from the twelfth century until the present. He holds that their doctrine of the imamate dominates Shiite jurisprudence to such an extent that they "maintain that the further elaboration of the law is the sole prerogative of their divinely inspired Imam." He claims that Shiite doctrine, again referring to the imamate in particular, makes Shiite law fundamentally different and sets it apart from that of the Sunnis: "the sectarian legal systems are, in the ultimate analysis, quite distinct from each other and from those of Sunnī Islam; for they derive their authority exclusively from those individual politico-religious beliefs by virtue of which the several sects and the Sunnites mutually regard each other as heretical." His statements are presented as holding for all periods of Shiite history; they are unqualified by such restrictions as "in the early period" or "before the Occultation." Perhaps as an afterthought, he goes on to deflate his detailed description of Shiite legal authority by saying that it is an ideal system, reserved for times when the imams are present, which has been in abeyance ever since the Occultation. He devotes only a short passage to the system which has functioned as a "temporary" replacement for the Imam-based system, observing:

> As far as the Ithnā-ʿasharites are concerned, it [the Imam-based system] has represented, since 874, an ultimate ideal which awaits the return of the hidden Imam for its implementation. During the protracted interregnum the exposition of law has been the task of qualified scholars (*mujtahids*), and however much they have been regarded as the agents of the Imam and working under his influence, their use of human reason (*ʿaql*) to determine the law has been accepted as necessary and legitimate.[19]

He admits here that this system is fundamentally different from that based on recourse to the imam.

Like Coulson, Eliash views the Twelver Shiite legal system at work during this prolonged period of Shiite history as a temporary, make-do framework of legislation without any authentic basis. He holds that Twelver

19. Noel J. Coulson, *A History of Islamic Law* (Edinburgh: Edingurgh University Press, 1964), 104, 105–6, 106–7, 108, 119.

Shiism does not allow for the delegation of authority to the jurists and claims, "it would be contrary to the very essence of Ithnā'asharī Shī'ism to regard the *mujtahid* as more than an ordinary *mukallaf* versed in the ordinances of the Sharī'ah and their application, and even more contrary to institute him as a performer of the functions of the Imam during the Great Occultation."[20] Eliash criticizes Leonard Binder's report that the Shiite *mujtahids* claim authority by virtue of their having been entrusted with the "general agency" (*niyābah 'āmmah*) of the imam, an argument they base on a hadith transmitted from the sixth imam, Ja'far al-Ṣādiq (d. 148/765).[21] Binder's findings are authentic, but Eliash refuses to grant them any weight because he feels that they go against the true spirit of Shiism and create an unacceptable discontinuity in the tradition.

In a 1979 article, Eliash, though he had since come across the hadith of 'Umar b. Ḥanẓalah on which the *mujtahids* base their claim to exclusive authority, continues to hold that such claims are invalid. The critical part of the tradition, as Eliash translates it, based on the version included in *al-Kāfi* by al-Kulaynī (d. 329/941), is the answer to a question put by 'Umar b. Ḥanẓalah to Ja'far al-Ṣādiq concerning whom Shiite believers should consult when settling legal disputes:

> They [should] look for him among you who has related our traditions, has examined what is lawful and what is unlawful according to us, and has known our decrees. They should accept him as a judge, for I appointed him a judge over you. If he would judge according to our ruling and his (judgment) would not be accepted, verily it is contempt for the ruling of God and rejection of us, and he who rejects us rejects God and is subject to the penalty for the attributing of partners to God.[22]

Eliash holds not only that the *mujtahids*' claims are historically invalid (i.e., that the imams had made no statement before the Occultation indicating that their functions would be entrusted exclusively to the *mujtahids* in their absence) but also that their claims are inconsistent with fundamental Shiite doctrines concerning the nature of authority during the Occultation. He holds that this hadith, if read in context, does not support the exclusive authority of the *mujtahids* and proclaims, "Twelver Shī'ī juridical principles do not vindicate an alleged designation of the *'ulamā'* by the Imams to wield the Imam's

20. Joseph Eliash, "The Ithnā'asharī-Shī'ī Juristic Theory of Political and Legal Authority," *Studia Islamica* 29 (1969):26.

21. Leonard Binder, "The Proofs of Islam: Religion and Politics in Iran," in *Arabic and Islamic Studies in Honor of Hamilton A. R. Gibb*, ed. George Makdisi (Leiden: E. J. Brill, 1965), 122–23.

22. Joseph Eliash, "Misconceptions Regarding the Juridical Status of the Iranian 'Ulamā'," *IJMES* 10 (1979): 14.

prerogatives." In Eliash's view, the Occultation is a time of suspended religious authority. During this period, the *mujtahids* have been providing some leadership of the community, but their entire legal system is a temporary measure, and the ruling of the *mujtahid* is "as fallible as any other *human* deed."[23] The best the *mujtahids* can hope to do is to institute rulings for the common good, to the best of their ability, while the Shiite community awaits the return of the Hidden Imam. Eliash believes that in Shiism in general, justice is reserved for the Utopia at the end of time, and meanwhile, no human efforts have any authoritative basis.

INVESTIGATION OF THE SHIITE LEGAL TRADITION

While there has been a steady flow of important works from the Shiite tradition since the nineteenth century, as lithograph editions were published in Iran and India, Western scholarship on Islam has tended to concentrate heavily on Sunnism and has relatively neglected the Shiites.[24] In 1871–72, Amédée Querry translated *Sharāʾiʿ al-Islām,* a manual of Twelver Shiite law by the thirteenth-century scholar al-Muḥaqqiq al-Ḥillī (d. 676/1277), and Ignaz Goldziher and Rudolf Strothmann published a number of important studies on Shiism in the late nineteenth and early twentieth centuries, but these stand out as exceptional efforts. Until recently, the only general introduction to the topic available in a Western language was Donaldson's 1933 work, *The Shi'ite Religion.* As recently as 1979, Joseph Eliash could write that the field of Twelver Shiite jurisprudence remained "all but unknown." Since the 1970s, significant progress has been made in the study of Shiism and a number of substantial studies have been completed. Āghā Buzurg's monumental catalogue of Shiite works, *al-Dharīʿah ilā taṣānīf al-shīʿah,* has provided an invaluable tool for research on the Shiite legal tradition in addition to other areas of Shiite thought. Quite thorough introductory presentations are now available in English, including Heinz Halm's *Shiism* and Moojan Momen's *An Introduction to Shiʿi Islam.* In the field of law, perhaps the most important work to appear has been Modarressi's *Introduction to Shīʿī Law;* it provides the best summary to date of the history of Shiite law and legal theory available in a European language in addition to an extensive bibliography of Shiite legal works. Kohlberg's work on Raḍī al-Dīn Ibn Ṭāwūs (d. 664/1266) is not only a thorough analysis of the methods of this thirteenth-century scholar but also an important resource for investigation of earlier scholarship in the Twelver tradition. Löschner made the first systematic presentation of Twelver legal theory

23. Ibid., 14, 15, 21, 23.

24. See Etan Kohlberg, "Western Studies of Shiʿa Islam," in *Shiʿism, Resistance, and Revolution,* ed. Martin Kramer (Boulder, Colorado: Westview Press, 1987), 31–34.

in a European language.[25] In addition, the publication of medieval Shiite works has accelerated in the last two decades, especially through the efforts of the Āyat Allāh Mar'ashī library in Iran.

The Iranian revolution of 1979 and the subsequent foundation of the Islamic Republic have made the world acutely aware of the power and importance of the Twelver Shiite legal establishment. Recent works which make the Shiite system of legal education, and particularly that of the center of learning at the city of Qum in Iran, accessible to the educated Western reader include Fischer's *Iran: From Religious Dispute to Revolution* and Mottahedeh's *The Mantle of the Prophet: Religion and Politics in Iran.*[26] Nevertheless, the workings of this complex system remain poorly understood and its history remains sketchy. Scholars have sensed that the juridical system found in modern Shiism differs radically from that based on recourse to an accessible imam that existed before the Occultation. These two faces of Shiite legal authority have created a great deal of confusion in the literature precisely because of the desire to see them as logically, necessarily linked. It is a common view that the modern legal system is somehow a mere extension of the system of authority in place when the imams were present.

This shortcoming in scholarship on the history of the Shiite legal system has begun to be remedied. In his 1980 doctoral dissertation, Calder treats the historical development of the Twelver Shiite *madhhab* and the establishment of the religious authority of the Twelver jurists. He identifies a trend toward greater and more explicit claims to juridical authority, providing historical data for its establishment in the theoretical discussion of specific areas of the law, including judgeship, the collection and distribution of *zakāt* and *khums* funds, the declaration of *jihād,* and the performance of Friday prayer. Beginning in the Buwayhid period, the prominent jurists al-Shaykh al-Mufīd, al-Sharīf al-Murtaḍā, and al-Shaykh al-Ṭūsī began asserting the authority of the qualified jurist (*faqīh*) over particular areas of the law. These claims were built up and extended in subsequent centuries, culminating in the theory of "general agency" (*niyābah 'āmmah*) first formulated in these exact terms by al-Shahīdal-Thānī (Zayn al-Dīn al-'Āmilī, d. 965/1558), though it was prefigured in the

25. Dwight M. Donaldson, *The Shi'ite Religion* (London: Luzac & Co., 1933); Eliash, "Misconceptions," 9; al-Ṭihrānī, Aghā Buzurg. *al-Dharī'ah ilā taṣānīf al-shī'ah,* 26 vols. (Beirut: Dār al-aḍwā', 1983); Heinz Halm, *Shiism* (Edinburgh: Edinburgh University Press, 1991); Moojan Momen, *An Introduction to Shi'i Islam* (New Haven: Yale University Press, 1985); Hossein Modarressi, *An Introduction to Shī'ī Law* (London: Ithaca Press, 1984); Etan Kohlberg, *A Medieval Muslim Scholar at Work* (Leiden: E. J. Brill, 1992); Harald Löschner, *Die dogmatischen Grundlagen des šī'itischen Rechts* (Cologne: Carl Heymanns Verlag, 1971).

26. Michael M. J. Fischer, *Iran* (Cambridge, Massachusetts: Harvard University Press, 1980); Roy Mottahedeh, *The Mantle of the Prophet* (New York: Simon and Schuster, 1985).

work of ʿAlī b. ʿAbd al-ʿĀlī al-Karakī (d. 940/1534). According to this theory, the fully qualified jurist is the exclusively entrusted "general deputy" (*al-nāʾib al-ʿāmm*) of the imam.[27]

Andrew Newman's 1984 dissertation examines the history of Shiite jurisprudence as a conflict between rationalist and traditionalist tendencies, represented by the Twelver Uṣūlīs and Akhbārīs, respectively. His discussion of the rise of the authority of the jurists supplements that of Calder, contributing greater detail for some periods. Newman also brings out the importance of the Akhbārīs and their rejection of the Uṣūlī jurists' authority.[28]

Algar and Cole both treat the role of the Twelver jurists vis-à-vis the state in specific historical and geographical contexts: Algar in Iran in Qajar Iran and Cole in Awadh India in the eighteenth and nineteenth centuries. Arjomand's complex and wide-ranging study, *The Shadow of God and the Hidden Imam,* analyzes the development of the Twelver legal system against the background of Iranian political and social history from the origins of Shiism until 1890. He argues that the development of Imami Shiism into a sectarian religion within the larger Islamic community led to a separation of religious and political authority. This separation manifested itself in various forms in the course of Iranian history and led, following the transformation of Shiism from a sectarian to a national religion during the Safavid period, to the consolidation in the nineteenth century of an autonomous hierocracy of jurists independent from the state. To Arjomand, the clear, normative demarcation between religious and political authority represents Shiism's main effect on the social structure of premodern Iran. In the course of his argument, he treats the history of the Twelver legal system in some detail, dealing briefly with the jurists of the Buwayhid and Ilkhanid periods and concentrating on the leading jurists of the Safavid period, particularly ʿAlī b. ʿAbd al-ʿĀlī al-Karakī. His analysis, building on that of Calder, stresses the establishment of an autonomous hierocracy which succeeded in dominating and suppressing other aspects of Shiite tradition, including Akhbārism, chiliasm, and mysticism.[29]

Sachedina's work *The Just Ruler in Shiite Islam* discusses the historical development of the comprehensive—including political—authority of the jurist in Twelver Shiite legal theory. The work reflects on the Shiite legal history

27. Norman Calder, "The Structure of Authority in Imāmī Shīʿī Jurisprudence," (Ph.D. diss., School of Oriental and African Studies, University of London, 1980).

28. Andrew Newman, "The Development and Political Significance of the Rationalist (Uṣūlī) and Traditionalist (Akhbārī) Schools in Imāmī Shīʿī History from the Third/Ninth to the Tenth/Sixteenth Century" (Ph. D. diss., University of California, Los Angeles, 1986).

29. Hamid Algar, *Religion and State in Iran* (Berkeley: University of California Press, 1969); Juan R. Cole, *Roots of North Indian Shīʿism in Iran and Iraq* (Berkeley: University of California Press, 1988); Said Amir Arjomand, *The Shadow of God and the Hidden Imam* (Chicago: University of Chicago Press, 1984); esp. 51–56, 122–70.

in a manner internal to the tradition, at times with an anachronistic and uncritical acceptance of established doctrine as historical truth. Sachedina argues that the concept of general representation through which Shiite jurists came to justify their authority derives, both historically and logically, from the concept of particular representation which existed during the period of the imams' presence. He thus uses as a historical argument what is in reality the modern Shiite doctrinal justification of this authority, a religious argument based on the projection of a later historical situation back to an earlier, more sacred period. The work notes some of the important theoretical discussions and major stages in the development of this theory, but does little to provide a framework for understanding the forces that brought about these changes. The work seems based on a presentist concern to justify the theory of *wilāyat al-faqīh,* or the comprehensive guardianship of the jurist, that has become so important in the late twentieth century.[30]

Ahmad Kazemi Moussavi's recent work *Religious Authority in Shi'ite Islam* seeks to explain the underpinnings of the Shiite jurists' religious authority through a historical examination of Twelver jurisprudence. In explaining the power of the modern Shiite jurists and the origins of the modern juridical hierarchy, the book narrates a steady progression from the "office" of *muftī*—jurisconsult—beginning before the Occultation, to that of *mujtahid*—jurist capable of reaching a legal opinion on the basis of independent reasoning—in the thirteenth century with the work of al-Muḥaqqiq al-Ḥillī (d. 676/1277) and al-'Allāmah al-Ḥillī (d. 726/1325), to the "institution" of *marji' al-taqlīd*—a "supreme exemplar" who serves as legal authority for the entire community and acts as the head of an informal hierarchy of Shiite jurists—in the nineteenth century. Moussavi identifies the major change in the history of Twelver jurisprudence as taking place not with the establishment of the theory of general agency in the sixteenth century but with the acceptance of *ijtihād* by al-Muḥaqqiq al-Ḥillī and al-'Allāmah al-Ḥillī in the thirteenth and early fourteenth centuries. He also brings out the role of the Akhbārīs, Shaykhīs, and mystics as challengers to the Uṣūlī jurists' authority and emphasizes the Uṣūlī jurists' use of popular religion as a means to influence the outcome of such conflicts.[31]

SUNNI AND SHIITE JURISPRUDENCE JUXTAPOSED

Discussions to date do not explain adequately how and why the institution of the Twelver Shiite legal *madhhab* was created. The tendency within the Shiite juridical tradition is to portray the legal system as a logical extension of the re-

30. Abdulaziz Abdulhussein Sachedina, *The Just Ruler in Shi'ite Islam* (Oxford: Oxford University Press, 1988).

31. Ahmad Kazemi Moussavi, *Religious Authority in Shi'ite Islam* (Kuala Lumpur: International Institute of Islamic Thought and Civilization, 1996).

ligious system of authority established during the time of the imams' presence. Traditions attributed to the imams, such as "We are obligated to provide you with general principles, and you must derive specific rules" (*'alaynā ilqā'u l-uṣūli ilaykum, wa-'alaykum bi't-tafrī'*), are cited to justify the activities of the later Shiite jurists.[32] Yet such reports do not account for the radical differences between the two systems. Scholars concerned with the history of Shiite jurisprudence often view it in isolation and seek to explain the rise of the Twelver legal *madhhab* in terms internal to Shiism, with little or no reference to the history of Islamic jurisprudence as a whole. Eliash, for example, attributes the establishment of the legal *madhhab* after the Greater Occultation of the imam to practical necessity and the rational character of Twelver Shiite theology.[33] Madelung makes a similar statement: "As a result of the loss of the absolute and infallible authority in religious and political matters vested in the Imams (after the disappearance of the Twelfth Imam), other sources and forms of authority and legitimacy were gradually accepted in theology, the religious law and the political sphere."[34] Both statements imply that the present-day system arose in order to fill a vacuum which existed in terms of religious authority and leadership—something had to make up for the effective absence of the imam. Yet to say this does not explain why the specific system that came into being works the way it does or adopted the particular features which characterize it.

There are numerous indications that the development of the Twelver Shiite legal *madhhab* and the rise of the legal system of authority in Shiism were influenced by the development of Sunni jurisprudence. Many features of the modern Shiite system of jurisprudence resemble those found in Sunni jurisprudence very closely, and some were even adopted after having at first been rejected by Shiites as incompatible with their own doctrine. Brunschvig, for example, notes certain temporal intervals (*décalages*) between the compilation of hadith collections and the systematization of jurisprudence in Sunnism and Shiism and posits influence.[35] The following are examples of some of the historical intervals between parallel developments in Sunni and Shiite jurisprudence.

The first books of Sunni hadith arranged according to the chapters of law for easy legal reference appeared in the ninth century.[36] The six such books

32. Modarressi, *Shī'ī Law,* 24; 'Amīd al-Dīn b. 'Abd al-Muṭṭalib al-A'rajī al-Ḥusaynī, *Munyat al-labīb fī sharḥ al-tahdhīb* (Lucknow: Maṭba' Ḍiyā' al-Riḍā, 1898–99), 1.

33. Eliash, "Misconceptions," 15.

34. Wilferd Madelung, "Authority in Twelver Shiism in the Absence of the Imam," in *La notion d'autorité au moyen âge,* ed. George Makdisi et al. (Paris: Presses universitaires de France, 1982), 173.

35. Robert Brunschvig, "Les Uṣūl al-Fiqh Imāmites à leur stade ancien (Xe et XIe siècles)," in *Le Shī'isme Imamite* (Paris: Presses universitaires françaises, 1970), 201–13.

36. Makdisi, *Rise of Humanism,* 19–20. Fuat Sezgin points out that it has been a common error to assume that al-Bukhārī's *al-Ṣaḥīḥ* was the first such book; others preceded it (*GAS* [Leiden: E. J. Brill, 1967–84], 1:115).

accepted by Sunnis as being the main works of reference are *al-Ṣaḥīḥ* by al-Bukhārī (d. 256/870), *al-Ṣaḥīḥ* by Muslim (d. 261/815), *al-Sunan* by Ibn Mājah (d. 273/886), *al-Sunan* by Abū Dā'ūd (d. 275/889), *al-Jāmiʿ al-ṣaḥīḥ* by al-Tirmidhī (d. 279/892), and *al-Sunan* by al-Nasā'ī (d. 303/915). All of them date from the mid- to late ninth century. The four such books accepted as the main works of reference by the Shiites are *al-Kāfī* by al-Kulaynī (d. 329/941), *Man lā yaḥḍuruhu 'l-faqīh* by Ibn Bābawayh al-Qummī (d. 381/991) and *Tahdhīb al-aḥkām* and *al-Istibṣār* by Muḥammad Abū Jaʿfar al-Ṭūsī (d. 460/1067). They date from the first half of the tenth century to the first half of the eleventh century. The Shiites came to refer to these books of hadith as *al-uṣūl al-arbaʿah* or *al-kutub al-arbaʿah*, "the four books," a nomenclature parallel to the Sunni terms *aṣ-ṣiḥāḥ as-sittah* or *al-kutub al-sittah*, "the six books."

The first integral text of Sunni *uṣūl al-fiqh* (methodology of law and jurisprudence) was written by al-Shāfiʿī (d. 204/820). While there is a considerable temporal gap between al-Shāfiʿī's text and the next extant Sunni work on *uṣūl al-fiqh—al-Fuṣūl fī al-uṣūl* by Abū Bakr Aḥmad b. ʿAlī al-Jaṣṣāṣ al-Rāzī (d. 370/980)[37]—the genre was solidly established by the early tenth century at the latest. The first extant work of *uṣūl al-fiqh* in the Twelver Shiite tradition is *al-Tadhkirah bi-uṣūl al-fiqh* by al-Shaykh al-Mufīd (d. 413/1022). With this work came the acceptance of the legal concept of *ijmāʿ*, "consensus," which dates back to the work of al-Shāfiʿī and even earlier in Sunni law.[38] Shiite jurists did not accept *qiyās* (analogy), widely accepted in Sunni jurisprudence, as one of the *uṣūl* or sources of jurisprudence, but they eventually developed Shiite *uṣūl al-fiqh* so that there would be four sources, substituting *dalīl al-ʿaql*, "the evidence of reason," for *qiyās*. Al-Shaykh al-Ṭūsī includes a statement in *al-ʿUddah*, written in the early eleventh century, that presents the four sources as the Koran, hadith, consensus, and *dalīl al-ʿaql*, corresponding to the usual Sunni order.[39] Al-Shāfiʿī's *Risālah* implies that the sources of law are the Koran, *sunnah*, *ijmāʿ*, and *qiyās*, although the structure of the work does not stress this point; it is clear, though, that this view became widely accepted among Sunni jurists by the first half of the tenth century.

The use of the term *ijtihād* to mean the ability to arrive at a legal ruling on the basis of individual investigation was at first rejected by Shiite jurisconsults

37. al-Jaṣṣāṣ, *al-Fuṣūl fī al-uṣūl*, 4 vols., ed. ʿUjayl Jāsin al-Nashmī (Kuwait: Wizārat al-awqāf wa'l-shu'ūn al-islāmīyah, 1985–93). See also al-Jaṣṣāṣ, *al-Fuṣūl fī al-uṣūl (abwāb al-ijtihād wa'l-qiyās)*, ed. Saeedullah Qazi (Lahore: al-Maktabah al-ʿilmīyah, 1981); Marie Bernand, "Ḥanafī *Uṣūl al-Fiqh* through a Manuscript of al-Ǧaṣṣāṣ," *JAOS* 105 (1985): 623–35.

38. Muḥammad b. Idrīs al-Shāfiʿī, *Islamic Jurisprudence*, trans. Majid Khadduri (Baltimore, Maryland: The Johns Hopkins Press, 1961), 285–87.

39. Muḥammad b. al-Ḥasan al-Ṭūsī, *ʿUddat al-uṣūl* (Tehran, 1896–97), 120–21. Modarressi states that the first Twelver Shiite work on *uṣūl al-fiqh* to present the four sources as the Koran, hadith, *ijmāʿ*, and *dalīl al-ʿaql* was *al-Sarā'ir al-ḥāwī li-taḥrīr al-fatāwī* by Ibn Idrīs al-Ḥillī (d. 598/1202) (*Shīʿī Law*, 3 n. 2).

but later incorporated into the Twelver Shiite legal system. Among Sunni jurisconsults, the term was used with this meaning as far back as the time of al-Shāfiʿī.[40] Al-Muḥaqqiq Jaʿfar b. al-Ḥasan al-Ḥillī (d. 676/1277) was the first to admit that Shiite jurisconsults practiced *ijtihād* and to incorporate the term into his works on jurisprudence.[41]

A major development in Sunni jurisprudence involved the compilation of works on *qawāʿid* "rules," in effect compendia of legal principles derived from the elaboration and comparison of the points of law in legal subfields, such as contracts, marriage, and so on, as opposed to prescriptive methodological rules given in the works on jurisprudence (*uṣūl al-fiqh*). While a few early works, such as *al-Uṣūl allatī ʿalayhā madār furūʿ al-ḥanafiyah* by Abū al-Ḥasan al-Karkhī (d. 340/952) and *Taʾsīs al-naẓar* by ʿUbayd b. ʿĪsā al-Dabūsī (d. 432/1041) follow similar principles,[42] the first work clearly belonging to the *qawāʿid* genre seems to have been *al-Qawāʿid fī furūʿ al-shāfiʿīyah* by the Shāfiʿī jurist Muʿīn al-Dīn Abū Ḥāmid Muḥammad b. Ibrāhīm al-Jājirmī, who died in 613/1216–17.[43] The genre subsequently became extremely popular in Sunni legal circles in the thirteenth and fourteenth centuries, and some of the best known exemplars are *Qawāʿid al-sharīʿah al-kubrā* by the Shāfiʿī ʿIzz al-Dīn ʿAbd al-ʿAzīz b. ʿAbd al-Salām al-Sulamī (d. 660/1262),[44] *al-Furūq* or *Anwār al-burūq fī anwāʿ al-furūq* by the Egyptian Mālikī Shihāb al-Dīn Aḥmad b. Idrīs al-Qarāfī (d. 684/1285),[45] and *al-Majmūʿ al-mudhahhab fī qawāʿid al-madhhab* by the Shāfiʿī jurist Ṣalāḥ al-Dīn Abū Saʿīd Khalīl b. Kaykaldī al-Dimashqī (d. 761/1359), which Ḥājjī Khalīfah identifies as the best work on *qawāʿid* in general.[46] The earliest Shiite work in this genre appears to be *ʿIqd al-jawāhir fī al-ashbāh waʾl-naẓāʾir* by Ḥasan b. ʿAlī b. Dāʾūd al-Ḥillī (d. ca. 740/1340).[47] The next known work is *al-Qawāʿid waʾl-fawāʾid* by al-Shahīd al-Awwal (d. 786/1384),[48] followed by *Jāmiʿ al-fawāʾid fī talkhīṣ al-qawāʿid* and

40. Muḥammad b. Idrīs al-Shāfiʿī, *al-Risālah,* 2d ed., ed. Aḥmad Muḥammad Shākir (Cairo: Dār al-turāth, 1979), 477.

41. Najm al-Dīn Jaʿfar b. al-Ḥasan al-Ḥillī, *Maʿārij al-uṣūl,* ed. Muḥammad Ḥusayn al-Riḍawī (Qum: Maṭbaʿat Sayyid al-shuhadāʾ, 1983), 177–82.

42. ʿUbayd al-Dabūsī, *Taʾsīs al-naẓar,* and al-Ḥasan al-Karkhī, *al-Uṣūl allatī ʿalayhā madār furūʿ al-ḥanafiyah,* ed. Muṣṭafā Muḥammad al-Qabbānī al-Dimashqī (Beirut: Dār Ibn Zaydūn, n.d.).

43. Ḥājjī Khalīfah, *Kashf al-ẓunūn fī asāmī al-kutub waʾl-funūn,* 7 vols., ed. Gustav Flügel (Leipzig and London, 1835–58), 4: 576.

44. Brockelmann, *GAL,* 1: 430.

45. Shihāb al-Dīn Aḥmad b. Idrīs al-Qarāfī, *al-Furūq,* 4 vols. (Beirut: ʿĀlam al-kitāb, n.d.).

46. Brockelmann, *GAL,* 2: 65, supp. 2: 68; Ḥājjī Khalīfah, *Kashf al-ẓunūn,* 4: 575–76.

47. Ibn Dāʾūd Taqī al-Dīn al-Ḥasan b. ʿAlī al-Ḥillī, *Kitāb al-rijāl* (Najaf: al-Maṭbaʿah al-ḥaydarīyah, 1972), 75.

48. Modarressi, *Shīʿī Law,* 116–17; Muḥammad b. Makkī al-Jizzīnī, *al-Qawāʿid waʾl-fawāʾid* (Tehran, 1890–91), with commentary by Bahāʾ al-Dīn al-ʿĀmilī (d. 1030/1621) in the margin, 2d ed., 2 vols., ed. al-Sayyid ʿAbd al-Hādī al-Ḥakīm (Qum: Maktabat al-mufīd, 1980).

Nadd al-qawāʿid by al-Fāḍil al-Miqdād (d. 826/1423)[49] and *Tamhīd al-qawāʿid* by Zayn al-Dīn al-ʿĀmilī in the sixteenth century.[50]

This short synopsis is enough to show that Schacht's portrayal of the history of Shiite law, according to which Shiism in the first three Islamic centuries was reasonably integrated into the Sunni community but broke off at about the time of the Occultation of the imam to form its own legal system, is seriously flawed.[51] After this early period, Schacht implies, Shiite law became somehow isolated from Sunni law, and the doctrinal similarities that exist date from the early period. The major developments just described, however, indicate that Shiite law and legal methodology started out quite different from Sunni law, but gradually conformed more and more to the Sunni system. Schacht was thinking primarily of the individual points of law rather than legal methodology and the organization of legal education and study when he propounded the diametrically opposed view.

Despite evidence suggesting Sunni influence on Twelver Shiite jurisprudence, this topic has yet to be studied in depth either as a general topic or in isolated instances. Coulson recognizes that the sectarian legal systems interacted extensively with the Sunni majority, particularly in the eighth and ninth centuries, and shared in the historical process of development which the Sunni schools of law underwent. He observes, "In fact, the sectarian legal systems, far from being wholly independent growths, often directly borrowed rules developed in the Sunnite schools." He notes that the developments of later Shiite jurisprudence have followed those in Sunni jurisprudence quite closely, but attributes this merely to the conservative nature of Shiite legal scholarship.[52]

A handful of scholars have made more specific assertions of Sunni influence on Shiite jurisprudence. Muḥammad Riḍā Muẓaffar states that Shiite scholars adopted the concept of *ijmāʿ*, or legal consensus, out of competition with Sunni scholars, but does not elaborate. Juan Cole suggests that it was probably in imitation of the Sunnis that the Twelvers developed four sources of law. Modarressi holds that the prominent Shiite jurist al-Shaykh al-Ṭūsī incorporated an important part of Sunni legal scholarship into Shiite law. He states that two of al-Ṭūsī's works, *Kitāb al-mabsūṭ* and *Kitāb al-khilāf*, are modeled

49. Modarressi, *Shīʿī Law*, 116; Miqdād b. ʿAbd Allāh al-Suyūrī al-Ḥillī, *Naḍd al-qawāʿid al-fiqhīyah ʿalā madhhab al-imāmīyah*, ed. al-Sayyid ʿAbd al-Laṭīf al-Kūhkamarī (Qum: Maktabat al-Marʿashī, 1983).

50. Zayn al-Dīn al-ʿĀmilī, *Tamhīd al-qawāʿid al-uṣūlīyah waʾl-ʿarabīyah li-tafrīʿ fawāʾid al-aḥkām al-sharʿīyah* (Tehran, 1855).

51. Joseph Schacht, *The Origins of Muhammadan Jurisprudence* (Oxford: Clarendon Press, 1950), 54, 99, 262.

52. Coulson, *A History of Islamic Law*, 104–5, 108.

on Sunni works, though he does not identify specific Sunni antecedents. He adds that the Shiite scholar Ibn al-Muṭahhar al-Ḥillī, known as al-ʿAllāmah, also drew on Sunni legal works. Madelung also mentions that al-ʿAllāmah introduced into Shiite law juridical principles adapted from Sunni law. Moussavi notes that al-Shaykh al-Ṭūsī and al-ʿAllāmah al-Ḥillī studied as youths under Sunni teachers, apparently what enabled them to write works on comparative law, such as *al-Mabsūṭ, al-Khilāf,* and *Tadhkirat al-fuqahāʾ.* He suggests that the theories of al-Muḥaqqiq and al-ʿAllāmah al-Ḥillī regarding *ijtihād* and *taqlīd* were drawn from Sunni works on jurisprudence, including the *Mankhūl* and *Mustaṣfā* of al-Ghazālī (d. 505/1111), the *Maḥṣūl* of Fakhr al-Dīn al-Rāzī (d. 606/1209), and the *Iḥkām* of Sayf al-Dīn al-Āmidī (d. 631/1233).[53] Beyond such indications, no detailed study has yet been done on the connections between Sunni and Shiite jurisprudence, nor have the important questions how and why Shiite scholars adapted Sunni juridical concepts been adequately addressed.

A clear instance of borrowing from the Sunni legal tradition may be seen in the work of al-Shahīd al-Thānī. One of the technical innovations in the Sunni legal tradition during the late medieval period was the invention of the interwoven commentary (*sharḥ mazj*). Rather than citing the original text in blocks or sentences and then commenting after each section, authors developed a new method of commentary whereby they would work the original text into their own sentences. The result was a more readable work that did not require constant glancing back and forth between the original text and its commentary. It is difficult to date this development precisely, but it became quite popular in the field of law by the fifteenth century in such works as the commentary on Tāj al-Dīn al-Subkī's *Jamʿ al-jawāmiʿ* by Jalāl al-Dīn al-Maḥallī (d. 864/1459).[54] Al-Shahīd al-Thānī was the first Shiite jurist to use this method. His best known works written in this manner are *Rawḍ al-jinān,* a commentary on al-ʿAllāmah's *Irshād al-adhhān,* and *al-Rawḍah al-bahīyah,* a commentary on *al-Lumʿah al-dimashqīyah* by al-Shahīd al-Awwal. His student and biographer Ibn al-ʿAwdī reports that al-Shahīd al-Thānī borrowed this method from the Sunnis; when he saw that they had interwoven commentaries and his fellows did not, zealous pride led him to write such works for the Shiites.[55] We also know that al-Shahīd al-Thānī studied al-Maḥallī's commentary in

53. Muḥammad Riḍā Muẓaffar, *Uṣūl al-fiqh,* 4 vols. (Najaf: Dār al-nuʿmān, 1966–67), 3: 97; Juan R. Cole, "Imami Jurisprudence and the Role of the Ulama," in *Religion and Politics in Iran: Shīʿism from Quietism to Revolution,* ed. Nikki R. Keddie (New Haven: Yale University Press, 1983), 35; Modarressi, *Shīʿī Law,* 44, 48; Madelung, "Authority in Twelver Shiism," 168; Moussavi, *Religious Authority,* 26, 30, 85, 164 n. 47, 170.

54. Tāj al-Dīn al-Subkī, *Jamʿ al-jawāmiʿ,* 2 vols., with commentaries by al-Maḥallī, al-Bannānī, and al-Shirbīnī (Cairo: ʿĪsā al-Bābī al-Ḥalabī, n.d.).

55. ʿAlī b. Muḥammad al-ʿĀmilī, *al-Durr al-manthūr min al-maʾthūr wa-ghayr al-maʾthūr,* 2 vols. (Qum: Maṭbaʿat mihr, 1978), 2: 185.

Cairo.[56] While this example has to do with a fairly simple technical innovation, it nevertheless indicates the important part borrowing from, imitation of, or competition with the Sunni system has played in the history of Shiite legal scholarship.

The 1984 dissertation of Aron Zysow treats Twelver Shiite jurisprudence within a larger typology of schools of Islamic legal thought. His short discussion of Twelver Shiite jurisprudence in the epilogue is one of the most important treatments to date of the relationship between Twelver Shiite and Sunni legal theory.[57] Using such criteria as the treatment of the isolated or unit tradition (*khabar al-wāḥid*), Zysow distinguishes two major types of Islamic legal systems: materialist systems, which require certainty on all legal issues, and formalist systems, which admit probability. The chief representative of formalism is the Ḥanafī *madhhab,* though Zysow takes formalism to be a fundamental feature of the three other standard Sunni *madhhabs*—Shāfiʿī, Mālikī, and Ḥanbalī—as well, and thus labels formal legal systems as "normal." He finds that the early Twelver jurists were materialists who required certainty in all areas of legal interpretation. Beginning with the jurists of the Buwayhid period, and particularly with al-Ṭūsī, formalism was incorporated into the Twelver legal system, and culminated in the work of al-ʿAllāmah al-Ḥillī, who recognized *ijtihād* and its extensive usefulness in a system of legal interpretation that was based on probability. Formalism was later challenged by the materialist Akhbārīs during the Akhbārī revival beginning in the seventeenth century, and the reaction to the Akhbārīs provoked a series of works on *uṣūl al-fiqh* upholding the formalist position, such as al-Bihbihānī's *al-Akhbār wa'l-ijtihād* and Murtaḍā al-Anṣārī's *Farā'id al-uṣūl,* which has continued until the present. Zysow recognizes an important discontinuity in the history of Shiite legal theory and relates that Twelver Shiite jurisprudence recapitulates the historical development of Sunni legal theory. Where his study differs from this one is that he uses the concept of probability rather than consensus as the basis for his typology. He attributes formalism's success in Shiism in part to its providing a more satisfactory justification for the authority of the jurists than did materialism, and he sees the eventual success of probabilistic methods in Twelver law as representative of the different fates of materialism and formalism in Islam at large.

SHIITE RESPONSES TO THE SUNNI LEGAL SYSTEM

This study is a reading of the history of Twelver Shiite reactions to the rise of the Sunni legal *madhhabs*. It not merely juxtaposes Sunni and Shiite legal systems, pointing out similar trends and parallels between them; it calls attention

56. Ibid., 162.

57. Aron Zysow, "The Economy of Certainty," Ph.D. diss., Harvard University, 1984, 497–511.

to some basic structural features of the Sunni legal system that shaped and controlled Shiite responses to it. These features did not determine the Shiite responses in an absolute manner but rather narrowed and defined not only the conceptual parameters within which Shiite responses would be framed but also forms and language in which they would be expressed. It highlights the specific stigma thrust upon heterodox Islamic groups by the Sunni juridical establishment and explores the strategies the Shiites used in order to react to this pressure.

Particularly in the tenth and eleventh centuries, orthodoxy came to be defined, in Sunni theory, as the consensus of the Sunni jurists (*ijmāʿ*). To go against or violate consensus (*mukhālafat al-ijmāʿ*) was to become an unbeliever or religious deviant. Only the opinions of those scholars who operated within one of the recognized legal *madhhab*s were considered as having value or authority in debates over religious questions. This rule became a structural or institutional feature of Islamic societies that would remain in force and indeed change very little until the twentieth century. By the tenth century, Islamic religious groups who originally had been defined by the issue of the imamate, such as the Shiites, as well as those groups defined by philosophical theological positions, such as the Muʿtazilah, felt the need to react to this new definition of heresy or else risk being excluded from the Islamic community. Thus began a complex negotiation, still going on today, between Shiite and Sunni jurists over the status of Shiism with respect to the Sunni legal system. The Shiite science of juridical methodology, designed to fill the vacuum in religious authority brought about by the Occultation of the twelfth imam, was created and shaped largely by these negotiations. It was inspired by the need to communicate and debate with Sunni jurists on common ground and was often based closely on Sunni texts of legal theory.

It is possible to identify three main types of response to the Sunni legal system of orthodoxy and the concept of consensus on which it was based. These responses correspond to the kinds of reactions typically expected from a stigmatized minority to the deviant status assigned to them within the majority community. In an effort to participate in the Sunni legal system, many Shiite scholars outwardly accepted the ground rules established by the Sunni theory of consensus, and, passing as Sunnis, joined the Shāfiʿī *madhhab*. The internal attitude of those who did so varied widely, ranging from scorn to nearly complete acceptance of the Sunni majority. For some it was a necessary evil, the main purpose of which was to defend the faith against the enemy. For others it was a chance to contribute to a sophisticated system of legal education and scholarship. A second response was the attempt to adopt the concept of consensus and modify it so that it would include the Twelver legal tradition. This response would allow the Twelvers to establish a Shiite legal *madhhab* parallel to those of the Sunnis. The development of a Shiite science of jurisprudence was not a blind adoption or servile imitation of Sunni concepts and methods. Concepts needed to be adapted to suit Shiite tradition and doctrine, and there always remained a tension between the goal of acceptance within the majority and the idea that Shiites were actually a chosen community, favored with special access to God's guidance. The Twelver Akhbārīs rejected Sunni legal consensus, holding instead to a system based more closely on the scripture itself that shunned rationalist methods and rejected the authority of the jurists. They thus opted to deviate from the Sunni majority, the third response. Though they would deny that religious authority could be located anywhere but in the sacred text itself, their program implied that Shiite scholars could serve as guides for the believers to consult, but in their capacity as hadith experts and not as rationalist jurists. While in the first three Islamic centuries, Shiites generally expressed their attitudes toward the majority community through their theory of the imamate, by the late tenth century they felt the need to do so also through the science of jurisprudence. The point is not that any one of the attitudes expressed toward the majority community in these responses was new, but that existing attitudes had to be expressed in new ways, in terms of the consensus, because of profound changes in the nature of religious authority and institutions which had taken place within the Sunni community.

This reading of the history of Shiite jurisprudence provides some indication of the extent to which the consolidation of the Sunni *madhhab*s controlled the subsequent history of Islamic religious doctrine and institutions not only within the Sunni community but also within the most prominent marginal or minority Islamic groups such as the Shiites and the Khārijīs. Examination of the Twelver Shiite tradition shows how the legal system functioned over the long run to create a large degree of similarity between disparate Islamic groups. The Sunni legal system and the theory of consensus on which it was based set the ground rules for marginal sects' negotiation of their identity and place with respect to Islamic legal orthodoxy and the international system of legal education in the Muslim world. Within this framework, the Twelver Shiite jurists developed legal and educational institutions that differ in relatively minor respects from those of the four Sunni *madhhab*s.

While this study employs many theories and concepts native to Islamic intellectual tradition and examined in Orientalist scholarship, including *takfīr* (declaration of unbelief), and *taqīyah* (dissimulation), and appeals to concepts familiar from Christian and general religious history, such as orthodoxy and heresy, it also draws on the theory of stigma proposed by Erving Goffman in *Stigma: Notes on the Management of Spoiled Identity*, first published in 1963.[58]

58. Erving Goffman, *Stigma* (New York: Simon and Schuster, 1986).

This theory is particularly applicable to Shiites, who have lived as a stigmatized minority dominated by a potentially hostile majority in most areas of the Muslim world and during most periods of Muslim history. Even in regions where Shiites constituted a majority or during periods when they held the reins of political power, such as under Buwayhid rule in Iraq and Iran or in Iran since the establishment of the Safavid Empire in the sixteenth century, the acute awareness of Shiism's minority status within a larger and potentially hostile Sunni majority has colored the thinking of Shiite laymen and religious leaders alike. Even in contemporary Iran, a nation at least 90 percent Shiite that is ruled after a fashion according to Shiite Islamic law and run under the aegis of top Shiite jurists, many policies are set with the reaction of the Muslim world's Sunni majority in mind.

Goffman's theory explains the strategies stigmatized groups are likely to adopt in their efforts to fit into a social system dominated by the majority and thus provides considerable insight into the historical actions and ideological choices not only of Shiite communities in general but also of Shiite religious scholars throughout the centuries. Applying the theory of stigma to the development of Shiite law, one may explain the major trends of Shiite jurisprudence as types of responses of a stigmatized group to a norm enforced by the potentially hostile majority. In sociological terms, the Shiite scholars were subject to widespread prejudice in an academic and social environment where adherence to Sunni Islam was the norm. The normative expectations which the Shiite scholars did not in general meet were determined by the definition of Sunni orthodoxy supported in that environment. In this situation, a number of strategies were open to the Shiites in their attempts to live and interact in a society in which their true identities were discredited, deprecated, or unacceptable.

This book includes seven chapters, of which this Introduction is the first. Chapter 2 discusses the system of religious authority adopted by the classical Sunni jurists, especially between the ninth and the eleventh centuries, showing how the concept of *ijmāʿ*, "consensus," anchored in the authority of the jurists as a restricted category of religious professionals, came to define orthodoxy. Consequently, *mukhālafat al-ijmāʿ*, "violation of consensus," constituted heresy or religious deviation according to this system of authority. The subsequent development of Twelver Shiite jurisprudence may be analyzed as comprising three types of historical response to the particular accusation that they violated consensus and were therefore heretical or deviant. These reactions include conformance to consensus, discussed in chapter 3; adoption of consensus, discussed in chapter 4; and rejection of consensus, discussed in chapter 5. Chapter 3 argues that Shiite jurists often claimed to belong to the Shāfiʿī *madhhab* in order to participate in the Sunni system of legal education. Chapter 4 treats Twelver Shiite attempts to participate in the Sunni system as equal partners, through the creation of an additional orthodox *madhhab,* parallel with the Sunni *madhhab*s. Chapter 5 treats Shiites' rejection of the jurists' exclusive authority and shows that it was usually based on the idea that the Sunni legal system violated fundamental Shiite principles. It examines the Akhbārī school within Twelver Shiism and shows how the Akhbārīs rejected the Shiite jurists' adoption of Sunni legal concepts as incompatible with Shiite faith, insisting that authentic Shiite religious authority was based on expertise in hadith rather than expertise in legal methodology. They completely rejected the Shiite establishment of a jurist-based system of authority, in their view a historical tragedy resulting from the illegitimate adoption of an essentially Sunni system. Chapter 6 is a brief comparison of the Twelver Shiite and Sunni legal systems, providing a general assessment of the historical results of the attempt to create a *madhhab* parallel with those of the Sunnis. Chapter 7 presents a conclusion for this study.

This study is primarily one of legal theory and institutions. It is based on an analysis of texts on law and legal theory, both Shiite and Sunni, as well as material dealing with the lives and thought of jurists in the Shiite tradition found in *ijāzah* documents, biographical dictionaries, chronicles, and the works of these scholars themselves. Historically it covers the period from the tenth until the eighteenth century. Geographically it concentrates on the areas of Iraq, Iran, and Syria, for these were the foremost centers of Twelver Shiite learning, where the formative works in the legal tradition were produced. Concern focuses on the realm of actual legal practice at the level of education and educational institutions. The general sociopolitical dimensions of Islamic sects and relations between sects on the popular level, though they deserve serious study, will not be addressed. A study in intellectual history, this reading of the Shiite legal tradition differs from earlier presentations in its consistent emphasis on the history of Sunni jurisprudence and legal institutions as a crucial backdrop for the formation of Shiite legal theory and institutions.

2

Islamic Legal Orthodoxy

"Whoever denies the consensus of the Community has denied the Prophet."[1]

Ibn al-Qāṣṣ (d. 335/946)

Through the formation and consolidation of the classical Sunni juridical *madhhabs*, traditionalist jurists were able to gain exclusive control over institutions of Islamic religious education and establish their collective authority for the interpretation of Islamic law. From the tenth century until the present, the Sunni *madhhabs* have dominated Islamic religious discourse. Their proponents have succeeded in marginalizing or subordinating other societal groups claiming religious authority, such as theologians, caliphs, and hadith experts, and have regularly attempted to prevent other religious groups perceived as heterodox from taking part in the legal system. In the community of interpretation constituted by the *madhhabs*, legal consensus (*ijmā'*), the unanimous opinion of qualified jurists, defines Islamic orthodoxy. Only the opinions of scholars who belong to one of the recognized *madhhabs*, and have completed study in a curriculum defined and controlled by the jurists, may be taken into account in debate on religious questions. All other opinions, whether supported by evidence or not, are considered heterodox. The violation of legal consensus (*mukhālafat al-ijmā'*)—the espousal of an opinion which goes against that held unanimously by the qualified jurists of the recognized *madhhabs*—represents an unacceptable deviation from orthodoxy.

Armed with this definition of Islamic legal heresy, Sunni jurists have historically attempted to restrict the boundaries of Islamic religious discourse and to prevent minority groups, including Mu'tazilīs, Shiites, and Khārijīs, from participating in the development of Islamic law. Beginning in the tenth

1. Cited in al-Khaṭīb al-Baghdādī. *Kitāb al-faqīh wa'l-mutafaqqih*, 2 vols., ed. Ismā'īl al-Anṣārī (Beirut: Dār al-kutub al-'ilmīyah, 1980), 2: 19.

century, the Twelver Shiites have reacted to this predicament in a number of ways that will be explored in the following chapters of this study. The specific norms used to exclude them have shaped the forms their reactions took, profoundly affecting the subsequent history of Twelver Shiite legal education, scholarship, and theory.

THE PROFESSIONALIZATION OF SUNNI LEGAL STUDY

Recent studies, correcting earlier views which date the *madhhabs* anachronistically back to their eponymous "founders," place the formation of the classical Sunni legal *madhhabs* as structured organizations engaged in the regular transmission of legal knowledge in the mid-ninth to early tenth centuries. The standard *muṣannaf* compilations of hadith, arranged according to legal topics, date from the mid-ninth century and were intended to serve as ready references for jurists, an implication that the legal profession was already active and beginning to organize at that time.[2] Calder identifies the tenth century as the major period of transition in the formalization of Islamic legal scholarship, characterized by the production of epitomes (*mukhtaṣars*) of law, the earliest element of a formal legal curriculum. The role of the *Epitomes* of the Ḥanafīs Aḥmad b. Muḥammad al-Ṭaḥāwī (d. 321/933) and Abū al-Faḍl Muḥammad b. Muḥammad al-Marwazī (d. 334/945–46), the *Talkhīṣ fī al-fiqh* of the Shāfiʿī Ibn al-Qāṣṣ (d. 335/946), and the *Epitome* of the Ḥanbalī Abū al-Qāsim al-Khiraqī (d. 334/945–46) as textbooks in regular processes of legal education is clear from the numbers of commentaries they generated.[3]

In his study of the formation of the classical Sunni schools of law, Melchert finds that the consolidation of the three main legal schools in Baghdad and the Islamic East—the Shāfiʿī, Ḥanbalī, and Ḥanafī *madhhabs*—may be dated to the late ninth and early tenth centuries. In order to discern the existence of the *madhhab* as an institution, Melchert uses as criteria the recognition of a *raʾīs* or chief scholar, the production of commentaries (*taʿlīqahs*) on standard legal epitomes (*mukhtaṣars*), and the regular transmission of legal knowledge, whereby students were recognized as having completed their legal education under a specific prominent jurist. He identifies the great law professors, the Shāfiʿī Ibn Surayj (d. 306/918), the Ḥanbalī al-Khallāl (d. 311/923), and the Ḥanafī Abū al-Ḥasan al-Karkhī (d. 340/952), as the virtual founders of their respective *madhhabs*. The Mālikī, Ẓāhirī, and Jarīrī *madhhabs* had limited success in the east and ceased to exist as coherent organizations in Baghdad by the early eleventh century. The Mālikī jurists of Baghdad during the ninth century, particularly Ismāʿīl b.

2. Makdisi, *Rise of Humanism*, 19–20.

3. Norman Calder, *Studies in Early Muslim Jurisprudence* (Oxford: Clarendon Press, 1993), 245–47.

Isḥāq (d. 282/896), established a system of legal education that maintained some continuity in the tenth century, but which would subsequently sputter out. Neither adherents of the Ẓāhirī school—followers of Dā'ūd b. 'Alī (d. 270/884)—nor those of the Jarrīrī school—followers of Muḥammad b. Jarīr al-Ṭabarī (d. 310/923)—produced, as far as the sources reveal, the regular commentaries which signal the existence of a functioning *madhhab.* The Mālikīs in the west subsequently and gradually incorporated the innovations that had taken place in the east.[4]

Several key developments in the professionalization of legal studies in the tenth and eleventh centuries have been identified by George Makdisi. He has shown that Sunni traditionalists established endowed colleges of law over which they maintained exclusive control, first in the form of *masjid-khān* complexes in the tenth century, then in the form of *madrasahs* per se in the eleventh. These new institutions entailed a framework of scholarly personnel also controlled by the jurists. They taught a formal legal curriculum, involving, in addition to the ancillary sciences, a regular four-year law course followed by a program of advanced study in law and disputation taking as long as ten to twenty years. The advanced student would write a *ta'līqah,* a commentary on his professor's method concerning the disputed questions of the law (*khilāf*). Upon completing his legal education, the student would receive the *ijāzat al-tadrīs wa'l-iftā',* "the license to teach law and grant legal *responsa,*" from his law professor, a master jurist. This license attested to the bearer's general competence as a jurist and ability to engage in independent legal research and interpretation. Makdisi likens it to a doctorate of law.[5] Jurists of the tenth and eleventh centuries were no longer merely scholars of the Koran and the traditions of the Prophet. They were trained professionals who had gone through a rigorous education in the law and related sciences. All those who had not completed this education were excluded from participating in the elaboration of the law.

Makdisi has argued that the traditionalist movement played a pivotal role in the formation of the Sunni *madhhabs* in an attempt to prevent what was seen as rationalist encroachments on religious interpretation at the expense of reliance on scripture. He points out several historical victories for the traditionalists in their struggle to limit the influence of speculative theology on the elaboration of Islamic doctrine. Near the turn of the ninth century, al-Shāfi'ī authored *al-Risālah,* a treatise on legal methodology that Makdisi characterizes as embodying a juridical theology designed to exclude the rationalist Mu'tazilīs

4. Melchert, "Formation of the Sunni Schools of Law."

5. Makdisi, *Rise of Colleges,* 1–223; idem, *Rise of Humanism,* 2–45; idem, "Muslim Institutions of Learning in Eleventh-Century Baghdad," *BSOAS* 24 (1961): 1–56.

as authorities on the religion.[6] The *miḥnah* or inquisition of the mid-ninth century (218–33/833–48) failed to impose the religious authority of the caliphs and Mu'tazilī theologians on society, and the heroic resistance of Aḥmad b. Ḥanbal set an example for them. The defection of the famous semirationalist theologian al-Ash'arī (d. ca. 324/935) to the traditionalist camp in his later years was also a triumph for the traditionalists. A century later Caliph al-Qādir (381–422/991–1031) promulgated decrees in 408/1017 and 409/1018 supporting the authority and views of the traditionalist legal scholars and rejecting Mu'-tazilī rationalist theology as well as Shiism. These decrees developed into the Qādirī Creed, a document read publicly in 409/1018 and on a number of other occasions during the caliphates of al-Qādir and his son al-Qā'im (422–67/1031–75). Makdisi interprets these historical events as landmarks in the process by which religious authority was concentrated in the hands of the traditionalist jurists. Largely in reaction to the philosophical methods of the Mu'tazilīs, the traditionalists succeeded in closing their ranks and arguing for the authenticity of the jurists' religious authority.[7] According to this portrayal, the traditionalists' struggle began at the turn of the ninth century, and was completed in the eleventh, coming to a close at the same time that the *madrasah*s or colleges of law were established.

Stressing the formal structure of the *madhhab*s as well as their autonomy and exclusivity, Makdisi has asserted that from the ninth century on, the *madhhab*s were in fact professional legal guilds.[8] While the appropriateness of this particular term may be subject to debate,[9] this insightful characterization nevertheless helps explain many aspects of subsequent Islamic religious and legal history, calling attention to the fact that the *madhhab*s were professional institutions with a considerable degree of formality and rigidity and not merely schools of thought or scholarly traditions carrying on the method of some

6. Makdisi, "The Juridical Theology of Shāfi'ī: Origins and Significance of Uṣūl al-fiqh," *Studia Islamica* 59 (1984): 5–47. Likewise, Norman Calder has characterized *al-Risālah* as a refutation of Mu'tazilī epistemology, asserting that revelation is a sufficient source of knowledge necessary for religious purposes. Al-Shāfi'ī's work, he suggests, was designed to defend and bolster the authority of the jurists, who claimed a monopoly of religious knowledge ("*Ikhtilāf* and *Ijmā'* in Shāfi'ī's *Risāla*," *Studia Islamica* 58 [1984]: 55–81, esp. p. 72).

7. Makdisi, *Rise of Humanism*, 2–8.

8. George Makdisi, "The Guilds of Law in Medieval Legal History," *Zeitschrift für Geshichte der Arabisch-Islamischen Wissenschaften* 1 (1984): 233–52; idem, "La corporation à l'époque classique de l'Islam," in *Présence de Louis Massignon: Hommages et témoignages*, ed. Daniel Massignon (Paris: Maisonneuve et Larose, 1987), 35–49; idem, *Rise of Humanism*, 16–23; idem, "Professionalized Higher Learning: Past and Present," paper presented at Symposium on Occidentalism, University of Pennsylvania, Philadelphia, March 23–24, 1990.

9. Some objections have been voiced by A. Kevin Reinhart in "Guilding the *Madhhab:* The 'Schools' of Islamic Law and Their Significance," paper presented at the American Oriental Society conference, Miami, March 1997.

great master of the past.[10] In a more recent study, Makdisi finds that *ṭabaqāt* works—biographical compendia arranged by "classes" or "generations"—were used by the jurists to establish the legitimacy of their *madhhabs*. On this basis, he concludes that the *madhhabs* indeed constituted professional legal guilds beginning in the late ninth or early tenth century. According to this article, the first guild to be established was that of the Ḥanbalīs, by the time of al-Khallāl (d. 311/923), who wrote a biographical work on the Ḥanbalīs entitled *Ṭabaqāt aṣḥāb Ibn Ḥanbal.* They were soon followed by the Mālikīs; the first author of a biographical work on Mālikī jurists was by the Andalusian Ibn Abī Dalim (d. 351/962). Subsequently, the Shāfi'īs and Ḥanafīs established their own guilds. The first Shāfi'ī *ṭabaqāt* works are those of al-Muṭṭawwi'ī (d. ca. 400/1009) and Abū al-Ṭayyib al-Ṭabarī (d. 450/1058), and the first Ḥanafī *ṭabaqāt* works are by al-Muhandis (d. 769/1367) or Ibn Abī al-Wafā' (d. 775/1373). The apparent delay in the case of the Shāfi'īs and Ḥanafīs is due, Makdisi holds, to internal conflict between the traditionalists and rationalists of those schools. The Ẓāhirīs also succeeded in establishing a guild by the eleventh century; its existence is signaled by the work *Akhbār ahl al-Ẓāhir* by Abū Bakr Ibn al-Akhḍar (d. 429/1038).[11] This account conflicts on several points with that of Melchert, who sets the foundation of the Shāfi'ī *madhhab* before that of the Ḥanbalīs and denies that the Ẓāhirīs succeeded in establishing a professional juridical *madhhab*.[12] It is perhaps risky to link the date of establishment of the professional *madhhabs* so closely with the production of a *ṭabaqāt* work on the jurists of that particular *madhhab,* for the legitimation of an institution does not necessarily coincide with its foundation. Nevertheless, the argument seems sound that *ṭabaqāt* of the jurists of a particular *madhhab,* designed as they were to legitimize the *madhhab* and establish the authority of its jurists, signals the existence of the *madhhab* as a self-conscious professional organization. Though the chronological order of the foundation of the *madhhabs* remains somewhat obscure, two points made in Makdisi's study stand out as reliable markers. The *ṭabaqāt* work of al-Khallāl probably reflects the organization of

10. In this study I have opted to use the Arabic term *madhhab* rather than "guild" to refer to the institutions of legal study because I am not entirely convinced that the *madhhabs* correspond to the European medieval guilds in all essential characteristics. More research is required on the nature and workings of the *madhhab* in the medieval Islamic world before this equation can be made reliably. There are problems with the use of the word *madhhab,* however, which has many denotations. The most significant problem for the present study is that the term is used to refer to both the personal schools of law before professionalization and the professional institutions of legal study—Makdisi's guilds. See his "*Ṭabaqāt*-Biography: Law and Orthodoxy in Classical Islam," *Islamic Studies* 32 (1993): 371–96, esp. 391. In the remainder of the work, I will use the term *madhhab* in the second sense: referring to organized, autonomous, exclusive associations engaged in the formation of professional jurists and the regular transmission of legal knowledge.

11. Ibid., 379–92.

12. Melchert, "Formation of the Sunni Schools of Law."

the Ḥanbalī *madhhab* by the late ninth or early tenth century, and the *Ṭabaqāt al-fuqahā'* of Abū Isḥāq al-Shīrāzī (d. 476/1083), giving the pedigrees of the jurists of his day, indicates the existence in the eleventh century of five organized juridical *madhhab*s, those of the Shāfi'īs, Ḥanafīs, Mālikīs, Ḥanbalīs, and Ẓāhirīs.

By the eleventh century, the jurists succeeded, to a large extent, in their attempts to establish a monopoly on Islamic religious authority. They refused to accept as authoritative the opinions of anyone who had not completed a legal education according to the methods they had established and who did not belong to a recognized *madhhab.* Only the opinions of these restricted groups were taken into account by the community of legal scholars as representing acceptable interpretations of the law. Makdisi argues that the Islamic doctorate of law, the *ijāzat al-tadrīs wa'l-iftā',* was crucial in enforcing such claims, for it not only attested to the competence of the jurist but also gave him sole jurisdictional authority in matters pertaining to the religious law.[13] During this period, the jurists also put forth strong arguments for their exclusive religious authority, citing scriptural authority texts from the Koran and hadith to back up their claims.[14] Through consolidation of the juridical *madhhab*s as autonomous, exclusive professional organizations, the traditionalist jurists were able to exert hegemony over Islamic religious discourse as never before.

JURISPRUDENCE AS A GENRE OF LEGAL LITERATURE

Jurists associated with the Sunni *madhhab*s expounded their views on jurisprudence or legal methodology in a genre of works that came to be termed *uṣūl al-fiqh,* "the sources of the law." A main concern of this genre seems to have been to present the interpretative methods of the jurists in a systematic manner, with the logical, theoretical, and philosophical sophistication of speculative theology. *Uṣūl al-fiqh* grew hand in hand with the consolidation of the legal *madhhab*s. Its establishment was intimately connected with the consolidation and theoretical justification of the *madhhab* system, for in a sense it embodies the sacred epistemology adopted by the jurists. This genre, more than any other, defines and acts as a forum for the "thought collective" of the jurists, a community of interpretation with shared goals, assumptions, and ways of thinking operating within particular institutional constraints. Despite the differences of opinion expressed therein, the genre of jurisprudence nevertheless set the boundaries and the framework for Islamic legal discourse from the tenth century on.

The *Epistle* (*al-Risālah*) of al-Shāfi'ī (d. 204/820) has long been recognized

13. Makdisi, *Rise of Humanism,* 26–29, 33–38.

14. One of the most sustained of such arguments for the authority of jurists is found in al-Khaṭīb al-Baghdādī, *Kitāb al-faqīh wa'l-mutafaqqih,* 1: 1–53. See chapter 6 for additional examples.

as the genre's first comprehensive work.[15] Striking, though, is the gap in time between al-Shāfiʿī's *Epistle* and the next extant works on jurisprudence: as much as a century and a half or even two. The differences between his work and the well-known *uṣūl al-fiqh* texts of the eleventh century, in both content and organization, are considerable. Makdisi sees the genre of *uṣūl al-fiqh* as inaugurated by al-Shāfiʿī in *al-Risālah,* with the classical tradition deriving directly from his work. While he recognizes the paucity of extant works on jurisprudence between the time of al-Shāfiʿī and the late tenth and early eleventh centuries, he holds that evidence for the existence of the genre may be gathered from later works on jurisprudence, such as *al-Musawwadah* by Ibn Taymīyah, his father, and his grandfather, which cite many earlier works in the genre. Makdisi recognizes the significant difference in content between al-Shāfiʿī's work and the later works of the classical *uṣūl al-fiqh* genre as well, but maintains that the original genre of *uṣūl al-fiqh* was transformed by the introduction of questions of legal theory and philosophy on the part of Muʿtazilī theologians.[16] This transformation, however, does not negate the basic continuity of the genre.

Recently, scholars have argued against this view, holding that *al-Risālah* should not be taken as the starting point of *uṣūl al-fiqh* as a recognized genre.[17] Hallaq insists that al-Shāfiʿī's *Risālah,* which treats the interpretation of sacred texts with a decided emphasis on the hadith of the Prophet, has little in common with the classical *uṣūl al-fiqh* works, which present a full-fledged legal methodology. He rejects the view that the genre of *uṣūl al-fiqh* begins with *al-Risālah,* claiming that no identifiable *uṣūl al-fiqh* texts were written during the ninth century. During this period, he states, *al-Risālah* met with "oblivion"; supposedly, it did not evoke any commentaries or refutations in the ninth century. It was only in the tenth century, in his view, that *uṣūl al-fiqh* became a recognized genre.[18]

Given the nature of available sources, it is risky to make claims about the development of jurisprudence in the ninth century based on the lack of evidence. Many works mentioned in the biographical and bibliographical sources have been lost, and many more, one must assume, have completely

15. Makdisi, "Juridical Theology," 5–47, esp. 6, 13, 14–17. Makdisi (6) holds that the original work must have been written before 198/813–14, because it was addressed to ʿAbd al-Raḥmān b. Mahdī, who died that year. Calder has argued that the *Risālah* cannot be dated accurately to al-Shāfiʿī's time since it was the product of organic growth and redaction, which continued long after his death. He suggests that it reached its present form ca. 300 A.H. (912–13 A.D.) (*Early Muslim Jurisprudence,* 221–44).

16. Makdisi, "Juridical Theology," 14–18.

17. Wael B. Hallaq, "Was al-Shāfiʿī the Master Architect of Islamic Jurisprudence," *IJMES* 25 (1993): 587–605; A. Kevin Reinhart, *Before Revelation* (Albany: State University of New York Press, 1995), 14–15.

18. Hallaq, "al-Shāfiʿī," 588–94.

escaped mention. For example, it is reported that the famous Shāfiʿī jurist Ibn Surayj wrote four hundred works, but extant sources mention only a handful of titles.[19] Even when the title of a book has been preserved, it is often difficult to tell whether it was devoted to *uṣūl al-fiqh*. Moreover, later works of jurisprudence often cite the opinions of a particular jurist without specifying the title of the work cited, if indeed it was an independent work. The Ḥanafī jurist Abū al-Ḥasan al-Karkhī is quoted so frequently in later works on jurisprudence that it seems nearly inconceivable that he did not write a work on *uṣūl al-fiqh*.[20] Nevertheless, the sources do not mention any. It is entirely posssible that the sources have failed to preserve mention of a number of ninth-century works that were crucial for the development of the *uṣūl al-fiqh* genre.

Hallaq's article includes a few tendentious interpretations designed to buttress the claim that *uṣūl al-fiqh* did not exist as such before the tenth century. His argument that al-Qāḍī al-Nuʿmān's mid–tenth-century refutation of Sunni juristic principles, *Ikhtilāf uṣūl al-madhāhib,* "confirms the data provided by the bio-bibliographical sources" is weak. First, the "data" provided by these sources is merely negative evidence—the failure to name and identify early works on *uṣūl al-fiqh*. Second, al-Qāḍī al-Nuʿmān mentions very few works by title in the course of his refutation: the Koran (passim), the Torah (p. 13), the Gospels (p. 13), *Adab al-qāḍī* and *Ikhtilāf al-Shāfiʿī wa-Mālik* by al-Shāfiʿī (p. 214), and *al-Mujarrad* by al-Ḥasan b. Ziyād al-Luʾluʾī (d. 204/819–20), a student of Abū Ḥanīfah (p. 41). Although none of these works is devoted to jurisprudence per se, the fact remains that al-Qāḍī al-Nuʿmān is arguing against a sophisticated system of jurisprudence which must have been presented in a highly developed tradition of Sunni works by his time. In order to claim that no works on *uṣūl al-fiqh* date to the ninth century, Hallaq must discount the works on jurisprudence attributed to al-Karābīsī (d. 248/862–63) and Ibn Surayj (d. 306/918) and ignore such figures as Abū Nuʿaym al-Astarābādī (d. 321/933) who lived a considerable portion of his life during the ninth century and could have written works on jurisprudence before 900 A.D. Similarly, he ignores the possibility that Abū Sahl al-Nawbakhtī (d. 311/924), an Imami theologian who wrote a refutation of al-Shāfiʿī's *Risālah,* may easily have done so before the tenth century.[21] Particularly egregious is the statement "it is indeed telling that even Ibn Surayj, with the intense detail of biographical

19. Abū Isḥāq al-Shīrāzī, *Ṭabaqāt al-fuqahāʾ,* ed. Iḥsān ʿAbbās (Beirut: Dār al-rāʾid al-ʿarabī, 1970), 109.

20. His opinions on topics in jurisprudence have been collected in Ḥusayn Khalaf al-Jubūrī, *al-Aqwāl al-uṣūliyah liʾl-Imām Abī al-Ḥasan al-Karkhī* (Medina: al-Jubūrī, 1989).

21. Hallaq reports that al-Nawbakhtī died in the 940s A.D., though it is not clear on what basis he does so ("al-Shāfiʿi," 595). Al-Nawbakhtī actually died in Shawwāl 311/January-February 924. See Wilferd Madelung, "Abū Sahl Nawbakhtī," *Encyclopaedia Iranica.*

notices he is accorded, is not reported to have written on *uṣūl* work proper."[22] The sources report that Ibn Surayj studied under al-Anmāṭī (d. 281/893–94?), debated Muḥammad b. Dā'ūd al-Ẓāhirī (d. 297/909–10), and served as qāḍī of Shiraz, but they say *very* little about his works. The notice of Ibn al-Nadīm gives five titles, that of al-Subkī two, and that of al-Shīrāzī none, though the latter states that the catalogue of his works includes four hundred titles[23]—which can hardly be described as "intense detail."

One must proceed with caution in tracing the early history of the genre, particularly since so many works from the ninth and tenth centuries have been lost. In any case, the categorical statement that *uṣūl al-fiqh* works were not written during the ninth century seems unwarranted. The following list, building on those of Makdisi and Hallaq, presents works of *uṣūl al-fiqh* mentioned in the sources as having been written after al-Shāfi'ī and up until the time of al-Qāḍī 'Abd al-Jabbār (d. 415/1024).[24]

Early Uṣūl al-Fiqh Works

1. Ḥusayn b. 'Alī al-Karābīsī (Shāfi'ī, d. 248/862–63), no title.[25]
2. Abū al-'Abbās Aḥmad b. 'Umar Ibn Surayj (Shāfi'ī, d. 306/918), *Kitāb al-i'dhār wa'l-indhār*[26] and *Risālat al-bayān 'an uṣūl al-aḥkām.*[27]
3. Abū Nu'aym 'Abd al-Malik b. Malik b. 'Adī al-Jurjānī al-Astarābādī (Shāfi'ī, d. 321/933), no title.[28]
4. Abū Bakr Muḥammad b. Ibrāhīm al-Ṣayrafī (Shāfi'ī, d. 330/942), *al-Bayān fī dalā'il al-a'lām 'alā uṣūl al-aḥkām.*[29]
5. Abū al-Faraj 'Umar b. Muḥammad (Mālikī, d. 331/943), *Kitāb al-luma' fī uṣūl al-fiqh.*[30]
6. Abū Manṣūr Muḥammad b. Muḥammad al-Māturīdī (Ḥanafī, d. 333/945), *Ma'khadh al-sharā'i' fī uṣūl al-fiqh* and *Kitāb al-jadal fī uṣūl al-fiqh.*[31]
7. Aḥmad b. Abī Aḥmad al-Ṭabarī Ibn al-Qāṣṣ (Shāfi'ī, d. 335/946–47), *Riyāḍ al-muta'allimīn.*[32]

22. Hallaq, "al-Shāfi'ī," 596.

23. Ibn al-Nadīm, *al-Fihrist* (Cairo: Maṭba'at al-istiqāmah, 1957), 313–14; al-Shīrāzī, *Ṭabaqāt al-fuqahā'*, 108–9; Tāj al-Dīn al-Subkī, *Ṭabaqāt al-shāfi'īyah al-kubrā,* 10 vols., ed. 'Abd al-Fattāḥ al-Ḥilw and Maḥmūd Muḥammad al-Ṭanāḥī (Cairo: Hajr, 1992), 3: 21–39.

24. See Makdisi, "Juridical Theology," 30–32; Hallaq, "al-Shāfi'ī," 595.

25. al-Shīrāzī, *Ṭabaqāt al-fuqahā'*, 102.

26. Makdisi, "Juridical Theology," 306, citing Badr al-Dīn al-Zarkashī (d. 794/1392).

27. al-Subkī, *Ṭabaqāt al-shāfi'īyah al-kubrā,* 3: 456–57.

28. Muḥammad b. Aḥmad al-'Abbādī, *Kitāb ṭabaqāt al-fuqahā' al-shāfi'īyah,* ed. Gösta Vitestam (Leiden: E. J. Brill, 1964), 55.

29. Ibn al-Nadīm, *al-Fihrist,* 314; al-Shīrāzī, *Ṭabaqāt al-fuqahā'*, 111.

30. Ibn al-Nadīm, *al-Fihrist,* 297.

31. Zayn al-Dīn Qāsim Ibn Quṭlūbughā, *Tāj al-tarājim fī ṭabaqāt al-ḥanafīyah* (Baghdad: Maṭba'at al-'Ānī, 1962), 59.

32. Makdisi, "Juridical Theology," 306, citing Badr al-Dīn al-Zarkashī.

8. Abū ʻAbd Allāh Muḥammad b. ʻĪsā, Ibn Abī Mūsā al-Faqīh al-Ḍarīr (Ḥanafī, d. 330s/940s), "he has eight volumes on *uṣūl al-fiqh.*"[33]
9. Abū Isḥāq Ibrāhīm b. Aḥmad al-Marwazī (Shāfiʻī, d. 340/951), *Kitāb al-fuṣūl fī maʻrifat al-uṣūl.*[34]
10. Abū Bakr Muḥammad b. ʻAbd Allāh al-Bardaʻī (Ḥanafī?, d. after 340/951–52), *Kitāb al-jāmiʻ fī uṣūl al-fiqh.*[35]
11. Ibn Abī Hurayrah, Abū ʻAbd Allāh al-Ḥasan b. al-Ḥusayn (Shāfiʻī, d. 345/956), no title.[36]
12. Abū al-Ḥasan ʻAlī b. al-Ḥusayn al-Masʻūdī (Shāfiʻī?, d. 345/956), *Kitāb naẓm al-adillah fī uṣūl al-millah* and *Kitāb naẓm al-aʻlām fī uṣūl al-aḥkām.*[37]
13. Abū Aḥmad Muḥammad b. Saʻīd b. Muḥammad b. ʻAbd Allāh b. Abī al-Qāḍī (Shāfiʻī, d. 343–49/954–60), *Kitāb al-hidāyah.*[38]
14. Abū Bakr al-Fārisī (Shāfiʻī, d. ca. 350/961–62), no title.[39]
15. Abū ʻAlī al-Ḥusayn b. al-Qāsim al-Ṭabarī (Shāfiʻī, d. 350/961–62), no title.[40]
16. Abū al-Ḥusayn b. al-Qaṭṭān (Shāfiʻī, d. 359/970), no title.[41]
17. Abū Ḥāmid Aḥmad b. Bishr al-ʻĀmirī (Shāfiʻī, d. 362/973), *Kitāb al-ishrāf ʻalā uṣūl al-fiqh.*[42]
18. Abū Bakr M. b. ʻAlī b. Ismāʻīl al-Qaffāl al-Shāshī (Shāfiʻī, d. 365/976), *Kitāb al-uṣūl.*[43]
19. Abū al-Ḥusayn al-Ṭawāʼifī al-Baghdādī (Shāfiʻī, fl. 4th/10th c.), no title.[44]

33. Ibn Quṭlūbughā, *Tāj al-tarājim,* 86.

34. Ibn al-Nadīm, *al-Fihrist,* 313; al-Shīrāzī, *Ṭabaqāt al-fuqahāʼ,* 112.

35. Ibn al-Nadīm, *al-Fihrist,* 344. The work was written before 340/951–52, because Ibn al-Nadīm met al-Bardaʻī and recorded the books he had authored in that year. Ibn al-Nadīm reports that al-Bardaʻī was a crypto-Khārijī who presented himself as a Muʻtazilī, but does not specify his adopted Sunni legal *madhhab.*

36. Makdisi, "Juridical Theology," 306, citing Badr al-Dīn al-Zarkashī; al-Subkī, *Ṭabaqāt al-shāfiʻīyah al-kubrā,* 3: 59.

37. Abū al-Ḥasan al-Masʻūdī, *Murūj al-dhahab wa-maʻādin al-jawhar,* 4 vols., ed. Qāsim al-Shammāʻī al-Rifāʻī (Beirut: Dār al-qalam, 1989), 1: 12–13; idem, *Kitāb al-tanbīh wa'l-ishrāf,* ed. M. J. De Goeje (Leiden: E. J. Brill, 1984), 4–5. Al-Masʻūdī was an Imami Shiite who participated in the Shāfiʻī legal *madhhab.* The works mentioned here may have been written from either a Shāfiʻī or an Imami Shiite perspective. See the discussions of al-Masʻūdī and his work in chapters 3 and 4.

38. al-Subkī, *Ṭabaqāt al-shāfiʻīyah al-kubrā,* 3: 164–66.

39. Aḥmad b. Yaḥyā Ibn al-Murtaḍā, *Kitāb ṭabaqāt al-muʻtazilah,* ed. Susanna Diwald-Wilzer (Beirut: Dār al-muntaẓar, 1988), 102. Al-Fārisī was a student of Ibn Surayj.

40. Makdisi, "Juridical Theology," 306, citing Badr al-Dīn al-Zarkashī; al-Subkī, *Ṭabaqāt al-shāfiʻīyah al-kubrā,* 3: 180–81; al-Shīrāzī, *Ṭabaqāt al-fuqahāʼ,* 115.

41. Makdisi, "Juridical Theology," 306, citing Badr al-Dīn al-Zarkashī.

42. Ibn al-Nadīm, *al-Fihrist,* 315; al-Shīrāzī, *Ṭabaqāt al-fuqahāʼ,* 114.

43. Ibn al-Nadīm, *al-Fihrist,* 317; al-Shīrāzī, *Ṭabaqāt al-fuqahāʼ,* 114; al-Subkī, *Ṭabaqāt al-shāfiʻīyah al-kubrā,* 3: 200.

44. Ibn al-Murtaḍā, *Ṭabaqāt al-muʻtazilah,* 109. Al-Ṭawāʼifī was a student of Abū Hāshim al-Jubbāʼī (d. 321/933).

20. Abū Bakr Aḥmad b. ʿAlī al-Jaṣṣāṣ al-Rāzī (Ḥanafī, d. 370/980), *al-Fuṣūl fī al-uṣūl.*[45]
21. Abū al-Ḥasan ʿAbd al-ʿAzīz b. al-Ḥārith al-Tamīmī (Ḥanbalī, d. 371/982), no title.[46]
22. Abū Bakr Muḥammad b. ʿAbd Allāh al-Abharī (Mālikī, d. 375/985), no title.[47]
23. Abū Bakr Muḥammad b. Isḥāq al-Qāsānī (Shāfiʿī, fl. 4th/10th c.) *Kitāb uṣūl al-futyā.*[48]
24. Abū ʿAbd al-Raḥmān (Shāfiʿī, fl. 4th/10th c.), *Kitāb al-maqālāt fī uṣūl al-fiqh.*[49]
25. Abū al-Ṭayyib Ibn al-Khallāl (Ẓāhirī, fl. 4th/10th c.), *Kitāb naʿt al-ḥikmah fī uṣūl al-fiqh.*[50]
26. Abū al-Faraj al-Muʿāfā al-Nahrawānī (Jarīrī, d. 390/1000) *Kitāb al-Taḥrīr wa'l-tanqīr(?) fī uṣūl al-fiqh* and *Kitāb al-ḥudūd wa'l-ʿuqūd fī uṣūl al-fiqh.*[51]
27. Abū Bakr Muḥammad b. Aḥmad b. ʿAbd Allāh Ibn al-Kawwāz (Mālikī, fl. 4th/10th c.), no title.[52]
28. Abū al-Ḥasan ʿAlī b. ʿUmar, Ibn al-Qaṣṣār al-Baghdādī (Mālikī, d. 398/1008), *al-Muqaddimah fī uṣūl al-fiqh.*[53]
29. Abū ʿAbd Allāh Muḥammad b. Aḥmad b. Ḥanīf (Ḥanafī, fl. 4th/10th c.), no title.[54]
30. Abū Naṣr b. Abī ʿAbd Allāh al-Ḥannāṭ al-Shīrāzī (Shāfiʿī, fl. 4th/10th c.), no title.[55]
31. Abū ʿAbd Allāh al-Ḥasan b. Ḥāmid al-Baghdādī (Ḥanbalī, d. 403/1012), no title.[56]

45. al-Jaṣṣāṣ, *al-Fuṣūl fī al-uṣūl.* See also idem, *al-Fuṣūl fī al-uṣūl, (abwāb al-ijtihād wa'l-qiyās);* idem, *al-Ijmāʿ,* ed. Zuhayr Shafīq Kabbī (Beirut: Dār al-muntakhab al-ʿarabī, 1993); Bernand, "Ḥanafī *Uṣūl al-Fiqh,*" 623–35.

46. Muḥammad Ibn Abī Yaʿlā, *Ṭabaqāt al-ḥanābilah,* 2 vols., ed. Muḥammad Ḥāmid al-Fiqī (Cairo: Maṭbaʿat al-sunnah al-muḥammadīyah, 1952), 2: 139; al-Qāḍī Abū Yaʿlā, *al-ʿUddah fī uṣul al-fiqh,* 5 vols., ed. Aḥmad b. ʿAlī Sayr al-Mubārakī (Riyāḍ, 1990), 3: 756, 4: 1257. Abū Yaʿlā reports that he had an autograph copy of this author's fascicle *(juz')* on *uṣūl al-fiqh* in his possession.

47. Ibn al-Nadīm, *al-Fihrist,* 297.

48. Ibid., 314. Written before 377/987–88.

49. Ibid., 314–15. Written before 377/987–88.

50. Ibid., 320. Written before 377/987–88.

51. Ibid., 343. Written before 377/987–88. The text reads *m-n-q-r* instead of *tanqīr.*

52. al-Shīrāzī, *Ṭabaqāt al-fuqahā',* 168.

53. Sezgin, *GAS,* 1: 481–82.

54. Ibn al-Murtaḍā, *Ṭabaqāt al-muʿtazilah,* 115. This scholar was a student of Abū ʿAbd Allāh al-Baṣrī (d. 369/979–80).

55. al-Shīrāzī, *Ṭabaqāt al-fuqahā',* 122.

56. Ibn Abī Yaʿlā, *Ṭabaqāt al-ḥanābilah,* 2: 171.

32. Abū Bakr Muḥammad b. al-Ṭayyib b. Muḥammad al-Bāqillānī (Mālikī, d. 403/1013), *al-Taqrīb wa'l-irshād fī tartīb ṭuruq al-ijtihād.*[57]
33. Abū al-Faḍl b. 'Abd al-'Azīz al-Tamīmī (Ḥanbalī, d. 410/1020), no title.[58]
34. al-Qāḍī 'Abd al-Jabbār b. Aḥmad al-Hamadhānī al-Asadābādī (Shāfi'ī, d. 415/1024), *al-Nihāyah, al-'Umad,* and volume seventeen of *al-Mughnī.*[59]

The earliest independent, comprehensive treatment of *uṣūl al-fiqh* that has come down to us is *al-Fuṣūl fī al-uṣūl* by Abū Bakr Aḥmad b. 'Alī al-Jaṣṣāṣ al-Rāzī (d. 370/980).[60] In both content and form, al-Jaṣṣāṣ's work is quite sophisticated, resembling later works in the *uṣūl al-fiqh* genre; it gives the impression of following a well-established tradition. Other than *al-Fuṣūl,* the earliest published texts on jurisprudence are al-Qāḍī 'Abd al-Jabbār's (d. 415/1024) treatment of *uṣūl al-fiqh* in the seventeenth volume of *al-Mughnī,* Abū al-Ḥusayn al-Baṣrī's (d. 436/1044) *al-Mu'tamad,* and the latter's commentary on al-Qāḍī 'Abd al-Jabbār's *al-'Umad.*[61] The *uṣūl al-fiqh* work *al-Taqrīb wa'l-irshād fī tartīb ṭuruq al-ijtihād* by al-Bāqillānī (d. 403/1013) is partially preserved in an abridgment, *al-Talkhīṣ,* by Imām al-Ḥaramayn al-Juwaynī (d. 478/1085).[62] These and other later *uṣūl al-fiqh* works give evidence of a rich tradition that developed in the course of the tenth century.

The list presented above indicates that jurisprudence was a thriving intellectual tradition in the late ninth century and throughout the tenth. Numerous works were written in the genre not only in the Shāfi'ī *madhhab* but also in the Ḥanafī, Mālikī, and Ḥanbalī *madhhabs*. By the late tenth century even Ẓāhirī and Jarīrī jurists wrote what appear to be comprehensive works on jurisprudence. The preponderance of Shāfi'īs in this list is partly a reflection of the extant and published sources, which are weighted heavily toward the Shāfi'īs. Nevertheless, it may be that the Shāfi'ī jurists led the development of the genre, which is intimated, at least, by the report that al-Karābīsī wrote an independent

57. Imām al-Ḥaramayn al-Juwaynī, *Kitāb al-ijtihād min kitāb al-talkhīṣ* (Damascus: Dār al-qalam, 1987).

58. Ibn Abī Ya'lā, *Ṭabaqāt al-ḥanābilah,* 2: 179; Abū Ya'lā, *al-'Uddah,* 2: 179.

59. Ibn al-Murtaḍā, *Ṭabaqāt al-mu'tazilah,* 113. The volume on jurisprudence of *al-Mughnī* has been published, though it is incomplete: al-Asadābādī al-Qāḍī 'Abd al-Jabbār, *al-Mughnī fī abwāb al-tawḥīd wa'l-'adl,* vol. 17, *al-Shar'īyāt,* ed. Ṭāhā Ḥusayn and Amīn al-Khōlī (Cairo: Wizārat al-thaqāfah, 1961). An incomplete version of *al-'Umad* is apparently extant in manuscript. See Sezgin, *GAS,* 1: 625.

60. al-Jaṣṣāṣ, *al-Fuṣūl fī al-uṣūl.* See also idem, *al-Fuṣūl fī al-uṣūl, (abwāb al-ijtihād wa'l-qiyās);* Bernand, "Ḥanafī *Uṣūl al-Fiqh,* 623–35.

61. Abū al-Ḥusayn Muḥammad b. 'Alī al-Baṣrī, *al-Mu'tamad fī uṣūl al-fiqh,* 2 vols., ed. Khalīl al-Mays (Beirut: Dār al-kutub al-'ilmīyah, 1983). His commentary on *al-'Umad,* which I was unable to consult, has been published as *Sharḥ al-'Umad,* 2 vols., ed. 'Abd al-Ḥamīd b. 'Alī Abū Zunayd (Medina: Maktabat al-'ulūm wa'l-ḥikam, 1989–90).

62. al-Juwaynī, *Kitāb al-ijtihād min kitāb al-talkhīṣ.*

work on jurisprudence. Hallaq and Reinhart single out Ibn Surayj as having played a leading role in the systematization of Islamic legal theory that shaped the development of *uṣūl al-fiqh*.[63] Certainly, his students, including al-Ṣayrafī, authored important works in the genre. There is nevertheless the possibility that scholars before Ibn Surayj played important roles in developing the genre. In fact, Ibn Abī Mūsā al-Faqīh, a Ḥanafī jurist who died in the 330s/940s, wrote an eight-volume work on *uṣūl al-fiqh,* indicating that the genre had, already by then, a long history. The attribution of a work on *uṣūl al-fiqh* to al-Karābīsī has already been mentioned. In addition, the frequency with which the jurists ʿĪsā b. Abān (d. 221/835–36), Dā'ūd b. ʿAlī al-Ẓāhirī, and Muḥammad b. Dā'ūd al-Ẓāhirī and the theologians al-Naẓẓām (d. 220–30/835–45) and Abū ʿAlī al-Jubbā'ī (d. 303/915–16) are cited in later works of jurisprudence suggests that they may already have played a significant role in the development of the genre in the course of the ninth century.

CONSENSUS: ISLAMIC LEGAL ORTHODOXY

Scholarship on Islam has long indicated that issues of religious conformance and deviance have something to do with *ijmāʿ*, "consensus" or "unanimous agreement." Goldziher senses the importance of *ijmāʿ* in determining orthodoxy and heterodoxy, although he does not explain how it functioned.

> *Ijmāʿ* is the key to a grasp of the historical evolution of Islam in its political, theological, and legal aspects. Whatever is accepted by the entire Islamic community as true and correct must be regarded as true and correct. To turn one's back on the *ijmāʿ* is to leave the orthodox community.[64]

To Goldziher, however, *ijmāʿ* seems a diffuse and nebulous principle, which he describes as "a nearly unconscious *vox populi*."[65] Bernard Lewis remarks that Islam has no ecclesiastical hierarchy and no councils or synods to decide questions of heresy, but only *ijmāʿ*, the workings of which are "barely definable."[66] Watt realizes that *ijmāʿ* played a role in defining heresy, but like Goldziher sees it as an ill-defined group feeling, though he notes that the *ʿulamā'* were the ones empowered to decide specific cases. In his view, the dynamics of Islamic orthodoxy and heresy are reminiscent of a tribal system; what determines whether a believer's unusual views are acceptable is merely the "feeling" of the commu-

63. Hallaq, "al-Shāfiʿī," 595–96; Reinhart, *Before Revelation,* 14–15. Hallaq rejects the view, however, that Ibn Surayj actually wrote a work on *uṣūl al-fiqh,* whereas Reinhart reports that he wrote a work on "Principles and Derivations" *(al-uṣūl wa'l-furūʿ).*

64. Goldziher, *Islamic Theology and Law,* 50.

65. Ibid., 51.

66. Bernard Lewis, "Some Observations on the Significance of Heresy in the History of Islam," *Studia Islamica* 1 (1953): 57–58.

nity's members, embodied in the principle of consensus. He concludes that "there is more communalistic thinking in Islam than is usually realized."[67]

While Goldziher, Watt, and others take consensus to be something like popular opinion, in actuality it is a well-defined legal principle cited, contested, and referred to constantly within the community of legal scholars. A number of recent studies on Islamic jurisprudence have increased our understanding of legal consensus considerably.[68] Commonly held views of *ijmā'* as the arbitrary basis of all Islamic law or as the basis for all customary practices and behaviors in the Muslim world have been corrected.[69] So, too, has the idea that the authority of consensus is based on a circular argument.[70]

The concept of legal consensus was fundamental to the juridical *madhhab* system that arose in the tenth century. In a sense it represented the guidelines which controlled Islamic legal discourse within the framework of the *madhhabs*. As a technical term in Islamic jurisprudence, *ijmā'* came to be defined by most jurists of the four Sunni *madhhabs* as the unanimous agreement of qualified Muslim jurists on a given point of the law.[71] It is opposed to *khilāf*, "dissent" or "disagreement." As a legal concept, consensus can be traced back to the eighth century. The Umayyad caliph 'Umar b. 'Abd al-'Azīz (99–101/717–20) is said to have written to provincial governors advising them that cases should be decided according to the consensus of the jurists of each region.[72] A letter from the Basran judge 'Ubayd Allāh al-Anbarī to the Abbasid caliph al-Mahdī (158–69/775–85) holds that cases should be decided with reference to the Koran, then the Sunnah, then the consensus of leading scholars, then by the

67. W. Montgomery Watt, "Conditions of Membership of the Islamic Community," *Studia Islamica* 21 (1964): 12.

68. Marie Bernand, "Idjmā'," *EI*²; idem, "L'Iǧmā' chez 'Abd Al-Ǧabbār et l'objection d'an-Naẓẓām," *Studia Islamica* 30 (1969): 27–38; idem, *L'accord unanime de la communauté comme fondement des statuts légaux de l'islam* (Paris, 1970); Calder, "*Ikhtilāf* and *Ijmā'*"; Eric Chaumont, "Bāqillānī, théologien ash'arite et uṣūliste mālikite," *Studia Islamica* 79 (1994): 79–102, esp. 87 ff.; Wael B. Hallaq, "On the Authoritativeness of Sunni Consensus," *IJMES* 18 (1986): 427–54; Ahmed Hasan, *The Doctrine of Ijmā' in Islam* (Islamabad: Islamic Research Institute, 1984); Georges F. Hourani, "The Basis of Authority of Consensus in Sunnite Islam," *Studia Islamica* 21 (1964): 13–60; Makdisi, *Rise of Colleges*, 105–12; idem, *Rise of Humanism*, 31–33; Abdel-Magid Turki, "L'Ijmā' Ummat al-Mu'minīn entre la doctrine et l'histoire," *Studia Islamica* 59 (1984): 4–78; Bernard G. Weiss, "Al-Āmidī on the Basis of Authority of Consensus," in *Essays on Islamic Civilization Presented to Niyazi Berkes*, 342–56, ed. Donald P. Little (Leiden: E. J. Brill, 1976); idem, *The Search for God's Law* (Salt Lake City: University of Utah Press, 1992), 181–258; Zysow, "Economy of Certainty," 198–281.

69. Zysow, "Economy of Certainty," 198–99, 259–61.

70. Hallaq, "Authoritativeness"; Hourani, " Basis of Authority"; Weiss, "Al-Āmidī"; idem, *Search for God's Law*, 195–212; Zysow, "Economy of Certainty," 202–10.

71. See, for example, Imām al-Ḥaramayn al-Juwaynī (Shāfi'ī), *al-Waraqāt* (Cairo: Maṭba'at al-madanī, n.d.), 11; Abū Ya'lā (Ḥanbalī), *al-'Uddah*, 1: 170; Abū al-Walīd al-Bājī (Mālikī), *Iḥkām al-fuṣūl fī aḥkām al-uṣūl*, ed. Abdel-Magid Turki (Beirut: Dār al-gharb al-islāmī, 1986), 459; al-Jaṣṣāṣ (Ḥanafī), *al-Fuṣūl fī al-uṣūl*, 3: 285.

72. Makdisi, *Rise of Colleges*, 106.

ijtihād of the governor in consultation with scholars.[73] Mālik (d. 179/795) held that the consensus of the people of Medina was binding, and al-Shāfiʿī (d. 204/820) rejects this view in *al-Risālah* and *Kitāb al-umm.*[74] According to Schacht, the ancient schools of law, represented by the Iraqi and Medinese jurists prior to al-Shāfiʿī, were dominated by the idea of consensus.[75]

In his *Risālah,* al-Shāfiʿī presents a theory of legal interpretation which would later be accepted, in its outlines, as the basis of nearly all Islamic jurisprudence. He proposes the doctrine that the law derives from four sources, the Koran (*kitāb*), tradition (*sunnah*), consensus (*ijmāʿ*), and analogical reasoning (*qiyās*).[76] Schacht devotes considerable attention to al-Shāfiʿī's theory of consensus, but the picture that emerges is far from clear. Unfortunately, al-Shāfiʿī's independent discussion of the issue, *Kitāb al-ijmāʿ,* has not survived.[77] According to Schacht, al-Shāfiʿī at first endorsed the consensus of the scholars, then qualified this view, expressing misgivings about its authority and assigning higher value to the consensus of the Muslims at large. Finally, he seems to have rejected its authority and even denied its existence, though he did not completely abandon the concept.[78] While a comprehensive study of al-Shāfiʿī's theory of consensus is beyond the scope of this study, a few observations may be made here based on the presentation of consensus in *al-Risālah.* Al-Shāfiʿī bases the authority of consensus on two traditions of the Prophet which stress the believer's obligation to "stick to the generality of Muslims" (*luzūm al-jamāʿat al-muslimīn*). He most often refers to the consensus of Muslims (*ijmāʿ al-muslimīn*), but he cites the consensus of Muslim scholars (*ijmāʿ ʿulamāʾ al-muslimīn*) together with *ijmāʿ al-muslimīn* in a context which indicates that the two are essentially equivalent. It is clear in other passages that al-Shāfiʿī makes an important distinction between Muslim commoners (*al-ʿāmmah*) and scholars or jurists in particular (*al-khāṣṣah,* "the elite," *ahl al-ʿilm,* "the people of learning," *al-ʿulamāʾ,* "the scholars," or *fuqahāʾ al-muslimīn,* "the jurists of the Muslims"). He distinguishes between the knowledge of Muslim commoners—which comprises such issues as the prohibition of adultery and the obligations to fast, perform the pilgrimage, and give alms—and the knowledge of scholars—which includes such matters as the set inheritance shares.[79] This distinction might imply, and some later

73. Crone and Hinds, *God's Caliph,* 93.

74. al-Shāfiʿī, *al-Risālah,* 534–35; idem, *Kitāb al-umm,* 7 vols. (Bulaq, 1902–6), 7: 147–48. Note that Calder attributes most of the material in *Kitāb al-umm* to after al-Rabīʿ (d. 270/883) and al-Muzanī (d. 264/878) (*Early Muslim Jurisprudence,* 104).

75. Schacht, *Muhammadan Jurisprudence,* 82.

76. al-Shāfiʿī, *al-Risālah,* 476, 598.

77. Ibn al-Nadīm, *al-Fihrist,* 310.

78. Schacht, *Muhammadan Jurisprudence,* 88–94.

79. al-Shāfiʿī, *al-Risālah,* 322, 357–60, 402–3, 457–58, 471–76, 527, 599.

works of jurisprudence adopt this view, that consensus for al-Shāfiʿī is of two types, general or lay consensus on such fundamental issues as the Ramaḍān fast and scholars' consensus on more arcane legal matters. Nevertheless, given that one of the main aims of *al-Risālah* is to bolster the authority of Muslim scholars, most of al-Shāfiʿī's discussions of consensus likely refer to the consensus of Muslim jurists.[80] According to Schacht, later theory, expressed in the classical works of jurisprudence, returned to older views recognizing the centrality of consensus for legal interpretation.[81]

According to the overwhelming majority of Sunni jurists since al-Shāfiʿī, *ijmāʿ* is a legitimate source (*aṣl* or *dalīl*) of Islamic law, after the Koran and the Sunnah of the Prophet (as embodied in hadith). The consensus of the Muslim community is a *ḥujjah,* that is, an incontrovertible argument. By the tenth century, consensus had become a standard part of Sunni legal doctrine; while many of the texts on *uṣūl al-fiqh* from this period, such as those of Ibn Surayj (d. 306/918) and al-Qaffāl al-Shāshī (d. 365/976), have been lost, the widespread adoption of consensus is clear from extant works on jurisprudence by later authors, such as al-Jaṣṣāṣ, al-Qāḍī ʿAbd al-Jabbār, and Abū al-Ḥusayn al-Baṣrī. The establishment of this doctrine went hand in hand with the creation of the *uṣūl al-fiqh* genre. It therefore probably became standard doctrine to the majority of Sunni jurists by the late ninth or early tenth century.

From the time of al-Jaṣṣāṣ, the *ḥujjīyah* or binding authority of consensus is generally taken to derive from scriptural proofs rather than any rational justification, since it is entirely possible, rationally, that a large community might agree unanimously on a falsehood (it is obvious, for example, that Jews and Christians all agree on their heretical beliefs).[82] Sunni legal theorists cite a number of Koranic verses and traditions of the Prophet as proofs of the binding authority of consensus; al-Āmidī (d. 631/1234), for example, cites five Koranic verses and sixteen hadith reports.[83] Among the most frequently cited

80. According to Calder, al-Shāfiʿī holds that the consensus relevant to a matter on which there is no revealed text is a consensus of Muslim commoners, despite the fact that it is only the scholars who can ratify such a consensus ("*Ikhtilāf* and *Ijmāʿ*," 55–81, esp. 78–79). The relevant text of al-Shāfiʿī"s *al-Risālah* (p. 472) is *wa-naʿlamu anna ʿāmmatahum lā tajtamiʿu ʿalā khilāfin li-sunnati rasūli Llāhi wa-lā ʿalā khaṭaʾin in shāʾa ʾLlāh.* I would suggest, however, that the word *ʿāmmah* here does not mean "commoners" as opposed to *khāṣṣah,* "elite, scholars," but rather that it simply means the generality or vast majority of Muslims. One might translate the text as follows: "We know that the generality of them (i.e., Muslims) do not reach an agreement which contradicts the tradition of the Prophet, or which is an error, God willing." The "generality of Muslims" here probably refers to the generality of Muslim *scholars* rather than commoners, just as the term *ijmāʿ al-muslimīn* means *ijmāʿ ʿulamāʾ al-muslimīn* elsewhere in al-Shāfiʿī's text (p. 322).

81. Schacht, *Muhammadan Jurisprudence,* 94–95.

82. al-Jaṣṣāṣ, *al-Fuṣūl fī al-uṣūl,* 3: 257.

83. Sayf al-Dīn al-Āmidī, *al-Iḥkām fī uṣul al-aḥkām,* 4 vols. (Cairo, n.d.), 1: 183–203; Weiss, *Search For God's Law,* 201–8.

Koranic verses are the following:

> Thus We have appointed you a middle nation (*ja'alnākum ummatan wasaṭan*), that you may be witnesses against mankind. (Q 2:143)
>
> And hold fast, all of you together, to God's bond, and do not separate from one another (*wa-lā tafarraqū*). (Q 3:103)
>
> You are the best community (*khayra ummatin*) that has been raised up for mankind. You enjoin right conduct and forbid indecency. (Q 3:110)
>
> Oh you who believe! Obey God, and obey the messenger and those of you who are in authority; and if you have a dispute concerning any matter, refer it to God and the messenger (*fa-in tanāza'tum fī shay'in fa-ruddūhu ilā 'Llāhi wa'r-rasūl*). (Q 4:59)
>
> And whoever opposes the Messenger (*yushāqiq ir-rasūla*) after the guidance has been manifested to him, and follows other than the way of the believers (*wa-yattabi' ghayra sabīli 'l-mu'minīna*), We appoint for him that to which he himself has turned, and expose him to Hell—a hapless end! (Q 4:115)

These verses are taken to express the special status God has bestowed on the Muslim community, the importance of following the generality of Muslims, and the prohibition of failing to do so. In addition, the jurists cite numerous hadith reports as proofs of the authority of consensus, including the famous report, "My community shall not agree on an error," and another, "Whoever separates from the group by so much as a span's length has removed the bond of Islam from his neck."[84] On the basis of proof-texts such as these, Sunni jurists conclude that the consensus of the Muslim community is guaranteed to be correct.

Although modern scholars have stressed the reference of consensus to the general agreement of all Muslim believers in addition to the agreement of the jurists,[85] most legal theorists limit consensus quite strictly to fully competent jurists. Even in al-Shāfi'ī's *al-Risālah,* there is a clear tendency to restrict to experts in the law the ability to issue reliable opinions on religious topics, and *ijmā'* refers to the consensus of these experts especially. Al-Jaṣṣāṣ, for example, holds the opinion that consensus is of two types. The first type, a general consensus, including both scholars (*al-khaṣṣah*) and the common people, covers basic issues of which all Muslims should be aware, such as the obligations to

84. al-Jaṣṣāṣ, *al-Fuṣūl fī al-uṣūl,* 3: 257–67; al-Baṣrī, *al-Mu'tamad,* 2: 4–16; al-Āmidī, *al-Iḥkām,* 1: 199.

85. For example, Bernand, "Idjmā'," 3: 1024.

fast during Ramaḍān, perform the pilgrimage to Mecca, and perform ablutions after a polluting incident, and the prohibitions of adultery, consumption of alcohol, and marrying one's mother or sister. The second more restricted type is the consensus of the scholars (*al-khāṣṣ min ahl al-ʿilm*) that covers technical points of law, such as the rates for the various types of alms (*zakāt*) or the prohibition of marrying both a paternal aunt and a brother's daughter. The opinions of the common people are not taken into consideration for this second type of consensus on the basis that they are not qualified to decide legal issues.[86] It is of course "elite or specialists' consensus" (*ijmāʿ al-khāṣṣah*), the consensus of *mujtahids* or qualifed legal experts, to which the bulk of the jurists' arguments on consensus are devoted. Al-Māwardī (d. 450/1058), al-Ghazālī (d. 505/1111), Ibn Taymīyah (d. 728/1328), and other jurists hold that there is no such thing as commoners' or general consensus, likening a layman's opinions on legal issues to those of a child, an unbeliever, or a madman.[87] This is the majority opinion among jurisprudents, according to al-Āmidī.[88] Al-Bāqillānī and al-Āmidī appear to be odd men out on this issue, for they argue that a consensus of the jurists becomes valid only through the concurrence of the commoners.[89]

In addition to laymen, the majority of legal theorists exclude from consideration in consensus those scholars who are not versed specifically in law and legal derivation. Al-Jaṣṣāṣ states that scholars like Dāʾūd al-Ẓāhirī and al-Karābīsī cannot be considered in consensus because they were incapable of rational methods of legal derivation. In his view, their status with respect to legal derivation was like that of the layman. Al-Jaṣṣāṣ also excludes scholars who are trained in the rational sciences but lack background in law and scripture from consideration in consensus.[90] Later jurists voice similar opinions, ex-

86. al-Jaṣṣāṣ, *al-Fuṣūl fī al-uṣūl*, 3: 285. Other jurists who propose similar views include Abū Isḥāq al-Shīrāzī al-Fayrūzābādī, *Kitāb al-lumaʿ fī uṣūl al-fiqh*, ed. Muḥammad Badr-al-Dīn al-Naʿsānī al-Ḥalabī (Beirut: Dār al-nadwah al-islāmiyah, 1987–88), 89; al-Bājī, *Iḥkām al-fuṣūl*, 459; al-Āmidī, *al-Iḥkām*, 1: 204; Muḥammad b. ʿAlī al-Shawkānī, *Irshād al-fuḥūl ilā taḥqīq ʿilm al-uṣūl*, ed. Abū Muṣʿab Muḥammad Saʿīd al-Badrī (Beirut: Muʾassasat al-Kutub al-thaqāfīyah, 1993), 159.

87. ʿAlī b. Muḥammad al-Māwardī, *Adab al-qāḍī*, 2 vols. (Baghdad: Maṭbaʿat al-irshād, 1971), 1: 456; Abū Yaʿlā, *al-ʿUddah*, 4: 1133–34; Abū Bakr Muḥammad al-Sarakhsī, *Uṣūl al-Sarakhsī*, 2 vols., ed. Abū ʾl-Wafāʾ al-Afghānī (Beirut: Dār al-maʿrifah, n.d.), 1: 312; Abū Ḥamid Muḥammad al-Ghazālī, *al-Mankhūl min taʿlīqāt al-uṣul* (Damascus: Dār al-fikr, 1980), 310; Shihāb al-Dīn Aḥmad b. Idrīs al-Qarāfī, *Sharḥ tanqīḥ al-fuṣūl fī ikhtiṣār al-maḥṣūl fī al-uṣūl* (Cairo: al-Maktabah al-azharīyah li'l-turāth, 1973), 342; Taqī al-Dīn Aḥmad Ibn Taymīyah, *al-Musawwadah fī uṣūl al-fiqh*, ed. Muḥammad Muḥyī al-Dīn ʿAbd al-Ḥamīd (Cairo: Maṭbaʿat al-madanī, 1964), 323.

88. al-Āmidī, *al-Iḥkām*, 1: 204.

89. al-Bājī, *Iḥkām al-fuṣūl*, 459; al-Āmidī, *al-Iḥkām*, 1: 204–7; Weiss, *Search for God's Law*, 212–14.

90. al-Jaṣṣāṣ, *al-Fuṣūl fī al-uṣūl*, 3: 296; al-Sarakhsī, *Uṣūl*, 1: 312; Muwaffaq al-Dīn ʿAbd Allāh Ibn Qudāmah al-Maqdisī, *Rawḍat al-nāẓir wa-jannat al-munāẓir* (Cairo: al-Maṭbaʿah al-salafīyah, 1965), 69–70; Ibn Taymīyah, *al-Musawwaddah*, 331. Al-Jaṣṣāṣ states that the opinions of *muḥaddithūn* unskilled in the legal sciences are]not to be taken into account. Al-Sarakhsī says the same of *mutakallimūn*, and attributes this opinion to Abū ʾl-Ḥasan al-Karkhī. Ibn Qudāmah and Ibn Taymīyah include both.

cluding experts in prophetic tradition (*muḥaddithūn*) and philosophical theologians (*mutakallimūn*) from consideration.[91] Nor do they consider the opinions of a scholar who is competent in legal theory alone (*uṣūlī*) or a jurist (*faqīh*) who is versed in the points of law but lacks an adequate background in jurisprudence.[92] The result is that only master jurists who have completed the rigorous training established by the *madhhab*s in law, its ancillary sciences, jurisprudence, and disputation could voice recognized opinions on Islamic legal questions.

Consensus is a principle governing legal interpretation within the Muslim community once a question has been examined and enters what one Shiite jurist calls "the battle of jurists' opinions."[93] A legal opinion that gains the approval, either tacit or explicit, of all contemporary qualified Muslim jurists takes on consensual status, and the unanimous agreement of the doctors of the law confers the sanction of binding authority on that legal opinion. Until such uniformity of opinion is reached, the individual jurist may choose among the various opinions that have been expressed on the issue. Afterwards, a case apparently falling under the specific legal rule subject to this consensus must be distinguished in some manner if the jurist pronounces a contrary ruling, unless he can show the claim that consensus actually exists to be false. For this reason, the requirements for *ijtihād* set by many Islamic legal theorists include the stipulation that the jurist must be aware of the points of law on which consensus exists so that he not give a contrary ruling.[94]

Consensus is most often established, Makdisi points out, negatively and retroactively, by the absence of dissenting opinion in the history of a particular legal issue; this feature is made clear by the existence of a prolific literature concerning *khilāf*, "dissent," or the disputed questions in the law, among other indications.[95] Al-Khaṭīb al-Baghdādī (d. 463/1071) states that only he who knows *khilāf* may know *ijmā'*.[96] *Ijmā'* and *khilāf* are therefore two sides of the same coin; they represent, together, the body of acceptable opinion on issues of the religious law. Some questions have been decided in favor of one opinion and thus are subject to consensus; others have not, and a number of authoritative variant opinions may be held concerning these questions. Ibn Qayyim al-Jawzīyah (d. 751/1350) observes the centrality of *khilāf* in the Islamic legal system:

91. Abū Ya'lā, *al-'Uddah*, 4: 1136–38; al-Sarakhsī, *Uṣūl*, 1: 312; Ibn Qudāmah al-Maqdisī, *Rawḍat al-nāẓir*, 69–70; Ibn Taymīyah, *al-Musawwadah*, 331.

92. al-Ghazālī, *al-Mankhūl*, 311; Ibn Qudāmah, *Rawḍat al-nāẓir*, 70; Ibn Taymīyah, *al-Musawwadah*, 331.

93. Muḥammad al-Bāqir al-Bihbihānī, *Risālat al-akhbār wa'l-ijtihād* (Tehran, n.d.), 7.

94. al-Shawkānī, *Irshād al-fuḥūl*, 420.

95. Makdisi, *Rise of Colleges*, 105–11; idem, *Rise of Humanism*, 32–33.

96. al-Khaṭīb al-Baghdādī, *Kitāb al-Faqīh wa'l-mutafaqqih*, 2: 21.

> When a jurisconsult or judge is faced with a case, he must first determine whether or not there is disagreement (*ikhtilāf*) concerning it. If there is no disagreement, he need not examine the Koran or the Sunnah, but rather gives his opinion or verdict on the case on the grounds of consensus. If there is disagreement concerning the case, he determines through personal effort (*ijtahad*) which of the opinions is closest to the evidence and gives his opinion or verdict accordingly.[97]

Notwithstanding, some scholars attempted to catalogue those questions on which consensus existed (*masā'il al-ijmā'*), as did Ibn al-Mundhir (d. 318/930), Ibn Ḥazm (d. 456/1064) in *Marātib al-ijmā'*, and Jalāl al-Dīn al-Suyūṭī (d. 911/1505) in *Tashnīf al-asmā' bi-masā'il al-ijmā'*.[98]

Makdisi has brought out the crucial role of consensus in the Sunni legal system, correcting a number of misconceptions concerning its definition and use. In his view, consensus defines Islamic orthodoxy:

> The bounds of orthodoxy are determined on the basis of the consensus of doctors of the law. Since there is no body of determinate character which could be convened for the purpose of polling the consensus, this principle operates negatively and retroactively. For this reason, consensus, ijmā', is determined, not by the yeas against the nays, for no clear count could actually be taken, but rather by whether voices of authoritative doctors of the law have been raised in the past *against* a particular doctrine. If not, then the doctrine was considered to have been accepted as orthodox.[99]

Makdisi's assessment of the role played by consensus and dissent in determining Islamic orthodoxy neatly explains many aspects of Islamic legal and religious history. This study modifies Makdisi's view by emphasizing that this definition of orthodoxy does not represent *the* single, all-encompassing definition of orthodoxy in Islamic history. Theologians, hadith experts, philosophers, and mystics held views concerning the definition and boundaries of appropriate belief in Islam that often differed markedly from those of the jurists. Nevertheless, for the majority of jurists in the recognized Sunni *madhhabs* from the tenth century on, consensus represented orthodoxy. As the legal

97. Ibn Qayyim al-Jawziyah, *I'lām al-muwaqqi'īn 'an rabb al-'ālamīn*, 4 vols. (Beirut: Dār al-Kutub al-'ilmīyah, 1991), 3: 174.

98. Ibn al-Mundhir, *al-Ijmā'*, ed. Fu'ād 'Abd al-Mun'im Aḥmad and 'Abd Allāh b. Zayd Āl Maḥmūd (al-Dawḥah, Qaṭar: Dār al-thaqāfah, 1987); Ibn Ḥazm, *Marātib al-ijmā' fī al-'ibādāt wa'l-mu'āmalāt wa'l-mu'taqadāt* (Beirut: Dār al-āfāq al-jadīdah, 1978); Jalāl al-Dīn al-Suyūṭī, *Kitāb al-taḥadduth bi-ni'mat Allāh*, in *Jalāl al-dīn al-Suyūṭī*, vol. 2, ed. Elizabeth M. Sartain (Cambridge: Cambridge University Press, 1975), 133. Brockelmann (*GAL*, supp. 1: 699) also lists a work entitled *Masā'il al-ijmā'* by the Zaydī scholar Shāh Sharījān Abū al-Ḥasan 'Alī b. al-Ḥusayn (fl. 5th/11th c.).

99. Makdisi, *Rise of the Colleges*, 106.

profession gained in power and influence, this version of orthodoxy, one among several espoused by claimants to religious authority, came to dominate Islamic religious discourse.

ORTHODOXY VS. ORTHOPRAXY

It is a common idea that Islam lacks well-defined religious authorities who oversee the community's religious life and set boundaries for acceptable practice and belief. Richard Burton voices this view categorically in the "Terminal Essay" to his translation of *The Thousand and One Nights:* "every father in al-Islam was made priest and pontiff in his own home, able unaided to marry himself, to circumcize (to baptise as it were) his children, to instruct them in the law and canonically to bury himself."[100] Goldziher writes, "In Islam there are no councils and synods that, after vigorous debate, fix the formulas that henceforth must be regarded as sound belief. There is no ecclesiastic office that provides a standard of orthodoxy."[101] It hardly seems possible, *a priori,* that definitions of orthodoxy and heresy together with religious authorities who define and set them simply do not exist in Islam. Any religion must regulate the exclusion of deviant elements from the community in some way, and there is ample evidence that this function has been exercised continually throughout Islamic history. While it is true that Islam does not have sacraments, a priesthood, or an ecclesiastical hierarchy, many well-defined groups, including that of the jurists, have acted as religious authorities during one historical and geographical context or another. They may have disagreed with other competing groups as to their legitimacy and jurisdiction, but they nevertheless have claimed, and exercised, the right to decide questions of acceptable and unacceptable belief.

The supposed lack of recognized religious authorities in Islam has led many scholars to balk at the use of the term "orthodoxy" in an Islamic context. Watt, for example, observes, "The word 'orthodox' is out of place in an Islamic context. . . . Indeed, Islam has had no machinery comparable to the Ecumenical Councils of the Christian Church which could say authoritatively what constitutes 'right doctrine.'"[102] Bernard Lewis, in a similar statement, maintains that

> the very idea of orthodoxy and heterodoxy is a quite specifically Christian notion. It has little or no relevance to the history of Islam, where there are no synods, churches, or councils to define orthodoxy and therefore none to

100. Sir Richard Francis Burton, "Terminal Essay," in *The Book of the Thousand Nights and a Night,* vol. 10 (London: Burton Club, n.d.), 181–82.

101. Goldziher, *Islamic Theology and Law,* 162–63.

102. W. Montgomery Watt, *The Formative Period of Islamic Thought* (Edinburgh: Edinburgh University Press, 1973), 5–6.

> define and condemn departure from orthodoxy, which we normally designate by such terms as heterodoxy and heresy.[103]

The complexity and unfamiliar workings of religious authority in Islam have led Watt and other scholars to claim that it is inappropriate, misleading, or even futile to attempt to describe Islamic religious history in these terms.[104] This is unfortunate and unnecessary, for to adopt such a stance is to shy away from a set of problems of fundamental importance in Islamic history. Rather than concealing the facts, as Dabashi suggests,[105] an understanding of Islamic orthodoxy reveals religious pressures at work within society and provides a better picture of intersectarian relations in Islamic history.

It has become common in scholarship on Islam to use the term "orthopraxy" rather than "orthodoxy" to refer to religious conformity. Though orthopraxy is by no means a new term—the *Oxford English Dictionary* reports its use as early as 1852—there seems to be considerable confusion concerning its meaning. In one usage, orthopraxy refers to the fact that religious conformity in Islam—and in Judaism as well—is based on legal rather than theological questions. While this idea is correct with regard to the religious system the jurists espoused, orthopraxy does not denote it accurately. In the second usage, orthopraxy is supposed to indicate that whereas in Christianity, one is concerned with belief, in Islam, one is concerned with acts. Two dichotomies are being erroneously conflated: theology/law and belief/practice. A clear example of this type of conflation is seen in the following statement by Esposito:

> For Christianity, the appropriate question is "What do Christians believe?" In contrast, for Islam (as for Judaism), the correct question is "What do Muslims do?" Whereas in Christianity, theology was the "queen of the sciences," in Islam, as in Judaism, law enjoyed pride of place, for "to accept or conform to the laws of God is *islām,* which means to surrender to God's law."[106]

The first part of this statement is false. Muslims and Jews are concerned with belief as well as practice, and Christianity is concerned with practice as well as belief. The second part, expressing the status of theology in Christianity and law in Islam, is accurate, but not logically tied to the first.

Scholars who use the terms "orthodoxy" and "orthopraxy" to refer to a

103. Bernard Lewis, "The Shiʿa in Islamic History," in *Shiʿism, Resistance, and Revolution,* 21–30, ed. Martin Kraemer (Boulder: Westview Press, 1987), 21.

104. See, for example, Dale Eickelmann, *The Middle East* (Englewood Cliffs, New Jersey: Prentice Hall, 1981), 213; Hamid Dabashi, *Authority in Islam* (New Brunswick, New Jersey: Transaction Publishers, 1989), 71–72.

105. Dabashi, *Authority in Islam,* 71.

106. John L. Esposito, *Islam* (Oxford: Oxford University Press, 1988), 68.

claimed dichotomy between Christian belief on the one hand and Islamic practice on the other are influenced by the common usage of the term "orthodoxy" to refer to accepted Christian dogma. Thus, in popular usage, orthodoxy is seen as meaning "correct theological belief," whereas, originally and etymologically, orthodoxy means simply "correct opinion," deriving as it does from Greek *doxa*, "opinion." There is nothing that restricts the literal meaning of orthodoxy to discussions of philosophical theology in particular. Orthopraxy, however, means "correct practice," and one cannot hold the opinion that practice in itself determines religious conformity in Islam. The vast majority of Muslim jurists, theologians, and other thinkers have argued against the view that true Muslims are simply those who pray toward Mecca (*ahl al-qiblah*). For example, al-Subkī remonstrates, "Do you not see that the hypocrites pray towards our *qiblah*, while they are unanimously held to be unbelievers (*kuffār*)?"[107]

In Sunni Islam in general, the commission of sin, which is incorrect practice, does not render one an unbeliever; only some Khārijī factions espoused this extreme view. Al-Ash'arī (d. ca. 325/937) states in one of his creeds that one cannot accuse a Muslim of unbelief because of a sin.[108] Najm al-Dīn al-Nasafī (d. 537/1142–43) states in his creed that neither a lesser nor a greater sin renders one an unbeliever. One is not considered a heretic in Islam for drinking alcohol, and one is not excluded irrevocably from the community of believers for doing so.[109] Drinking alcohol is a sin for which atonement or a specific punishment is prescribed. It is heretical, rather, *to consider it permissible* to drink alcohol. To hold the opinion that it is not sinful and forbidden to drink alcohol is to go against the consensus and leave the community of believers. Al-Nasafī, for example, using a phrase common in Islamic religious literature, holds that considering that which is forbidden lawful constitutes unbelief.[110] Similarly, the Qādirī Creed demonstrates that it is an opinion, and not an act, which renders one an unbeliever: "L'homme ne doit pas déclarer un autre homme infidéle pour l'omission d'aucune obligation, sauf la seule priére prescrite dans le Livre de Dieu....Quant à toutes les autres oeuvres, on ne le déclarera pas infidèle pour les avoir négligés, même s'il commet le péché, à moins qu'il ne les nie."[111] Sinning does not make one an unbeliever, but denial of specific religious obligations does, and denial is clearly a mental operation, an expression of opinion or belief as opposed to practice. Of all legal obliga-

107. al-Subkī, *Ṭabaqāt al-shāfi'iyah al-kubrā*, 1: 99.

108. MacDonald, *Development of Muslim Theology*, 296.

109. Ibid., 311.

110. Ibid.

111. George Makdisi, *Ibn 'Aqīl et la résurgence de l'islam traditionaliste au XIe siècle (Ve siècle de l'Hégire)* (Damascus: Institut français de Damas, 1963), 307.

tions, only omission of the prescribed prayer causes one to be considered an unbeliever. A hadith attributed to Ja'far al-Ṣādiq shows the significance of giving up prayer in particular. Someone asked the imam why one may label as an unbeliever (*kāfir*) a Muslim who has abandoned prayer (*tārik al-ṣalāt*) but not an adulterer or a drinker of alcohol. Ja'far replies that the drinker of alcohol and the adulterer might be driven to commit those sins out of lust or physical urges, whereas this cannot be the case with someone who fails to pray; the man in question must have abandoned prayer because he does not take the obligation seriously (*istikhfāfan bihā*).[112] It is thus the conviction that prayer is unnecessary which makes him an unbeliever.

Evidence of a heretical opinion may be produced in Islam, as in Christianity, through word or deed. Al-Subkī states, "Whoever utters unbelief (*talaffaẓ bi 'l-kufr*) or performs the acts of unbelief is a disbeliever in God the Almighty and will spend eternity in Hell."[113] A jurist who gives a legal opinion declaring alcohol permissible may be declared a heretic. A Muslim who utters unacceptable statements concerning God or the Prophet is equally subject to a declaration of heresy. Thus, there is an Islamic literature on blasphemy, termed *alfāẓ al-kufr*, literally "utterances of unbelief," that describes and codifies the statements the utterance of which renders one a heretic.[114] Similarly, actions such as the worship of false gods or the desecration of religious symbols render one an unbeliever. In either case, the evidence—actions or words—is viewed as a sign of belief or conviction and is not considered an end in itself. Thus, the term "orthodoxy" may apply as aptly to Islam as to Christianity, for both religions are fundamentally concerned with belief. Moreover, the special place of law in Islam as opposed to Christianity is not accurately reflected in the term "orthopraxy."

THE VIOLATION OF CONSENSUS: ISLAMIC LEGAL HERESY

Heresy is poorly understood in scholarship on Islam. It is a common belief that a Muslim who utters the fundamental creed (*shahādah*), "I witness that there is no god but God and that Muḥammad is the prophet of God," thereby avoids any accusation of heresy. Ismail Faruqi expresses this view as follows:

> Every law court of Islam is bound to recognize as a Muslim in good standing, and hence entitled to all privileges and rights of a Muslim and bound by all the duties and obligations of Islamic law, every adult male and fe-

112. Ibn Bābawayh al-Qummī, *'Ilal al-sharā'i'*, ed. Muḥammad Ṣādiq Baḥr al-'Ulūm (Najaf: al-Maṭba'ah al-ḥaydariyah, 1963), 339.

113. al-Subkī, *Ṭabaqāt al-shāfi'iyah al-kubrā*, 1: 91.

114. An example is *Kitāb alfāẓ al-kufr* by Muḥammad b. Ismā'īl Badr al-Rashīd (d. 786/1366) (Brockelmann, *GAL*, 2: 80).

> male who consciously and solemnly witnesses that "there is no God but God and Muhammad is the Prophet of God." Fulfillment of this simple definition of "Islamicity" is all that Islamic law requires for membership in the Muslim community. Once a person is put to the test and witnesses responsibly to the twin declarations of God being the only God and Muḥammad being His Prophet, no more can be legally required as proof of faith and, consequently, that person enjoys all the rights and is obligated by all the duties under Islamic law.[115]

Such a view, however, does not accurately present Islamic doctrine and is belied by myriad heresy trials, polemics, and other episodes in Islamic religious history. It is clear that simply declaring one's belief in Islam is not enough. Ibn Taymīyah states, "It has been established by the Koran, the Sunnah, and the consensus of the Muslim community that one must fight against whoever has transgressed the religious law of Islam, even though he utters the two *shahādahs*."[116] Al-Ghazālī adds important restrictions to the statement that the requirement to be a Muslim is to repeat the *shahādah*. For the creed to have full effect, the one who makes it must sincerely believe in it (*ṣādiq bihā*) and not otherwise contradict it (*ghayr munāqiḍ lahā*).[117] It is this last restriction which begs attention, for it indicates that someone who claims to be a Muslim through the utterance of the creed may prove to be a heretic since he contradicts his statement in some other way.

But what constitutes a contradiction of the creed? Obvious contradictions include statements directly opposed to the content of either of its phrases: that is, to deny God's existence, admit the existence of a plurality of gods, or deny Muḥammad's prophecy. Persons making these statements would not be apt to consider themselves Muslims or present themselves as such in the first place and would therefore not fall in the category under discussion, that of Muslim heretics. Al-Ghazālī provides the following definition of Islamic heresy: "Unbelief (*al-kufr*) is to give the lie to the Prophet (*takdhīb ar-rasūl*) with regard to anything which he brought, and faith (*al-īmān*) is to believe him regarding all that which he brought."[118] Thus, Islamic orthodoxy involves a certain attitude not only toward God and the Prophet Muḥammad but also toward the body of material that Muḥammad is seen as having conveyed, whether scripture, law, or doctrine.

115. Ismāʿīl Faruqi, *Islam* (Brentwood, Maryland: International Graphics, 1984), 4.

116. Taqī al-Dīn Aḥmad Ibn Taymīyah, *al-Siyāsah al-sharʿiyah fī iṣlāḥ al-raʿiyah* (Beirut: Dār al-āfāq al-jadīdah, 1983), 109.

117. Abū Ḥāmid Muḥammad al-Ghazālī, *Fayṣal al-tafriqah bayn al-islām wa'l-zandaqah* (Cairo: Maṭbaʿat al-saʿādah, 1907), 4.

118. Ibid.

One legal definition of al-Ghazālī's "giving the lie to the Prophet" (*takdhīb al-rasūl*) that was widely upheld by medieval Muslim jurists (though not by al-Ghazālī) was the violation of consensus. As we have seen above, consensus defines Islamic legal orthodoxy, at least according to strict adherents to the system of religious authority promoted by the jurists. Consequently, the violation of consensus (*mukhālafat al-ijmāʿ*), also termed breach of consensus (*kharq al-ijmāʿ*) or deviation from consensus (*al-khurūj ʿan al-ijmāʿ*), is tantamount to heresy or unbelief. While some thinkers stopped short of this position, holding that the violation of consensus should be treated as a lesser type of religious deviance, the equation of the violation of the consensus with unbelief was explicitly upheld by many legal scholars throughout the medieval period. This position, it is claimed, dates back to the time of al-Shāfiʿī. Pressed to find a scriptural basis for the authority of consensus, he supposedly cited the following verse:

> Whoever opposes the Messenger (*man yushāqiq ir-rasūl*) after (God's) guidance has been revealed to him, and follows a way other than that of the believers, We will appoint for him that to which he himself has turned, and will let him burn in Hell—a terrible end. (Q 4:115)

According to his interpretation, abandonment of the consensus of the Muslims is equivalent to opposing the Prophet.[119] Al-Ghazālī reports that prohibitions of the violation of consensus (*taḥrīm mukhālafat al-ijmāʿ*) had become common by the time of the Muʿtazilī scholar al-Naẓẓām (d. 220–30/835–45).[120] The equation of violating the consensus with heretical belief may be seen in the statement of the famous Shāfiʿī jurist Ibn al-Qāṣṣ (Abū ʾl-ʿAbbās Aḥmad b. Aḥmad al-Ṭabarī, d. 335/946): "Whoever denies the consensus of the Community has denied the Prophet."[121] The tenth-century Ismāʿīlī scholar al-Qāḍī al-Nuʿmān (d. 363/974) remarks on Sunni jurists' reliance on consensus: "according to them, it is an authoritative argument (*ḥujjah*). They must have recourse to it and refrain from departing from it." He adds that the Sunnis consider going against consensus forbidden and tantamount to heresy: "Consensus is a fundamental principle of the religion (*aṣl min uṣūl al-dīn*). One must follow and obey it, and to go against it is not lawful" (*lā yaḥillu mukhālafatuh*). In somewhat stronger terms, he reports, "Some of them have declared those who deviate from it unbelievers" (*wa-kaffara baʿḍuhum man kharaja ʿanhu*).[122]

119. Imām al-Ḥaramayn al-Juwaynī, *al-Burhān fī uṣūl al-fiqh*, 2 vols. (Cairo, 1980), 1: 677. The earliest reference to al-Shāfiʿī's use of this verse as a justification for consensus found by Hallaq is *Aḥkām al-Qurʾān* by al-Bayhaqī (d. 458/1065). Hallaq asserts, though, that al-Shāfiʿī probably did not consider this verse a convincing argument for consensus ("Authoritativeness," 432, 452 n. 34).

120. Abū Ḥamid Muḥammad al-Ghazālī, *al-Mustaṣfā min ʿilm al-uṣūl*, 2 vols. (Cairo, 1906), 1: 173.

121. al-Khaṭīb al-Baghdādī, *Kitāb al-Faqīh waʾl-mutafaqqih*, 2: 19.

122. al-Qāḍī al-Nuʿmān, *Ikhtilāf uṣūl al-madhāhib*, ed. S. T. Lokhandwalla (Simla, India: Indian Institute of Advanced Study, 1972), 56.

By the tenth century at the latest, the authority of consensus was a solidly established principle in Sunni jurisprudence. Consequently, the violation of consensus represented a serious infraction of Sunni norms and involved a risk of accusation of heresy.

Eleventh-century authors attest that consensus constitutes orthodoxy and cannot be violated. Abū al-Muẓaffar al-Isfarā'inī (d. 471/1078–79) states, "The consensus is true. Whatever the community agrees upon is true, and its truth is irrefutable (*maqṭū' 'alayh*), whether it be word or deed."[123] Al-Khaṭīb al-Baghdādī holds that consensus is of two types: lay consensus (*ijmā' al-'āmmah*) and consensus of the jurists (*ijmā' al-khāṣṣah*). The former refers to such points as the obligations to pray toward the Ka'bah, to fast during Ramaḍān, to perform ablutions, to pray at specific times, and to give alms. The latter refers to such issues as the rule that sexual intercourse renders a pilgrimage or Ramaḍān fast invalid, the rule that the plaintiff must produce proof and the defendant take an oath, and so on. He holds that whoever denies the first type of consensus should be given the opportunity to repent; if he does not, he should be killed. Whoever rejects the second type of consensus and continues to do so wittingly should be told, "You are a man who stubbornly opposes the truth and those who uphold it" (*anta rajulun mu'ānidun li'l-ḥaqqi wa-ahlih*).[124] Even in the latter case, violation of the consensus is a grave form of religious deviance.

Imām al-Ḥaramayn al-Juwaynī (d. 478/1085) stresses the centrality of consensus to Islamic law, writing, "The consensus is the binding strap of the Law and its pillar, whence it derives its support" (*al-ijmā'u 'iṣāmu 'sh-sharī'ati wa-'imāduhā wa-ilayhi 'stinādubā*). Equating violation of consensus with religious deviance, though short of unbelief, he reports, "Those whose opinions are considered in consensus have declared with certainty that whoever violates the consensus (*man yukhālif al-ijmā'*) should be censured." He adds:

> We have found that the generations of the past and the extinct nations were in agreement that whoever violates the consensus of the scholars of the age (*man yukhālifu ijmā'a 'ulamā'i 'd-dahr*) should be reproached, and they continually deemed such violators guilty of deviance, recalcitrance, and disobedience. They do not consider this a trifling matter, but rather see the audacity of going against the scholars as blatant miscreance (*ḍalāl mubīn*).[125]

The violator of consensus is therefore, in al-Juwaynī's view, a particularly intractable deviant. Though he stops short of labeling such a deviant an unbe-

123. Abū al-Muẓaffar al-Isfarā'inī, *al-Tabṣīr fī al-dīn wa-tamyīz al-firqah al-nājiyah 'an al-firaq al-hālikīn*, ed. Muḥammad Zāhid b. al-Ḥasan al-Kawtharī (Cairo: Maktabat al-Khānjī, 1955), 159.

124. al-Khaṭīb al-Baghdādī, *Kitāb al-Faqīh wa'l-mutafaqqih*, 1: 172.

125. al-Juwaynī, *al-Burhān*, 1: 679, 718, 681.

liever, many jurists of his time, he reports, equate violation of the consensus directly with unbelief: "The jurists very commonly state that the violator of consensus should be declared an unbeliever" (*fashā fī lisāni 'l-fuqahā'i anna khāriqa 'l-ijmā'i yukaffar*).[126] Al-Ghazālī ridicules jurists who make accusations of unbelief relying solely on their knowledge of *fiqh*, for, according to his view, such decisions involve extensive expertise in logic, philosophical categories, and rules of interpretation which most jurists lack. In his early work on jurisprudence, *al-Mankhūl*, al-Ghazālī gives the opinion that the breacher of consensus (*khāriq al-ijmā'*) should not be declared an unbeliever on the grounds that the Muslims have disagreed on the validity of consensus as a source of law in the first place. He then adds that when the jurists describe the violater of consensus as an unbeliever, they intend only that consensus which is based on an irrefutable source text, whether a Koranic verse or a prophetic tradition reported through many chains of transmission.[127] His remarks imply, however, that his contemporaries were much less reluctant to label opponents heretics on the basis of legal opinions alone. Equating violating the consensus with unbelief was not uncommon after the eleventh century; the late author al-Shawkānī (d. 1250/1832), for example, deems the violator of consensus an unbeliever (*kāfir*) and a sinner (*fāsiq*).[128]

The work of Makdisi has brought out the historical role of the jurists as a collective body who claimed and wielded religious authority beginning in the ninth century, firmly establishing their dominance over Islamic religious discourse by the eleventh century. The *madhhab*s were autonomous, excluding all outsiders such as the philosophical theologians and the caliph from participating in the law. They established a monopoly, claiming sole jurisdiction over matters pertaining to the law. In the system they developed orthodoxy was defined by consensus and decided by the continual process of disputation in which the jurists championed variant opinions. A scholar could uphold legitimate dissenting opinions on the law if he had completed the proper course of legal education within the *madhhab*s and had been recognized by his qualified masters as a fully competent jurist. The absence of dissent on a particular issue signaled that a consensus had been reached; otherwise, any of the views which the jurists had supported was equally valid. Though Makdisi does not treat questions of heresy specifically, it follows from his discussion that in the system established by the jurists heresy may be defined as the violation of consensus.

In order for a scholar's opinion on the religious law to be taken into consideration, it was necessary for him to be considered a qualified jurist. This

126. Ibid., 724.

127. al-Ghazālī, *Fayṣal al-tafriqah*, 5–15, 19; idem, *al-Mankhūl*, 309.

128. al-Shawkānī, *Irshād al-fuḥūl*, 138.

stipulation is apparently why Ibn Jarīr al-Ṭabarī did not include Aḥmad b. Ḥanbal in his *Ikhtilāf al-fuqahā'*; in his view, Ibn Ḥanbal was merely an expert in tradition, and this did not render his opinion on the law worthy of consideration. As the *madhhab* system became more rigid, one needed to belong to an established legal *madhhab* in order to ensure that one's opinions would be based on a recognized methodology and tradition of legal teaching. Only then would one's dissenting opinions be accepted as valid. Otherwise, dissenting opinions were considered violations of consensus, and by espousing them, one risked setting oneself outside the pale of orthodoxy.

By the early tenth century it became necessary for scholars to affiliate with a particular legal *madhhab* in order to gain recognition as competent jurists who could voice legal opinions with authority. The coalescence of the *madhhabs* as regular teaching institutions and as organizations that restricted religious authority to a limited group of experts trained in the law was designed to keep out a number of groups, including the Mu'tazilīs and the Shiites. Within this institutional framework, the norm used to exclude the Shiites from attaining religious authority was that of the consensus. Shiites were deemed violators of the consensus if their opinions differed from Sunni positions and did not have a valid basis in terms of legal methodology. A typical legal issue taken as evidence of the Shiites' deviance or outright heresy was that of temporary or fixed-duration marriage (*zawāj al-mut'ah*). Shiites held that this type of marriage was permissible and that it had been practiced during the time of the Prophet but was abolished by 'Umar b. al-Khaṭṭāb, the second caliph. The jurists of the Sunni *madhhabs* held that *mut'ah* marriage was forbidden and that the Shiites who allowed it were in violation of consensus. Many of these Sunni critics claimed not only that the Shiites were wrong on this particular point of law but also that they were miscreants and unbelievers for insisting on an opinion which plainly violated the consensus of qualified jurists. Because the Shiites did not belong to a recognized legal *madhhab*, their opinions on matters of the law would not be taken into consideration. Unless they repented and recanted these opinins, they were to be treated as unbelievers who had no legitimate place in Muslim society.

SHIITE RESPONSES TO THE SUNNI LEGAL SYSTEM

Throughout their existence, the Imami or Twelver Shiites have been acutely aware of the pressure and scrutiny of the Sunni majority. Their constant attention to the Sunni restrictions on their community is as evident in their legal theory as it is in other areas of Shiite scholarship and custom. In their religious texts, they often refer to the Sunnis as *mukhālifūnā*, "our opponents" or "those who disagree with us," emphasizing the historical confrontation between the two groups. They also term the Sunnis *al-'āmmah*, "the majority" or "the generality," as opposed to the Shiites themselves, termed *al-khāṣṣah*, "the minority" or "the select group." The Sunnis, by virtue of number and political power, determine the norms of society and often confront the Shiites or show them open hostility. Even in modern Iran, a majority Shiite society under a Shiite religious regime since the 1979 revolution, there is an acute awareness that Shiites are a minority in the Islamic world and that they must adjust their behavior with a view to the potential hostility or ill will of that majority.

As a community accused of religious deviance, the Twelver Shiites were under continual criticism and attack by members of the Sunni majority. The level and frequency of criticism varied widely according to social, political, and economic circumstances, but self-styled guardians of Sunni orthodoxy have frequently attempted either to remove Shiism from the public sphere or to force conformance to Sunni norms. The exact form and content of the criticisms, however, have been shaped not only by economic and political factors but also by the concepts and ideologies espoused by Sunni religious scholars. With the rise in power and influence of the juridical *madhhabs*, the views of the Sunni jurists provided a new basis for criticism directed at the Shiites: the accusation of violating the consensus. Since consensus renders an opinion binding or irrefutable, to argue against it is not only incorrect but also impermissible. Hence the ruling that to go against consensus is tantamount to unbelief. The implication, in the Sunni jurists' view, is that the Shiites must retract their opinions or else be excluded from the community of opinion which constitutes Islamic orthodoxy.

While statements that it is illegal to go against the consensus (*taḥrīm mukhālafat al-ijmāʿ*) may date back to as early as the first half of the ninth century, it appears that pressure on Twelver Shiites to conform to Sunni legal consensus became particularly acute in the course of the tenth century. The Sunni *madhhabs* were in the process of closing their ranks and the Shiites were in danger of being left out. Against this background, the establishment of Buwayhid hegemony in Iraq and Iran in the mid-tenth century allowed Shiite religious rituals, doctrines, and practices to enter the public sphere more freely. In reaction, Sunni traditionalists forcefully opposed the Shiites' increasingly open display of their beliefs. The result was a prolonged series of confrontations between the Shiites and their conservative Sunni opponents that lasted throughout the period of Buwayhid hegemony. Such confrontations had existed before and would exist after Buwayhid rule, but they occurred with greater frequency and regularity during those years. The resurgence of the Sunni traditionalist movement in the late tenth and early eleventh century redoubled the pressure to conform to Sunni norms.

Among the criticisms directed at the Shiites during the Buwayhid period was the assertion that their legal system was inadequate. This issue is evident from a number of works by prominent Shiite scholars of the time, including al-Shaykh al-Mufīd, al-Sharīf al-Murtaḍā, al-Shaykh al-Ṭūsī, and al-Najāshī, wherein they cite Sunni criticisms of their legal tradition and state that they are writing in response to their accusers. Al-Najāshī, for example, frames his bibliography of works in the Shiite tradition as a response to Sunni interlocutors who claimed, *innahu lā salafa lakum wa-lā muṣannaf:* "You (Shiites) have neither predecessors (from whom your legal tradition derives) nor comprehensive works arranged by chapter."[129] The violation of consensus was one of the most prominent issues raised in such criticisms. Al-Shaykh al-Mufīd's treatise *al-Masā'il al-ṣāghānīyah* is a response to the accusation on the part of a Sunni contemporary that a number of Shiite positions on the law, including the position on *zawāj al-mut'ah* or fixed-duration marriage, represent a violation of consensus (*khurūj 'an al-ijmā'*) and that Shiites are therefore unbelievers.[130] Similarly, al-Sharīf al-Murtaḍā's legal work *Kitāb al-Intiṣār* responds to Sunni accusations that many Shiite legal opinions violated consensus and were therefore heretical, describing them as "vituperous attacks." The Sunnis claimed that a prior consensus had been reached which excluded such Shiite opinions and, on this basis, refused to debate the Shiites or consider their legal opinions.[131]

Accusations of violating the consensus became a regular structural feature of the Sunni *madhhab* system and were frequently directed against the Shiites from the tenth century on. Ibn al-Jawzī, writing in the twelfth century, remarks that the Shiite rulings on the points of law discussed by al-Sharīf al-Murtaḍā violate the consensus and are therefore unacceptable.[132] The Shiites wrote many works on their well-known dissenting legal positions in response to Sunni claims that they were heretical for violating the consensus. For example, the well-known Safavid author Bahā' al-Dīn al-'Āmilī (d. 1030/1621) wrote *Taḥrīm dhabā'iḥ ahl al-kitāb* in response to an accusation conveyed by the Ottoman ambassador that a traditional Shiite legal position—that it is forbidden for Muslims to eat meat slaughtered by Christians and Jews—violated the consensus.[133] Such accusations always carried the implication not only that the individual legal opinion held by the Shiites was wrong but also that by holding such opinions the Shiites were operating outside all recognized juridical *madh-*

129. Abū al-'Abbās Aḥmad b. al-Najāshī, *Kitāb al-rijāl* (Qum: Markaz-i nashr-i kitāb, n.d.), 2.

130. Muḥammad b. Muḥammad b. al-Nu'mān al-Shaykh al-Mufīd, *al-Masā'il al-ṣāghānīyah fī al-radd 'alā Abī Ḥanīfah* (Najaf: al-'Adl al-islāmī, n.d.), passim.

131. al-Sharīf al-Murtaḍā, *al-Intiṣār*, ed. Sayyid Muḥammad Riḍā b. Ḥasan al-Kharsān (Beirut: Dār al-aḍwā, 1985), 1–5.

132. Ibn al-Jawzī, *al-Muntaẓam fī tārīkh al-mulūk wa'l-umam*, 18 vols., ed. Muḥammad 'Abd al-Qādir 'Aṭā and Muṣṭafā 'Abd al Qādir 'Aṭā (Beirut: Dār al-kutub al-'ilmīyah, 1992), 15: 294. For an accusation of violating the consensus from the eighteenth century, see 'Abd Allāh b. al-Ḥusayn al-Suwaydī, *Mu'tamar al-Najaf* (Cairo: al-Maṭba'ah al-salafīyah, 1973), 42.

133. Bahā' al-Dīn Muḥammad al-'Āmilī, *Ḥurmat dhabā'iḥ ahl al-kitāb*, ed. Zuhayr al-A'rajī (Beirut: Mu'assasat al-a'lamī li'l-maṭbū'āt, 1990).

habs with an illegitimate legal methodology and were therefore heretics. Writing in the seventeenth century, a Shiite scholar states that the Sunnis had agreed many centuries earlier that there were only four recognized legal *madhhabs* and that anyone who went against the rulings espoused within these *madhhabs* was a heretic. Unless he repented, his life and property would be forfeit. Ever since the time of the Ayyūbid ruler Ṣalāḥ al-Dīn (564–89/1169–93), he reports, no judge or *mudarris* could be appointed unless he belonged to one of the four Sunni *madhhabs*.[134] The Sunni jurists upheld consensus as a norm regulating interpretation of the law within the Muslim community, and the Shiites were at risk of being excluded from participation in Islamic religious, academic, and social life on the grounds that they violated it.

As part of the Islamic community under regular scrutiny and attack, it was inevitable that the Shiites, Twelvers included, react to this challenge. The definition of orthodoxy espoused by the Sunni juridical establishment was, in sociological terms, an identity norm that defined the Muslim believer and placed the Shiite community in a dilemma or normative predicament.[135] On the one hand, Shiites considered themselves to be believers and perfectly good Muslims, entitled to participate fully and freely in Muslim society. On the other hand, society was threatening to exclude them as heretics for failing to conform to the consensus of the Sunni jurists. Though the threat of execution was usually remote, it is clear that the Shiites were indeed marked out as deviants who held unacceptable beliefs and were under considerable social pressure to conform. On both popular and elite levels, they were subject to systematic discrimination. Linked to this general social pressure was what may be termed academic pressure. While Shiite laymen often suffered abuse in the social arena, Shiite scholars were threatened with being excluded from the community of interpretation formed by qualified Muslim jurists, a community that became more and more rigidly defined in the course of the ninth, tenth, and eleventh centuries.[136] In order to conform, it seemed, the Shiites would have to give up what they felt was an inalienable part of their identity, yet it was necessary that they respond in some fashion to avoid utter marginalization.

The Twelver Shiites' historical reactions to the predicament presented by the Sunni legal definition of heresy may be described under three main rubrics, each of which played an important role in the subsequent history of Shiite jurisprudence and legal education. One way of reacting to the challenge of the

134. Shihāb al-Dīn al-Karakī, *Hidāyat al-abrār ilā ṭarīq al-a'immah al-aṭhār*, ed. Ra'ūf Jamāl al-Dīn (Najaf, 1977), 182–83.

135. Erving Goffman, *Stigma*, 127.

136. Melchert presents evidence that Muslim sectaries, including Shiites, were systematically excluded from the Sunni community in the ninth century ("Sectaries in the Six Books," *The Muslim World* 82 [1992]: 287–95).

madhhab system was to acknowledge consensus publicly, practicing dissimulation (*taqīyah*), but to adhere inwardly and privately to Shiite doctrine. The use of *taqīyah* in this manner would allow Shiites to participate in the Sunni legal system—as a Sunni system—by selectively suppressing or modifying information about themselves, their beliefs, and their community. In reference to the general predicament of stigmatized social groups, Goffman calls strategies of this type "passing."[137] Makdisi has discussed a similar course of action adopted by the theological schools of Mu'tazilism and the Ash'arism, also threatened with exclusion from the *madhhab* system. The adherents of suspect groups would adopt one of the established legal *madhhab*s in order to participate in the system of education through which the jurists maintained their monopoly of religious authority. Makdisi has shown that the Mu'tazilīs adopted the Ḥanafī *madhhab,* while the Ash'arīs adopted the Shāfi'ī *madhhab.*[138] Once having completed a legal education within this system, the Mu'tazilī scholar could profess his opinions on the law, not as a Mu'tazilī, but as a Ḥanafī, and the Ash'arī scholar could profess his legal opinions as a Shāfi'ī. Their opinions, then legitimate variants, would have to be taken into account for the evaluation of the consensus and dissent of the jurists. Like the Mu'tazilīs and the Ash'arīs, Shiites participated in the Sunni legal system by adopting and adhering outwardly to one of the four Sunni *madhhab*s. As it turns out, the Twelvers affiliated primarily with the Shāfi'ī *madhhab* and the Zaydīs with the Ḥanafī *madhhab.*

A second method was to adopt the concept of legal consensus, but, while doing so, to interpret it in such a way that Twelver Shiite opinions did not have to be retracted. Shiite jurists thus accepted the Sunni jurists' exclusionary norm in principle, but maintained that the norm itself had to be adjusted in order to take their religious tradition into account. The acceptance of the principle of consensus was the key step in the attempt to establish Twelver Shiism as a legitimate coordinate *madhhab* parallel to the Sunni *madhhab*s. The creation of the Imami or Twelver *madhhab* in this manner was undertaken to allow Twelver Shiites to participate openly in Islamic society and in the community of legal interpretation as the Sunni *madhhab*s exerted ever greater hegemony over religious discourse.

A third type of reaction was for the Twelver Shiites to reject the system of legal orthodoxy embodied in consensus and based on the exclusive authority of the jurists belonging to the Sunni *madhhab*s. In so doing, they were opting for deviance, refusing to uphold the norm espoused by society at large. This strategy is one of the possible solutions to the normative predicament: for the

137. Goffman, *Stigma,* 73–91.

138. George Makdisi, "Ash'arī and the Ash'arites in Islamic Religious History," *Studia Islamica* 17 (1962): 37–80, 18 (1963): 19–39; idem, *Rise of Humanism,* 39–43.

individual who cannot maintain an identity norm to alienate himself from the community that upholds the norm or to refrain from developing an attachment to the community in the first place.[139] The adherents of this tendency within Shiism would perform dissimulation as a practical, defensive measure when necessary, yet hold, inwardly and within their own community, that the Sunnis were fundamentally misguided and that their entire legal system was in plain error. They held that study of the law and legal methodology did not suffice to grant religious authority. In their view, it was more historically authentic and more consonant with fundamental Shiite doctrine, particularly the belief in the imamate, that religious truth be sought in the hadith of the imams, that the believers consult experts in the traditions of the imams rather than legal scholars, and that the consensus of jurists was meaningless, if not blatantly false, for the truth was limited to the imams' teachings. Shiites who chose this alternative believed it did not matter what opinions the Sunnis held, since they were heretics who denied the true source of religious authority in the first place. This stance was generally adopted in medieval Ismāʿīlī Shiism. It exists to this day in Ismāʿīlism's modern branches, the Khojas, who recognize a living imam—the Agha Khan—as the source of authority, and the Bohras, who recognize a representative of the imam—the *dāʿī muṭlaq* or "supreme missionary"—as the conduit of authority from their Hidden (*mastūr*) Imam. It is also the view adopted by many proponents of the traditionalist trend within Twelver Shiism, most often designated as Akhbārīs. Their position attracted a considerable following in the tenth and eleventh centuries, but subsequently lost ground until the Akhbārī revival of the seventeenth and eighteenth centuries, when it played a prominent role in Shiite intellectual history.

Throughout Islamic history, the Shiites have harbored conflicting attitudes toward the Sunni majority. On the one hand, many Shiites felt wronged by the majority and held that Sunni Islam should be rejected, in either a quietist or an openly hostile fashion. On the other hand, there was a strong tendency to support the concept of Muslim unity, accept the Sunni majority, and strive to be accepted within the circle of Islamic orthodoxy. While these attitudes had existed before the rise of the Sunni system of juridical *madhhabs*, they came to be expressed in different ways after its establishment. After the Occultation of the twelfth imam, opposition to the Sunni caliph was no longer a crucial issue facing the Shiites. The pressure to confront Sunni theology effectively remained significant in the tenth and eleventh centuries, but abated with time as the philosophical theologians became increasingly marginalized. The theological questions that remained prone to contention

139. Goffman, *Stigma*, 127.

between Sunnis and Shiites were those related to the issue of the imamate, which had originated as an immediate political issue but, largely divorced from contemporary political considerations by the tenth century, had developed into a question of theological belief concerning the early historical caliphate. Chief among the questions related to this issue was the status of the Companions whom the Shiites consider enemies of ʿAli and the family of the Prophet. Vilification of the Companions assumed a preeminent role in the public expression of Shiite identity throughout the medieval period and into modern times, and was one of the chief signs adopted by the Sunnis as evidence of their heretical beliefs. Notwithstanding, while law has certainly not been the only area of conflict with the majority Sunni community which the Shiites have had to face in the course of Islamic history, the pressure to conform or react to the Sunni legal system has remained strong from the tenth century until the present. It is difficult to gain an adequate understanding of Shiite legal history without taking this fundamental structural feature of Islamic societies into account.

This study treats what has generally been seen as the result of a break in the system of authority in Twelver Shiism caused by the Occultation of the imam as a sustained reaction to the Sunni system of legal orthodoxy that developed between the ninth and eleventh centuries. The pressure or predicament which Twelver Shiites faced as a result of the establishment of the *madhhab*s was most succinctly expressed in the accusation that they violated the consensus and were therefore deviants or unbelievers. As a means of explaining aspects of Twelver Shiite intellectual history, legal education, and legal theory for which other studies have failed to account adequately, the following chapters treat the history of Shiite jurisprudence under the rubrics of the three types of reaction to the Sunni *madhhab* system outlined above. This particular reading, of course, represents a generalization; the three types of reaction outlined here, though they have all been important in Shiite intellectual and institutional history, have not necessarily figured significantly within the Shiite community in all areas and periods. Moreover, the three tendencies have not been mutually exclusive, and are interrelated in important ways elaborated in the following discussion. They nevertheless serve as a useful framework for the examination of the Twelver Shiite legal tradition.

3

Conformance to Consensus

Twelver Shiite Participation in the Shāfiʿī *Madhhab*

"*Taqīyah* is the shield of the believer and his fortress."[1]
Jaʿfar al-Ṣādiq

One option open to Shiite scholars, faced as they were with exclusion from the Sunni juridical system and from the process of disputation that defined Islamic legal orthodoxy, was to adopt one of the Sunni *madhhabs* while inwardly still holding to Shiite beliefs. In this way they could complete an education in law and legal methodology, contribute to legal scholarship, and even serve as legal authorities within the Sunni majority community. This strategy was a form of outward capitulation to adverse circumstances, a conformance to the consensus defined by the Sunni *madhhabs* which explicitly excluded Shiites' opinions. If Shiites were denounced for not belonging to one of the established Sunni *madhhabs* and for espousing legal opinions not represented therein, it served their purposes actually to join one of them and thereby avoid the accusation altogether. Makdisi has argued that the theological schools of Muʿtazilism and Ashʿarism adopted a similar strategy in response to the growing power of the traditionalist Sunni jurists. At first excluded from the *madhhabs*, they later infiltrated them, the Ashʿarīs entering the Shāfiʿī *madhhab* and the Muʿtazilīs, the Ḥanafī *madhhab*.[2] Shiites, faced with a situation parallel to that of the philosophical theologians, often reacted in a similar fashion, "infiltrating" the Sunni legal *madhhabs*. The term "infiltration," which suggests that the actors involved were trying to undermine the Sunni legal system, need not be used here. "Affiliation" or "participation" might more aptly express the na-

1. Muḥammad b. Yaʿqūb al-Kulaynī, *al-Kāfī*, 8 vols. (Beirut: Dār al-aḍwāʾ, 1985), 2: 221.
2. Makdisi, "Ash ʿari"; idem, *Rise of Colleges*, 8.

ture of the relationship. In general, the Twelver Shiites chose affiliation with the Shāfiʿī *madhhab,* while the Zaydī Shiites chose affiliation with the Ḥanafī *madhhab.*

Twelver Shiites have often remarked that, of the Sunni *madhhab*s, the law of the Shāfiʿī *madhhab* is closest to their own, and Western scholars have made similar observations.[3] While one might suppose this a mere coincidence, it may also point to a more profound relationship between the Shāfiʿī *madhhab* and the Twelver Shiite legal tradition. A significant connection is suggested by the number of attested instances where Shiite scholars claimed to be Shāfiʿīs when on trial for heresy. Muḥammad b. Makkī al-Jizzīnī, executed in Mamluk Damascus in 786/1384, claimed to be a Shāfiʿī at his heresy trial.[4] The Iranian scholar Shihāb al-Dīn ʿAbd Allāh b. Maḥmūd al-Tustarī (d. 997/1588–89), captured by the Uzbeks during an attack on the Safavid province of Khurasan and subsequently executed as a heretic in Bukhara, also claimed to be a Shāfiʿī at his trial.[5] Al-Qāḍī Nūr Allāh al-Shushtarī, executed on 18 Jumādā II 1019/7 September 1610 at the court of the Moghul Jahāngīr in India, claimed to be a Shāfiʿī when accused of heresy.[6] One may explain this phenomenon as an expedient used by Shiite scholars when in danger of losing their lives and due, primarily, to the agreement of a number of well-known Shāfiʿī positions on the points of law with those of the Twelver Shiites. There are, however, further indications of a more important connection between Twelver Shiism and the Shāfiʿī *madhhab* that profoundly affected the transmission of legal knowledge in pre-modern Islamic societies.

Twelver Shiite jurists participated extensively in the Shāfiʿī *madhhab.* Their participation involved much more than simply reading books by Shāfiʿī authors[7] or claiming affiliation with the Shāfiʿīs under duress. Twelver Shiite

3. al-Karakī, *Hidāyat al-abrār,* 152–53; Muḥammad b. al-Ḥasan al-Ḥurr al-ʿĀmilī, *al-Fawāʾid al-ṭūsīyah,* ed. Mahdī al-Lājiwardī al-Ḥusaynī and Muḥammad Durūdī (Qum: al-Maṭbaʿah al-ʿilmīyah, 1983), 467–70; Goldziher, *Islamic Theology and Law,* 205.

4. Taqī al-Dīn Abū Bakr b. Aḥmad Ibn Qāḍī Shuhbah al-Asadī al-Dimashqī, *Tārīkh Ibn Qāḍī Shuhbah,* vol. 1, ed. ʿAdnān Darwīsh (Damascus: al-Maʿhad al-ʿilmī al-faransī li ʾl-dirāsāt al-ʿarabīyah, 1977), 134–35.

5. Iskandar Beg Munshī, *Tārīkh-i ʿālam-ārā-yi ʿabbāsī,* 2 vols. (Tehran: Chāpkhānah-yi gulshan, 1971), 1: 154–55. See also Muḥammad Bāqir al-Khwānsārī, *Rawḍāt al-jannāt fī aḥwāl al-ʿulamāʾ waʾl-sādāt,* 8 vols. (Beirut: al-Dār al-islāmīyah, 1991), 4: 224–28.

6. Saiyid Athar Abbas Rizvi, *A Socio-Intellectual History of the Isnā ʿAsharī Shīʿīs in India,* 2 vols. (Canberra, Australia: Maʿrifat Publishing House, 1986), 1: 377–78.

7. Shiite scholars commonly read books by authors from all the Sunni *madhhabs*. See, for example, Kohlberg's list of books found in the library of Raḍī al-Dīn ʿAlī b. Mūsā Ibn Ṭāwūs (d. 664/1266), which includes a number of works by Shāfiʿīs, Ḥanafīs, and Ḥanbalīs, less so Mālikīs *(Medieval Muslim Scholar at Work),* 89 and in index, s.v. "Ḥanafīs", "Ḥanbalīs", "Mālikīs", "Shāfiʿīs").

jurists read Shāfiʿī legal texts, trained under Shāfiʿī professors, and studied and taught in Shāfiʿī institutions. Moreover, they did so as part of a long and self-conscious tradition. While not emphasized in scholarship on Shiite intellectual history to date, this tradition was nevertheless quite strong in many periods, and boasts some of the foremost figures in the Shiite legal tradition, such as al-ʿAllāmah al-Ḥillī, al-Shahīd al-Awwal, and al-Shahīd al-Thānī.

THE SHIITE TRADITION OF LEGAL STUDY IN SUNNI CIRCLES

Many Twelver Shiite scholars are known to have studied under Sunni teachers, and this chapter presents short synopses of the careers of the most important participants in this tradition. The aim here is to demonstrate not only that extensive study under Sunni teachers has been a regular phenomenon in Shiite intellectual history but also that it merits recognition as an established tradition. While Shiite scholars studied a wide range of topics, including grammar, rhetoric, recitation of the Koran, and logic with Sunni teachers, they also made considerable efforts to study doctrinally marked topics, such as hadith and law. When they studied the legal sciences per se, they tended to study within the Shāfiʿī *madhhab*. Their legal studies and related activities often led them to participate quite extensively, as Shāfiʿī students, professors, authors, and jurists, in Sunni educational and juridical institutions.

A brief look at the medieval Islamic organization of learning is necessary before examining the Twelver Shiite Shāfiʿī tradition. The sciences were divided into two main groups: the rational sciences and the scriptural or traditional sciences. The latter were divided into five areas: the study of the Koran, hadith, philosophical theology, law, and the literary arts, considered ancillary to the first four fields. The rational sciences or the sciences of the ancients—a designation that acknowledged the accomplishments of the Greeks in these fields—included mathematics, geometry, astronomy, philosophy, medicine, and so on. For the most part, the rational sciences were not taught in the *madrasah,* the main function of which was to produce scholars of the law, and were not part of the standard curriculum. Expertise in them, necessary for a few subsidiary areas of the law, was usually relegated to specialists. Mathematics was important for inheritance law; astronomy and geometry, for the determination of the *qiblah* and the times for prayer. Study of the rational sciences was therefore optional or tangential to the study of the law. An important exception was logic, which, though a rational science, was often considered the foundation of legal argumentation and the science of dialectic (*jadal*). Therefore the legal curriculum often included logic. The ancillary literary arts included Arabic morphology, syntax, rhetoric, lexicography, and other sciences which enabled one to understand the legal source material, the text of the Koran and the hadith. The ancillary arts were not doctrinally marked, nor was logic. Sunnis and Shiites, Ḥanafīs and Shāfiʿīs could study the same books in these fields without any tensions arising.

The source material, however, could be doctrinally marked. The Koran, for the most part, was not. Although some Shiites accused Caliph ʿUthmān of altering the text of the Koran or omitting key passages from it, Shiite legal scholars have by and large accepted the received text of the Koran.[8] The Shiites have a relatively independent tradition of *tafsīr,* or exegesis of the Koran, and the science of variant readings of the Koran was fairly underdeveloped among the Shiites as opposed to that among the Sunnis. More important, though, Shiite hadith constitutes a corpus distinct from Sunni hadith, since the Shiites recognize as scripture traditions attributed to any of the twelve imams as well as those which go back to the Prophet himself. In addition, the science of hadith criticism remained relatively underdeveloped among the Shiites until the work of Jamāl al-Dīn Aḥmad b. Ṭāwūs (d. 673/1274–75) and Ibn al-Muṭahhar al-Ḥillī in the thirteenth and fourteenth centuries and al-Shahīd al-Thānī in the sixteenth century.[9]

Tafsīr and hadith were thus doctrinally marked to a great extent, and the sciences of *qirāʾāt* and hadith criticism were not well represented within Shiite tradition. A number of Sunni hadith works, termed *ṣiḥāḥ* (sing. *ṣaḥīḥ*), were compiled in the ninth century primarily to serve as references for legal scholars and were therefore arranged according to the standard chapter divisions of legal compendia. Six *ṣiḥāḥ* became standard reference manuals for Sunni scholars, while the Twelver Shiites recognized their own standard reference manuals, four in number, by the end of the eleventh century. The study of hadith as a field in itself was often relatively ignored as part of the legal curriculum, as was *tafsīr.* In legal texts listing the requirements for *ijtihād,* it is often stated that one need not have memorized the required hadith texts or Koranic verses with legal content as long as one knows where to find them in the standard manuals.[10] The twentieth-century Shiite scholar Muḥsin al-Amīn voices a standard complaint when he states that contemporary jurists neglect the study of hadith and

8. See Löschner, *Dogmatischen Grundlagen,* 70–72; Etan Kohlberg, "Some Notes on the Imāmite Attitude to the Qur'ān," in *Islamic Philosophy and the Classical Tradition,* ed. S. M. Stern et al. (Oxford: Cassirer Press, 1972) 209–24.

9. See Asma Afsaruddin, "An Insight into the Ḥadīth Methodology of Jamāl al-Dīn Aḥmad b. Ṭāwūs," *Der Islam* 72 (1995): 25–46; Zayn al-Dīn al-ʿĀmilī, *Sharḥ al-bidāyah fī ʿilm al-dirāyah* (n.p., 1891–92); Ḥusayn b. ʿAbd al-Ṣamad al-Ḥārithī al-ʿĀmilī, *Wuṣūl al-akhyār ilā uṣūl al-akhbār,* ed. ʿAbd al-Laṭīf al-Kūhkamarī (Qum: Maṭbaʿat al-khayyām, 1981); Bahāʾ al-Dīn Muḥammad al-ʿĀmilī, *al-Wajīzah,* ed. Muḥammad al-Mishkāt (Tehran: Maṭbaʿat al-majlis al-shūrī, 1937).

10. Jamāl al-Dīn al-Ḥasan b. Yūsuf Ibn al-Muṭahhar al-Ḥillī, *Tahdhīb al-wuṣūl* (Tehran, 1890), 101; al-Aʿrajī al-Ḥusaynī, *Munyat al-labīb,* 359.

11. Muḥsin al-Amīn, *Aʿyān al-shīʿah,* 10 vols. (Beirut: Dār al-taʿāruf li'l-maṭ būʿāt, 1984), 10: 352.

hadith criticism, merely relying on the standard compilations.[11] In addition to the hadith manuals, manuals of commentary on the five hundred or so verses of the Koran related to legal topics, called *āyāt al-aḥkām,* were also compiled.

Al-Ḥurr al-ʿĀmilī gives a good indication of which topics were doctrinally marked in premodern scholarly circles when he complains that, unless absolutely necessary, Shiites should not study Sunni works in four fields: "the two *uṣūl*s"—philosophical theology (*uṣūl al-dīn*) and legal methodology (*uṣūl al-fiqh*)—Koranic exegesis (*tafsīr*), and hadith.[12] Legal topics per se were not only doctrinally marked, either Shiite or Sunni, but also segregated, to a large extent, by individual *madhhab.* Ḥanafīs generally read Ḥanafī manuals of *fiqh,* Ḥanafī textbooks of *uṣūl al-fiqh,* and *khilāf* works written from the Ḥanafī point of view. The same could be said, *grosso modo,* for the Shāfiʿīs, Ḥanbalīs, and Mālikīs. The main centers for the teaching of *fiqh* and *uṣūl al-fiqh* were the *madrasah*s, and by attending a certain *madrasah,* registering for a stipend, and following the curriculum taught by the professor of law there, each student would declare a choice of *madhhab.*

al-Faḍl b. Shādhān al-Nīsābūrī (d. 260/873–74)

Al-Faḍl b. Shādhān al-Nīsābūrī[13] was a prominent Shiite jurist and theologian of Nishapur. He wrote, in addition to a number of treatises on philosophical and theological issues, a work on the imamate and several works on Shiite *fiqh,* treating inheritance law, temporary marriage, divorce, and the polemic issue of the wiping of one's inner boots (*al-masḥ ʿalā al-khuffayn*). His works witness to his intense involvement in the major polemics of the time and include refutations of Muḥammad b. Karrām, al-Iskāfī, dualism, philosophers, the Murji'ah, extremist Shiites (*Ghulāt*), literalists (*Ḥashwīyah*), the Khārijīs Yazīd b. Bazīʿ and Yamān b. Rabāb, Aḥmad b. Yaḥyā, al-Aṣamm, al-Ḥasan al-Baṣrī, Abū ʿUbayd, al-Bāṭinīyah, and al-Qarāmiṭah. Al-Faḍl also wrote a legal work, perhaps touching on issues of legal theory in addition to the points of law, which his student ʿAlī b. Muḥammad b. Qutaybah posthumously named *Kitāb al-dībāj.* In it al-Faḍl collected the opinions of al-Shāfiʿī, Abū Thawr (d. 240/854), and Dāwūd b. Khalaf al-Iṣfahānī (d. 269/882), the founder of the Ẓāhirīs. The book presents the opinions of the three prominent jurists mentioned here but is not designated as a refutation (*radd*), like so many of al-Faḍl's other works, which suggests that he had some important connections to the currents of legal thought that constituted the nascent Shāfiʿī *madhhab.*

12. al-Ḥurr al-ʿĀmilī, *al-Fawā'id al-ṭūsīyah,* 252.

13. Muḥammad b. al-Ḥasan al-Ṭūsī, *Fihrist kutub al-shīʿah,* ed. Sayyid Muḥammad Ṣādiq Baḥr al-ʿUlūm (Najaf: al-Maṭbaʿah al-ḥaydarīyah), 150–51; al-Najāshī, *Kitāb al-rijāl,* 235–36; Ibn Shahrāshūb, *Maʿālim al-ʿulamā'* (Tehran, 1934), 80–81.

Abū 'l-Ḥasan 'Alī b. al-Ḥusayn al-Mas'ūdī (d. 345/956)

Al-Mas'ūdī,[14] most famous as author of the history *Murūj al-dhahab,* participated in the Shāfi'ī legal *madhhab* while at the same time espousing Imami Shiism.[15] He was born in Baghdad shortly before 280/893 to a Shiite family from Kūfah. He spent his youth in Baghdad, studying with both Shiite and Sunni teachers, including the Shiite theologian Abū Sahl Ismā'īl al-Nawbakhtī (d. 311/923) and the Shāfi'ī jurist Ibn Surayj (d. 306/918). After his early years in Baghdad, he traveled to Iran and India, then returned to Iraq. In 306/918, he was in attendance at the *majlis* of Ibn Surayj. He later went to Syria, returned to Iraq, and settled during his later years in Fusṭāṭ, Egypt. His allegiance to Shiism is clear, for he wrote a number of expressly Shiite works, including a number of works on the imams, such as *al-Istibṣār fī al-imāmah* and *al-Ṣafwah fī al-imāmah.*[16] In addition, his *Kitāb al-ibānah 'an uṣūl al-diyānah* explains the differences between Imāmī Shiite and Mu'tazilī theology. Al-Mas'ūdī's involvement with the Shāfi'ī *madhhab* in Baghdad is equally clear, especially given his connection with Ibn Surayj, the leading Shāfi'ī jurist of the period. It seems that al-Mas'ūdī was studying with Ibn Surayj just before he died. Al-Subkī reports that he possessed a copy of a work on *uṣūl al-fiqh* entitled *Risālat al-bayān 'an uṣūl al-aḥkām,* which Ibn Surayj composed at the request of legal scholars from central Asia (Shāsh and Farghānah), but was unable to finish dictating to his students because of his illness. The work was therefore read out loud while Ibn Surayj listened. The manuscript in al-Subkī's possession, about fifteen folios, he reports, was al-Mas'ūdī's own record of the work.[17] In addition, al-Mas'ūdī wrote a number of legal works, several of which appear to treat *uṣūl al-fiqh,* including *Kitāb naẓm al-adillah fī uṣūl al-millah* and *Kitāb naẓm al-a'lām fī uṣūl al-aḥkām.* These works may have been written within the

14. See al-Mas'ūdī, *Murūj al-dhahab;* idem, *Kitāb al-tanbīh wa'l-ishrāf;* Ibn al-Nadīm, *al-Fihrist,* 225–26; al-Najashi, *Kitāb al-rijāl,* 192; Yāqūt al-Ḥamawī, *Irshād al-arīb ilā ma'rifat al-adīb,* 7 vols. ed. D. S. Margoliouth (London: Luzac, 1907), 5: 147–49; Jamāl al-Dīn al-Ḥasan b. Yūsuf Ibn al-Muṭahhar al-Ḥillī, *Rijāl al-'Allāmah al-Ḥillī* (*Khulāṣat al-aqwāl fī 'ilm al-rijāl*) (Najaf: al-Maṭba'ah al-haydarīyah, 1961), 100; al-Subkī, *Ṭabaqat al-shāfi'īyah al-kubrā,* 3: 456–57; Muḥammad b. al-Ḥasan al-Ḥurrr al-'Āmilī, *Amal al-āmil fī 'ulamā' Jabal 'Āmil,* 2 vols. (Baghdad: Maktabat al-andalus, 1965–66), 2: 180–81; Mīrzā 'Abd Allāh Afandī al-Iṣfahānī, *Riyaḍ al-'ulamā' wa-ḥiyaḍ al-fuḍalā',* 6 vols., ed. Aḥmad al-Ḥusaynī (Qum: Maṭba'at al-khayyām, 1980), 3: 428–32; al-Khwānsārī, *Rawḍāt al-jannāt,* 4: 272–80; al-Amīn, *A'yān al-shī'ah,* 8: 220–26; André Miquel, *La Géographie humaine du monde musulman jusqu'au milieu du XIe siècle* (Paris: Mouton, 1967), 202–12; Tarif Khalidi, *Islamic Historiography* (Albany: State University of New York Press, 1975); A. Shboul, *Al-Mas'ūdī and His World* (London: Ithaca Press, 1979); Charles Pellat, "al-Mas'ūdī," *EI*[2] 6:784–89.

15. André Miquel's suggestion that al-Mas'ūdī was an Ismā'īlī *dā'ī* seems unwarranted (*Géographie humaine,* 207).

16. The well-known Shiite work *Kitāb Ithbāt al-waṣīyah li'l-Imām 'Alī b. Abī Ṭālib* (printed Najaf, 1955, and many times since) cannot be attributed to him with any certainty.

17. al-Subkī, *Ṭabaqāt al-shāfi'īyah al-kubrā,* 3: 456–57.

Shāfiʿī tradition, though it is also possible that they treated *uṣūl al-fiqh* from a Shiite point of view. That al-Masʿūdī wrote works dealing with Shiite law is also known; his work *Kitāb al-wājib fī al-furūḍ al-lawāzib* (or *al-lawāzim*) treats legal *khilāf* between Sunnis and Shiites, including such points as fixed-duration marriage (*mutʿah*) and *al-masḥ ʿalā al-khuffayn.*

While fairly little is known of al-Masʿūdī's legal writings, one cannot agree with Shboul, who holds that it is not possible to determine the legal *madhhab* to which al-Masʿūdī belonged.[18] It seems fairly clear that al-Masʿūdī was an Imami Shiite who affiliated with the Shāfiʿī *madhhab.*

Muḥammad b. Aḥmad b. Ibrāhīm b. Yūsuf al-Kātib (b. 281/894)

In his famous bibliographical catalogue, *al-Fihrist,* the Twelver Shiite bookseller Ibn al-Nadīm (d. early fifth/eleventh c.) mentions a jurist who was both a Shāfiʿī and a Shiite. Abū al-Ḥasan Muḥammad b. Aḥmad b. Ibrāhīm b. Yūsuf al-Kātib was born in 281/894-95 in al-Ḥasanīyah, a town in northern Iraq two days' journey east of Mosul.[19] This scholar studied law as a Shāfiʿī, presumably in Baghdad, professing Shāfiʿī opinions outwardly but holding Shiite opinions secretly (*kāna yatafaqqahu ʿalā madhabi 'sh-Shāfiʿīyi fī 'ẓ-ẓāhir, wa-yarā raʾya sh-shīʿati 'l-imāmīyati fī 'l-bāṭin*). He wrote in both traditions; Ibn al-Nadīm mentions his works in two separate sections of the *Fihrist,* one on Shāfiʿī legal works and the other on Shiite legal works. The famous Shiite jurist al-Shaykh al-Ṭūsī also mentions this scholar in his Shiite bibliographical catalogue, *Fihrist kutub al-shīʿah,* drawing on Ibn al-Nadīm. He, too, records that Muḥammad b. Aḥmad studied both Shiite and Shāfiʿī law, but gives the titles of only his Shiite works.[20] The titles Ibn al-Nadīm lists as Shāfiʿī works are *Kitāb al-baṣāʾir, Kitāb al-ablā, Kitāb al-radd ʿalā al-Karkhī,* and *Kitāb al-mufīd fī al-hadith.* He presents the following titles as Shiite works: *Kitāb kashf al-qināʿ, Kitāb al-istiʿdād, Kitāb al-ʿuddah, Kitāb al-istibṣār, Kitāb naqḍ al-ʿAbbāsīyah, Kitāb al-maqtal, Kitāb al-mufīd fī al-ḥadīth,* and *Kitāb al-ṭarīq.*[21] Two works, *Kitāb naqḍ al-ʿAbbāsīyah* and *Kitāb al-maqtal,* are identifiably Shiite from their titles; they presumably relate to the Shiite theory of the imamate, the first aiming to refute Abbasid claims to the caliphate since Abbasids were of course usurpers in the Shiites' estimation, and the second relating to the martyrdom of Imam Ḥusayn and perhaps the other imams as well. The *Kitāb al-radd ʿalā al-Karkhī* is apparently an anti-Ḥanafī work attacking the well-known Ḥanafī jurist Abū 'l-

18. Shboul, *Al-Masʿūdī,* 57.

19. Ibn al-Nadīm, *al-Fihrist,* 292, 315; Yāqūt al-Ḥamawī, *Muʿjam al-buldān,* 7 vols. (Beirut: Dār al-kutub al-ʿilmīyah, 1990), 2: 300.

20. al-Ṭūsī, *Fihrist kutub al-shīʿah,* 159–60.

21. Ibn al-Nadīm, *al-Fihrist,* 292, 315. It is interesting to note that two of these titles, *Kitāb al-ʿuddah* and *Kitāb al-istibṣār,* would later be used by al-Shaykh al-Ṭūsī, one for his work on *uṣūl al-fiqh* and the other for one of his famous compilations of hadith.

Ḥasan ʿUbayd Allāh al-Karkhī (d. 340/952). It is interesting to note that one work, *Kitāb al-mufīd fī al-ḥadīth,* appears in both lists, perhaps because it included reports transmitted by both Sunnis and Shiites. Ibn al-Nadīm's remarks show that he conceived of the legal traditions as separate entities and recognized at least one scholar who participated in both. Given that Ibn al-Kātib was born in 281/894-95, his affiliation with the Shāfiʿī *madhhab* must have occurred early in the tenth century. Ibn al-Nadīm, who was writing the *Fihrist* in 377/987–88, does not give a death date for Ibn al-Kātib. Al-Subkī also includes him in his *Ṭabaqāt,* but provides no additional information.[22]

Abū Jaʿfar Muḥammad b. al-Ḥasan al-Ṭūsī (d. 460/1067)

Abū Jaʿfar Muḥammad b. al-Ḥasan al-Ṭūsī[23] was one of the three most important Twelver jurists of the Buwayhid period. Born in Ṭūs, next to Mashhad in northeastern Iran, in Ramaḍān 385/October 995, he came to Baghdad in 408/ 1017–18. He studied under al-Shaykh al-Mufīd until the latter's death in 413/ 1022, and then under al-Sharīf al-Murtaḍā (d. 436/1044). Upon al-Murtaḍā's death he became the leading jurist of the Twelver Shiites and the focal point of Shiite legal studies in Baghdad until the Seljuk conquest of 447/1055. Al-Ṭūsī fled to Najaf, where he spent the rest of his days. He died on 22 Muḥarram 460/1 December 1067 in Najaf and was buried in his house there.[24]

Despite his fame as the leading jurist of the Twelvers during his day, al-Shaykh al-Ṭūsī appears in al-Subkī's *Ṭabaqāt al-shāfiʿīyah al-kubrā,* where the author explicitly claims that al-Ṭūsī was a Shāfiʿī.[25] In the biographical notice he devotes to al-Ṭūsī, al-Subkī makes it clear that he knew al-Ṭūsī was an important Shiite jurist as well. He states that al-Ṭūsī was the jurist of the Shiites and author of their reference works (*faqīh al-shīʿah wa-muṣannifuhum*), but this does not deter him from claiming that al-Ṭūsī affiliated himself with the Shāfiʿī guild: "He used to claim adherence to the *madhhab* of al-Shāfiʿī" (*kāna yantamī ilā madhhabi 'sh-Shāfiʿī*). Al-Subkī also states, "He came to Baghdad and studied law following the *madhhab* of al-Shāfiʿī" (*qadima baghdāda wa-tafaqqaha ʿalā madhhabi 'sh-Shāfiʿī*), implying that al-Ṭūsī first claimed membership in the Shāfiʿī *madhhab* on coming to Baghdad and that he studied Shāfiʿī law under teachers there. Al-Subkī also remarks that al-Ṭūsī transmitted

22. al-Subkī, *Ṭabaqāt al-shāfiʿīyah al-kubrā,* 3: 63, citing the *Ṭabaqāt al-fuqahāʾ* of Ibn Bāṭish al-Mawṣilī (d. 655/1257).

23. al-Ṭūsī, *Fihrist kutub al-shīʿah,* 188–90; al-Najāshī, *Kitāb al-rijāl,* 316; Ibn al-Muṭahhar al-Ḥillī, *Rijāl al-ʿAllāmah al-Ḥillī,* 148; Yūsuf al-Baḥrānī, *Luʾluʾat al-Baḥrayn,* ed. Muḥammad Ṣadiq Baḥr al-ʿUlūm (Najaf: Maṭbaʿat nuʿmān, 1966), 293–98; al-Amīn, *Aʿyān al-shīʿah,* 9: 159–67.

24. al-Muṭahhar al-Ḥillī, *Rijāl al-ʿAllāmah al-Ḥillī,* 148.

25. al-Subkī, *Ṭabaqāt al-shāfiʿīyah al-kubrā,* 4: 126–27.

hadith from Hilāl al-Ḥaffār (d. 414/1023), a well-known Sunni traditionist.[26] It could be that al-Subkī based the conclusion that al-Ṭūsī studied Shāfiʿī law on this last fact alone. He may, however, have had evidence which is no longer available that al-Ṭūsī studied law under Shāfiʿī professors. While al-Subkī's information is not corroborated by earlier sources, it did not deter him from including a famous Shiite scholar in his grand history of the Shāfiʿī *madhhab.*

'Imād al-Dīn and Tāj al-Dīn al-Jaʿfarī (fl. 6th/12th c.)

ʿImād al-Dīn Abū al-Qāsim Jaʿfar b. ʿAlī b. ʿAbd Allāh al-Jaʿfarī al-Zaynabī was a member of the prominent Jaʿfarī sayyid family from Qazvin who were known to be Twelver Shiites. He apparently adopted the Ḥanafī *madhhab* and was appointed *muftī* of Dihistān in northeastern Iran. His son Tāj al-Dīn ʿAlī also adopted the Ḥanafī *madhhab* and studied with scholars in Khwārazm, including, presumably, Ḥanafī jurists. In Rayy, he studied with the famous philosopher and Shāfiʿī jurist Fakhr al-Dīn al-Rāzī (d. 606/1209). Tāj al-Dīn, like his father, was appointed *muftī* of Dihistān. Muntajab al-Dīn writes that they both adopted the Ḥanafī *madhhab* out of *taqīyah.*[27]

Najm al-Dīn al-Baʿlabakkī (d. 699/1300)

Najm al-Dīn Aḥmad b. Muḥassin, known as Ibn Millī[28] al-Baʿlabakkī, was a Twelver jurist particularly well integrated into Sunni legal circles.[29] Born in Ramaḍān 617/November 1220 in the town of Baʿlabakk, he studied primarily in Damascus, spent some time in Baghdad, and traveled to Egypt several times. Both Tāj al-Dīn al-Subkī and al-Isnawī include him in their biographical dictionaries of Shāfiʿī scholars, and al-Subkī praises him highly, reporting that he excelled in debate, had an incredible memory, taught students in law, and

26. al-Subkī, *Ṭabaqāt al-shāfiʿīyah al-kubrā,* 4: 127. Abū al-Fatḥ Hilāl b. Muḥammad b. Jaʿfar al-Ḥaffār was a well-known traditionist who taught in Baghdad and lived on the east side, near al-Ḥaṭṭābīn. He was born in 322/934 and died in Ṣafar 414/April-May 1023. See al-Khaṭīb al-Baghdādī, *Tārīkh Baghdād aw Madīnat al-salām,* 14 vols. (Cairo: Maktabat al-Khānjī, 1931), 14: 75.

27. Muntajab al-Dīn ʿAlī b. ʿUbayd Allāh b. Bābawayh al-Rāzī, *Fihrist asmāʾ ʿulamāʾ al-shīʿah wa-muṣannifīhim (Fihrist Muntajab al-Dīn),* ed. ʿAbd al-ʿAzīz al-Ṭabāṭabāʾī (Beirut: Dār al-aḍwāʾ, 1986), 41, 116.

28. The name M-L-Y or M-L-A is uncommon, and it is difficult to determine its correct voweling. Other possibilities include Malī, Mallī or Mullā.

29. The most complete and accessible biography of al-Baʿlabakkī is found in the recent work of Jaʿfar al-Muhājir, *Sittat fuqahāʾ abṭāl* (Beirut: al-majlis al-islāmī al-shīʿī al-aʿlā, 1994), 46–78. The main sources for his biography include al-Subkī, *Ṭabaqat al-shāfiʿīyah,* 8: 31–32; ʿImād al-Dīn Ismāʿīl b. ʿUmar Ibn Kathīr, *Ṭabaqāt al-fuqahāʾ al-shāfiʿīyīn,* 3 vols., ed. Aḥmad ʿUmar Hāshim and Muḥammad Zaynhum Muḥammad Gharb (Cairo: Maktabat al-thaqāfah al-dīnīyah, 1993), 2: 941; Jalāl al-Dīn ʿAbd al-Raḥmān al-Isnawī, *Ṭabaqāt al-shāfiʿīyah,* 2 vols., ed. Kamāl Yūsuf al-Ḥūt (Beirut: Dār al-kutub al-ʿilmīyah, 1987), 2: 256–57; ʿAbd al-Ḥayy Ibn al-ʿImād al-Ḥanbalī, *Shadharāt al-dhahab fī tārīkh man dhahab,* 8 vols. (Cairo: Maktabat al-Qudsī, 1932–33), 5: 444–45.

served as a *muftī*. Al-Isnawī adds that he was accused of Shiite heresy (*rafḍ*) and that his native region of Ba'labakk was populated by Shiites. It is fairly clear that al-Ba'labakkī was Shiite by background. In his early years in Ba'labakk, he studied with the Shiite jurist 'Izz al-Dīn b. Ma'qil al-Muhallabī al-Ḥimṣī (d. 644/1246). The historian al-Yūnīnī (d. 726/1325), also a native of Ba'labakk, records that al-Ba'labakkī acted as a legal authority for both local Shāfi'īs and local Shiites.[30]

During his years in Damascus, al-Ba'labakkī studied hadith with a number of teachers, grammar with the famous grammarian Ibn al-Ḥājib (d. 646/1249), and law with the famous Shāfi'ī jurist 'Izz al-Dīn 'Abd al-'Azīz b. 'Abd al-Salām (d. 660/1262). This time period must have been before 639/1241 when Ibn al-Ḥājib and Ibn 'Abd al-Salām were expelled from Damascus and left for Egypt after their protest against the Ayyubid ruler al-Ṣāliḥ Ismā'īl (637–43/1239–45). Al-Ba'labakkī taught hadith in Damascus and Aleppo. Subsequently, he settled in Baghdad, where he held a post as repetitor (*mu'īd*) at the Niẓāmīyah *madrasah*.

When the Mongols invaded Syria in 658/1256, al-Ba'labakkī, back in his native region, led popular resistance to the occupation. Following the Mongol withdrawal in 1260, he traveled to Egypt. The fact that al-Ba'labakkī chose to spend time in Upper Egypt corroborates his Shiite identity, for during this period there remained substantial Shiite communities in Upper Egypt, in Isnā and other nearby towns.[31] He settled in Aswan, also an important Shiite center during this period, and taught law at the Bābāsīyah *madrasah* there. He eventually returned to his native region, and died in the village of Bakh'ūn in Jibāl Ẓinnīyin (modern al-Ḍinnīyah) in Jumādā I 699/February 1300.

Sulaymān b. 'Abd al-Qawī al-Ṭūfī (d. 716/1316)

Sulaymān b. 'Abd al-Qawī al-Ṭūfī[32] is something of an exception in the Shiite tradition of legal study in Sunni environments in that he was involved with the Ḥanbalī *madhhab* rather than the Shāfi'ī. He was born in the 670s/1270s

30. al-Muhājir, *Sittat fuqahā' abṭāl,* 50–54.

31. al-Isnawī, *Ṭabaqāt al-shāfi'īyah,* 2: 331–32.

32. The most detailed account of al-Ṭūfī's life and career is that of Ibn Rajab 'Abd al-Raḥmān b. Aḥmad al-Baghdādi, *Kitāb al-dhayl 'alā ṭabaqāt al-ḥanābilah,* 2 vols., ed. Muḥammad Ḥāmid al-Fiqī (Cairo: Maṭba'at al-sunnah al-muḥammadīyah, 1953), 2: 366–70. He cites the unpublished work of Ibn Maktūm (Tāj al-Dīn Aḥmad b. 'Aqil, d. 749/1348), *al-Jam' al-mutanāh fī akhbār al-lughawīyīn wa'l-nuḥāh.* See Brockelmann, *GAL,* 2: 110, supp. 2: 137. Other accounts, largely derivative, include Ibn Ḥajar al-'Asqalānī, *al-Durar al-kāminah fī a'yān al-mi'ah al-thāminah,* 4 vols. (Haydarābād: Maṭba'at majlis al-ma'ārif al-'uthmānīyah, 1930), 2: 154–57; Jalāl al-Dīn al-Suyūṭī, *Bughyat al-wu'āt fī ṭabaqāt al-lughawīyīn wa'l-nuḥāt* (Cairo: Maṭba'at al-sa'ādah, 1908), 262; Ibn al-'Imād al-Ḥanbalī, *Shadharāt al-dhahab,* 6: 39–40; Brockelmann, *GAL,* 2: 108–9, supp. 2: 133–34. See also Sulaymān b. 'Abd al-Qawī al-Ṭūfī, *'Alam al-jadhal fī 'ilm al-jadal,* ed. Wolfhart Heinrichs (Wiesbaden: Franz Steiner, 1987); Muṣṭafā Zayd, *al-Maṣlaḥah fī al-tashrī' al-islāmī wa-Najm al-Dīn al-Ṭūfī* (Cairo: Dār al-fikr al-'arabī, 1964).

in the village of Ṭūf (or Ṭūfā) near the town of Ṣarṣar, not far from Baghdad. He first studied in his native town and memorized the *Mukhtaṣar* of ʿUmar b. al-Ḥusayn al-Khiraqī (d. 334/945), the standard epitome of Ḥanbalī law. In 691/1291–92 he entered Baghdad and passed an oral exam on the work with Taqī al-Dīn ʿAbd Allāh b. Muḥammad al-Zarīrātī (d. 729/1329), then the leading Ḥanbalī jurist in Baghdad and professor of Ḥanbalī law at the Mustanṣirīyah *madrasah*.[33] He studied in Baghdad for a number of years, then traveled to Damascus in 704/1304–5. He apparently did not enjoy his stay in Damascus, for he wrote several poems complaining about the miserable conditions he experienced there and expressing his antipathy for the city's inhabitants. In 705/1305–6, he traveled to Cairo, where he studied under the chief Ḥanbalī judge, Saʿd al-Dīn Masʿūd b. Aḥmad al-Ḥārithī (d. 711/1312), also a native Iraqi. Having succeeded in winning al-Ḥārithī's favor, he obtained an appointment as repetitor (*muʿīd*) of Ḥanbalī law as al-Ḥārithī's deputy at the Manṣūrīyah and Nāṣirīyah *madrasahs* in Cairo. At some point after his appointment and before 14 Dhū al-Ḥijjah 711/22 April 1312, when al-Ḥārithī died, al-Ṭūfī was accused and convicted of Shiite heresy (*rafḍ*). He immediately lost his positions. Upon conviction, he was beaten, publicly humiliated, then imprisoned for a time. Afterwards, he was exiled to Syria. He apparently was loathe to go to Damascus after having lampooned the Syrians in his poetry, so he traveled as far as Damietta, then turned back and headed for Upper Egypt. He settled in Qūṣ for a number of years, then made the pilgrimage to Mecca in 714/1315. After staying in the Ḥijāz throughout the next year, he set out for Syria in 716/1316, but died on the way in al-Khalīl (Hebron) in Rajab/September–October of that year.

The accusations of Shiism were not unwarranted. The evidence used to convict al-Ṭūfī of Shiite heresy in Cairo was poems in his hand, obtained by an informer, which contained blasphemies against Abū Bakr, ʿĀʾishah, and other Companions. Al-Ṭūfī also wrote an anti-Sunni polemical work entitled *al-ʿAdhāb al-wāṣib ʿalā arwāḥ al-nawāṣib* ("Perpetual Torment for the Souls of the Sunni Heretics")[34] and, according to Ibn Rajab, Shiite tendencies are evident in many of his other works. His commentary on al-Nawawī's *Arbaʿūn ḥadīth* contains a passage which suggests that the conflicts over variant hadith traditions arose in Islam because ʿUmar b. al-Khaṭṭāb prevented the Companions from recording hadith in written form, despite the fact that the Prophet had encouraged them do so. Ibn Rajab sees this as a terrible blasphemy and a sly attempt on al-Ṭūfī's part to promulgate heretical Shiite opinions without explicitly ac-

33. On al-Zarīrātī, see Ibn Rajab, Kitāb al-dhayl, 2: 410–13.

34. The phrase *al-ʿadhāb al-wāṣib*, "Perpetual Torment," is an allusion to Qurʾān 37:9. The word *nāṣibī* is used by Shiites as a derogatory term for Sunnis, referring to the unjust appointment of Abū Bakr as caliph instead of ʿAlī. Shiites take the term to mean enemies or detesters of *ahl al-bayt*, the descendants of the Prophet. It is the counterpart of the common medieval Sunni term, *rāfiḍī*, for Shiites.

knowledging his Shiism. That al-Ṭūfī took refuge in Upper Egypt, which harbored a significant Shiite minority at the time, also suggests his Shiite allegiances. In addition, when al-Ṭūfī stayed in the Ḥijāz in 715/1315–16, he associated with Shiites in Medina, including the Damascene al-Sakākīnī (d. 721/1321), described as *Shaykh al-rāfiḍah* ("the chief scholar of the Shiites").[35]

al-ʿAllāmah al-Ḥillī (648–726/1250–1325)

Ḥasan b. Yūsuf Ibn al-Muṭahhar al-Ḥillī,[36] known in Shiite scholarly tradition as al-ʿAllāmah ("the Consummate Scholar"), lived in Iraq and Iran during the period of the Ilkhanid dynasty (654–754/1256–1353) and produced a number of the most influential works in the Twelver Shiite legal tradition. He was born on 27 or 29 Ramaḍān 648/23 or 25 December 1250, and was the nephew of the renowned jurist Najm al-Dīn Jaʿfar al-Ḥillī, known as al-Muḥaqqiq ("the Precise Scholar," d. 676/1276). Though his early studies were completed in al-Ḥillah under Shiite teachers, including his father, his uncle al-Muḥaqqiq, Jamāl al-Dīn Ibn Ṭāwūs (d. 673/1274), and others, and though he became a renowned authority on Shiite law in his later years, he had extensive training in Shāfiʿī law as a young man, mostly in Baghdad.

On 15 Shaʿbān 723/19 August 1323, a few years before his death, al-ʿAllāmah wrote a very long *ijāzah* for members of the Shiite Banū Zuhrah family from Aleppo who had come to Iraq, and this document contains valuable information on al-Ḥillī's studies with Sunni scholars.[37] Though it is likely that al-Ḥillī performed the pilgrimage during his lifetime, there is no documentation of his traveling to Damascus or Cairo, and it appears that his movements and studies were limited to Iraq and Iran. He mentions six Sunni teachers, one with whom he studied in Kūfah, one with whom he studied in Azerbaijan, and four others with whom he probably studied in Baghdad. His statements imply that he studied for a considerable period of time in Baghdad itself.

While still a youth, al-Ḥillī probably attended the scientific academy at Marāghah attached to the observatory founded by Hulagu (654–63/1256–65)

35. See Ibn Ḥajar al-ʿAsqalānī, *al-Durar al-kāminah*, 3: 410–11.

36. The best single account of al-Ḥillī's life and career is Sabine Schmidtke, *The Theology of al-ʿAllāma al-Ḥillī* (d. 726/1325) (Berlin: Klaus Schwarz Verlag, 1991). For a general biography of al-Ḥillī, see Ibn al-Muṭahhar al-Ḥillī, *Rijāl al-ʿAllāmah al-Ḥillī*, 45–49; Ibn Ḥajar al-ʿAsqalānī, *al-Durar al-kāminah*, 2: 71; al-Ḥurr al-ʿĀmilī, *Amal al-āmil*, 2: 81–85; al-Iṣfahānī, *Riyāḍ al-ʿulamāʾ*, 1: 358–90; al-Baḥranī, *Luʾluʾat al-Baḥrayn*, 210–27; al-Khwānsārī, *Rawḍāt al-jannāt*, 2: 264–80; al-Amīn, *Aʿyān al-shīʿah*, 5: 396–407; Brockelmann, *GAL*, 2: 164, supp. 2: 206–9; S. H. M. Jafri, "al-Ḥillī," *EI*²; Michel M. Mazzauoi, *The Origins of the Ṣafawids* (Weisbaden: Franz Steiner, 1972), 27–34.

37. Muḥammad Bāqir Majlisī, *Biḥār al-anwār*, 110 vols. (Tehran: al-Maktabah al-islāmīyah, 1956–72), 107: 60–137.

in 657/1258–59. There he studied logic, theology, and astronomy with Naṣīr al-Dīn al-Ṭūsī (d. 672/1274), the founder and head of the academy.[38] There is some question about Naṣīr al-Dīn's religious affiliation, but it appears that he was a Twelver Shiite who had adopted Ismāʿīlism under the patronage of the new line of Nizārī imams at Alamut. Al-Ḥillī wrote commentaries on several of Naṣīr al-Dīn's works, including *al-Jawhar al-naḍīd fī sharḥ kitāb al-tajrīd*, a commentary on al-Ṭūsī's *Tajrīd* on logic, and *Kashf al-murād fī sharḥ tajrīd al-iʿtiqād*, a commentary on al-Ṭūsī's *Tajrīd al-iʿtiqād* on theology.

Also at Marāghah, al-Ḥillī studied with the Shāfiʿī scholar Najm al-Dīn ʿAlī b. ʿUmar al-Kātibī al-Qazwīnī, known as Dabīrān.[39] Al-Kātibī was one of the four top scholars whom Naṣīr al-Dīn al-Ṭūsī had requested Hulagu to invite to Marāghah when the observatory was founded. He was an expert in logic and philosophy. His most famous work, a treatise on logic entitled *al-Risālah al-shamsīyah fī al-qawāʿid al-manṭiqīyah,* is still used in the traditional Shiite legal curriculum. Of this scholar al-Ḥillī writes,

> He was one of the learned men of the age, and the most accomplished in logic. He had written many works. I read all of *Sharḥ al-Kashf* with him except for a short section. He had a pleasant disposition and excelled in disputation. He was one of the most learned Shāfiʿī scholars and an expert in philosophy (*ḥikmah*).[40]

Al-Kātibī left Marāghah and returned to his native town of Juwayn just a few years before he died in 675/1276–77. Al-Ḥillī wrote a commentary on *al-Risālah al-shamsīyah* entitled *al-Qawāʿid al-jalīyah fī sharḥ al-risālah al-shamsīyah,* which he completed in Rabīʿ II 679/July-August 1280.[41] Al-Ḥillī must have been quite young when he studied at Marāghah. Given that Naṣīr al-Dīn al-Ṭūsī died in 672/1274, al-Ḥillī must have come to Marāghah to study when he was under twenty-four years of age.

Al-Ḥillī's studies at Marāghah were mostly philosophical and scientific; it was primarily in Baghdad that he worked with Sunni teachers in the Islamic religious fields. Ibn Kathīr mentions al-Ḥillī's studies in Baghdad prominently.[42] Al-Ḥillī studied with one Sunni teacher, Taqī al-Dīn ʿAbd Allāh b. Jaʿfar b. ʿAlī b. al-Ṣabbāgh al-Kūfī, in Kūfah, but his contact with this scholar seems to have been less important than his studies in Baghdad. Of him, al-Ḥillī writes, "This

38. Ibid., 62.

39. Brockelmann, *GAL*, 1. 466, supp. 1: 845; M. Mohaghegh, "al-Kātibī," *EI*², 4:762.

40. Majlisī, *Biḥār al-anwār*, 107: 66.

41. Schmidtke, *Theology*, 61.

42. The text reads: *kāna ʾshtighāluhū bi-baghdāda wa-ghayrihā min al-bilād* (ʿImād al-Dīn Ismāʿīl b. ʿUmar Ibn Kathīr, *al-Bidāyah wa'l-nihāyah fī al-tārīkh*, 14 vols. [Cairo: Maṭbaʿat al-saʿādah, 1939], 14: 125).

master was an upright man, a Ḥanafī jurist in al-Kūfah."[43] Al-Ḥillī transmits *al-Kashshāf*, the famous *tafsīr* of al-Zamakhsharī (d. 538/1134), through him.[44]

Al-Ḥillī's teachers in Baghdad included Jamāl al-Dīn Ḥusayn b. Ayāz al-Baghdādī al-Naḥwī, the lecturer on grammar (*shaykh al-naḥw*) at the Mustanṣirīyah *madrasah*. Al-Ḥillī records, "This Master was the most learned of his age in syntax and morphology, and has good works on *adab*." Al-Ḥillī transmits the *Mukhtaṣar* of Ibn al-Ḥājib, the well-known Sunni *uṣūl al-fiqh* text, from him.[45] Ibn Ayāz died in Baghdad in 681/1282–83.[46]

Al-Ḥillī's most important teacher of Sunni law was the Shāfiʿī jurist Shams al-Dīn Muḥammad b. Muḥammad b. Aḥmad al-Kīshī. Concerning this scholar, he writes:

> This Master was one of the most learned scholars of the Shāfiʿīs, and was one of the fairest jurists in debate. I used to study under him and occasionally raise objections to him. He would reflect, then answer sometimes, and other times say, 'So that I might contemplate this matter, ask me this question again later.' I would ask him again one, two, or three days later, and sometimes he would answer and sometimes he would admit, 'I am unable to answer this question.'[47]

Al-Kīshī was born in 615/1218–19 in Kīsh, an island off the coast of Fars in the Persian Gulf.[48] He came to Baghdad in 665/1266–67 and was appointed professor of Shāfiʿī law at the Niẓāmīyah *madrasah* in that year. After teaching there for a number of years, he left to seek the patronage of the vizier Bahā' al-Dīn Muḥammad b. Shams al-Dīn al-Juwaynī in Isfahan.[49] He seems to have spent his remaining years in Iran, and died in Shiraz in 695/1295–96.[50] Al-Kīshī must have left Baghdad to go to Isfahan before 678/1279–80, the year Bahā' al-Dīn al-Juwaynī died. He probably left in 672/1273–74, since Naṣīr al-Dīn al-Fārūthī was appointed professor at the Niẓāmīyah that year.[51] In all likelihood al-Ḥillī studied under al-Kīshī at the Niẓāmīyah *madrasah*. Given that the Niẓāmīyah was a Shāfiʿī institution, al-Ḥillī presumably claimed adherence to the Shāfiʿī *madhhab* at this point in his career.

43. Majlisī, *Biḥār al-anwār*, 107: 67. This scholar is not Ṣāliḥ b. ʿAbd Allāh al-Asadī, born in 639/1241, as Schmidtke states, but rather Ṣāliḥ's father (*Theology*, 22 n. 94).

44. Majlisī, *Biḥār al-anwār*, 107: 103.

45. Ibid., 65, 104.

46. ʿAbd al-Razzāq Ibn al-Fuwaṭī, *al-Ḥawādith al-jāmiʿah wa'l-tajārib al-nāfiʿah fī al-miʾah al-sābiʿah* (Baghdad: Maṭbaʿat al-Furāt, 1932), 426; Brockelmann, *GAL*, 1: 303, supp. 1: 531.

47. Majlisī, *Biḥār al-anwār*, 107: 66.

48. al-Ḥamawī, *Muʿjam al-buldān*, 4: 497.

49. Ibn al-Fuwaṭī, *al-Ḥawādith*, 358.

50. Ṣalāḥ al-Dīn Khalīl b. Aybak al-Ṣafadī, *al-Wāfī bi'l-wafayāt*, 17 vols. (Istanbul: Maṭbaʿat al-dawlah, 1931), 2: 141.

51. Ibn al-Fuwaṭī, *al-Ḥawādith*, 376, 410.

Al-Ḥillī studied dialectic with the Ḥanafī jurist Burhān al-Dīn Muḥammad b. Muḥammad al-Nasafī. He relates:

> This Master was extremely accomplished and an ascetic. He wrote on dialectic and developed discussions of difficult new questions. I studied some of his works on disputation. He has many works.[52]

Al-Nasafī was born ca. 600/1203–4, and came to Baghdad in order to perform the pilgrimage in 675/1276–77. He probably taught at the Mustanṣirīyah from then until his death in 687/1288.[53]

Al-Ḥillī studied with another Shāfiʿī teacher, ʿIzz al-Dīn Abū ʾl-ʿAbbās b. Ibrāhīm b. ʿUmar al-Fārūthī al-Wāsiṭī, probably at a later date.[54] Al-Wāsiṭī was born in Dhū al-Qaʿdah 614/February 1218 in Wāsiṭ. He spent most of his life in Damascus, and became the leading *khaṭīb* of the city for about a year in 691/1291–92. In 692/1293, he left to make the pilgrimage with the Iraqi pilgrimage caravan. It is possible that he stayed in Baghdad and came into contact with al-Ḥillī at this time. He died in Wāsiṭ two years later, in 694/1294–95. Al-Ḥillī probably studied with him during this two-year period; there is no indication that al-Ḥillī ever traveled to Syria.[55] Al-Fārūthī's brother, Naṣīr al-Dīn ʿAbd Allāh b. ʿUmar, had been appointed professor of Shāfiʿī law at the Mustanṣirīyah in 682/1283–84.[56]

From the information al-Ḥillī provides, it is clear that he studied law and other related fields in Baghdad during his earlier years. He must have been in Baghdad before 672/1273–74, the year al-Kīshī left for Isfahan, and he must have stayed there until at least 675/1276–77, the year al-Nasafī arrived in Baghdad. Given that al-Kīshī was the professor of law at al-Niẓāmīyah, officially a Shāfiʿī institution, it seems clear that al-Ḥillī studied Shāfiʿī law in particular. Though the sources do not provide explicit evidence, it is likely that al-Ḥillī studied in the Niẓāmīyah and the Mustanṣirīyah *madrasahs*, both officially Sunni institutions. He probably claimed adherence to the Shāfiʿī *madhhab* in order to do so.

In his later years, however, al-Ḥillī's Shiism could have been no secret. He came to be recognized as the leading jurist of the Twelver Shiites, and he seems

52. Majlisī, *Biḥār al-anwār,* 107: 66–67.

53. See Schmidtke, *Theology,* 20–21; Brockelmann, *GAL,* 1: 615; supp. 1: 849; al-Ṣafadī, *al-Wāfī,* 1: 282–83.

54. al-Majlisī, *Biḥār al-anwar,* 107:67; Schmidtke, *Theology,* 21. This scholar may have been confused with Naṣīr al-Dīn b. ʿUmar, who became professor of law at the Niẓāmīyah in 672 A.H. (Ibn al-Fuwaṭī, *al-Ḥawādith,* 376).

55. Muḥammad b. Muḥammad al-Jazarī, *Ghāyat al-nihāyah fī ṭabaqāt al-qurrā',* 3 vols., ed. G. Bergstrasser (Cairo: Maṭbaʿat al-saʿādah, 1933), 1: 34–35; Ibn al-ʿImād al-Ḥanbalī, *Shadharāt al-dhahab,* 5: 425.

56. Ibn al-Fuwaṭī, *al-Ḥawādith,* 429.

to have participated in legal debates in Baghdad quite freely. Ibn Rajab relates that al-Ḥillī held discussions with Taqī al-Dīn ʿAbd Allāh b. Muḥammad al-Zarīrātī (d. 729/1329), the leading Ḥanbalī jurist and the professor of Ḥanbalī law at the Mustanṣirīyah. He states that al-Zarīrātī

> was recognized as the top scholar in Baghdad by both friend and foe. Jurists from all sects would meet with him and learn from him concerning their own legal traditions. They would treat him with great respect and consult his opinions and citations of their own legal traditions. He would get them to rescind legal opinions they had issued; they would concede to him, adopt his opinion, and admit to him the benefit to their schools of what he had imparted to them. Even Ibn al-Muṭahhar, the leading Shiite scholar (*shaykh al-shīʿah*) did so. Master Taqī al-Dīn used to point out to him mistakes he had made in citing earlier Shiite legal sources (*naqluh li-madhhab al-shīʿah*), and [Ibn al-Muṭahhar] would concede to him.[57]

Al-Ḥillī also engaged in scholarly exchanges with other Shāfiʿī scholars. An exchange of letters between al-Qāḍī al-Bayḍāwī (d. 685/1286) and al-Ḥillī is recorded in the sources.[58] While serving as *qāḍī* in Shiraz, al-Bayḍāwī wrote to al-Ḥillī objecting to his legal reasoning on a point included in the section on ritual purity in his work *Qawāʿid al-aḥkām.* Specifically, he objected to al-Ḥillī's use of *istiṣḥāb,* "presumed continuity of *status quo ante,*" in arguing a particular point of law. Al-Ḥillī wrote a reply justifying his legal reasoning and explaining that the argument was not based on *istiṣḥāb.* Both letters include flattering formulas of praise for their recipients.

Later in his career, al-Ḥillī had contact with Sunni scholars at the court of the Ilkhanid ruler Muḥammad Khudābandah Uljaytū, who reigned from 703/1304 until 716/1316. Uljaytū converted to Shiism in Shaʿbān 709/January–February 1310. He issued coins bearing the names of the twelve imams and the inscription "ʿAlī is the ward of God" (ʿAlī walī Allāh) and suppressed the mention of the first three Sunni caliphs in the Friday sermon.[59] The Shiite claim that al-Ḥillī played a crucial role in Uljaytū's conversion is not confirmed by contemporary chronicles. Nevertheless, it is clear that al-Ḥillī was held in particular esteem at the Ilkhanid court during this period and had close contact with Uljaytū himself. Between 709/1309 and 716/1316, he spent most of his time with the court, together with his son Muḥammad (682–771/1283–1369). In Rajab 709/December 1309, he accompanied Uljaytū on a visit to the tomb

57. Ibn Rajab, *Kitāb al-dhayl,* 2: 411.

58. al-Iṣfahānī, *Riyāḍ al-ʿulamāʾ,* 1: 382–83, citing the work *Lisān al-khawāṣṣ* by Āghā Raḍī al-Dīn Muḥammad b. al-Ḥasan al-Qazwīnī (d. 1096/1684–85).

59. Jafri, "al-Ḥillī," *EI*².

of Salmān al-Fārisī at al-Madā'in.[60] An ijāzah al-Ḥillī issued to Tāj al-Dīn Maḥmūd b. Zayn al-Dīn Muḥammad b. al-Qāḍī Sadīd al-Dīn 'Abd al-Wāḥid al-Rāzī places him in Sulṭānīyah, Uljaytū's planned capital in northwestern Iran, at the end of Rabī' II 709/October 1309.[61] He engaged in a debate at court on 25 Dhū al-Qa'dah 710/14 April 1311. In 712/1312, the vizier Rashīd al-Dīn awarded al-Ḥillī a riding horse with saddle, a shoulder belt, and two thousand dinars. He issued another ijāzah to Quṭb al-Dīn al-Rāzī (d. 766/1365) in Varāmīn, north of Rayy, in 713/1313.[62] Al-Ḥillī was made a professor in the madrasah sayyārah, a type of mobile college created by Rashīd al-Dīn that traveled with Uljaytū's retinue. He dedicated four of his works—Istiqṣā' al-baḥth wa'l-naẓar fī al-qaḍā' wa'l-qadar, Kashf al-ḥaqq wa-nahj al-ṣidq, Kashf al-yaqīn fī faḍā'il Amīr al-mu'minīn, and Minhāj al-karāmah fī ma'rifat al-imāmah to Uljaytū, and one—al-Risālah al-sa'dīyah—to the minister Sa'd al-Dīn, who was executed on 10 Shawwāl 711/19 February 1312.[63] In debates at court and in the mobile madrasah, al-Ḥillī seems to have engaged freely in exchanges with Sunni scholars, not only because of Uljaytū's patronage and conversion to Shiism but also because of the Mongols' high level of tolerance for open religious differences in comparison with that of the Seljuks, Mamluks, or subsequent Sunni regimes.

Quṭb al-Dīn Muḥammad b. Maḥmūd al-Rāzī (d. 766/1365)

Quṭb al-Dīn al-Rāzī[64] was a native of Rayy and the author of several important works on logic and dogma, including an excellent commentary, which became a popular textbook, on al-Kātibī's compendium of logic, *al-Risālah al-shamsīyah.* The town of Rayy was divided between Sunnis and Shiites, yet al-Rāzī was generally known as a Shāfi'ī Sunni scholar and al-Subkī includes him in his biographical dictionary of the Shāfi'īs, *Ṭabaqāt al-shāfi'īyah al-kubrā.*[65] An *ijāzah* preserved in al-Majlisī's *Biḥār al-anwār* shows that al-Rāzī studied with al-'Allāmah al-Ḥillī in Varāmīn, north of Rayy, in 713/1313 and read *Qawā'id al-aḥkām,* one of al-'Allāmah's works on Shiite law.[66] This probably

60. Schmidtke, *Theology,* 27; G. Levi della Vida, "Salmān al-Fārisī," *EI*[1], 7: 426–28; al-Amīn, *A'yān al-shī'ah,* 7: 279.

61. Majlisī, *Biḥār al-anwār,* 107: 142.

62. Ibid., 138–40.

63. For a description of al-Ḥillī's connection with the Ilkhanids, see Mazzaoui, *Origins of the Ṣafawids,* 27–34; Schmidtke, *Theology,* 24–32.

64. For a general biography, see Brockelmann, *GAL,* 1: 290, 454, 466–67, 2: 209; supp. 2: 293; al-Amīn, *A'yān al-shī'ah,* 9: 413; al-Baḥrānī, *Lu'lu'at al-Baḥrayn,* 194–99; al-Ḥurr al-'Āmilī, *Amal al-āmil,* 2: 300–301; al-Iṣfahānī, *Riyāḍ al-'ulamā',* 5: 168–72; al-Subkī, *Ṭabaqāt al-shāfi'īyah al-kubrā,* 9: 274–75; al-Khwānsārī, *Rawḍāt al-jannāt,* 6: 37–47.

65. al-Subkī, *Ṭabaqāt al-shāfi'īyah al-kubrā,* 9: 274–75.

66. Majlisī, *Biḥār al-anwār,* 107: 138–40.

took place when al-Ḥillī was teaching with the *madrasah sayyārah* that traveled with Uljaytū's retinue. After al-Rāzī moved to Damascus in 763/1362, the famous Shiite jurist Muḥammad b. Makkī al-Jizzīnī (al-Shahīd al-Awwal) was able to obtain an *ijāzah* from him at the end of Sha'bān 766/May 1365. Al-Shahīd al-Awwal records that he found that al-Rāzī was indeed a Shiite when he met him in Damascus. He states, "He was an Imami beyond any doubt. He stated so explicitly and I heard him say this."[67] Al-Rāzī died on 12 or 16 Dhū al-Qa'dah 766/1 or 5 August 1365.[68] Yūsuf al-Baḥrānī reports that a Damascene Shiite scholar later edited Quṭb al-Dīn al-Rāzī's marginal notes on al-Ḥillī's legal work *Qawā'id al-āhkām* and that the resulting work became known as *al-Ḥawāshī al-quṭbīyah.*[69]

al-Shahīd al-Awwal (d. 786/1384)

Shams al-Dīn Muḥammad Abū 'Abd Allāh b. Makkī al-Jizzīnī al-'Āmilī[70] is known as al-Shahīd al-Awwal (the "First Martyr") in Shiite tradition because he was executed as a heretic in Damascus. He was born in Jizzīn in what is now southern Lebanon in 734/1333–34, grew up there, and studied with his father. He went to Iraq at a young age, primarily to study with Shiite teachers in al-Ḥillah. *Ijāzahs* mentioned in al-Shahīd al-Awwal's *Arba'ūn ḥadīth,* completed on 18 Dhū 'l-Ḥijjah 782/15 March 1381,[71] show that he studied in Iraq between 751/1350, when he was only seventeen years old, and 756/1355.[72] He studied un-

67. Ibid., 141.

68. Ibid., 140–41; Brockelmann, *GAL,* supp. 2: 293; al-Subkī, *Ṭabaqāt al-shāfi'īyah al-kubrā,* 9: 275.

69. al-Baḥrānī, *Lu'lu'at al-Baḥrayn,* 199.

70. For a general biography, see Muḥammad Riḍā Shams al-Dīn, *Ḥayāt al-imām al-Shahīd al-Awwal* (Najaf: Maṭba'at al-gharī al-ḥadīthah, 1957); al-Amīn, *A'yān al-shī'ah,* 10: 59–64; al-Ḥurr al-'Āmilī, *Amal al-āmil,* 1: 181–83; al-Baḥrānī, *Lu'lu'at al-Baḥrayn,* 143–48; al-Iṣfahānī, *Riyāḍ al-'ulamā',* 5: 185–91; al-Khwānsārī, *Rawḍāt al-jannāt,* 7: 5–21.

71. Muḥammad b. Makkī al-Jizzīnī, *Arba'ūn ḥadīth* (Tehran, 1900–1901), 213.

72. He received an *ijāzah* from the son of al-'Allāmah al-Ḥillī Abū Ṭālib Muḥammad, known as Fakhr al-Muḥaqqiqīn, in his house in Ḥillah on 20 Sha'bān 751/23 October 1350 (ibid., 184). He received an *ijāzah* from al-Murtaḍā 'Amīd al-Dīn 'Abd al-Muṭṭalib b. Muḥammad b. 'Alī al-A'rajī al-Ḥusaynī, the well-known author of *al-Sharḥ al-'Amīdī,* in Karbalā' on 19 Ramaḍān 751/20 November 1350 (183, 207). He received an *ijāzah* in Ḥillah from Abū Muḥammad al-Ḥasan b. Aḥmad b. Najīb al-Dīn Muḥammad Ibn Namā al-Ḥillī in Rabī' II 752/June 1351 (185). He received an *ijāzah* from Tāj al-Dīn Abū Ja'far Muḥammad b. al-Qāsim b. al-Ḥusayn b. Mu'ayyah al-Dībājī in Ḥillah on 15 Shawwāl 753/24 December 1352 (186–87). He received an *ijāzah* from Zayn al-Dīn Abū al-Ḥasan 'Alī b. Aḥmad b. Ṭirād al-Maṭārābādī in Ḥillah on 6 Rabī' II 754/11 May 1353 (186, 205). He received another *ijāzah* from Ibn Mu'ayyah al-Dībājī in Ḥillah on 16 Sha'bān 754/16 September 1353 (190). He received another *ijāzah,* part of which is preserved in Majlisī's *Biḥār al-anwār* (107: 182) from Ibn Mu'ayyah on Saturday, 11 Shawwāl 754/9 November 1353. He received two other *ijāzahs* from Fakhr al-Dīn Muḥammad the son of al-'Allāmah at his house in Ḥillah, one on Friday, 3 Jumādā I 756/16 May 1355, and one on 6 Shawwāl 756/14 October 1355 (al-Jizzīnī, *Arba'ūn ḥadīth,* 194, 208). He received another *ijāzah,* preserved in Majlisī's *Biḥār al-anwār* (107: 177–78), from the same professor in his house in Ḥillah on this last date.

der al-'Allāmah's son Muḥammad, known as Fakhr al-Muḥaqqiqīn, "Pride of the Precise Scholars" (d. 771/1369), as well as with a number of al-'Allāmah's former students. Fakhr al-Muḥaqqiqīn taught at his home, in the *majlis* where al-'Allāmah himself used to teach.[73]

In several *ijāzahs*, al-Shahīd al-Awwal reports that he studied with a large number of Sunni scholars. On 13 Ramaḍān 784/20 September 1382 in Damascus, he issued a long *ijāzah* to Zayn al-Dīn 'Alī b. al-Ḥasan, known as Ibn al-Khāzin since his father was the keeper of the shrine of Imam Ḥusayn at Karbalā'. In this *ijāzah* he records that he studied with about forty Sunni teachers from Mecca, Medina, Baghdad, Cairo, Damascus, Jerusalem, and Hebron. It is not clear why, in the long *ijāzah* which he issued to Muḥammad b. Tāj al-Dīn 'Abd 'Alī, known as Ibn Najdah, on 10 Ramaḍān 770/18 April 1369, he states only that he studied with many scholars in Damascus, Iraq, and the Ḥijāz.[74]

Al-Shahīd al-Awwal made the pilgrimage of 754/1353–54, presumably with the Baghdad pilgrimage caravan.[75] He took the opportunity to benefit from the presence of important Sunni teachers. In Medina on 22 Dhū al-Ḥijjah 754/18 January 1354 he received an *ijāzah* from 'Izz al-Dīn 'Abd al-'Azīz b. Muḥammad b. Ibrāhīm Ibn Jamā'ah al-Kinānī al-Shāfi'ī (d. 767/1366), the chief judge (*qāḍī al-quḍat*) of the Shāfi'is in Egypt.[76] Elsewhere he reports that he relates al-Zamakhsharī's *tafsīr, al-Kashshāf,* from this same judge; this work may also have been included in the *ijāzah* he received on the pilgrimage in 754/1354. Also in Medina in Dhū al-Hijjah 754/January 1354, he received an *ijāzah* from 'Afīf al-Dīn 'Abd Allāh b. Muḥammad al-Khazrajī al-Madanī al-Maṭarī, another Egyptian scholar. He received an *ijāzah* for *Ṣaḥīḥ al-Bukhārī* from a third Egyptian scholar, Sirāj al-Dīn al-Damanhūrī, in Mecca at the Ka'bah itself, but does not mention the date.[77]

On the return trip, al-Shahīd al-Awwal probably passed through Palestine and Syria before returning to Iraq. Documents do not place him back in Ḥillah until 3 Jumādā I 756/16 May 1355.[78] In the *ijāzah* to Ibn Najdah, al-Shahīd

73. al-Jizzīnī, *Arba'ūn ḥadīth,* 184, 194, 208; Majlisī, *Biḥār al-anwār,* 107: 177–78.

74. Majlisī, *Biḥār al-anwār,* 107: 186–201.

75. The *ijāzahs* mentioned above from Ibn Mu'ayyah al-Dībājī place al-Shahīd al-Awwal in Ḥillah on 16 Sha'bān 754/16 September 1353 (al-Jizzīnī, *Arba'ūn ḥadīth,* 190) and also, probably in Ḥillah, though the place is not mentioned, on Saturday, 11 Shawwāl 754/9 November 1353 (Majlisī, *Biḥār al-anwār,* 107: 182). Al-Shahīd al-Awwal would not have had time to return to Damascus to join the pilgrimage caravan there.

76. Majlisī, *Biḥār al-anwār,* 109: 70. 'Izz al-Dīn 'Abd al-'Azīz Ibn Jamā'ah held the post of chief Shāfi'ī judge in Cairo for twenty-five years—with one interruption—beginning in 738/1340. See K. S. Salibi, "Ibn Djamā'a," *EI*², 4: 748–49; idem, "The Banū Jamā'a: a Dynasty of Shāfi'ī Jurists in the Mamluk Period," *Studia Islamica* 9 (1958): 97–109; Brockelmann, *GAL,* 2: 72, supp. 2: 78.

77. Majlisī, *Biḥār al-anwār,* 107: 71, 191, 200.

78. al-Jizzīnī, *Arba'ūn ḥadīth,* 194.

al-Awwal reports that he studied the *Alfiyah* of Ibn Mālik with Shihāb al-Dīn Abū 'l-'Abbās Aḥmad b. al-Ḥasan al-Ḥanafī in Jerusalem, whom he describes as "jurist of the dome of the rock" (*faqīh al-ṣakhrah al-sharīfah*). He also studied this work with Burhān al-Dīn Ibrāhīm b. 'Umar al-Ja'barī in Hebron and received an *ijāzah* for it. He studied *al-Shāṭibīyah*, a famous work on Koranic recitation, with many scholars, including the famous Shāfi'ī jurist Burhān al-Dīn Ibrāhīm Ibn Jamā'ah (d. 764/1363), with whom he read the work in Jerusalem, as well as a professional Koran reciter in Jerusalem, Ghars al-Dīn Khalīl al-Nāqūsī.[79] Given that Burhān al-Dīn Ibn Jamā'ah died in 764/1363, al-Shahīd al-Awwal must have gone to Palestine before that date, presumably in 755/1354, just after he had performed the pilgrimage.

After returning to Ḥillah and studying with Fakhr al-Muḥaqqiqīn for a time in 756/1355, al-Shahīd al-Awwal apparently studied with Sunni teachers in Baghdad, as al-'Allāmah al-Ḥillī had done before him. He studied Koranic recitation under students of the famous Koranic scholar Ibn al-Mu'min, probably in Baghdad.[80] In the *ijāzah* to Ibn al-Khāzin, he mentions that under Sunni teachers he studied many works on hadith, including the *Ṣaḥīḥ* of al-Bukhārī, the *Ṣaḥīḥ* of Muslim, the *Musnad* of Abū Dā'ūd, *al-Jāmi'* by al-Tirmidhī, the *Musnad* of Aḥmad b. Ḥanbal, *al-Muwaṭṭa'* by Mālik, the *Musnad* of Ibn Mājah, *al-Mustadrak 'alā al-ṣaḥīḥayn* by al-Ḥākim al-Nīsābūrī, and others. He studied *al-Shāṭibīyah* with the Baghdādī Ḥanbalī scholar Shams al-Dīn Muḥammad b. 'Abd Allāh al-Baghdādī. He relates *al-Jāmi' al-ṣaḥīḥ* of al-Bukhārī and the *Ṣaḥīḥ* of Muslim not only through his Shiite teacher Fakhr al-Muḥaqqiqīn but also through Sharaf al-Dīn Muḥammad b. Biktāsh al-Tustarī, a Shāfi'ī, he reports, who settled in Baghdad and held the post of professor of Shāfi'ī law at the Niẓāmīyah *madrasah*. He also transmits al-Bukhārī's *Ṣaḥīḥ* from Shams al-Dīn Muḥammad b. 'Abd Allāh al-Baghdādī al-Ḥanbalī, Fakhr al-Dīn Muḥammad b. al-A'azz al-Ḥanafī, and Shams al-Dīn Abū 'Abd al-Raḥmān Muḥammad b. 'Abd al-Raḥmān, a professor of Mālikī law at the Mustanṣirīyah *madrasah*. He received an *ijāzah* from Jamāl al-Dīn 'Abd al-Ṣamad b. Ibrāhīm al-Baghdādī al-Ḥanbalī, the lecturer on hadith at the *Dār al-ḥadīth* in Baghdad.[81]

In Baghdad in early Jumādā I 758/April 1357, al-Shahīd al-Awwal received an *ijāzah* from the Shāfi'ī scholar Shams al-Dīn Muḥammad b. Yūsuf b. 'Alī al-Kirmānī al-Baghdādī al-Qurashī.[82] The text of the *ijāzah*, preserved in its entirety in al-Majlisī's *Biḥār al-anwār*, states that it was issued in the teacher's house on Darb al-Mas'ūd. The works mentioned in the document are *al-*

79. Majlisī, *Biḥār al-anwār*, 107: 199; 109: 55–56.
80. al-Jazarī, *Ghāyat al-nihāyah*, 2: 65.
81. Majlisī, *Biḥār al-anwār*, 107: 191, 200; 109: 72–74.
82. Ibid., 107: 183–84.

Mawāqif al-sulṭānīyah, al-Fawā'id al-ghiyāthīyah, and *Sharḥ mukhtaṣar al-muntahā,* all by the renowned scholar 'Aḍud al-Dīn 'Abd al-Raḥmān b. Zayn al-Dīn Aḥmad al-Ījī (d. 756/1355). The *Sharḥ mukhtaṣar al-muntahā,* a commentary on Ibn al-Ḥājib's *Mukhtaṣar,* was a standard Shāfi'ī textbook of *uṣūl al-fiqh.* Al-Kirmānī had spent his youth in Kirmān, then studied under al-Ījī himself in Shiraz for twelve years. He settled in Baghdad after performing the pilgrimage ca. 756/1355. After teaching in Baghdad for about thirty years, he died in 786/1384 on the return trip from the pilgrimage.[83] It is evident from the *ijāzah* that al-Shahīd al-Awwal avoided giving his *nisbah* as al-Jizzīnī and claimed the *nisbah* al-Dimashqī instead, apparently to conceal his Shiite identity.

The contemporary Sunni scholar al-Jazarī (d. 833/1429) reports that al-Shahīd al-Awwal studied Koranic recitation with the students of Ibn al-Mu'min (d. 740/1340), the most accomplished Koran reader in Iraq during his day, and that he studied for many years under Ibn al-Labbān (d. 776/1374), a Damascene Shāfi'ī jurist and an expert on the Koran. A statement by Ibn al-Labbān concerning him shows that he was known even among Sunnis as an expert on law; he reports that al-Shahīd al-Awwal was "a leading scholar (*imām*) in law, syntax, and recitation of the Koran." The specific terms Ibn al-Labbān uses to describe his relationship with al-Shahīd al-Awwal indicate that he was an advanced student and well integrated into the Sunni scholarly community: "He was my fellow for a lengthy period, and I never heard from him anything contrary to the [beliefs of the] Sunnis" (*ṣaḥibanī muddatan madīdah, fa-lam asma' minhu mā yukhālifu 's-sunnah*).[84] The verb *ṣaḥiba* "to be the fellow of someone" is of particular importance here, because it is a technical term which designates the relationship between a teacher and his advanced students, termed *aṣḥāb* (sing. *ṣāḥib*), "fellows."[85] Ibn al-Labbān was the leading Koran expert of his day in Damascus. In 764/1362–63, he was appointed the head Koran reader at the tomb of Umm al-Ṣāliḥ in Damascus, and the endowment deed stipulated that the incumbent be the most learned reader in the city. He had studied in Jerusalem, Cairo, and Alexandria, but spent most of his career in Damascus, where he died on 2 Rabī' I 776/11 August 1374.[86]

Al-Shahīd al-Awwal probably spent most of his later years between Damascus and his native town, Jizzīn.[87] In Damascus in Sha'bān 766/May 1365, he

83. Ibn Ḥajar al 'Asqalānī, *al-Durar al-kāminah,* 4: 310–11; Ibn al-'Imād al-Ḥanbalī, *Shadharāt al-dhahab,* 6: 294; Brockelmann, *GAL,* supp. 2: 211–12.

84. al-Jazarī, *Ghāyat al-nihāyah,* 2: 65.

85. See Makdisi, *Rise of Colleges,* 128–29.

86. al-Jazarī, *Ghāyat al-nihāyah,* 2: 72–73.

87. Ibn Qāḍī Shuhbah reports that prior to his arrest and subsequent execution, al-Shahīd al-Awwal was residing in Jizzīn (*Tārīkh Ibn Qāḍī Shuhbah,* 134–35).

received an *ijāzah* from Quṭb al-Dīn al-Rāzī, as mentioned above.[88] It is reported that al-Shahīd al-Awwal, performing *taqīyah* assiduously, engaged constantly in teaching Sunni works and Koranic recitation, and had very little opportunity to teach Shiite works. He was able to teach Shiite works only in private in an underground room between the *maghrib* and *'ishā'* prayers.[89]

Several accounts show that al-Shahīd al-Awwal claimed to belong to the Shāfi'ī *madhhab*. Shams al-Dīn b. al-Jazarī, the author of *Ṭabaqāt al-qurrā'*, writes that al-Shahīd al-Awwal claimed to be a Shāfi'ī jurisconsult. Specifically, he states that al-Shahīd al-Awwal attached the *nisbah* "al-Shāfi'ī" to his name in a written petition for an *ijāzah* (*istad'ā*) he sent to the author.[90]

Two contemporary accounts describing al-Shahīd al-Awwal's heresy trial and execution in some detail make it clear that he claimed to be a Shāfi'ī in the course of the proceedings. One account was recorded by a Sunni Damascene historian, Ibn Qāḍī Shuhbah (d. 851/1448),[91] and the other was recorded by one of al-Shahīd al-Awwal's Shiite students, al-Fāḍil al-Miqdād b. 'Abd Allāh al-Suyūrī al-Ḥillī (d. 826/1423).[92] He was tried at *Dār al-sa'ādah* in the presence of the leading judges and scholars of Damascus after having been imprisoned for a year in the citadel. An affidavit filed with the *qāḍī* of Beirut and signed by a large number of men from Jabal 'Āmil and the adjacent coastal region accused him of uttering blasphemies concerning Abū Bakr, 'Umar, and 'Ā'ishah, holding heretical beliefs and opinions, such as the permissibility of drinking alcohol, and issuing legal *responsa* in accordance with those opinions.[93] It appears that al-Shahīd was tricked at the trial, for both accounts state that he was led to confess, thinking that he would be given the opportunity to recant afterwards. Instead, the Shāfi'ī chief judge, Burhān al-Dīn Ibrāhīm b. 'Abd al-Raḥīm Ibn Jamā'ah (d. 790/1388), rather than giving his own verdict, required the Mālikī chief judge, Burhān al-Dīn al-Tādhalī (d. 803/1400–1401), to give the verdict according to Mālikī law. [94] Al-Tādhalī ruled

88. The *ijāzah* section of Majlisī's *Biḥār al-anwār* (107: 140–41) mentions two *ijāzah*s that al-Shahīd al-Awwal received, but they include contradictory information. In one passage, al-Shahīd al-Awwal reports that he received an *ijāzah* from al-Rāzī in Sha'bān 766/April–May 1365 and that al-Rāzī died later that same year, on 12 Dhū al-Qa'dah 766/1 August 1365. In another passage, the text reports that he received the *ijāzah* in Damascus in 768/1366–67 (107: 188). Clearly, both accounts cannot be true, and either the death of al-Rāzī did not occur in 766/1365 or the date of the second *ijāzah* is wrong.

89. al-Iṣfahānī, *Riyāḍ al-'ulamā'*, 5: 189.

90. Ibn Qāḍī Shuhbah, *Tārīkh Ibn Qāḍī Shuhbah*, 1: 151.

91. Ibid., 134–35.

92. Majlisī, *Biḥār al-anwār*, 107: 184–86; al-Baḥrānī, *Lu'lu'at al-Baḥrayn*, 146–48.

93. Majlisī, *Biḥār al-anwār*, 107: 185.

94. On Ibn Jamā'ah see Ibn Qāḍī Shuhbah, *Tārīkh Ibn Qāḍī Shuhbah*, 248–51. He was the chief Shāfi'ī judge in Damascus from 773/1371 until his death in 790/1388, with two interruptions, in 779 A.H. and 784 A.H. On Burhān al-Dīn Ibrāhīm b. Muḥammad b. 'Alī al-Tādhalī, see Muḥammad b. 'Abd al-Raḥmān al-Sakhāwī, *al-Ḍaw' al-lāmi' li-ahl al-qarn al-tāsi'*, 12 vols. (Cairo: Dār al-kitāb al-islāmī, n.d.), 1: 155–56.

that the defendant be executed since the Mālikīs do not accept the repentance of a proven heretic. After praying two cycles, uttering the *shahādah,* and blessing the Companions, al-Shahīd was beheaded in the open area below the citadel. His body was subsequently crucified, stoned, and burned by the mob. Ibn Qāḍī Shuhbah gives the date of the execution as 10 Jumādā I 786/30 June 1384.[95] The concern here is not with the details of the trial, but rather with the fact that during the proceedings, al-Shahīd al-Awwal claimed to belong to the Shāfiʿī *madhhab.* He is reported to have addressed Burhān al-Dīn Ibn Jamāʿah: "I am of the Shāfiʿī *madhhab,* and you are the foremost jurist (*imām*) and judge of the Shāfiʿī *madhhab.* Give your verdict concerning me according to your *madhhab.*"[96]

ʿAlī b. ʿAbd al-ʿĀlī al-Karakī (d. 940/1534)

ʿAlī b. ʿAbd al-ʿĀlī al-Karakī,[97] known in Shiite scholarly tradition as al-Muḥaqqiq al-Thānī ("the Second Precise Scholar") was one of the most influential Shiite scholars in the history of the early Safavid Empire and associated closely with Shah Ismāʿīl I (907/1501–930/1524) and his successor Shah Ṭahmāsb (930/1524-984/1576). He was a native of Karak Nūḥ, situated in the Biqāʿ valley near Zaḥlah, at the foot of Mount Lebanon.[98] The exact date of his birth is not known, but al-Ḥurr al-ʿĀmilī reports that he was over seventy when he died, which would imply that he was born before 870/1466.[99] He studied first with Shiite teachers in Jabal ʿĀmil, completed his studies under the leading jurist in Najaf at the time, ʿAlī b. Hilāl al-Jazāʾirī, and became the top authority in Najaf on al-Jazāʾirī's death—between 909/1504 and 914/1508. Before that, however, he had studied with Sunni scholars in Damascus, Jerusalem, and Cairo.

Al-Karakī must have studied first in a Shiite context in his native region, but little is known of his academic career. At the age of about thirty, he received an *ijāzah* from Ibn Khātūn al-ʿĀmilī on 19 Dhū al-Ḥijjah 900/10 September 1495. He had probably studied with Ibn Khātūn for some time prior to this in

95. Ibn Qāḍī Shuhbah, *Tārīkh Ibn Qāḍī Shuhbah,* 134–35. A short account written by one of al-Shahīd al-Awwal's sons states that he was executed and then burned below the citadel of Damascus on Thursday, 9 Jumādā I 786/29 June 1384 (Majlisī, *Biḥār al-anwār,* 107: 186).

96. Majlisī, *Biḥār al-anwār,* 107: 185.

97. On this scholar in general, see al-Ḥurr al-ʿĀmilī, *Amal al-āmil,* 1: 121–23; al-Iṣfahānī, *Riyāḍ al-ʿulamāʾ,* 3: 441–60; al-Baḥrānī, *Luʾluʾat al-Baḥrayn,* 151–54; al-Khwānsārī, *Rawḍāt al-jannāt,* 4: 346–60; al-Amīn, *Aʿyān al-shīʿah,* 8: 208–13; Wilferd Madelung, "al-Karakī," *EI*[2]; Erika Glassen, "Schah Ismāʿīl I. und die Theologen seine Zeit," *Der Islam* 48 (1972): 262–68; Elke Eberhard, *Osmanische Polemik gegen die Safawiden im 16. Jahrhundert nach arabischen Handschriften* (Freiburg: Klaus Schwarz Verlag, 1970); Caroline J. Beeson, "The Origins of Conflict in the Ṣafawī Religious Institution," Ph.D. diss., Princeton University, 1982; Newman, "Development and Political Significance," 748–57; idem, "The Myth of Clerical Migration to Safawid Iran," *Die Welt des Islams* 33 (1993): 66–112.

98. See Dominique Sourdel, "Karak Nūḥ," *EI*[2].

99. al-Ḥurr al-ʿĀmilī, *Amal al-āmil,* 1: 122.

ʿĪnāthā, that teacher's native town in Jabal ʿĀmil. In Damascus, on 16 Ramaḍān 903/8 May 1498, he issued an *ijāzah* to a Shiite student, Ḥusayn b. Muḥammad al-Ḥurr al-ʿĀmilī. He issued another *ijāzah* to an Iranian Shiite student, Ḥusayn b. Muḥammad al-Astarābādī, who had read al-Muḥaqqiq al-Ḥillī's legal work *Qawāʿid al-aḥkām* with him, on 11 Shawwāl 907/19 April 1502.[100]

Al-Karakī traveled to Iraq, then under Aqqoyunlu rule, in 909/1503–4, and received an *ijāzah* from ʿAlī b. Hilāl al-Jazāʾirī, the leading jurist at the Shiite center of learning in Najaf during this period, on 15 Ramaḍān 909/2 March 1504.[101] Al-Karakī seems to have spent the subsequent years in Iraq. When the Safavids advanced on Iraq in 914/1508, he was imprisoned by the Aqqoyunlu ruler in Baghdad during the hostilities and later freed by Shah Ismāʿīl I. From that date on, he spent his time in Shiite environments, either at Safavid court in Iran or in southern Iraq, which the Safavids controlled until after his death. During the years 916–17/1511, he was in Khurasan with the Safavid royal entourage.[102] *Ijāzah*s place him back in Najaf in 928/1522 and 929/1528.[103] He made a second trip to Iran in 931–32/1525–26, was in Najaf in 933/1527, in Baghdad in 934/1528, and back in Najaf in 935/1528.[104] He traveled to Khurasan in 936/1529–30 and returned to Kāshān. He then proceeded to Isfahan, where he gave an *ijāzah* on 9 Ramaḍān 937/26 April 1531. He issued an *ijāzah* to al-Sayyid Shams al-Dīn al-Mashhadī in Qum on 11 Dhū ʾl-Ḥijjah 937/26 July 1531. Apparently still in Iran, he gave an *ijāzah* to Kamāl al-Dīn Darwīsh Muḥammad al-Iṣfahānī, an ancestor of the famous Muḥammad Bāqir al-Majlisī, in 939/1532–33.[105] Shah Ṭahmāsb issued a decree granting al-Karakī land and tax immunities in Iraq, as well as revenue from the mint at al-Ḥillah, in 939/1533.[106] Al-Karakī died on 13 Dhū ʾl-Hijjah 940/25 June 1534 in Najaf.

Al-Karakī claims to have expended great efforts in the study of Sunni

100. Majlisī, *Biḥār al-anwār,* 108: 20–27, 53, 57.

101. Ibid., 108:34, 69. Some sources report that al-Jazāʾirī traveled to Karak Nūḥ and settled there, but this is unlikely, in my opinion, and is not supported by documented evidence. Al-Karakī probably received this *ijāzah* from al-Jazāʾirī after arriving in Najaf in 909/1504, rather than receiving it from al-Jazāʾirī in Karak Nūḥ and then traveling to Najaf later that same year.

102. Newman, "Development and Political Significance," 749.

103. He issued an *ijāzah* to Pīr Ḥabīb Allāh b. Muḥammad al-Jūzdānī on 11 Ṣafar 928/10 January 1522 in Najaf (Majlisī, *Biḥār al-anwār,* 108: 59). In Jumādā II 928/May 1522, also in Najaf, he issued an *ijāzah* to Aḥmad b. Abī Jāmiʿ al-ʿĀmilī after having taught him *al-Alfiyah* by al-Shahīd al-Awwal on ritual prayer along with the glosses of al-Karakī himself (108: 60–1). Also in Najaf, he issued an *ijāzah* to ʿAbd al-ʿAlī b. Aḥmad b. Saʿd al-Dīn Muḥammad al-ʿĀmilī on 16 Ramaḍān 929/29 July 1523 (108: 68).

104. Newman, "Development and Political Significance," 749, 753. Al-Karakī taught in Iraq for a number of years. He issued an *ijāzah* to ʿAlī b. ʿAbd al-ʿĀlī al-Maysī and his son Ibrāhīm in Baghdad on 9 Jumādā II 934/1 March 1528 (Majlisī, *Biḥār al-anwār,* 108: 49).

105. Majlisī, *Biḥār al-anwār,* 108: 80, 81, 83, 84.

106. Said Amir Arjomand, trans., "Two Decrees of Shah Ṭahmāsp Concerning Statecraft and the Authority of Shaykh ʿAlī Al-Karakī," in *Authority and Political Culture in Shiʿism,* ed. Said Amir Arjomand (Albany: State University of New York Press, 1988), 250–62.

works, especially in the fields of *fiqh*, hadith, *tafsīr*, lexicography, and the literary arts. He received *ijāzah*s to transmit these works from both Shiite and Sunni scholars, having studied with Sunni scholars for considerable periods of time in Damascus, Jerusalem, Mecca, and Cairo. In an *ijāzah* dated 9 Ramaḍān 937/26 April 1531 and issued in Isfahan, al-Karakī reports that he had studied a number of Sunni works. He transmitted *Kashshāf ḥaqā'iq al-tanzīl* by al-Zamakhsharī, *al-Ṣiḥāḥ* by Ismā'īl b. Ḥammād al-Jawharī, *Jamharat al-lughah* by al-Ḥasan b. Durayd al-Azdī, *al-Shāṭibīyah* on Koranic recitation, and *al-Nashr* and *al-Nūnīyah* on the ten *qirā'āt* by al-Jazarī. His Sunni teachers included two prominent Shāfi'ī jurists, Kamāl al-Dīn Abū 'Abd Allāh Muḥammad b. Abī Sharīf al-Maqdisī (d. 906/1501) and Abū Yaḥyā Zakarīyā al-Anṣārī (d. 926/1520). Al-Karakī collected his Sunni *ijāzah*s and recorded his Sunni paths of transmission in several places and adds that he copied the entire *mashyakhah* or catalogue of al-Anṣārī's teachers while he was in Egypt.[107] This must have been the *thabat* or catalogue in which al-Anṣārī recorded over one hundred and fifty teachers who had granted him *ijāzah*s.[108]

Kamāl al-Dīn Muḥammad b. Muḥammad Ibn Abī al-Sharīf al-Maqdisī was a prominent Shāfi'ī jurist who belonged to a large family of accomplished jurists in Jerusalem. He was born in Jerusalem on 5 Dhū al-Ḥijjah 822/23 December 1419 and completed his early studies there. He traveled to Cairo to study in 839/1435–36 and returned there a number of times to study and teach. During his later years in Cairo, he taught jurisprudence, particularly al-Maḥallī's commentary on al-Subkī's *uṣūl al-fiqh* work, *Jam' al-jawāmi'*. The last period he spent there was from Rajab 881/October-November 1476 until 890/1485, when Qā'it Bāy appointed him to the *mashyakhah* of his *madrasah* in Jerusalem to replace Shihāb al-Dīn Aḥmad b. 'Umar b. Khalīl al-'Umayrī after the latter died on 9 Rabī' I 890/26 March 1485.[109] During this period he taught law at the Mu'ayyadīyah *madrasah*. He apparently remained in Jerusalem after returning in 890/1485, where he died on 25 Jumādā II 906/16 January 1501. His extant works include a commentary on *Jam' al-jawāmi'* entitled *al-Durar al-lawāmi'*.[110] Al-Karakī may have studied with him at the tail end of his last stay in Cairo—al-Karakī would have been about twenty years old then—or he may have studied with him later in Jerusalem.

Zakarīyā b.Muḥammad al-Anṣārī was the leading jurist in Cairo and the *ra'īs* or head man of the Shāfi'ī *madhhab* in Egypt during his day. Born in the

107. Majlisī, *Biḥār al-anwār*, 108: 76, 79–80.

108. Najm al-Dīn al-Ghazzī, *al-Kawākib al-sā'irah bi-a'yān al-mi'ah al-'āshirah*, 3 vols. (Beirut: al-maṭba'ah al-amīrkānīyah, 1954–58), 1: 198.

109. al-Sakhāwī, *al-Ḍaw' al-lāmi'*, 2: 52–53; Ibn al-'Imād al-Ḥanbalī, *Shadharāt al-dhahab*, 8: 29–30.

110. al-Sakhāwī, *al-Ḍaw' al-lāmi'*, 9: 64–67; Brockelmann, *GAL*, 2: 89, 118; supp. 2: 105.

village of al-Sunaykah in the Sharqīyah region of the Nile delta in 823/1420, he was very long-lived. According to al-Sha'rānī, by the time of his death all the scholars in Egypt were either his students or his students' students. He saw his students' students become leading scholars, and collected so many posts as professor and other positions that his daily income was reckoned at three thousand *dirhams* even before he had accepted any judgeships. The Mamluk Sultan al-Ashraf Qā'it Bāy (872–901/1468–96) appointed him chief judge in Rajab 886/September 1481, but soon dismissed him for accusing the sultan of injustices. Al-Anṣārī taught his most popular textbook on Shāfi'ī law, *Sharḥ al-bahjah,* fifty-seven times. He died on 3 Dhū al-Qa'dah 926/15 October 1520, and his funeral was the biggest al-Sha'rānī had ever seen.[111] Under al-Anṣārī, al-Karakī must have studied Shāfi'ī law in particular, perhaps at al-Azhar.

al-Shahīd al-Thānī (d. 965/1558)

A native of Jabal 'Āmil in what is now southern Lebanon, Zayn al-Dīn al-'Āmilī[112] was born on Tuesday, 13 Shawwāl 911/ February 7, 1506. His native village was Jubā' in the region of Ṣaydā (Sidon).[113] The Ottomans wrested his native region from the Mamluks in 922/1516 during his youth, and he came to be known as al-Shahīd al-Thānī in the Shiite tradition because he was executed by the Ottomans many years later in 965/1558. Like al-Karakī, Zayn al-Dīn studied with Sunni teachers in Jerusalem, Damascus, and Cairo.

Zayn al-Dīn completed his early studies in private contexts with Shiite teachers in Jabal 'Āmil. He first studied with his father 'Alī b. Aḥmad (d. 925/1519) in Jubā', then with his uncle (his mother's sister's husband) 'Alī b. 'Abd al-'Ālī al-Maysī (d. 938/1531–32) in the village of Mays, then with Sayyid Ja'far b. Ḥasan al-Karakī (d. 936/1530) in Karak Nūḥ. In 937/1530–31, he went to study in Damascus. Under Shams al-Dīn Muḥammad b. Makkī, whom he terms a philosopher, he studied several works on medicine, including a commentary on *al-Mūjaz al-Nafīsī* and a work by Muḥammad b. Makkī himself, *Ghāyat al-qaṣd fī ma'rifat al-faṣd,* as well as *Fuṣūl al-Far'ānī* on astronomy, and some of al-

111. 'Abd al-Wahhāb al-Sha'rānī, *al-Ṭabaqāt al-ṣughrā* (Cairo: Maktabat al-qāhirah, 1970), 37, 45; al-Ghazzī, *al-Kawākib al-sā'irah,* 1: 196–207; Ibn al-'Imād al-Ḥanbalī, *Shadharāt al-dhahab,* 8: 134–36.

112. The most detailed biographical source is 'Ali al-'Āmilī, *al-Durr al-manthūr,* 2: 149–99. For other biographies, see al-Ḥurr al-'Āmilī, *Amal al-āmil,* 1: 85–91; al-Iṣfahānī, *Riyāḍ al-'ulamā',* 2: 365–86; al-Baḥrānī, *Lu'lu'at al-Baḥrayn,* 28–36; al-Khwānsarī, *Rawḍāt al-jannāt,* 3: 337–68; al-Amīn, *A'yān al-shī'ah,* 7: 143–58; Āghā Buzurg al-Ṭihrānī, *Ṭabaqāt a'lām al-shī'ah,* ed. 'Alī Naqī Munzavī (Tehran: Dānishgāh-i Tihrān, 1987), 90–92; Beeson, "Origins of Conflict," 111–14; Marco Salati, "Ricerche sulo sciismo nell'Impero ottomano," *Oriente Moderno* 9 (1990): 81–92; Devin J. Stewart, "A Biographical Notice on Bahā' al-Dīn al-'Āmilī (d. 1030/1621)," *JAOS* 111 (1991): 564–65; idem, "Ḥusayn b. 'Abd al-Ṣamad al-'Āmilī's Treatise for Sultan Suleiman and the Shi'i Shāfi'ī Legal Tradition," *Islamic Law and Society* 4 (1997): 156–99; al-Muhājir, *Sittat fuqahā',* 131–86.

113. 'Alī al-'Āmilī, *al-Durr al-manthūr,* 2: 158, 159, 189.

Suhrawardī's *Ḥikmat al-ishrāq*.[114] According to 'Ālī al-'Amilī, Muḥammad b. Makkī died in Jumādā I 938/December 1531–January 1532. Najm al-Dīn al-Ghazzī refers to him as the head of the doctors' guild (*shaykh al-aṭibbā'*), knowledgeable in astronomy and geometry as well as medicine, and identifies him as a Shāfi'ī, though reporting that he was suspected of Shiism (*wa-kāna yunsabu ilā 'r-rafḍ*). Al-Ghazzī reports his death on a different date: 9 Jumādā II 938/18 January 1532, at an age of over eighty.[115] Also during this first stay in Damascus, Zayn al-Dīn studied Koranic recitation with a scholar named Aḥmad b. Jābir. He read *al-Shāṭibīyah* on Koranic recitation and learned the variant readings of Nāfi', Ibn Kathīr, Abū 'Amr, and 'Āṣim. In 938/1531–32 he returned to Jubā' and stayed there until the beginning of 942/1535, when he went to Damascus for a second time.[116]

During his second stay in Damascus, Zayn al-Dīn studied the *Ṣaḥīḥ*s of Muslim and al-Bukhārī with the well-known historian and hadith scholar, the Ḥanafī Shams al-Dīn Muḥammad b. Ṭūlūn (d. 953/1546), at the Salīmīyah *madrasah* in the Ṣāliḥīyah quarter. He received an *ijāzah* for these two works from Ibn Ṭūlūn in Rabī' I 942/30 August–28 September 1535 (but it must have been before 13 September, when he left for Egypt).[117] At that time Ibn al-'Awdī, a younger Shiite scholar and a native of Jizzīn in Jabal 'Āmil, was Zayn al-Dīn's student-servitor (*khādim*). He attended these lessons along with Zayn al-Dīn, and also received an *ijāzah* from Ibn Ṭūlūn.[118] Ibn Ṭūlūn seems to have had some Shiite sympathies, for he wrote a work on the Twelver Imams entitled *al-Shadharāt al-dhahabīyah fī tarājim al-a'immah al-ithnā-'ashar 'ind al-imāmīyah*.[119]

While in Damascus, Zayn al-Dīn decided to travel to Cairo to continue his studies. There is no evidence that he had studied *fiqh* according to the Sunni *madhhab*s in Damascus, and it seems that he went to Egypt primarily for this purpose. Several of his students, including Ḥusayn b. 'Abd al-Ṣamad al-Ḥārithī and the latter's cousin, 'Alī b. Zuhrah, accompanied him to Egypt. The Shiite al-Ḥājj Shams al-Dīn b. Hilāl, perhaps a wealthy merchant from Jabal 'Āmil or Damascus, paid the expenses involved in the trip. Zayn al-Dīn and his companions left Damascus heading for Egypt on Sunday, 15 Rabī' I 942/13 September 1535. On the way to Egypt they passed through Ramlah,

114. Ibid., 159.

115. Ibid.; al-Ghazzī, *al-Kawākib al-sā'irah*, 2: 59–60.

116. 'Alī al-'Āmilī, *al-Durr al-manthur*, 2: 159. The text has *miṣr* instead of Damascus. The context, including the teachers mentioned, shows that Damascus is intended.

117. Ibid. On Ibn Ṭūlūn, see W. M. Brinner, "Ibn Ṭūlūn," EI^2, 3: 957–58; Muḥammad Ibn Ṭūlūn, *al-Fulk al-mashḥūn fī aḥwāl Muḥammad ibn Ṭūlūn* (Damascus: Maṭba'at al-taraqqī, 1929).

118. 'Alī al-'Āmilī, *al-Durr al-manthūr*, 2: 160.

119. This work on the Twelver Imams by Ibn Ṭūlūn has been published under the title *al-A'immah al-ithnā 'ashar*, ed. Ṣalāḥ al-Dīn al-Munajjid (Beirut, 1958).

then proceeded to Gaza, where Zayn al-Dīn met a scholar named Muḥyī al-Dīn 'Abd al-Qādir b. Abī al-Khayr al-Ghazzī. The two held learned discussions and debates, and al-Ghazzī issued him an *ijāzah*. Before Zayn al-Dīn left, al-Ghazzī invited him to choose a book to take from his library. Zayn al-Dīn chose without looking, and picked a book by the famous Shiite jurist al-'Allāmah al-Ḥillī. He considered it a good omen to have chosen a Shiite book from the Sunni scholar's library. They arrived in Cairo on Friday, 15 Rabī' II 942/13 October 1535.[120]

By going to study in Cairo, Zayn al-Dīn was following in the footsteps of al-Karakī, who had studied in Cairo several decades earlier. During the short period of a year and a half, Zayn al-Dīn accomplished a great deal, as is attested to by the list of his teachers and the works he read while in Cairo. He may have already studied many of the works on his own in Jabal 'Āmil or with Shiite teachers, and was simply reviewing or presenting what he had already learned in order to get certificates of study. All together, Zayn al-Dīn reports the names of sixteen Sunni teachers with whom he studied in Cairo, though he claims that this list is incomplete.[121] In his work on education, *Munyat al-murīd fī ādāb al-mufīd wa al-mustafīd,* he mentions that one of his teachers in Cairo directed him to study with other teachers rather than discouraging him from looking elsewhere out of jealousy, a fault he attributed to most teachers of his day.[122] He studied the ancillary sciences, including syntax, morphology, rhetoric, and logic, as well as Koranic recitation, hadith, *tafsīr,* mathematics, and astronomy, and in most cases gives the titles of the works he studied with each teacher.

While in Cairo, Zayn al-Dīn studied a great deal of Sunni legal material, primarily that of the Shāfi'ī *madhhab.* With the Shāfi'ī jurist Shihāb al-Dīn Aḥmad al-Ramlī al-Anṣārī, he studied *al-Minhāj,* a standard textbook of Shāfi'ī *fiqh* by al-Nawawī (d. 676/1278), and a number of Shāfi'ī textbooks of *uṣūl al-fiqh.* These included *Mukhtaṣar al-uṣūl* by Ibn al-Ḥājib, together with its commentary *al-Sharḥ al-'Aḍudī* by 'Aḍud al-Dīn al-Ījī and the supercommentaries of Sa'd al-Dīn al-Taftazānī and al-Sharīf al-Jurjānī (d. 816/1413), al-Ramlī's own commentary on *al-Waraqāt* by Imām al-Ḥaramayn al-Juwaynī (d. 478/1085), and *Jam' al-jawāmi'* by Tāj al-Dīn al-Subkī (d. 771/1370), with the commentary of Jalāl al-Dīn al-Maḥallī (d. 864/1459). He received an *ijāzah* for these and other works in 943/1536-37.[123] Shihāb al-Dīn al-Ramlī, originally from a small village in the area of al-Manūfiyah, was Zayn al-Dīn's most im-

120. 'Alī al-'Āmilī, *al-Durr al-manthūr,* 2: 160–62.

121. Ibid., 162–68.

122. Zayn al-Dīn al-'Āmilī, *Munyat al-murīd fī ādāb al-mufīd wa'l-mustafīd,* (Najaf: Maṭba'at al-gharī, 1950–51), 73.

123. 'Alī al-'Āmilī, *al-Durr al-manthūr,* 2: 162.

portant Egyptian teacher in the legal sciences. Al-Ramlī had been a favorite student of Zakarīyā al-Anṣārī, the leading Shāfiʿī jurist and law professor of the previous generation, and was granted the responsibility of editing al-Anṣārī's works. According to the contemporary biographer ʿAbd al-Wahhāb al-Shaʿrānī, al-Ramlī became the leading Shāfiʿī legal authority not only for Egypt but for Syria and the Ḥijāz as well. Al-Ramlī died on Friday, 1 Jumādā II 957/18 May 1550, and al-Shaʿrānī reports that his funeral was so large that those attending the funeral prayer could not fit in the mosque of al-Azhar.[124]

With Abū al-Ḥasan ʿAlī b. Muḥammad al-Bakrī al-Ṣiddīqī, also a Shāfiʿī jurist, Zayn al-Dīn studied *fiqh* and *tafsīr.* Al-Bakrī was the hereditary leader of the Bakrī Sufi order and a very important man in Cairo. He died there in 953/1546–47, and was buried near the tomb of al-Shāfiʿī.[125] Zayn al-Dīn read some of al-Bakrī's commentary on *al-Minhāj* by al-Nawawī.[126] It appears that he knew this teacher particularly well, for he later accompanied him on the pilgrimage.

Zayn al-Dīn also studied with the prominent Shāfiʿī jurist Shihāb al-Dīn Aḥmad b. ʿAbd al-Ḥaqq al-Sinbāṭī al-Miṣrī al-Shāfiʿī. Al-Sinbāṭī was a popular preacher (*wāʿiẓ*) at the mosque of al-Azhar. In addition, he was an expert on the disputed questions of the law and the opinions held in the various *madhhab*s. He became the professor of law at the Khashshābīyah *madrasah,* a post supposed to be given to the most learned Shāfiʿī jurist, after the death of Shams al-Dīn Muḥammad b. Shaʿbān al-Ḍayrūṭī in 949/1543. He was known for declaring coffee forbidden and for ordering the destruction of several churches. He died at the end of Ṣafar 950/early June 1543.[127] Zayn al-Dīn does not specify the works he studied under al-Sinbāṭī.

Zayn al-Dīn left Cairo with the pilgrimage caravan on 17 Shawwāl 943/29 March 1537, in the company of his teacher Abū al-Ḥasan al-Bakrī. After performing the pilgrimage, he returned to his native village Jubāʿ, arriving on 24 Ṣafar 944/2 August 1537.[128]

Zayn al-Dīn's studies in Cairo represent a crucial stage in his intellectual formation and his exposure to Sunni tradition. His second stay in Damascus lasted only about two and a half months. His first stay there could not have been more than a year.[129] Sources do not indicate that he studied law during

124. See al-Shaʿrānī, *al-Ṭabaqāt al-ṣughrā,* 67–69; Ibn al-ʿImād, *Shadharāt al-dhahab,* 8: 316.

125. al-Shaʿrānī, *al-Ṭabaqāt al-ṣughrā,* 78–80; al-Ghazzī, *al-Kawākib al-sāʾirah,* 2:194–97; Ibn al-ʿImād, *Shadharāt al-dhahab,* 8: 292–93; ʿAlī al-ʿĀmilī, *al-Durr al-manthūr,* 2: 165. Al-Ghazzī and Ibn al-ʿImād give his death date as 952 A.H. instead of 953 A.H., the date given in *al-Ṭabaqāt al-ṣughrā* and *al-Durr al-manthūr.*

126. ʿAlī al-ʿĀmilī, *al-Durr al-manthūr,* 2: 165.

127. al-Shaʿrānī, *al-Ṭabaqāt al-ṣughrā,* 77–78; al-Ghazzī, *al-Kawākib al-sāʾirah,* 2: 111–12; Ibn al-ʿImād, *Shadharāt al-dhahab,* 8: 292–93.

128. ʿAlī al-ʿĀmilī, *al-Durr al-manthūr,* 2: 167–68.

129. Ibid., 159.

either of these stays, although he studied hadith with Ibn Ṭūlūn in the Salīmīyah *madrasah.* In Cairo, however, Zayn al-Dīn was able to study law with at least three teachers: Shihāb al-Dīn Aḥmad al-Ramlī al-Anṣārī, Abū al-Ḥasan al-Bakrī, and Shihāb al-Dīn Aḥmad b. ʿAbd al-Ḥaqq al-Sinbāṭī al-Miṣrī. All three of these scholars were Shāfiʿīs, as were the authors of the works they taught Zayn al-Dīn, including *al-Minhāj* by al-Nawawī, *al-Waraqāt* by Imam al-Ḥaramayn al-Juwaynī, and *Sharḥ Jamʿ al-jawāmiʿ* by al-Maḥallī. Ibn al-Ḥājib was a Mālikī, but his *Mukhtaṣar,* and particularly the commentary by the Shāfiʿī al-Ījī, had become a standard part of the Shāfiʿī curriculum. While Zayn al-Dīn does not state so explicitly, it seems clear that he and his Shiite companions were passing as Shāfiʿī law students during their stay in Cairo and that, as a result of their studies, they were able to establish a high level of competence in Shāfiʿī law.

In 948/1541–42, Zayn al-Dīn made a short trip to Jerusalem. There he met the Shāfiʿī *muftī* of Jerusalem, the jurist Shams al-Dīn Ibn Abī al-Luṭf al-Maqdisī, read some of the *Ṣaḥīḥ* of al-Bukhārī and the *Ṣaḥīḥ* of Muslim, and obtained an *ijāzah.*[130] It appears that he did not stay in Jerusalem long and that his most serious studies under Sunni teachers had taken place in Damascus and especially Cairo. Zayn al-Dīn was probably anxious to collect *ijāzah*s from prominent Shāfiʿī jurists for an important undertaking on which he would embark several years later.

In 952/1545 Zayn al-Dīn, together with his student and companion Ḥusayn b. ʿAbd al-Ṣamad al-ʿĀmilī, traveled to Istanbul and successfully petitioned officials connected with the court of Sultan Suleiman (926–74/1520–66) for positions as law professors. As a result, Zayn al-Dīn was appointed to the Nūrīyah *madrasah* in Baʿlabakk and Ḥusayn to an unspecified *madrasah* in Baghdad. Muḥammad b. ʿAlī Ibn al-ʿAwdī al-Jizzīnī, the servitor (*khādim*) of Zayn al-Dīn, studied with him during this period (from 10 Rabīʿ I 945/6 August 1538 until 10 Dhū al-Qaʿdah 962/26 September 1555) and subsequently wrote a biography of his teacher entitled *Bughyat al-murīd min al-kashf ʿan aḥwāl al-Shaykh Zayn al-Dīn al-shahīd* ("The Seeker's Goal, Revealing the Circumstances of the Martyred Master, Zayn al-Dīn"). In the extant portions of this work, he provides a fairly detailed account of the trip to Istanbul in 952/1545, drawing on Zayn al-Dīn's autobiographical notes.[131] Zayn al-Dīn and Ḥusayn left Jubaʿ on 12 Dhū ʾl-Ḥijjah 951/24 February 1545 and, after making extended stops in Damascus, Aleppo, and Tokat along the way, arrived in Istanbul on 17 Rabīʿ I 952/29 May 1545. Before meeting with anyone, Zayn al-Dīn spent eighteen days writing a treatise on ten topics in ten different fields, including law, Koranic exegesis, and the rational sciences. This

130. Ibid., 169–70.

131. Ibid., 170–82, 191; see also Salati, "Ricerche sulo sciismo nell'Impero ottomano."

treatise would serve to establish Zayn al-Dīn's credentials and in a sense replace the *'arḍ al-qāḍī,* a document one was expected to obtain from the judge of one's local district, which served as a type of recommendation in the Ottoman system. Zayn al-Dīn had decided against asking for this document from the judge of Ṣaydā, Ma'rūf al-Shāmī, perhaps for fear that the judge would expose him as a Shiite. He sent the treatise to the *qāḍī al-'askar,* Muḥammad b. Quṭb al-Dīn b. Muḥammad b. Qāḍī-zādah al-Rūmī (d. 957/1550), who recognized Zayn al-Dīn's talent, praised him highly, and eagerly supported his petition. After twelve days, the *qāḍī al-'askar* sent him the record book of professorships and other positions (*waẓā'if wa-madāris*) and told him he could choose any position he wanted in Damascus or Aleppo. Zayn al-Dīn opted for a position as professor of law at the Nūrīyah *madrasah* in Ba'labakk. The Qāḍī al-'askar petitioned Sultan Suleiman on Zayn al-Dīn's behalf, and the sultan wrote a decree granting Zayn al-Dīn the position and assigning him the monthly stipend stipulated by the founder, the Ayyubid ruler Nūr al-Dīn Maḥmūd b. Zangī (541–69/1146–74). All together, Zayn al-Dīn spent three and a half months in Istanbul; he left on 11 Rajab 952/18 September 1545.

Ḥusayn and Zayn al-Dīn then traveled to Iraq before returning to Jabal 'Āmil on 15 Ṣafar 953/17 April 1546. Soon afterwards, they went to Ba'labakk, where Zayn al-Dīn assumed his post at the Nūrīyah *madrasah.* For nearly two years, Zayn al-Dīn taught law and other topics at the *madrasah* and also held a regular lesson at the adjacent mosque. They returned to Jubā' before the end of 954/February 1548.[132]

Not only Ottoman officials but also the endowment document of the *madrasah* itself would have required that Zayn al-Dīn belong to one of the four recognized *madhhabs*. The Nūrīyah *madrasah* in Ba'labakk was officially a Shāfi'ī institution and was one of the four Shāfi'ī *madrasahs*—in Baa'labakk, Ḥimṣ, Ḥamāh, and Manbij—that Nūr al-Dīn had built after 550/1155–56 for the prominent Shāfi'ī jurist Sharaf al-Dīn 'Abd Allāh b. Muḥammad Ibn Abī 'Aṣrūn (d. 585/1189–90).[133] Zayn al-Dīn stresses, concerning his stipend, that the Ottoman officials followed the dictates of the original endowment of Nūr al-Dīn, and the same document must have stated explicitly that Zayn al-Dīn be a Shāfi'ī jurist in order to be appointed *mudarris.* Hence, Zayn al-Dīn must have presented himself as a Shāfi'ī jurist in order to obtain the position. His official duties must have been to teach Shāfi'ī law and ancillary subjects. Notwithstanding, he apparently taught Shiite law there as well.

132. 'Alī al-'Āmilī, *al-Durr al-manthūr,* 2: 182. The mosque, like the *madrasah,* was built by Nūr al-Dīn Maḥmūd b. Zangī. The modern Lebanese scholar Ja'far al-Muhājir reports that both the mosque and the *madrasah,* which stood just east of it, are now in ruins (*Sittat fuqahā' abṭāl,* 153).

133. Nikita Elisséeff, "Les Monuments de Nūr ad-Dīn," *Bulletin d'études orientales* 13 (1949–51): 5–49, esp. 17, 31–33; idem, *Nūr al-Dīn,* 3 vols. (Damascus: Institut français de Damas, 1967), 3: 933–34.

Zayn al-Dīn states that the time he spent at the Nūrīyah *madrasah* was especially pleasant and rewarding, adding that he taught law there according to the five *madhhabs*—that is, according to the Twelver Shiite tradition in addition to the four Sunni *madhhabs*:

> Then we stayed in Ba'labakk and taught there for a time in the five *madhhabs* and in many subsidiary fields (*funūn*). We associated with its inhabitants in the best manner, irrespective of their opinions, and lived among them in an ideal fashion. Those were days of good fortune and times of joy, the likes of which our fellows [i.e., Twelver Shiites] have never seen, in any age.[134]

His student Ibn al-'Awdī adds to this description:

> I was in his service in those days, and I will never forget how he enjoyed the highest status, [serving as] an authority for the people and a recourse for high and low alike, granting legal opinions to each group according to its *madhhab,* and teaching the works of each *madhhab.* He held a lesson in the Great Mosque in addition to that which he has mentioned above, and all the inhabitants of the town came to follow him and obey his wishes, with hearts filled with affection and kindness for him as well as faith in him. The market of learning prospered there as well as one could possibly wish, learned men would come from far and wide to consult him, and the honor of Sayyids and our fellows increased. For them, those days were like festivals.[135]

These statements show that Zayn al-Dīn taught both Sunni and Twelver Shiite law and imply in addition that he granted legal opinions to both Sunnis and Shiites. He subsequently left the position, returning to a life of private teaching and writing in Jubā'. He was executed by Ottoman officials about ten years later, in 965/1558.

Ḥusayn b. 'Abd al-Ṣamad al-'Āmilī (d. 984/1576)

Ḥusayn b. 'Abd al-Ṣamad al-'Āmilī[136] was a companion of al-Shahīd al-Thānī and also a native of the town of Jubā'. He eventually became a leading legal authority in the Safavid Empire during the reign of Shah Ṭahmāsb, and served as *shaykh al-islām* of the capital, Qazvin. In his younger years he accompanied al-Shahīd al-Thānī to Egypt, along with his cousin 'Alī b. Zuhrah, and pursued an education there similar if not identical to that described above, in-

134. 'Alī al-'Āmilī, *al-Durr al-manthūr,* 2: 182.

135. Ibid.

136. On this scholar in general, see Devin J. Stewart, "The First *Shaykh al-Islām* of the Safavid Capital Qazvin," *JAOS* 116 (1996): 387–405, and the sources cited therein.

cluding extensive work in Shāfi'ī law and legal theory. He traveled twice to Istanbul to petition for a teaching position at a Sunni *madrasah,* once on his own in 945/1539, and again in 951–52/1545–46 with al-Shahīd al-Thānī. On both occasions, Ḥusayn presumably presented himself as an accomplished Shāfi'ī jurist.

Ḥusayn was born on 1 Muḥarram 918/19 March 1512 in Jubā'.[137] He completed his studies and travels in his younger years as a constant companion of al-Shahīd al-Thānī.[138] He studied first with Sayyid Ja'far al-Karakī (d. 936/1530) in Karak Nūḥ.[139] Later, he studied with al-Shahīd al-Thānī in Jubā' and received a lengthy *ijāzah* from him on 3 Jumādā II 941/10 December 1534.[140] The sources do not report that Ḥusayn studied with Al-Shahīd al-Thānī in Damascus during the latter's first stay there, in 937/1530–31, but it seems very likely that he accompanied him there during his second stay, in 942/1535, since they left for Egypt directly from Damascus. In Cairo, Ḥusayn presumably followed a course of study quite similar to that recorded by al-Shahīd al-Thānī. Like al-Shahīd al-Thānī, he probably studied Shāfi'ī law and legal methodology with Shihāb al-Dīn al-Ramlī, Abū al-Ḥasan al-Bakrī, and Shihāb al-Dīn Aḥmad b. 'Abd al-Ḥaqq al-Sinbāṭī. The works he studied must have included al-Nawawī's *Minhāj al-ṭālibīn,* the standard Shāfi'ī legal text of the day, al-Ījī's commentary on the *Mukhtaṣar* of Ibn al-Ḥājib, al-Juwaynī's *Waraqāt,* and al-Subkī's *Jam' al-jawāmi'.* Like al-Shahīd al-Thānī, he probably collected a number of *ijāzah*s from his Sunni teachers to attest to his accomplishments in law and other fields.

In 945/1539, not long after returning to Jubā' from his studies in Cairo and a subsequent pilgrimage to Mecca, Ḥusayn traveled to Istanbul, probably in order to petition for a post as *mudarris.* He wrote an anthology on ethical topics entitled *Nūr al-ḥaqīqah wa-nawr al-ḥadīqah,* "The Light of Truth and the Blossoms of Paradise," which he directed to a Sunni audience and dedicated to the Ottoman sultan, Suleiman. In the work, Ḥusayn presented himself as a Shāfi'ī jurist. In the autographed copy he presented to Ottoman officials, he signed his name "Ḥusayn b. 'Abd al-Ṣamad al-'Āmilī *al-Shāfi'ī* al-Ḥārithī al-Hamdānī," explicitly claiming adherence to the Shāfi'ī legal *madhhab.* He may have been successful in this plea and been appointed to a *madrasah* in Iraq, but the sources are reticent on this point.[141]

137. al-Iṣfahānī, *Riyāḍ al-'ulamā',* 2: 110.

138. 'Alī al-'Āmilī, *al-Durr al-manthūr,* 2: 149–98.

139. See Ḥusayn b. 'Abd al-Ṣamad al-Ḥārithī al-'Āmilī, *Arba'ūn ḥadīth,* ed. Ḥusayn 'Alī Maḥfūz (Tehran: Maṭba'at al-ḥaydarī, 1957), 2; idem, *Wuṣūl al-akhyār ilā uṣūl al-akhbār,* 39. Zayn al-Dīn reports that he went to Karak Nūḥ to study with this same teacher from Dhū al-ḥijjah 933/September 1527 until Jumādā II 934/February-March 1528.

140. Majlisī, *Biḥār al-anwār,* 108: 146–71.

141. See Stewart, "Ḥusayn b. 'Abd al-Ṣamad al-'Āmilī's Treatise."

Seven years later, in 952/1545, Ḥusayn traveled once again to Istanbul, this time accompanied by al-Shahīd al-Thānī. On this trip, they both obtained appointments as professors of law, al-Shahīd al-Thānī at the Nūrīyah *madrasah* in Ba'labakk and Ḥusayn at a *madrasah* in Baghdad. Ḥusayn was not pleased when he found that the *madrasah* to which the *qāḍī al-'askar* had assigned him lacked adequate endowment funds, and he stayed behind three weeks trying to exchange his position for a different one. He and al-Shahīd al-Thānī then traveled to Iraq and may have evaluated Ḥusayn's new position. It appears that Ḥusayn did not assume the post after all, returning to Jubā' instead.[142] He then accompanied al-Shahīd al-Thānī to Ba'labakk, where the latter was teaching at the Nūrīyah *madrasah*.[143] Ḥusayn presumably served as a repetitor or teaching assistant for al-Shahīd al-Thānī during his time at the Nūrīyah.

Bahā' al-Dīn al-'Āmilī (d. 1030/1621)

Bahā' al-Dīn Muḥammad al-'Āmilī,[144] the son of Ḥusayn b. 'Abd al-Ṣamad, became famous as the *shaykh al-islām* of Isfahan and the leading legal authority in Safavid Iran for most of the reign of Shah 'Abbās (995–1038/1587–1629). He was born in Ba'labakk in 953/1547 and raised in Iran after his father emigrated there ca. 960/1552–53. He completed his studies in Iran and became the *shaykh al-islām* or *muftī* of Isfahan ca. 984/1576. Already a jurist and scholar of some standing, he returned to Ottoman territory in 991/1583, following the example of his father and al-Shahīd al-Thānī, in order to engage in learned exchanges with scholars in Aleppo, Damascus, Cairo, Jerusalem, and Mecca. Bahā' al-Dīn's travels and studies in the Ottoman Empire between 991/1583 and 993/1585 indicate that he was particularly interested in Sunni hadith and *tafsīr* and that he went to considerable lengths to present himself as a Sunni scholar. He wrote a treatise on the exegesis of verse 23 of *Sūrat al-baqarah* which he probably dedicated to the Ottoman sultan Murād III (982–1003/1574–95) and in which he presented himself as a Sunni. He received an *ijāzah* from the Shāfi'ī *muftī* of Jerusalem, which shows that he claimed to be a Sunni and presumably a Shāfi'ī as well; the document states that he was a descendant of the famous Shāfi'ī jurist al-Ghazālī.[145] According to some reports, Bahā' al-Dīn pretended to be a Shāfi'ī in an encounter with a Sunni scholar in Damascus.[146]

142. 'Alī al-'Āmilī, *al-Durr al-manthūr*, 2: 175, 177, 182.

143. We know of Ḥusayn's whereabouts because his son Bahā' al-Dīn Muḥammad was born in Ba'labakk on 27 Dhu 'l-ḥijjah 953/18 February 1547 (al-Iṣfahānī, *Riyāḍ al-'ulamā'*, 2: 110).

144. On Bahā' al-Dīn al-'Āmilī in general, see Andrew Newman, "Towards a Reconsideration of the 'Isfahan School of Philosophy,'" *Studia Iranica* 15 (1986): 165–99; Etan Kohlberg, "Bahā' al-Dīn 'Āmelī," *Encyclopaedia Iranica* (1989), 3: 429–30; Stewart, "Biographical Notice"; idem, "*Taqiyyah* as Performance," *Princeton Papers in Near Eastern Studies* 4 (1996): 1–70, and the sources cited therein.

145. See Stewart, "Taqiyyah as Performance."

146. al-Khwānsārī, *Rawḍāt al-jannāt*, 7: 71.

These brief synopses present the most salient figures in the Twelver Shiite tradition of participation in the Shāfiʿī *madhhab*. The list is by no means exhaustive, and further research will undoubtedly reveal other participants in the tradition from various historical periods and regions of the Islamic world. Al-Muḥaqqiq al-Ḥillī and Ibn Dā'ūd al-Ḥillī, like al-ʿAllāmah al-Ḥillī, probably studied Sunni law in Baghdad, and Muḥammad b. Abī Bakr al-Sakākīnī (d. 721/1321) probably studied Sunni law in Damascus, though the sources do not provide explicit indications that they did so. This tradition did not stop with Bahā' al-Dīn al-ʿĀmilī in the seventeenth century, but continued intermittently until the innovation of the field of "comparative law" in the twentieth century made the study of Sunni and Shiite law possible within a different, somewhat less polemic, framework. In fact, the famous nineteenth-century reformer Jamāl al-Dīn al-Afghānī may be seen as a participant in this tradition. A native Iranian who hid his Shiite background by claiming to hail from Afghanistan, al-Afghānī benefited from a traditional Shiite religious training before engaging in reform activities in Afghanistan and Egypt. Though his career differs from most of those scholars mentioned above in that he claimed affiliation with the Ḥanafī *madhhab* rather than the Shāfiʿī and did not participate in the Shiite legal tradition in his later career, he nevertheless followed strategies similar to those used by earlier Twelver jurists.

SHIITES IN SUNNI COLLEGES OF LAW

Shiite scholars participated in legal studies, both as students and teachers, in Sunni *madrasahs*. That Shiites studied and taught in Sunni *madrasahs* in addition to more private settings, such as teachers' homes, indicates they were probably passing as Sunnis while doing so and claiming to have adopted one of the Sunni *madhhabs*. Because the *madrasahs* were exclusive institutions, "admitting students who belonged to one or the other juridical *madhhab*, to the exclusion of all others,"[147] a student who enrolled to receive a stipend from the endowment funds of the *madrasah* had to declare an affiliation with a particular Sunni *madhhab*. Twelver Shiites generally opted for affiliation with the Shāfiʿī *madhhab* while studying in these Sunni institutions.

There are many explicit indications that Shiites studied and taught in Sunni *madrasahs*. To summarize: Ibn Millī al-Baʿlabakkī held a position as repetitor at the Niẓāmīyah *madrasah*, an expressly Shāfiʿī institution, in Baghdad. He held a post as *mudarris* at the Bābāsīyah *madrasah* in Aswan. Al-Ṭūfī taught as a repetitor of Ḥanbalī law in the Manṣūrīyah and Nāṣirīyah *madrasahs* in Cairo. Al-Shahīd al-Thānī studied hadith under Ibn Ṭūlūn in the Salīmīyah *madrasah* in al-Ṣāliḥīyah in Damascus. He was accompanied by

147. Makdisi, "Guilds of Law," 1: 233–52, esp. 242.

his student-servitor Bahā' al-Dīn Muḥammad al-'Awdī and perhaps other Shiite companions as well. Both al-Shahīd al-Thānī and Ḥusayn b. 'Abd al-Ṣamad al-'Āmilī obtained appointments as professors of law at Sunni *madrasahs* from the Ottoman government in 952/1545, al-Shahīd al-Thānī at the Shāfi'ī Nūrīyah *madrasah* in Ba'labakk and Ḥusayn at a *madrasah* in Baghdad. Al-Shahīd al-Thānī taught at the Nūrīyah *madrasah* for nearly two years, and Ḥusayn accompanied him there and perhaps taught at the *madrasah* as a repetitor or assistant. It is clear in the bulk of these cases that the Twelver Shiite scholars in question were passing as Sunni jurists and Shāfi'īs in particular; and that enabled them to gain access to exclusive environments.

Additional circumstantial evidence suggests that Shiite scholars studied in Sunni *madrasahs* more extensively than we have realized. Ibn Millī al-Ba'labakkī probably was enrolled as a Shāfi'ī student at a *madrasah* when he studied under the famous Shāfi'ī jurist 'Abd al-'Azīz b. 'Abd al-Salām in Damascus. Al-Ṭūfī probably studied Ḥanbalī law under al-Zarīrātī at the Mustanṣirīyah in Baghdad. Ibn al-Muṭahhar al-Ḥillī does not mention any *madrasahs* when he lists his Sunni teachers, but Jamāl al-Dīn Ḥusayn b. Ayāz al-Naḥwī was the lecturer on grammar at the Mustanṣirīyah, Shams al-Dīn Muḥammad b. Muḥammad b. Aḥmad al-Kīshī was the professor of Shāfi'ī law at the Niẓāmīyah, and Burhān al-Dīn al-Nasafī probably taught at the Mustanṣirīyah as well. It seems quite likely that al-Ḥillī studied at both institutions.

Al-Shahīd al-Awwal does not state explicitly that he studied at a *madrasah*, but he mentions both the Niẓāmīyah and the Mustanṣirīyah in Baghdad. He relates al-Bukhārī's *Ṣaḥīḥ* through Sharaf al-Dīn Muḥammad b. Biktāsh al-Tustarī, a Shāfi'ī who had settled in Baghdad and become the professor of Shāfi'ī law at the Niẓāmīyah. He also relates this hadith compilation through Shams al-Dīn Abū 'Abd al-Raḥmān Muḥammad b. 'Abd al-Raḥmān, a Mālikī professor of law at the Mustanṣirīyah. Al-Shahīd al-Awwal mentions the Mustanṣirīyah twice, and both times writes the blessing "May God be pleased with its founder" (*riḍwānu 'Llāhi 'alā munshi'ihā*) following the name of the *madrasah*.[148] This blessing shows that he had some respect for the Abbasid caliph al-Mustanṣir (623–40/1226–42), something quite odd given the typical Shiite view of the Abbasid caliphs as usurpers of an office that rightfully belonged to the Shiite imams. Al-Shahīd al-Awwal's expressed attitude might suggest that he had studied there, perhaps as the recipient of a stipend from the endowment, and consequently felt a debt of gratitude toward the *madrasah*'s founder. In addition, it would seem unnecessary or superfluous for him to mention that these two professors taught in these *madrasahs* unless he

148. Majlisī, *Biḥār al-anwār*, 107: 200.

had studied with them in that context or to include such a blessing on mentioning the *madrasah* unless he wished to express some degree of appreciation for the institution itself.

While in Cairo in the late fifteenth century, ʿAlī b. ʿAbd al-ʿĀlī al-Karakī studied with the leading jurist of the Shāfiʿīs, Zakarīyā al-Anṣārī, probably at one of Cairo's prominent *madrasahs*, perhaps at the great mosque-*madrasah* of al-Azhar. Al-Karakī's studies with Kamāl al-Dīn Ibn Abī Sharīf may have taken place at the Mu'ayyadīyah *madrasah* in Cairo or at a *madrasah* in Jerusalem. Al-Shahīd al-Thānī studied Shāfiʿī law and legal methodology with the leading Shāfiʿī jurist of his day, Shihāb al-Dīn Aḥmad al-Ramlī, and several other leading Shāfiʿī jurists during his stay in Cairo in 942–43/1535–37. His companions Ḥusayn b. ʿAbd al-Ṣamad and ʿAlī b. Zuhrah presumably studied under the same teachers. They probably studied under al-Ramlī at al-Azhar, as al-Karakī had before them under al-Anṣārī. In addition, their legal studies under Shihāb al-Dīn Aḥmad b. ʿAbd al-Ḥaqq al-Sinbāṭī and Abū al-Ḥasan al-Bakrī almost certainly took place at Shāfiʿī *madrasahs* in Cairo.

SHĀFIʿĪ/SHIITE LEGAL TEXTBOOKS

It is not surprising that the Shiite curriculum of legal study included Sunni works on the preparatory sciences, such as Arabic syntax and morphology, rhetoric, and logic, but that Sunni works on *uṣūl al-fiqh* became standard textbooks in the Shiite legal curriculum raises important questions. Two Sunni works on jurisprudence became extremely influential in the Twelver Shiite legal tradition, and, judging from the evidence, formed a standard part of the Shiite legal curriculum from the fourteenth until the end of the eighteenth century. These two works were the *Mukhtaṣar* of the thirteenth-century grammarian and Mālikī jurist Ibn al-Ḥājib and the commentary on this work, known as *al-Sharḥ al-ʿAḍudī*, by the fourteenth-century theologian and Shāfiʿī jurist ʿAḍud al-Dīn ʿAbd al-Raḥmān al-Ījī. Muḥsin al-Amīn notes that for a lengthy period the standard *uṣūl al-fiqh* works studied in the Shiite curriculum were al-ʿAllāmah al-Ḥillī's *Tahdhīb al-wuṣūl*, followed by the *Mukhtaṣar* of Ibn al-Ḥājib and *al-Sharḥ al-ʿAḍudī*. He adds that Ḥasan b. Zayn al-Dīn al-ʿĀmilī's work *Maʿālim al-Dīn*, completed in the late sixteenth or early seventeenth century, eventually replaced *Tahdhīb al-wuṣūl* in the curriculum.[149] The two Sunni works were replaced first by *Qawānīn al-uṣūl*, completed in 1205/1791 by Mīrzā Abū 'l-Qāsim al-Qummī (d. 1231/1816), then, during Muḥsin al-Amīn's own lifetime, by *al-Kifāyah* of Mullā Kāẓim al-Khurāsānī (d. 1329/1911).[150]

149. In recent scholarship, a number of authors erroneously attribute *al-Maʿālim* to al-Shahīd al-Thānī rather than his son: Sachedina, *Islamic Messianism;* Said Arjomand, *Shadow of God*, 140.

150. Mīrzā Abū al-Qāsim al-Qummī, *Qawānīn al-uṣūl* (Tehran, 1275/1858–59), 446; Muḥsin al-Amīn, *Khiṭaṭ Jabal ʿĀmil*, ed. Ḥasan al-Amīn (Beirut: al-Dār al-ʿālamīyah, 1983), 188.

Ibn Ḥājib was a Mālikī jurist, but his *Mukhtaṣar*—an abridgment of one of his own works, entitled *Muntahā al-sūl wa'l-amal fī 'ilmayy al-uṣūl wa'l-jadal*—was used by scholars of all the Sunni *madhhabs*, and became particularly influential in the Shāfi'ī *madhhab*. Al-Ījī's commentary on the work, completed in 734/1334, became one of the most important Shāfi'ī textbooks of *uṣūl al-fiqh*, as is evident from the large number of supercommentaries on the work written by such Shāfi'ī jurists as Sa'd al-Dīn al-Taftazānī and al-Sharīf al-Jurjānī.[151] The use of these works as textbooks in Shiite circles is attested to by the large number of commentaries and supercommentaries that Shiite scholars wrote on them as a result of teaching and studying them repeatedly.

Al-'Allāmah al-Ḥillī transmitted the *Mukhtaṣar* of Ibn al-Ḥājib through his Shāfi'ī teacher, Ibn Ayāz al-Naḥwī, as mentioned above. He did not merely obtain permission to transmit the work; his extensive involvement with Sunni legal scholarship is demonstrated by the commentary he wrote on the *Mukhtaṣar*, entitled *Ghāyat al-wuṣūl wa-īḍāḥ al-subul fī sharḥ Mukhtaṣar Muntahā al-sūl wa'l-amal*, which he completed on 12 Rajab 697/25 April 1298.[152] The Damascene Sunni scholar Ibn Kathīr (d. 774/1373–74) states that this commentary was the most famous of al-Ḥillī's works among law students, indicating that it was known and used in Sunni circles, but adds that it did not entirely deserve its excellent reputation.[153] Ibn Ḥajar al-'Asqalānī (d. 852/1449) reports that the commentary conveyed the meaning of the original work excellently and made it easily accessible to the student.[154]

The Shiite scholar Tāj al-Dīn Ḥusayn b. Shams al-Dīn al-Ṣā'idī wrote a supercommentary on al-Sharīf al-Jurjānī's commentary on the *Mukhtaṣar* of Ibn al-Ḥājib in 977/1569–70. He had studied the commentary of al-Jurjānī with Manṣūr Rāst-gū b. al-Mawlā 'Abd Allāh al-Shīrāzī in 969/1561–62. Manṣūr Rāst-gū also wrote a supercommentary on al-Jurjānī's commentary.[155] Supercommentaries on *al-Sharḥ al-'Aḍudī* are known to have been written by the following Shiite scholars:[156]

1. Mullā Kamāl al-Dīn Ḥusayn b. 'Abd al-Ḥaqq al-Ālihī (d. 950/1543–44), who also wrote a *ta'līqah* on the same.
2. Mīrzā Jān Ḥabīb Allāh al-Bāghawī al-Shīrāzī (fl. 10th/16th c.).
3. Aḥmad b. Muḥammad al-Muqaddas al-Ardabīlī (d. 993/1585).
4. Mullā 'Abd al-Wāḥid b. 'Alī al-Tustarī (fl. late 16th c.).

151. See Brockelmann, *GAL*, 1: 306, supp. 1: 537–38.
152. al-Ṭihrānī, *al-Dharī'ah*, 16: 13, 24–25.
153. Ibn Kathīr, *al-Bidāyah wa'l-nihāyah*, 14: 125.
154. Ibn Ḥajar al-'Asqalānī, *al-Durar al-kāminah*, 2: 71.
155. al-Ṭihrānī, *al-Dharī'ah*, 6: 128, 129.
156. Ibid., 129–32.

5. Mullā ʿAbd Allāh b. al-Ḥusayn al-Tustarī (d. 1021/1612).
6. Bahāʾ al-Dīn Muḥammad b. Ḥusayn al-ʿĀmilī (d. 1030/1621).[157]
7. Mīr Muḥammad Bāqir b. Muḥammad al-Dāmād (d. 1040/1631).
8. Sulṭān al-ʿUlamāʾ Mīr ʿAlāʾ al-Dīn Ḥusayn b. Rafīʿ al-Dīn al-Ḥusaynī al-Āmulī al-Iṣfahānī (d. 1064/1653–54).
9. Mullā Muḥammad Ṣāliḥ b. Aḥmad al-Māzandarānī (d. 1081/1670–71).
10. Muḥammad b. al-Ḥasan al-Shīrwānī (d. 1098/1687–88).
11. Mīrzā Rafīʿ al-Dīn Muḥammad b. Ḥaydar al-Ḥusaynī al-Ṭabāṭabāʾī al-Nāʾīnī (d. 1099/1688).
12. Āghā Jamāl al-Dīn b. Ḥusayn al-Khwānsārī (d. 1125/1712–13).
13. Mīrzā ʿAbd Allāh al-Iṣfahānī, author of *Riyāḍ al-ʿulamāʾ* (d. ca. 1130/1717–18).
14. Āghā Muḥammad Mahdī b. Muḥammad Hādī b. Ṣāliḥ al-Māzandarānī (d. 1134/1722).
15. Mīrzā Abū al-Qāsim al-Qummī (d. 1231/1816).

The famous jurist Muḥammad Bāqir al-Waḥīd al-Bihbihānī, who died in 1205/1791, wrote a commentary on the above-mentioned supercommentary of al-Shīrwānī.[158] This list provides a mere indication of the importance of *al-Sharḥ al-ʿAḍudī* in the Shiite tradition. Many other Shiite jurists' commentaries on the work are probably extant in collections in Iraq and Iran that Āghā Buzurg al-Ṭihrānī did not consult, and many others have been lost.

As seen above, al-Shahīd al-Awwal studied *al-Sharḥ al-ʿAḍudī* with a Sunni scholar in Baghdad. Al-Shahīd al-Thānī studied this work in Cairo with Egypt's leading Shāfiʿī jurist. Ḥasan b. Zayn al-Dīn al-ʿĀmilī and Muḥammad b. Abī al-Ḥasan al-ʿĀmilī studied *al-Sharḥ al-ʿAḍudī* with the Shiite jurist Aḥmad al-Ardabīlī (d. 993/1585) in Iraq in the late sixteenth century. A large number of students were studying this work with al-Ardabīlī at the time; they were supposedly jealous of the two ʿĀmilīs' superior command of Arabic.[159] Muḥammad Amīn al-Astarābādī (d. 1036/1627) studied this work in Shiraz in the late sixteenth or early seventeenth century, referring to it as a Shāfiʿī text and identifying it as the best Sunni work on *uṣūl al-fiqh*.[160] Writing in 1073/1662, Ḥusayn b. Shihāb al-Dīn al-Karakī (d. 1076/1665–66) goes so far as to state that, during his day in Iran, no Shiite scholar is considered versed in jurisprudence unless he has studied *al-Sharḥ al-ʿAḍudī* and its commentaries, just as any scholar of *tafsīr* must have studied the exegesis of al-Bayḍāwī, and any

157. See also al-Ḥurr al-ʿĀmilī, *Amal al-āmil*, 1: 155.
158. al-Ṭirānī, *al-Dharīʿah*, 6: 76.
159. ʿAlī al-ʿĀmilī, *al-Durr al-manthūr*, 2: 201.
160. Muḥammad Amīn al-Astarābādī, *al-Fawāʾid al-madanīyah* (Tehran, 1904), 18–19.

philosopher or theologian must have spent a lifetime studying the works of al-Dawwānī and others.[161] In one of his legal textbooks, al-Shahīd al-Thānī advises that the legal scholar does not have to expend a great deal of effort studying the methods of logical proof (*sharā'iṭ al-dalīl*), for most of the relevant information is contained in the shorter works on *uṣūl al-fiqh*, such as al-'Allāmah al-Ḥillī's work *Tahdhīb al-wuṣūl* and the *Mukhtaṣar* of Ibn al-Ḥājib.[162] That Twelver Shiite jurists studied *al-Sharḥ al-'Aḍudī* from the fourteenth until the late eighteenth century and wrote such a substantial number of commentaries on the work demonstrates the extent of the *madhhab* system's influence on Shiite legal education and indicates a more than coincidental or random link between Shiite jurisprudence and the Shāfi'ī *madhhab* in particular.

Al-'Allāmah's work *Tahdhīb al-wuṣūl*, which became a standard textbook of *uṣūl al-fiqh* in the Shiite curriculum, was considered by a seventeenth-century Shiite scholar to be a product of the Sunni tradition of *uṣūl al-fiqh* works.[163] Ibn Kathīr mentions that he examined one of al-Ḥillī's works on *uṣūl al-fiqh* besides the commentary on Ibn al-Ḥājib's work, although he does not give the exact title: "I have seen two volumes by him on *uṣūl al-fiqh*, written according to the method of *al-Maḥṣūl* and *al-Iḥkām*. It was quite good (*fa-lā ba's bihā*), for it contained extensive citations (*naql kathīr*) and excellent explanations (*tawjīh jayyid*)."[164] The work in question must have been one of al-Ḥillī's works on Shiite *uṣūl al-fiqh*, probably *Nihāyat al-wuṣūl ilā 'ilm al-uṣūl*, his most extensive discussion of legal methodology, which he completed on 8 Ramaḍān 704/4 April 1305.[165] Coming from a Sunni jurist, Ibn Kathīr's comparison of *al-Nihāyah* with the Shāfi'ī *uṣūl al-fiqh* texts of Fakhr al-Dīn al-Rāzī and Sayf al-Dīn al-Āmidī is high praise for a Twelver Shiite legal work.

DISSIMULATION AND THE SHIITE SHĀFI'Ī TRADITION

Dissimulation, or *taqīyah*, has played a major role in the Shiite Shāfi'ī tradition.[166] The Shiite jurists introduced above often concealed their true beliefs and modified their identities in order to participate more fully in Sunni education and juridical institutions. While it is difficult to gauge from the historical record to what extent they dissimulated, it is clear that many of the participants in this tradition studied and taught in environments where open admis-

161. al-Karakī, *Hidāyat al-abrār*, 95, 220.

162. Zayn al-Dīn al-'Āmilī, *al-Rawḍah al-bahīyah fī sharḥ al-lum'ah al-dimashqīyah*, 10 vols. (Najaf: Maṭba'at al-ādāb, 1967), 3: 65.

163. al-Astarābādī, *al-Fawā'id al-madanīyah*, 277–78.

164. Ibn Kathīr, *al-Bidāyah wa'l-nihāyah*, 14: 125.

165. Schmidtke, *Theology*, 66.

166. On this topic, see Stewart, "Taqiyyah as Performance"; idem, "Ḥusayn b. 'Abd al-Ṣamad's Treatise."

sion of Shiite faith would have discredited them among their colleagues if not put them in grave danger. That this danger was real is shown not only by the experiences of the two martyrs Muḥammad b. Makkī al-Jizzīnī and Zayn al-Dīn al-ʿĀmilī but also by al-Ṭūfī's loss of his teaching position, punishment, imprisonment, and subsequent banishment. Particular methods that Shiite jurists adopted in their performances of *taqīyah* may nevertheless be identified through careful reading of the sources. Salient methods included the modification of one's name, particularly the *nisbah,* the adjectival appellation often designating one's place of origin or residence. Al-Shahīd al-Awwal, for example, avoided revealing his *nisbah* al-Jizzīnī to his Sunni teacher al-Kirmānī in Baghdad, instead using the *nisbah* al-Dimashqī. Similarly, both Ḥusayn b. ʿAbd al-Ṣamad al-ʿĀmilī and his son Bahāʾ al-Dīn avoided using the *nisbah* al-ʿĀmilī when addressing Sunni audiences, using instead the *nisbah* al-Ḥārithī al-Hamdānī derived from the name of their reputed ancestor al-Ḥārith b. ʿAbd Allāh al-Aʿwar of the Arab tribe of Hamdān (d. 65/684–85), a companion of ʿAlī b. Abī Ṭālib.[167] On occasion, performers modified their genealogy (*nasab*) as well; Bahāʾ al-Dīn on at least one occasion claimed descent from the renowned Shāfiʿī jurist al-Ghazālī.

Documents served as props for maintaining a Sunni identity. Many Shiite jurists, including al-Shahīd al-Awwal, ʿAlī al-Karakī, al-Shahīd al-Thānī, Ḥusayn b. ʿAbd al-Ṣamad al-ʿĀmilī, and Bahāʾ al-Dīn al-ʿĀmilī, assiduously collected *ijāzahs* from Sunni scholars, and in a number of cases must have presented themselves as Sunnis in doing so. For example, al-Shahīd al-Awwal sent a written petition for an *ijāzah (istidʿāʾ)* to the Koran expert al-Jazarī with his name signed "al-Shāfiʿī." Bahāʾ al-Dīn al-ʿĀmilī also presented himself as a Sunni when requesting an *ijāzah* from Ibn Abī al-Luṭf al-Maqdisī, the Shāfiʿī *muftī* of Jerusalem. In addition, many Shiite jurists wrote books and treatises which were ostensibly Sunni in ideological content as part of their performances of *taqīyah.* Ḥusayn b. ʿAbd al-Ṣamad's *Nūr al-ḥaqīqah wa-nawr al-ḥadīqah,* which he dedicated to the Ottoman sultan Suleiman in 945/1539, presents itself as a Sunni text written by a Shāfiʿī author. The treatise al-Shahīd al-Thānī wrote in Istanbul for the Qāḍī al-ʿaskar Muḥammad b. Quṭb al-Dīn Qāḍī-zādah al-Rūmī, when seeking an appointment in 952/1545, must have been similar. Yet another ostensibly Sunni text is the treatise on *tafsīr* Bahāʾ al-Dīn al-ʿĀmilī probably dedicated to the Ottoman sultan Murād III.

Much information concerning Shiite jurists who passed as Sunnis and the measures they adopted in doing so has been lost, and much information has evidently been suppressed either by the claimants themselves or by later scholars in the Shiite tradition. We know from Bahāʾ al-Dīn's treatise on *tafsīr,* from

167. On al-Ḥārith, see al-Amīn, *Aʿyān al-shīʿah,* 4: 365–70.

the Chester Beatty MS of Ḥusayn b. ʿAbd al-Ṣamad's work *Nūr al-ḥaqīqah,* and from other less direct indications that Shiite jurists often suppressed information concerning the extent to which they dissimulated their Shiite identity.[168] This practice of course makes it more difficult to identify Shiite jurists who passed as Shāfiʿīs and to examine the methods they used in doing so. Careful examination of extant works and documents, both published and unpublished, may nevertheless provide additional glimpses of the Twelver Shiite tradition of participation in the Shāfiʿī *madhhab.*

TWELVER SHIITE ATTRACTION TO THE SHĀFIʿĪ *MADHHAB*

The historical evidence presented above reveals a tradition of association with the Shāfiʿī *madhhab* on the part of Twelver Shiite jurists that lasted from the beginning of the tenth until the seventeenth century and probably beyond. Why, in the overwhelming majority of cases, Twelvers preferred association with the Shāfiʿī *madhhab* in particular remains to be explained. Societal pressure to claim affiliation with one of the Sunni *madhhabs* is clear, but if this were the only factor one would expect to find a more or less even distribution of affiliations among the Shiites, determined, for the most part, by geographic origin or opportunism. In a few cases, such circumstances may have been the determining factor. ʿImād al-Dīn and Tāj al-Dīn al-Jaʿfarī probably adopted the Ḥanafī *madhhab* expressly in order to benefit from Seljuk patronage and gain positions as *muftīs*. Al-Ṭūfī, from the area of Ṣarṣar near Baghdad, chose affiliation at a very early stage with the Ḥanbalī *madhhab* perhaps because that was the dominant *madhhab* in the immediate vicinity. Jamāl al-Dīn al-Afghānī claimed affiliation with the Ḥanafī *madhhab* perhaps because that was the leading *madhhab* in Ottoman Egypt and because to do otherwise would contradict the persona he had constructed out of *taqīyah.* It was well known that Afghanistan, his supposed country of origin, was entirely a Ḥanafī region. Al-Ḥurr al-ʿĀmilī reports that it would do no good for a Shiite scholar to claim to be a Shāfiʿī in the Maghrib because the region was entirely Mālikī. If adopted merely as a protective measure to avoid accusations of heresy or religious deviance, one's choice of *madhhab* would of course be influenced by the surrounding environment. Thus, the Khārijīs of North Africa, for example, must have claimed adherence to the Mālikī *madhhab* when necessary.

Nevertheless, the examples of al-Ṭūfī, the Jaʿfarīs, and al-Afghānī remain isolated cases in a long tradition that spanned many centuries, political regimes, and social environments. The maintenance of such a strong affiliation with the Shāfiʿī *madhhab* throughout the centuries and in different areas cannot be explained merely as opportunism or an ad hoc safety measure. It

168. See Stewart, "Ḥusayn b. ʿabd al-Ṣamad al-ʿĀmilī's Treatise."

made sense, perhaps, for al-Baʿlabakkī, al-Jizzīnī, and al-Karakī to adopt the Shāfiʿī *madhhab,* for they lived under Ayyubid and Mamluk rule when Shāfiʿism was officially recognized by the government as the leading *madhhab.*[169] It would have been more advantageous, however, for Zayn a-Dīn al-ʿĀmilī and Ḥusayn b. ʿAbd al-Ṣamad to adopt the Ḥanafī *madhhab,* since to do so would have increased their opportunities to benefit from Ottoman patronage. Similarly, the choice for earlier scholars, such as al-ʿAllāmah al-Ḥillī, al-Masʿūdī, and Muḥammad b. Aḥmad al-Kātib, to adopt the Shāfiʿī *madhhab* could not have been dictated merely by the circumstances of their environment.

It is widely held by the Twelvers themselves that the Shāfiʿī *madhhab* is the closest to their own, particularly with respect to the rulings on specific points of law. Writing in the late seventeenth century, Shihāb al-Dīn al-Karakī held that it was this similarity which attracted Shiite jurists to the Shāfiʿī legal tradition.[170] This claim seems based on a few salient legal issues and is not true in all areas of the law. Twelver Shiite law occasionally agrees more closely with Ḥanafī or Ḥanbalī law in certain areas such as dietary law or the law of sales. Only extensive investigation may provide a more accurate assessment of the relationship between the law of the *madhhabs* for particular periods, works, or legal topics; for the moment one should caution that a blanket statement that the Shāfiʿī *madhhab* is the Sunni legal tradition closest to that of the Twelver Shiites ignores the historical development of the law and risks anachronism. In addition, given the extensive involvement of Twelver jurists in the Shāfiʿī *madhhab* just outlined, one might argue that the similarities between Twelver and Shāfiʿī law developed over time as a result of exchange and borrowing—in either direction—rather than arguing that the Twelver Shiite jurists chose affiliation with the Shāfiʿī *madhhab* because that *madhhab* was from the beginning the closest to their own.

Jaʿfar al-Muhājir, one of the few modern scholars who have drawn attention to the tradition of affiliation with the Shāfiʿī legal school among Twelver Shiite jurists, suggests that when Shiites were forced to hide their true *madhhab* outside their own environment, they always pretended to be Shāfiʿīs and never members in any other legal *madhhab.* This is not entirely the case, as the examples of ʿImād al-Dīn al-Jaʿfarī, Tāj al-Dīn al-Jaʿfarī, and al-Ṭūfī show, but it is a reasonable generalization. He mentions as participants in this tradition al-

169. Heinz Halm identifies the periods of Ayyubid and Baḥrī Mamluk rule in Egypt and Syria—that is, from 549/1169 until 784/1382—as the high point in the spread of the Shāfiʿī *madhhab* (*Die Ausbreitung der šāfiʿitischen Rechtsschule von den Anfangen bis zum 8./14. Jahrhundert* (Weisbaden: L. Reichert, 1974), 7.

170. al-Karakī, *Hidāyat al-abrār,* 152–53; see also al-Ḥurr al-ʿĀmilī, *al-Fawāʾid al-ṭūsīyah,* 467, 470.

Ba'labakkī, al-Shahīd al-Awwal, 'Alī b. 'Abd al-'Ālī al-Karakī, and Bahā' al-Dīn al-'Āmilī. The only reason Ja'far al-Muhājir proposes to explain this phenomenon is al-Shāfi'ī's reputation for Shiite sympathies.[171] Indeed, Twelvers widely hold that al-Shāfi'ī himself was sympathetic to the Shiites and particularly revered the descendants of the Prophet. The sixteenth-century Iranian scholar Mīrzā Makhdūm al-Shīrāzī holds that the Shāfi'īs were well known for their love of *ahl al-bayt,* and Ibn al-Nadīm states in *al-Fihrist* that al-Shāfi'ī was a staunch Shiite (*wa-kāna'sh-Shāfi'īyu shadīdan fi 't-tashayyu'*).[172] Several selections of poetry attributed to al-Shāfi'ī are cited as evidence of his reverence for the descendants of the Prophet, particularly the following verse, which uses the pejorative term *rāfiḍī* "(heretic) Shiite" in a positive sense:

> *in kāna rafḍan ḥubbu āli Muḥammadin*
> *fa-l-yashhad ith-thaqalāni annī rāfiḍī*

> "If love for Muḥammad's family is Shiite heresy (*rafḍ*), then may jinn and men alike bear witness that I am a Shiite heretic (*rāfiḍī*)."[173]

Al-Muhājir remarks that, given al-Shāfi'ī's attachment to *ahl al-bayt,* the Shiite jurist would not feel that by pretending in this way he had undertaken something that was beyond his power.[174] This statement suggests the possibility that by claiming allegiance to al-Shāfi'ī, Shiite jurists could intend, by a sort of mental reservation or verbal ambiguity, that they shared his allegiance to *ahl al-bayt,* rather than confessing literally that they were Sunni jurists, though of course that would be the meaning understood by their Sunni interlocutors. Shāfi'ī's reputed special reverence for the descendants of the Prophet, however, is not a sufficient explanation. The Zaydīs loved *ahl al-bayt* just as much as the Twelvers, yet this did not prevent them from preferring association with the Ḥanafī *madhhab* over the Shāfi'ī *madhhab.* If al-Shāfi'ī's reputed Shiite tendencies were the deciding factor in determining the choice of the Shāfi'ī *madhhab,* one assumes that the Zaydīs would have made the same choice.

Shiite jurists' affiliation with the Shāfi'ī *madhhab* was a tradition, and not simply a series of coincidences. The participants in this tradition were aware that they were following the example of their predecessors, who included some of the most brilliant scholars in Shiite legal history. It could not have been otherwise; they were careful historians of the journeys, studies, and works of their

171. al-Muhājir, *Sittat fuqahā' abṭāl,* 54–55.

172. Mīrzā Makdūm al-Shīrāzī, "al-Nawāqiḍ fī al-rawāfiḍ" (MS, Princeton University Library, Garrett Collection 2629), 139b; Ibn al-Nadīm, *al-Fihrist,* 309.

173. al-Subkī, *Ṭabaqāt al-shāfi'īyah,* 1: 299; al-Khwānsārī, *Rawḍāt al-jannāt,* 7: 261–63.

174. al-Muhājir, *Sittat fuqahā' abṭāl,* 54–55.

predecessors and expended great efforts to collect the *ijāzah*s, notes, and other texts that documented their careers. Al-Shahīd al-Awwal must have been aware of al-ʿAllāmah al-Ḥillī's Shāfiʿī legal studies, and ʿAlī b. ʿAbd al-ʿĀlī al-Karakī knew he was following the example of al-ʿAllāmah al-Ḥillī and al-Shahīd al-Awwal, and so on. These scholars, as well as al-Shahīd al-Thānī, Ḥusayn b. ʿAbd al-Ṣamad, and Bahāʾ al-Dīn al-ʿĀmilī, were consciously participating in an established tradition which they knew had existed for centuries. In order to explain the Twelver Shiite attraction to the Shāfiʿī *madhhab,* one must go back to the beginning of the tradition and examine its early participants who chose that affiliation in particular.

Affiliation with the Shāfiʿī *madhhab* among Twelver or Imāmī Shiites goes back to the tenth century in Baghdad, as the examples of al-Masʿūdī and Muḥammad b. Ibrāhīm al-Kātib demonstrate. Particularly in Baghdad itself, Ḥanbalīs were the great enemies of the Shiites and a constant thorn in their side. Their intolerance would have precluded Shiite participation in the Ḥanbalī *madhhab* at that time. The Ẓāhirī *madhhab* was dwindling, and became extinct in the east in the eleventh century. The same was true of the Jarīrī *madhhab,* of which some of the latest representatives were the judge al-Muʿāfā al-Nahrawānī (d. 390/1000) and the deputy judge Ibrāhīm b. Makhlad (d. 410/1020).[175] The Mālikī *madhhab* as well began waning in the east during this period. The real choices open to Shiites in Baghdad—and in Syria, Iraq, and Iran in general—were the two largest and strongest *madhhab*s in the region: the Shāfiʿī and the Ḥanafī. As mentioned, the Zaydīs tended to side with the Ḥanafīs and the Twelvers with the Shāfiʿīs.

One might suppose that the Twelvers sided with the Shāfiʿīs because the Abbasid caliphs, their Turkish soldiery, and the subsequent regimes of the Ghaznavids, the Seljuks, and the Ottomans, all more or less enemies of the Shiites, traditionally supported the Ḥanafī *madhhab,* and the Shiites naturally chose the opposite. This supposition, however, would fail to explain why the Zaydīs, who opposed the Abbasid caliphs as much if not more fervently than did the Twelvers, ended up affiliating with the Ḥanafī *madhhab.* If opposition to the official *madhhab* of the Abbasids were the key issue, this alliance would not have occurred. It is true that the Buwayhid *amīr*s lent some support to the Shāfiʿīs at the expense of the Ḥanafīs, which may be taken as evidence that the Shiites preferred to deal with the Shāfiʿīs among the Sunni legal schools.[176] In particular, shortly after the Buwayhid conquest of Iraq, Abū al-Sāʾib ʿUtbah b. ʿUbayd Allāh (d. 350/961) became the first Shāfiʿī to be appointed *qāḍī* of Baghdad, serving from 338/949–50 until his death. Before then, the *qāḍī* had always been a Ḥanafī. During the period of Buwayhid control over Baghdad, the

175. Melchert, "Formation of the Sunni Schools of Law," 333.
176. Heribert Busse, *Chalif und Grosskönig* (Weisbaden: Franz Steiner, 1969), 432.

qāḍī of Karkh, the Shiite quarter, was generally a Shāfiʿī. Holders of this office included Muḥammad b. Muḥammad Ibn al-Daqqāq al-Baghdādī (d. 392/1002), al-Bayḍāwī (d. 424/1033), and Abū al-Ṭayyib Ṭāhir b. ʿAbd Allāh al-Ṭabarī (d. 450/1058).[177]

The main reason, it appears, for the Twelvers' decision to follow the Shāfiʿī *madhhab* rather than the Ḥanafī *madhhab* was their traditional rejection of and deep-seated aversion to *qiyās* or analogy, which they associated primarily with the Ḥanafī *madhhab* and very strongly with Abū Ḥanīfah himself. Ḥanafī jurisprudence was characterized by the extensive use of *raʾy*, literally "opinion," and hence its adherents were often labeled *aṣḥāb al-raʾy* as opposed to *aṣḥāb al-ḥadīth*. The Twelvers traditionally viewed the use of *raʾy* with regard to Islamic legal issues as reprehensible and invalid. They had inherited strong warnings against the use of analogy from their imams, and in particular from Jaʿfar al-Ṣādiq.[178] Al-Kulaynī's collection of hadith, *al-Kāfī*, compiled in the early tenth century, includes a section which rejects the use of *raʾy* and *qiyās*.[179] Al-Ṭūsī relates that the Shiites know through reliable sources that the Imams Muḥammad al-Bāqir and Jaʿfar al-Ṣādiq both rejected *qiyās*.[180] Al-Shaykh al-Mufīd, al-Sharīf al-Murtaḍā, and al-Shaykh al-Ṭūsī all rejected the methods of *raʾy*, *ijtihād*, and *qiyās* as being equivalent to arbitrary personal opinion. They considered the Ḥanafīs the chief representatives of unbridled use of arbitrary personal opinion in the law and held that they preferred rational considerations to scriptural texts. They could therefore not justify association with the Ḥanafī *madhhab*.

The Twelvers' aversion to the Ḥanafī *madhhab* and Abū Ḥanīfah himself is quite clear during the Buwayhid period, and spawned literature devoted solely to denigrating the person of Abū Ḥanīfah along with his legal methods. Al-Sharīf al-Murtaḍā criticized Abū Ḥanīfah for arriving at opinions through *raʾy* without offering any textual evidence or precedents.[181] Al-Shaykh al-Mufīd wrote a work entitled *al-Shaykh al-ḍāll* ("The Erring Master"), in which he recounted the disgraces (*faḍāʾiḥ*) of Abū Ḥanīfah.[182] In his treatise *al-Masāʾil al- ṣāghānīyah*, he compares Abū Ḥanīfah unfavorably to Jaʿfar al-Ṣādiq and claims that he willfully contradicted the Prophet, agreeing instead with the devil. He describes Abū Ḥanīfah as "al-Nuʿmān, who is universally held to be outside the pale of faith" (*al-Nuʿmān al-māriqu biʾl-ijmāʿi ʿan il-īmān*).[183] Shiite accounts, perhaps apocryphal, depict Jaʿfar al-Ṣādiq, the sixth

177. Halm, *Ausbreitung*, 157.
178. Zysow, "Economy of Certainty," 498.
179. al-Kulaynnī, *al-Kāfī*, 1: 54–59.
180. al-Ṭūsī, *ʿUddat al-uṣūl*, 263.
181. al-Murtaḍā, *al-Intiṣār*, 3.
182. Ibn Shahrāshūb, *Maʿālim al-ʿulamāʾ*, 101.
183. al-Mufīd, *al-Masāʾil al-ṣāghānīyah*, 15–16.

imam, debating with Abū Ḥanīfah and criticizing him for the use of analogy in religious matters.[184] A Shiite account from the seventeenth century reports that Abū Ḥanīfah was so determined to adopt legal positions contrary to those of Ja'far al-Ṣādiq that he wanted to know whether the imam closed his eyes or opened them when he performed *rukū'* so that he could espouse the opposite opinion.[185] While one may question the authenticity of such reports, the Twelver aversion to analogy clearly dates back at least to the ninth century, and the acerbity of al-Shaykh al-Mufīd's criticisms of Abū Ḥanīfah is striking.

Twelver jurists apparently preferred the more traditionalist methods of the Shāfi'īs, who did not give rational considerations such free rein and relied heavily on scripture, especially hadith reports. In their view, the jurists in the Shāfi'ī tradition took a more moderate position on the relationship of reason to revelation. The Shāfi'ī *madhhab* included a traditionalist branch that allowed for the adoption of a circumspect position with regard to analogical reasoning compatible with the Shiite jurists' own ideology. The antirationalist Ẓāhirīs, who rejected *qiyās* altogether, came out of Shāfi'ī circles and in a way represented the extreme traditionalist wing of the Shāfi'ī *madhhab*.[186] Schacht observes that al-Shāfi'ī recognized *qiyās* only begrudgingly and felt that it left too much room for human authority to shape the interpretation of Islamic law.[187] Later Shāfi'ī scholars who adopted a strong traditionalist position include al-Khaṭīb al-Baghdādī (d. 463/1071), the well-known jurist and hadith expert. He asserts in his presentation of *uṣūl al-fiqh* that there are only three sources of the law—the Koran, the Prophet's *sunnah*, and consensus—and that *qiyās* is acceptable only if used in severely restricted circumstances.[188] It was probably this factor, above all, that made the Shāfi'ī *madhhab* look most appealing to the Twelvers.

The Twelvers' choice of affiliation with the Shāfi'ī *madhhab* was already established in the tenth century. This may be gathered from the Twelver jurists' rejection of the work of Ibn al-Junayd al-Iskāfī. Ibn al-Junayd was a prolific Shiite jurist who lived and taught in Baghdad in the generation before al-Shaykh al-Mufīd, but whose works were repudiated and for the most part ignored by the later Twelver legal tradition. He wrote a twenty-volume work on Shiite law entitled *Tahdhīb al-shī'ah li-aḥkām al-sharī'ah* and arranged according to the method of the jurists (*'alā ṭarīqat al-fuqahā'*). It must have been the most advanced work on Shiite law at the time. He accepted the concepts of

184. For example, see the exchange Ignaz Goldziher reports in *Die Ẓâhirîten* (Leipzig: O. Schulze, 1884), 15.

185. Ni'mat Allāh al-Jazā'irī, *Zahr al-rabī'* (Beirut: Mu'assasat al-balāgh, 1990), 602.

186. Goldziher, *Ẓâhirîten;* idem, *The Ẓāhirīs,* trans. W. Behn (Leiden: E. J. Brill, 1971).

187. Schacht, *Muhammadan Jurisprudence,* 122.

188. al-Khaṭīb al-Baghdādī, *al-Faqīh wa'l-mutafaqqih,* 1: 54, 177, 178–216.

qiyās and *ijtihād,* and wrote works entitled *The Removal of Distortion and Deception for Gullible Shiites Concerning Analogical Reasoning (Kitāb kashf al-tamwīh wa'l-ilbās 'alā aghmār al-shī'ah fī amr al-qiyās)* and *Disclosing Traditions from the Imams Concerning Ijtihād that Our Stubborn Opponents Have Suppressed (Kitāb iẓhār mā satarahu ahl al-'inād min al-riwāyah 'an a'immat al-'itrah fī amr al-ijtihād).*[189] According to al-Shaykh al-Mufīd, Shiite scholars rejected his works and did not pay any attention to them because of his use of *qiyās;* al-Ṭūsī makes a similar statement.[190] Ibn al-Junayd was accepted to a certain extent much later by such jurists as al-'Allāmah al-Ḥillī, but by then most of his works had been lost. Ibn al-Junayd's legal opinions cited in later works such as al-'Allāmah al-Ḥillī's work on Shiite *khilāf, Mukhtalaf al-shī'ah,* show that he made wide use of analogy and often agreed with Ḥanafī positions. It seems likely that he had studied Ḥanafī law extensively. According to al-Mufīd's Ḥanafī interlocutor in *al-Masā'il al-ṣāghānīyah,* Ibn al-Junayd plagiarized his works from Ḥanafī jurists with Mu'tazilī leanings.[191] This accusation corroborates the idea that Ibn al-Junayd had established some sort of affiliation with the Ḥanafī *madhhab.* The shape the Twelver legal tradition was to take over the next several centuries was determined by the Buwayhid jurists al-Shaykh al-Mufīd, al-Sharīf al-Murtaḍā, and al-Shaykh al-Ṭūsī. Their rejection of Ibn al-Junayd's work, which prevented his acceptance as an authority in the Twelver tradition, shows the importance in their legal ideology of the rejection of analogy and, with it, association with the Ḥanafī *madhhab* and Ḥanafī methods of jurisprudence.

Ibn al-Junayd worked in, if not established, a tradition of Shiite jurisprudence with close associations with the Ḥanafī *madhhab.* As it turns out, this tradition was cut off in the history of Twelver law by the end of the tenth century. The same tradition, however, began at roughly the same time and flourished among the Zaydīs. Already in the tenth century, Zaydī jurists opted for affiliation with the Ḥanafī *madhhab* just as Twelver Shiite jurists opted for affiliation with the Shāfi'ī *madhhab.* Among the participants in the Zaydī Ḥanafī tradition was the Zaydī Imam Abū 'Abd Allāh al-Dā'ī Muḥamad b. al-Ḥasan b. al-Qāsim (d. 360/970–71), who studied law with the famous Ḥanafī jurist Abū al-Ḥasan al-Karkhī in Baghdad.[192] The involvement of Zaydīs with Mu'tazilism, which was closely associated with the Ḥanafī legal *madhhab,* is evident in that the Zaydī scholar Sayyid Mānakdīm Aḥmad al-Ḥusaynī (d. 425/1034) wrote a commentary on the Mu'tazilī theology of al-Qāḍī 'Abd

189. al-Ṭūsī, *Fihrist kutub al-shī'ah,* 160; al-Najāshī, *Kitāb al-rijāl,* 301.
190. al-Mufīd, *al-Masā'il al-ṣāghānīyah,* 18; al-Ṭūsī, *Fihrist kutub al-shī'ah,* 160.
191. al-Mufīd, *al-Masā'il al-ṣāghānīyah,* 17.
192. Ibn al-Murtaḍā, *Kitāb Ṭabaqāt al-mu'tazilah,* 113–14.

al-Jabbār.[193] Both the Twelvers and the Zaydīs maintained these traditions for many centuries, even under circumstances which would have dictated otherwise.

CONCLUSION

From the tenth until the seventeenth century, a series of Twelver Shiite jurists, including a number of the most accomplished and innovative thinkers in the history of Twelver jurisprudence, maintained a tradition of participation in the Shāfiʿī *madhhab.* While the historical record of this tradition is spotty, and many traces of it have been lost, neglected, or covered up, it remains discernible in biographical sources. Twelver Shiite jurists did not merely study an occasional work with a teacher who happened to be affiliated with the Shāfiʿī *madhhab.* They participated extensively in the system of Sunni legal education and in the institutions of the *madrasah* and the *madhhab.* They attended advanced courses in law with the leading Shāfiʿī jurists of their day, studying the standard texts of Shāfiʿī law and legal methodology. *Ijāzah*s they collected proved their competence in Shāfiʿī law and other fields and preserved information about the background of their Sunni teachers. Indeed, some Shiite jurists taught as recognized professors of Sunni Islamic law, served as legal authorities in Sunni circles, and wrote well-received works on the Islamic sciences within the Sunni tradition—in most cases by performing *taqīyah,* or religious dissimulation, establishing and maintaining affiliation with the Shāfiʿī *madhhab* while holding to Shiite beliefs inwardly. It is difficult to gauge from extant sources how dangerous it was for them to admit their Shiite allegiances to teachers, colleagues, or the public in general, or how they negotiated their identity successfully while claiming membership in the Shāfiʿī *madhhab.* In any case, it is clear that many participants in the Shiite Shāfiʿī tradition became accomplished Shāfiʿī jurists after spending years of study to attain that competence. In doing so, they were following one of the courses left open to Shiites by the Sunni definition of legal heresy and the Sunni system of legal *madhhab*s. The Sunni doctrine of consensus threatened to exclude them from participation in the elaboration of Islamic law on the grounds that their tradition did not constitute a recognized and legitimate legal *madhhab.* They therefore chose affiliation with and participation in the Shāfiʿī *madhhab* as a way out of this predicament, even though it often involved concealing or denying their Shiite ideological commitments.

193. Sayyid Mānakdīm Aḥmad al-Ḥusaynī, *Sharḥ al-uṣūl al-khamsah,* ed. ʿAbd al-Karīm ʿUthmān (Cairo: Maṭbaʿat wahbah, 1965). Al-Qāḍī ʿAbd al-Jabbār was of course a Shāfiʿī rather than a Ḥanafī, but he was an exception in this regard.

4

Adoption of Consensus

The Foundation of the Twelver Shiite *Madhhab*

"It is not permissible for the Muslim Community to agree on an error."[1]

al-Shaykh al-Ṭūsī (d. 460/1067)

The previous chapter described one type of reaction to the normative predicament facing the Shiites as a result of the charge that they were violating the consensus. As we have seen, many Shiite jurists conformed to consensus, at least outwardly, by adopting the Shāfiʿī legal *madhhab*. This chapter covers a second type of reaction, the adoption of consensus. Scholars who followed this course, many of whom were also important participants in the Shiite Shāfiʿī tradition, tried to adjust or remove the stigma itself, so they could profess their true beliefs openly and participate as equals within the Islamic legal system without facing discrimination, persecution, or rejection. The strategy they adopted was to establish a Twelver Shiite legal *madhhab* on a par with the Sunni *madhhab*s. The first major step or the key theoretical operation in doing so was to accept the principle of consensus. In order to be accepted as equal members within the Sunni legal system, the Shiite jurists had to accept the general norms on which that system was based. They had to adjust these norms, however, in order to be accepted without assimilating, giving up their religious identity. They embraced the concept of consensus while at the same time arguing that the Sunnis should recognize the Shiite legal tradition and take their jurists' legal opinions into account. The claim that the Twelver Shiite legal system represents a legal *madhhab* not only implies that Shiism has a structure of legal authority which conforms to that of the Sunni jurists' con-

1. al-Ṭūsī, *'Uddat al-uṣūl*, 232.

ception of legal authority but also that it can be accepted as a legitimate alternative within the circle of Islamic orthodoxy.

TWELVER SHIISM AS A COORDINATE *MADHHAB*

The conception of Twelver Shiism as a fifth *madhhab* has occasionally surfaced as an important issue in the history of the Islamic world. Twelver and Zaydi Shiite law were accepted as orthodox in 1959 at al-Azhar.[2] Nādir Shah Afshār, who ruled Iran from 1148/1736 until 1159/1747, attempted to have Twelver Shiism accepted as the Ja'farī *madhhab*. He tried several times to get the Ottoman sultan to recognize Shiism as a fifth *madhhab* and permit an additional Persian *amīr al-ḥajj* to lead pilgrims to Mecca. After conquering Iraq, Nādir Shah arranged a debate in Najaf on 25 Shawwāl 1156/12 December 1743 between Sunni and Shiite scholars of his realm, at which the Shiite scholars renounced what were perceived as heretical opinions.[3] Nādir Shah's short-lived policies regarding this matter are usually interpreted as a ploy designed to quell dissidence among the Sunni Afghanis and others in his army and to defuse Ottoman hostility toward Iran. It is not generally recognized that the concept of the fifth *madhhab* had any prior recognition within Shiism or that it had any sound basis in Shiite theory or scholarship. In fact, it is often portrayed as being completely inconsistent with Shiite views.[4]

The concept of the fifth *madhhab* is considerably older within Shiite tradition than is generally recognized. Moreover, it has considerable support in Shiite legal theory. In the sixteenth century, the Shiite jurist Nūr Allāh al-Shushtarī referred to Twelver Shiism as constituting the Ja'farī *madhhab* and made a detailed statement holding that the Shiite *madhhab* was equivalent to those of the Sunnis.[5] Before that, al-Shahīd al-Thānī reported that when he held his teaching position at the Nūrīyah *madrasah* in Ba'labakk ca. 953–54/1546–47 he taught law there according to the "five *madhhabs*" (*fī al-madhāhib al-khamsah*),

2. For an overview, see F. R. G. Bagley, "The Azhar and Shi'ism," *Muslim World* 50 (1960): 122–29; Muḥammad Taqī al-Qummī, *"Qiṣṣat al-taqrīb," Risālat al-islām*, 11 (1959): 348–59; Kate Zebiri, *Maḥmūd Shaltūt and Islamic Modernism* (Oxford: Clarendon Press, 1993), 24–27, 36 n. 96. The Egyptian scholar Maḥmūd Shaltūt, who served as rector of al-Azhar between 1957 and 1963, recognized the Zaydī and Twelver Shiite legal traditions as orthodox and included them in the curriculum of al-Azhar in 1959. His *fatwā* proclaiming this decision was published in *Risālat al-islām*, 11 (1959): 227–28. With the end of Shaykh Shaltūt's tenure as rector of al-Azhar and increased Saudi influence over the institution, the acceptance of the Shiite legal traditions has fallen by the wayside. 'Abd al-Ḥalīm Maḥmūd, the rector of al-Azhar between 1973 and 1978, was much less accepting of the Shiite legal tradition.

3. The section of al-Suwaydī's work which treats the events surrounding the debate as well as the debate itself has been printed as *Mu'tamar al-Najaf* (Cairo: al-Maṭba'ah al-salafiyah, 1973). It was first printed under the title *al-Ḥujaj al-qāṭi'ah l'ittifāq al-firaq al-islāmīyah* (Cairo: Maṭba'at al-sa'ādah, 1905).

4. Laurence Lockhart, *Nadir Shah* (London: Luzac & Co., 1938), 99–101, 279.

5. Rizvi, *Socio-Intellectual History*, 1: 365–67.

meaning the four Sunni *madhhabs* and the Twelver Shiite *madhhab.*[6] Several centuries earlier, Ibn Dā'ūd al-Ḥillī (d. ca. 740/1340) wrote *Khilāf al-madhāhib al-khamsah,* apparently dealing with the points of law disputed between the four Sunni *madhhabs* and the Twelver Shiite *madhhab.*[7] The term thus appears by the fourteenth century in the writings of Twelver jurists.

Nevertheless, the concept of a Twelver Shiite legal *madhhab* parallel to the Sunni *madhhabs* dates back still further. Without citing specific sources, Claude Cahen writes of the Twelver Shiite scholars of the Buwayhid period, "It is said that at this moment when the four schools remaining to the Sunnis were beginning to be defined by them as exclusively orthodox, they would have wished that their form of Shiism might be recognized in the heart of the *umma* as a sort of fifth authorized school." This statement, while expressing a legitimate idea, is anachronistic.[8] The terms "the fifth *madhhab*" or "the five *madhhabs*" were not used during the Buwayhid period for the simple reason that the idea that there were only four Sunni *madhhabs*, indicating the limits of Sunni legal orthodoxy, had not yet been firmly established. The dust had not yet settled on the last of the other Sunni *madhhabs*, such as the Jarīrī and Ẓāhirī *madhhabs*, so the Twelver *madhhab* was not termed "the fifth *madhhab*" specifically. Nevertheless, the concept of Twelver Shiite law forming a *madhhab* similar in form and function to the Sunni *madhhabs* is evident in the works of al-Shaykh al-Mufīd, al-Sharīf al-Murtaḍā, and al-Shaykh al-Ṭūsī in the late tenth and early eleventh century.

Yet the development of a Shiite juridical *madhhab* like those of the Sunnis would appear illogical, given the Shiite theory of the imamate, and unexpected, given widespread views concerning the nature of Shiism held by Islamists. The formation of a class of experts claiming authority to decide religious questions on the basis of their training in the legal sciences seems incompatible with fundamental Shiite beliefs. In the introduction to his work on jurisprudence, *Ghunyat al-nuzūʿ,* the twelfth-century Shiite jurist Ibn Zuhrah al-Ḥalabī (d. 585/1189–90) reports the question of an unnamed Sunni interlocutor who doubts the relevance of the science of *uṣūl al-fiqh* for Shiism:

6. ʿAlī al-ʿĀmilī, *al-Durr al-manthūr,* 2: 182.

7. Ibn Dā'ūd al-Ḥillī, *Kitāb al-rijāl,* 75.

8. Claude Cahen, "Buwayhids," *EI*², 1: 1350–57. Nevertheless, the use of the term fifth *madhhab* in this context has some support in Shiite sources. The nineteenth-century Shiite scholar Tunkābunī reports that during the Buwayhid period, al-Sharīf al-Murtaḍā pleaded with the sultan of the time to recognize the Jaʿfarī *madhhab* as the fifth legitimate *madhhab* in addition to the four Sunni *madhhabs.* The sultan agreed on the condition that al-Murtaḍā pay the sum of two hundred thousand tomans. Al-Murtaḍā paid one hundred thousand tomans of his own money, but was unable to raise the rest, so the Jaʿfarī *madhhab* was not accepted. While Tunkābunī claims that he heard of this event from one of his teachers, citing a reliable work, it seems clearly apocryphal. Mīrzā Muḥammad Tunkābunī, *Qiṣaṣ al-ʿulamā'* (Shiraz: Intishārāt ʿilmīyah islāmīyah, 1964), 406–7; Donaldson, *Shi'ite Religion,* 287.

"Since, in matters of the religious law, you follow nothing but the opinion of the Infallible Imam, then what need have you of legal methodology (*uṣūl al-fiqh*)? Your discussion of this discipline is mere folly, and serves no purpose."[9] This query reflects the intuitive understanding that the Twelver Shiite legal system, rather than following naturally or logically from the tradition established by the imams, somehow contradicts the Shiites' reliance on an imam for religious guidance. The origin of Shiite legal methodology and the rise of the organized Twelver legal *madhhab* thus beg an explanation. In order to provide this explanation, we must turn our attention to the Shiite jurists of Baghdad during the Buwayhid period.

In order to understand the establishment of the Twelver Shiite legal *madhhab*, there are several reasons for concentrating on Baghdad. Political and commercial capital of the Abbasid Empire, Baghdad had become the leading cultural and intellectual center of the Islamic world. Certainly, other centers such as Cordoba, Qayrawān, Cairo, and Rayy were also important during this period, and it is wrong to take Baghdad's primacy as given or assume that the situation which held there represents the contemporary situation of the Islamic lands as a whole. Nevertheless, in the ninth and tenth centuries, the major legal institutional developments in the outlying regions tended to follow those which occurred in Baghdad.[10] Baghdad was the primary intellectual center of the Shiites as well. Southern Iraq had been the historical center of the Shiite community from the time of the caliphate of ʿAlī. The Abbasid caliphs' policy to keep the Shiite imams, beginning with Mūsā al-Kāẓim, under their close supervision in Baghdad and Samarra had increased the Shiite community's focus on Iraq. The major Shiite shrines were located in Iraq, and had since become sites of devotion and pilgrimage. With the founding of the capital city of Baghdad, a thriving Shiite merchant community grew up in the suburb of al-Karkh and provided considerable patronage for Shiite scholars. Other centers were important for Shiite intellectual life during this period, particularly Cairo in Egypt, Aleppo in Syria, and Rayy in Iran, but relatively few works produced by Twelvers writing in those regions have been preserved, not the least surprising because of the great book burnings that took place when Maḥmūd of Ghaznah conquered Rayy in 420/1029 and when the Ayyūbid dynasty overthrew the Fatimids in Egypt. Most of the canonical Shiite legal works from the tenth and eleventh centuries, those which shaped the subsequent tradition of Shiite legal scholarship to the greatest degree, were written by the Shiite jurists of Baghdad.

9. Ḥamzah b. ʿAlī Ibn Zuhrah al-Ḥalabī, *Ghunyat al-nuzūʿ*, in *al-Jawāmiʿ al-fiqhīyah* (Qum: Maktabat al-Marʿashī al-Najafī, 1983–84), 461.

10. Melchert, "Formation of the Sunni Schools of Law," 340–41.

THE TWELVER JURISTS OF BUWAYHID BAGHDAD

Al-Shaykh al-Mufīd, al-Sharīf al-Murtaḍā, and al-Shaykh al-Ṭūsī were the foremost Twelver jurists of their time, and held, in succession, a position of leadership within the Twelver Shiite scholarly community in Baghdad. Together, their careers spanned nearly the entire period of Buwayhid control over the imperial capital—that is, from the mid-tenth century until 447/1055, when the Seljuks conquered Baghdad and al-Shaykh al-Ṭūsī fled to Najaf for safety. It is during this period, and in the works of these jurists, that the foundations for the subsequent tradition of Shiite jurisprudence which has continued until the present were set.

Muḥammad b. Muḥammad b. al-Nuʿmān al-ʿUkbarī, known as Ibn al-Muʿallim and al-Shaykh al-Mufīd in the sources, was born in the town of ʿUkbarā in Iraq on 11 Dhū al-Qaʿdah 336/23 May 948. He came to Baghdad with his father at the age of twelve, in about 348/950. In Baghdad he studied with a large number of Shiite hadith experts, including Jaʿfar b. Muḥammad b. Qawlawayh (d. 368/978–79). He also studied with the leading theologians of his time, including the Sunni Muʿtazilīs Abū ʿAbd Allāh al-Ḥusayn b. ʿAlī al-Baṣrī, known as al-Juʿl (d. 369/979–80), and ʿAlī b. ʿĪsā al-Rummānī (d. 384/994-95) and the Shiite Abū al-Ḥubaysh al-Muẓaffar b. Muḥammad al-Balkhī. In 355/965–66 he received an *ijāzah* from the well-known Shiite hadith expert, Ibn Bābawayh al-Qummī (d. 381/991), probably in Baghdad. He soon became the leading Shiite theologian and jurist in Baghdad; Ibn al-Nadīm, writing in 377/987–88, refers to him as the *raʾīs* or leading scholar of the Shiites. He lived on Darb al-Riyāḥ in al-Karkh, the main Shiite quarter on the west side of Baghdad, and taught at the mosque he had built adjacent to his house. He held a regular *majlis,* which was attended by the eminent scholars of his day and prominent figures, including the Buwayhid ruler ʿAḍud al-Dawlah (367–72/978–83). Among the scholars whom he debated were al-Bāqillānī (d. 403/1013) and al-Qāḍī ʿAbd al-Jabbār (d. 415/1024). He remained the leading theologian and jurist of the Twelvers until his death on 2 Ramaḍān 413/29 November 1022. Al-Sharīf al-Murtaḍā performed the ritual washing of the corpse; it is reported that a crowd of eighty thousand Shiites attended the funeral.[11]

ʿAlī b. al-Ḥusayn al-Mūsawī, known as al-Sharīf al-Murtaḍā, was born in Rajab 355/June–July 966 to a prominent Alid family. As a youth, he studied

11. The most accessible biography of al-Shaykh al-Mufīd is provided by Martin J. McDermott, *The Theology of al-Shaikh al-Mufīd (d. 413/1022)* (Beirut: Dār al-mashriq, 1978). The main Arabic sources are Ibn al-Nadīm, *al-Fihrist,* 266, 293; al-Ṭūsī, *Fihrist kutub al-shīʿah,* 186–87; al-Najāshī, *Kitāb al-rijāl,* 311–16; Ibn Shahrāshūb, *Maʿālim al-ʿulamāʾ,* 100–102; Ibn al-Muṭahhar al-Ḥillī, *Rijāl al-ʿAllāmah al-Ḥillī,* 147; al-Ḥurr al-ʿĀmilī, *Amal al-āmil,* 2: 304; al-Iṣfahānī, *Riyāḍ al-ʿulamāʾ,* 5: 176–79; al-Baḥrānī, *Luʾluʾat al-Baḥrayn,* 356; al-Khwānsārī, *Rawḍāt al-jannāt,* 6: 142–66; al-Amīn, *Aʿyān al-shīʿah,* 9: 420–24; al-Khaṭīb al-Baghdādī, *Tārīkh Baghdad,* 3: 231; Ibn al-Jawzī, *al-Muntaẓam,* 15: 33, 58–59, 157.

under al-Shaykh al-Mufīd along with his brother al-Sharīf al-Raḍī. While they were both accomplished in the fields of law, theology, and poetry, al-Raḍī excelled particularly in poetry and al-Murtaḍā became better known as a jurist and theologian. Their family dominated the position of Alid *naqīb,* "syndic" or "marshall of the nobility," during the Buwayhid period. Al-Murtaḍā's father Abū Aḥmad al-Ḥusayn b. Mūsā was appointed *naqīb* on 4 Jumādā I 354/8 May 965, and held the office intermittently for about forty years until he died in 400/1009–10. Al-Raḍī then held the office until his own death in 406/1015. On 16 Muḥarram 403/7 August 1012, al-Raḍī was promoted, as it were, and made *naqīb* of the Ṭālibīyīn throughout the territories under Abbasid sovereignty. He was the first Alid *naqīb* to receive an honorary robe in black, the color of the Abbasid dynasty.[12] Al-Murtaḍā assumed the office of *naqīb* on his brother's death and held it for thirty years until his own death in 436/1044. His nephew ʻAdnān b. ʻAlī held the office of *naqīb* from 436/1044 until 450/1058.[13]

Members of the family held additional official positions: In 366/976–77, al-Sharīf Abū Aḥmad was sent by ʻIzz al-Dawlah (356–67/967–78) as an ambassador to ʻAḍud al-Dawlah. In 380/990–91, he was appointed leader of the pilgrimage caravan to Mecca (*amīr al-ḥājj*) and supervisor of the grievance council (*nāẓir al-maẓālim*) in addition to his duties as Alid *naqīb;* al-Murtaḍā and al-Raḍī were appointed as deputies to their father. They were removed from these offices in Dhū al-Qaʻdah 384/December 994–January 995, but regained them in 394/1004. In Rabīʻ II 402/November 1011, Caliph al-Qādir had a document drawn up denouncing the Fatimids as illegitimate claimants to the caliphate who had falsified their genealogy. Both al-Raḍī and al-Murtaḍā, along with a number of other scholars, signed this document. On 3 Ṣafar 406/23 July 1015, al-Sharīf al-Murtaḍā was appointed *naqīb, amīr al-ḥājj,* and supervisor of the grievance council. An official ceremony, attended by the leading judges and jurists, was held at Dār al-mulk, the Buwayhid prince's palace, and an official letter of appointment was issued by al-Qādir.[14]

When al-Shaykh al-Mufīd died in 413/1022, al-Sharīf al-Murtaḍā became the leading Shiite jurist in Baghdad in addition to being an important notable and political figure. He lived first in al-Ṣurāh but, when his house there was burned in 415/1024, he moved to Darb Jamīl. He often appears as mediator in the various conflicts between the caliph, the Buwayhid ruler, the army, the gang leaders (*ʻayyārūn*), and the inhabitants of al-Karkh. For example, he was

12. Ibn al-Jawzī, *al-Muntaẓam,* 15: 89.

13. On the office of *naqīb* during this period and its incumbents see Busse, *Chalif und Grosskönig,* 280–97; Louis Massignon, "Cadis et naqībs Baghdadiens," *Weiner Zeitschrift für die Kunde des Morgenlandes,* 51 (1948): 106–15. Reprinted in his *Opera Minora,* vol. 1, ed. Y. Moubarac (Beirut: Dār al-maʻārif, 1963), 263–64.

14. Ibn al-Jawzī, *al-Muntaẓam,* 15: 43, 82–83, 111–12, 248, 344, 369.

entrusted with taking an oath of allegiance to the Buwayhid ruler Musharrif al-Dawlah (412–16/1021–25) from the Turkish soldiery in 415/1024. Just following ʿĪd al-aḍḥā 420/23 December 1029, al-Murtaḍā led a delegation of notables to the caliphal palace to apologize for a Shiite attack on a Sunni preacher the caliph had appointed to preach at the Shiite Barāthā mosque. When the Turkish garrison showed signs of rebellion in 424/1033 and again in 427/1036, Jalāl al-Dawlah (416-35/1025–44) took refuge in al-Murtaḍā's house. On 13 Shawwāl 425/31 August 1034 al-Murtaḍā was requested to summon the gang leaders to his house and to have them swear to serve the sultan or else leave the city.[15] He died in Rabīʿ I 436/September-October 1044.[16]

Abū Jaʿfar Muḥammad b. al-Ḥasan al-Ṭūsī was born in Ṭūs, next to Mashhad in northeastern Iran, in Ramaḍān 385/October 995. In 408/1017–18 he came to Baghdad, where he studied under al-Shaykh al-Mufīd until the latter's death in 413/1022. During this period he began his major hadith work, *Tahdhīb al-aḥkām,* which used al-Mufīd's epitome of law, *al-Muqniʿah,* as a basis. He then studied under al-Sharīf al-Murtaḍā, receiving a handsome stipend of twelve dinars a month. Upon al-Murtaḍā's death in 436/1044, he became the leading jurist of the Twelver Shiites and the focal point of Shiite legal studies in Baghdad until the Seljuk conquest in 447/1055. To escape popular attacks, which the Sunni Seljuk regime failed to stop, al-Ṭūsī fled to Najaf, where he spent the rest of his days. His house in al-Karkh was looted, and his notebooks and a chair from which he used to lecture were burned along with three white banners that Shiite pilgrims used to carry to al-Kūfah.[17] He died on 22 Muḥarram 460/1 December 1067 in Najaf and was buried in his house there. He holds such a prominent place in the Shiite legal tradition that he is known as *Shaykh al-ṭāʾifah* ("the Master of the Sect") or simply al-Shaykh ("*the* Master").[18]

15. Ibid., 15: 171, 201, 235, 241 254.

16. al-Ṭūsī, *Fihrist kutub al-shīʿah,* 125–26; al-Najāshī, *Kitāb al-rijāl,* 206–7; Ibn Shahrāshūb, *Maʿālim al-ʿulamāʾ,* 61–63; Ibn al-Muṭahhar al-Ḥillī, *Rijāl al-ʿAllāmah al-Ḥillī,* 94–95; al-Iṣfahānī, *Riyāḍ al-ʿulamāʾ,* 4: 14–65; al-Baḥrānī, *Luʾluʾat al-Baḥrayn,* 313–22; al-Khwānṣārī, *Rawḍāt al-jannāt,* 4: 284–301; al-Amīn, *Aʿyān al-shīʿah,* 8: 213–19; Abū Manṣūr ʿAbd al-Malik al-Thaʿālibī al-Nīsābūrī, *Tatimmat al-yatīmah,* vol. 1 (Tehran: Maṭbaʿat fardīn, 1934), 53–56; al-Khaṭīb al-Baghdādī, *Tārīkh Baghdād,* 11: 402–3; Ibn al-Jawzī, *al-Muntaẓam,* 15: 294–300; Yāqūt al-Ḥamawī, *Muʿjam al-udabāʾ aw Irshād al-arīb ilā maʿrifat al-adīb,* 6 vols. (Beirut: Dār al-kutub al-ʿilmīyah, 1991–93), 4: 76–82.

17. Ibn al-Jawzī, *al-Muntaẓam,* 16: 8, 16. Ibn al-Jawzī reports that al-Ṭūsī fled and that his house was looted in 448/1056, the year after the Seljuks arrived in Baghdad. Then he reports that al-Ṭūsī's house was looted again and his books burned in Ṣafar 449/April–May 1057.

18. al-Ṭūsī, *Fihrist kutub al-shīʿah,* 188–90; al-Najāshī, *Kitāb al-rijāl,* 316; Ibn Shahrāshūb, *Maʿālim al-ʿulamāʾ,* 102–3; Ibn al-Muṭahhar al-Ḥillī, *Rijāl al-ʿAllāmah al-Ḥillī,* 148; al-Baḥrānī, *Luʾluʾat al-Baḥrayn,* 293–98; al-Khwānṣārī, *Rawḍāt al-jannāt,* 6: 201–31; al-Amīn, *Aʿyān al-shīʿah,* 9: 159–67; Ibn al-Jawzī, *al-Muntaẓam,* 16: 110; al-Subkī, *Ṭabaqāt al-shāfiʿīyah al-kubrā,* 4: 126–27; Ibn Ḥajar al-ʿAsqalānī, *Lisān al-mīzān,* 7 vols. (Ḥaydarābād: Maṭbaʿat majlis dāʾirat al-maʿārif al-niẓāmīyah, 1971), 5: 135.

THE SHIITES' POSITION IN BUWAYHID BAGHDAD

During what has been termed "the Shiite century"—ca. 950–1050 A.D.—Shiite governments ruled the greater part of the Muslim world. The Buwayhids ruled over Iraq and Iran, the Hamdanids over northern Syria, and the Fatimids over Egypt, the Hijaz, much of the Levant, and for a time Sicily and parts of North Africa. The Qarāmiṭah held large areas in the Arabian peninsula and along the Persian Gulf. They repeatedly raided southern Iraq, and had even attacked Mecca in the early tenth century, carrying off the Black Stone and holding it for ransom for over two decades. Smaller principalities were established by a number of lesser Shiite dynasties, such as the Mazyadids in southern Iraq and the ʿUqaylids and Mirdāsids in northern Iraq and Syria. The tremendous power that Shiites wielded at this time brought about a heightened presence of Shiism in public life, both political and social.

The Buwayhids, originally from the region of Daylam, conquered most of Iran and Iraq in the early tenth century, establishing capitals at Rayy, Shiraz, and Baghdad. It is generally agreed that they converted to Twelver Shiism, though they were Zaydī by background. Pursuing a policy of conciliation between the Sunnis and Shiites, they nevertheless patronized the Twelvers to an unprecedented extent and supported popular displays of Shiite belief.[19] Scholars have noted, among the various manifestations of religious and intellectual life that particularly stand out in the Buwayhid period, two which are especially relevant for this study. One the one hand, Shiite communities, including the Twelvers, experienced a cultural renaissance, part of the general heightened cultural and intellectual activity of the time. Especially during the period of Buwayhid control of Iraq, from 334/945 until 447/1055, economic success and political support allowed Shiites numerous opportunities to express their views more openly, abandoning traditional postures associated with dissimulation which were necessary in more oppressive times.[20] On the other hand, Sunni traditionalists—especially the Ḥanbalīs, but others as well—vehemently opposed the Shiite regime and the increased presence of Shiism and Shiite beliefs in the public sphere. This opposition gave rise not only to religious polemics but also to many attacks on Shiites and riots between Sunni and Shiite factions.[21]

19. On the Buwayhids (or Buyids) in general, see Busse, *Chalif und Grosskönig;* Cahen, "Buwayhids," 1: 1350–57; ʿAlī Aṣghar Faqihī, *Āl-i Būyah va-awḍāʿ-i zamān-i ishān* (Tehran: Intishārāt-i ṣabā, 1986); Joel L. Kraemer, *Humanism in the Renaissance of Islam,* 2d revised ed. (Leiden: E. J. Brill, 1992); Roy Mottahedeh, *Loyalty and Leadership in an Early Islamic Society* (Princeton: Princeton University Press, 1980.

20. Busse, *Caliph und Grosskönig,* 415–31, 448–50; Faqihi, *Āl-i Būyah,* 450–82; Kramer, *Humanism,* 41–43, 65–68.

21. Makdisi, *Ibn ʿAqīl,* 293–384; Simha Sabari, *Mouvements Populaires à Bagdad à l'époque ʿAbbaside, IXe-XIe Siècles* (Paris: Maisonneuve, 1981), 101–20.

Both the high profile of Shiites and Shiism in public life and Sunni opposition thereto had existed, to a lesser extent, even before the advent of the Buwayhids. In the early tenth century, several members of the Shiite Banū Furāt family served as vizier under the Abbasid caliphs. In 305/917–18, the vizier Ibn al-Furāt had instituted the office of *naqīb* of the Alids or Ṭālibīyīn, intended to be parallel to the office of *naqīb* of the Hāshimīyīn that had been established by the early Abbasids. Visitations to the tombs of the imams; the "two Kāẓims," Mūsā al-Kāẓim and Muḥammad Jawād in Baghdad; Ḥusayn in Karbalā'; and 'Alī in Kūfah had become popular public rituals before the advent of Buwayhid rule.

Ḥanbalī attacks on the Shiites and others date to the early tenth century, when they were led by the jurist and preacher Abū Muḥammad al-Barbahārī (d. 329/941).[22] When the prominent jurist Muḥammad b. Jarīr al-Ṭabarī, eponym of the Jarīrī *madhhab,* died in 310/323, the Ḥanbalīs prevented his burial and accused him of Shiite heresy (*rafḍ*).[23] They were sworn enemies of al-Ṭabarī because he had refused to recognize Ibn Ḥanbal as a jurist, asserting that he was merely an expert in hadith, and before his death, the Ḥanbalīs had prevented followers from visiting him.[24] The historian Ibn Miskawayh records that by 323/935 the Ḥanbalīs had made visits to the tomb of Aḥmad b. Ḥanbal into a devotional ritual designed to rival Shiite pilgrimages to the tombs of the imams. In 323/935, a particularly severe Ḥanbalī attack on the Shiites provoked a crackdown on the Ḥanbalīs in Baghdad by order of the Caliph al-Rāḍī bi'Llāh (322–29/934–40). The decree the caliph issued on the occasion, threatening the Ḥanbalīs with military suppression for causing unrest in Baghdad, relates that al-Barbahārī and his followers had attacked the Shiites and accused them of unbelief (*kufr*) and miscreance (*ḍalāl*). The caliph imprisoned a number of the Ḥanbalīs and forbade them to assemble in public.[25]

With the advent of the Buwayhids in 334/945, the public presence of Shiism and, with it, the opposition of the Ḥanbalīs and Sunni traditionalists increased. As seen above, Shiite notables, such as al-Sharīf Abū Aḥmad and his sons, were appointed to important positions, including Alid marshall, leader of the pilgrimage caravan, and supervisor of the grievance council. In 352/963–64

22. See Henri Laoust, "al-Barbahārī," *EI*², 1: 1039–40.

23. Ibn Miskawayh, *Tajārib al-umam,* 2 vols. (Tehran: Intishārāt zarrīn, 1987), 1: 84. In this and later periods, *rafḍ* is a general pejorative term for Shiites *(rāfiḍah, rawāfiḍ, rafaḍah),* referring most often to Imāmīs but used also to refer to Isma'ilis. It is taken to refer more specifically to the Shiites' rejection of the Prophet's Companions, especially Abū Bakr, 'Umar, and 'Ā'ishah, which they express by insulting them, cursing them, declaring them unbelievers, or relating deprecatory accounts concerning them.

24. 'Izz al-Dīn 'Alī b. Muḥammad Ibn al-Athīr, *al-Kāmil fī al-tārīkh,* 13 vols. (Beirut: Dār ṣādir and Dār bayrūt, 1965–66), 8: 134, 135.

25. Ibn Miskawayh, *Tajārib al-umam,* 1: 322–23.

the Buwayhid ruler Mu'izz al-Dawlah (334–56/945–67) inaugurated public rituals for the Shiite holidays of 'Āshūrā' (10 Muḥarram 352/8 February 963) and Ghadīr Khumm (18 Dhū al-Ḥijjah 352/7 January 964), and these holidays continued to be celebrated publicly throughout the Buwayhid period. Other public manifestations of Shiism were the dawn call to prayer, which included the phrase *ḥayya 'alā khayri 'l-'amal,* "come to the best of works," instead of the phrase *aṣ-ṣalātu khayrun min an-nawm,* "prayer is better than sleep." On such occasions as 'Āshūrā' the Shiites hung up plaques with the inscription *Muḥammad wa-'Alī khayr al-bashar,* "Muḥammad and 'Alī are the best of mankind," or engraved or painted similar phrases, and probably curses of the Companions as well, on walls and doors. In Rabī' II 351/May–June 962, for example, the Shiites wrote curses of the Companions on the mosques in Baghdad. The curses mentioned only Mu'āwiyah by name, but referred to Abū Bakr, 'Umar, 'Uthmān, and 'Ā'ishah indirectly.[26]

During the Buwayhid period, al-Shaykh al-Mufīd and other Shiite scholars in major centers of learning, such as Baghdad and Rayy, debated openly with the great Sunni scholars of their day. Kings attended their lectures and princes studied at their feet. Shiites entered into the fray of intellectual and religious debate more directly, freely, and visibly than had been or would be possible in most other periods of Islamic history. They therefore had to engage, more intensely than had often been the case, with Sunni thought in the various disciplines, particularly in the religious disciplines where such engagement was more prone to stir up controversy. They also had to defend their own positions more regularly and in a more convincing manner now that they were available for public scrutiny by the Sunnis. They wrote many works presenting and justifying traditional Shiite views on the religious sciences.

While the Shiite century produced an intellectual flowering for the Shiites, it also produced many disgruntled Sunnis, who felt that their political and cultural hegemony was being challenged if not undermined. To them, the high public profile of Twelver Shiism and the Twelver Shiites, not to mention Mu'tazilīs and others, with their impressive economic success and their increased access to public institutions and patronage, were unacceptable and painfully visible signs of a concerted attack on Sunni cultural and religious values. To this threat was added that of clandestine proselytism on the part of the Fatimids and Qarāmiṭah, whom some Sunni traditionalists saw as allies with the Zaydi and Twelver Shiites in a nefarious plot to control the Muslim world. The traditionalist movement, the major goal of which was to remove Shiism and Mu'tazilism from the public sphere, became especially strong in the last decades of the tenth century. An atmosphere of rivalry between Sunnis and Shiites manifested itself at all levels, including political office, trade, acade-

26. Ibn al-Jawzī, *al-Muntaẓam,* 14: 140, 150; Ibn al-Athīr, *al-Kāmil,* 8: 542–43, 549–50.

mics, crime, and even sports. The Sunni Marʿūsh and the Shiite Faḍl, two famous runners whom Muʿizz al-Dawlah had hired to run the postal route between Baghdad and Rayy, became the focus of an enormous rivalry between Sunni and Shiite fans.[27]

Numerous feuds, riots, and attacks between the Shiites of al-Karkh and Bāb al-Ṭāq and the Sunnis in the surrounding quarters are recorded in the annals between 334/995 and 447/1055, when Baghdad was under Buwayhid rule. In these conflicts, which sometimes continued for months, many people were wounded and killed, markets and neighborhoods were pillaged or destroyed, and entire quarters of the city were burned.[28] The key figures in many of the physical raids and attacks were Ḥanbalī and other Sunni traditionalist activists who had declared themselves the guardians of Sunni orthodoxy and who were centered in the quarters of Bāb al-Baṣrah and Sūq al-Qallāʾīn, adjacent to al-Karkh. The Ḥanbalīs pursued a regular program of social and religious activism during this period designed to restrict the public discussion of religious topics and to define the boundaries of the authoritative community of interpretation. Attacks on and feuds with the Shiites represented a major aspect of this program; as Makdisi remarks, "Ce sont les ḥanbalites qui représentèrent les sunnites à Bagdad dans la lutte entre les deux sectes."[29] These conflicts had clear political implications. The Buwayhids patronized the Shiites of Baghdad in order to provide political backing for themselves in the capital. The Sunni traditionalists attacked the Shiites in part as a means of protest against Buwayhid rule. The conflict pitted the Shiites, the Buwayhid *amīrs*, and the Daylamī soldiery against the traditionalist Sunnis, the Abbasid caliph, and the Turkish soldiery.

The Ḥanbalīs and other traditionalists in Baghdad expended enormous efforts to compete with Shiites at the popular level and in particular to develop religious ceremonies to rival Shiite public rituals. The Shiite holidays of ʿĀshūrāʾ and Ghadīr Khumm, celebrated beginning in 352/963–64, became prime occasions for Sunni attacks. On ʿĀshūrāʾ the next year (28 January 964), there were violent altercations between Sunnis and Shiites at Qaṭīʿat Umm Jaʿfar and the road to the Quraysh cemetery, in which many people were wounded and property was looted.[30] In 389/999, Sunnis began to perform additional

27. Ibn al-Jawzī, *al-Muntaẓam*, 14: 43; Ibn al-Athīr, *al-Kāmil*, 8: 575–76.

28. Some sort of conflict, battle, or riot between Shiites and Sunnis occurred in each of the following years: 338/949, 340/952, 348/959, 349/960, 353/964, 354/965, 362/972–73, 363/973–74, 380/990–91, 382/992, 392/1001–2, 393/1002, 398/1008, 408/1017, 409/1018, 415–16/1024–26, 417/1026, 420/1029, 421/1030, 422/1031, 431/1040, 437/1045, 441/1049, 443/1051, 444/1053, 445/1053, 447/1055. See the chronicles of Ibn al-Jawzī, *al-Muntaẓam;* Ibn al-Athīr, *al-Kāmil;* and Ibn Kathīr, *al-Bidāyah wa'l-nihāyah,* under the years in question.

29. Makdisi, *Ibn ʿAqīl*, 293–384, esp. 310–27; Sabari, *Mouvements Populaires*, 101–20, esp. 106–10.

30. Ibn al-Jawzī, *al-Muntaẓam*, 14: 155; Ibn al-Athīr, *al-Kāmil*, 8: 558.

rituals in Baghdad as an expression of protest against the Shiite celebrations in order to spite their rivals. They mourned the death of Muṣʻab b. Zubayr on 18 Muḥarram, eight days after ʻĀshūrā'. On 26 Dhū 'l-Ḥijjah, eight days after Yawm al-Ghadīr, they celebrated Yawm al-Ghār, commemorating the occasion when Abū Bakr hid together with the Prophet in a cave, taken by Sunnis as a sign of his special relationship with the Prophet and his right to succeed him as leader of the Muslim community. On 1 Ramaḍān 425/20 July 1034, the Ḥanbalīs instituted a ritual pilgrimage to the tomb of Muṣʻab b. al-Zubayr in order to counter the Shiite ritual pilgrimage to the shrine of al-Ḥusayn at Karbalā' on the 15th of Shaʻbān. Sunni-Shiite riots ensued.[31]

The popular conflicts often ended up involving the prominent Shiite jurists, including al-Shaykh al-Mufīd and al-Sharīf al-Murtaḍā. In 392/1001–2, conflicts between rival Sunni and Shiite gangs wreaked havoc in Baghdad, and Bahā' al-Dawlah (379–403/987–1012) sent ʻAmīd al-Juyūsh Abū ʻAlī b. Ustādh Hurmuz to reestablish public order. After having Sunni and Shiite toughs bound together and drowned in the Tigris, the commander forbade the Sunnis and Shiites from holding public displays and banished al-Shaykh al-Mufīd temporarily from the city. On 10 Rajab 398/21 March 1008, there were riots between the inhabitants of Karkh and the law students of Qaṭīʻat al-Rabīʻ, who had vilified al-Shaykh al-Mufīd at his mosque in Darb al-Riyāḥ. The Shiite students retaliated by attacking the houses of Abū Muḥammad b. al-Akfānī (d. 405/1014), the prominent Ḥanafī jurist and chief Qāḍī of Baghdad, and Abū Ḥāmid al-Isfarā'inī (d. 406/1015), the leading Shāfiʻī jurist. The next month, Shaʻbān 398/April 1008, the caliph ordered the execution of a Shiite who had protested the burning of a copy of the Koran giving the variant readings of Ibn Masʻūd. A Shiite mob formed in al-Karkh and attacked the house of Abū Ḥāmid yet again, shouting *Yā Ḥākim! Yā Manṣūr!* in expressing allegiance to the reigning Fatimid caliph. In the ensuing conflict, the district next to Nahr al-Dajāj was burned and al-Karkh was attacked. ʻAmīd al-Juyūsh came to restore order in Baghdad in late Ramaḍān 398/May 1008 and temporarily banished al-Shaykh al-Mufīd.[32] In 409/1018 al-Shaykh al-Mufīd was banished once more after another series of riots.[33]

Al-Sharīf al-Murtaḍā appears many times as a mediator, and occasionally as a victim, in connection with Sunni-Shiite disturbances. After riots between the inhabitants of al-Karkh and Bāb al-Shaʻīr in 406/1015, Fakhr al-Mulk reprimanded the Shiites and banned wailing on ʻĀshūrā' and the hanging of plaques. Al-Murtaḍā mediated in the conflict. In the course of continual conflicts from Rajab 415/September 1024 until the end of 416/February 1026,

31. Ibn al-Jawzī, *al-Muntaẓam*, 15: 14, 241.

32. Ibn al-Jawzī, *al-Muntaẓam*, 15: 58–59, 125–26; Ibn al-Athīr, *al-Kāmil*, 9: 208.

33. Ibn Kathīr, *al-Bidāyah wa'l-nihāyah*, 9: 88.

al-Sharīf al-Murtaḍā's house in al-Ṣurāh was burned. Following riots on 20 Muḥarram 417/13 March 1026 in which al-Karkh, al-Qaṭī'ah, and Darb Riyāḥ were looted and parts of al-Karkh were burned, al-Sharīf al-Murtaḍā interceded with Caliph al-Qādir to forgive the Shiites for their role in the conflict. Al-Qādir imposed a fine of one hundred thousand dinars on al-Karkh. In the aftermath of Sunni-Shiite disturbances on 'Āshūrā 421/18 January 1030, al-Sharīf al-Murtaḍā was asked to have someone take down the Shiites' plaques. In Rabī' I 422/March 1031, al-Qādir outfitted a contingent of fighters against the Byzantines led by the Sufi Madhkūr al-Khazlajī (?). Before they left Baghdad, fighting broke out between them and the inhabitants of al-Karkh. The *ghāzīs* broke into the house of al-Murtaḍā in Darb Jamīl and burned two of his boats. The following day, Sunni commoners crossed over to the west side along with Turkish troops to attack al-Karkh; many markets were burned or destroyed.[34]

The Sunni attacks on the Shiites were not merely popular riots. Religiously motivated at least in part, they expressed vehement criticism of Shiite opinions and beliefs, and were often condoned or supported by Sunni jurists and other religious leaders. They were conducted within a discourse which labeled Shiites as deviants and unbelievers and rejected their legal and theological traditions as heretical. In 313/925, the headman (*ra'īs*) of the Shiites in al-Karkh, a certain al-Ka'kī, was accused of being a propagandist for the Qarāmiṭah. He was whipped three hundred lashes and paraded around Baghdad on a camel. That same year, Caliph al-Muqtadir (295–320/908–32) had the Barāthā mosque, one of the six principal mosques of Baghdad and the one most frequented by Shiites—they claimed that 'Alī b. Abī Ṭālib had prayed at the site—raided and razed, and the worshippers there imprisoned. In order to justify this act, a number of Sunni jurists had issued a *fatwā* declaring that the mosque was a haven for unbelievers and propagandists for the Qarāmiṭah.[35] The decree of al-Rāḍī bi'Llāh in 323/935 shows that already in the early tenth century the Ḥanbalīs were waging an organized program of attacks against the Shiites and accusing them not only of religious deviance but also of outright unbelief.[36]

During the late tenth and early eleventh centuries, the Sunni traditionalists joined forces with Caliph al-Qādir (381–422/991–1031) in what would prove to

34. Ibn al-Jawzī, *al-Muntaẓam,* 15: 111, 171, 175, 204, 213–14; Ibn al-Athīr, *al-Kāmil,* 9: 263.

35. Ibn al-Jawzī, *al-Muntaẓam,* 13: 247–48, 14: 4–5. The mosque lay in ruins for fifteen years, until the Abbasid caliph al-Rāḍī (322–29/934–40) rebuilt it in 328/939–40. It then remained in use until ca. 451/1059, a few years after the Seljuk conquest.

36. Mottahedeh, in considering this incident, deems it unlikely that Ḥanbalī thinkers would have declared Shiites unbelievers, but other data concerning the Ḥanbalīs' activities suggests that they would not have hesitated to do so (*Loyalty and Leadership,* 25). Mottahedeh's text gives 322/934 rather than 323/935.

be an organized movement opposed to Shiism and the rationalist theology of the Mu'tazilīs. Despite the backing of the powerful Buwayhid *amīrs*, Shiites were subject to numerous ideological and physical attacks. The movement gained strength when Maḥmūd b. Sebuktegin, self-styled champion of Sunnism, took control of Khurasan in 387/997 and pledged allegiance to al-Qādir. The caliph promulgated a campaign against heresies, including Shiism and Mu'tazilism, in 408/1017, 409/1018, and 420/1029. In 408/1017, he called the Mu'tazilīs and Shiites to repent, and forbade them to lecture, debate, or teach Mu'tazilī or Shiite views. The pressure brought to bear as a result of such measures was significant. In 1017/1026, the Ḥanafī jurist and Mu'tazilī theologian al-Ṣaymarī had to abjure his Mu'tazilism in order to retain his post as judge. The Ghaznavid ruler Maḥmūd pledged support for al-Qādir's religious policies and promised to enforce them in the territory under his control.[37]

In the year 420/1029, Caliph al-Qādir promoted religious conformity with particular vigor. He had creeds denouncing Mu'tazilī and Shiite beliefs read at the palace on three separate occasions, on 18 Sha'bān/1 September, 10 Ramaḍān/22 September, and 1 Dhū al-Qa'dah/11 November. The main jurists, judges, and sayyids were in attendance at these proclamations and were required to sign statements attesting that they were present and had heard the creed so that they would be bound by its contents. At the last of these proclamations, the Shiite *khaṭīb* of the Barāthā mosque was arrested and accused of blasphemy. The caliph appointed Abū Manṣūr Ibn Tammām, a well-known Sunni preacher, to give the next Friday sermon at the Barāthā mosque in his stead. During the sermon, Ibn Tammām offended the Shiite audience by rapping the *minbar* with the hilt of his sword at the beginning of the sermon, omitting mention of 'Alī, and concluding the sermon with the statement, "Oh God, forgive the Muslims and those who claim that 'Alī is their master." When he finished, they pelted him with bricks, dislocating his shoulder and breaking his nose. After the incident, the caliph summoned Shiite leaders, including al-Sharīf al-Murtaḍā and al-Sharīf Abū al-Ḥasan Muḥammad b. 'Alī al-Zaynabī, and asked the commander of the garrison and the vizier Abū 'Alī b. Mākūlā to punish the perpetrators, whom he described as unbelievers. Two days later, a Shiite gang broke into Ibn Tammām's house, looted it, and stripped Ibn Tammām and his entire family. The caliph then forbade Friday prayer at the Barāthā mosque. Only after al-Sharīf al-Murtaḍā and the notables of al-Karkh interceded was prayer reinstated, on 1 Muḥarram 421/9 January 1030. The Sunni preacher the caliph appointed was ordered not to rap the *minbar* with his sword and had to read a prepared text free of offensive statements.[38]

37. Ibn al-Jawzī, al-Muntaẓam, 15: 125–26, 128, 197–98; Makdisi, *Ibn 'Aqīl,* 300; idem, "*Ṭabaqāt*-Biography," 381.

38. Ibn al-Jawzī, *al-Muntaẓam,* 15: 197–201; Ibn al-Athīr, *al-Kāmil,* 9: 393.

Maḥmūd b. Sebuktegin's conquest of Rayy in 420/1029 was a tremendous blow to the Shiites, not only politically but also intellectually. Rayy had been the most important Buwayhid capital next to Baghdad, and under the patronage of the Buwayhid *amīrs* and the fabulously wealthy vizier al-Ṣāḥib Ibn 'Abbād, it had became a thriving intellectual center for Mu'tazilīs and Zaydi, Ismā'īlī, and Twelver Shiites. The epistle Maḥmūd sent to Caliph al-Qādir on 1 Jumādā II 420/17 June 1029, two weeks after the conquest, describes the measures he took to suppress heresy in the city. Maḥmūd's forces had gathered outside Rayy on 16 Jumādā I 420/2 June 1029. The Shiite Daylamī army surrendered, along with their leader Rustam b. 'Alī al-Daylamī, and supposedly confessed to rejection of the Companions (*rafḍ*) and unbelief (*kufr*). The groups the conquerors treated as heretics included Mu'tazilīs and Shiites—Zaydis, Ismā'īlīs, and Twelvers. Extensive heresy trials were held in which the Sunni jurists were consulted. Many of the defendants were declared renegades, miscreants, or unbelievers. They were executed, mutilated, or banished; Mu'tazilī, Shiite, and philosophical books were burned. The Ismā'īlī *dā'īs* were expelled from the region, as were the leading Mu'tazilī and Twelver Shiite scholars.[39]

In 433/1041–42, al-Qādir's successor al-Qā'im (422–67/1031–65) had the Qādirī Creed read once again in the caliphal *dīwān*. The leading scholars were again required to be present, and had to sign statements saying, "This is the creed of the Muslims; whoever violates it is a sinner and an unbeliever (*wa-man khālafahū fa-qad fasaqa wa-kafar*)."[40]

SUNNI CRITICISM OF TWELVER LEGAL SCHOLARSHIP

Traditionalist attacks on the Twelvers during the Buwayhid period included the accusation that they lacked an adequate legal system. Al-Najāshī (d. 450/1058) frames his biobibliography of Shiite scholars as a response to Sunni interlocutors who taunted the Shiites: *innahu lā salafa lakum wa-lā muṣannaf,* "You have neither predecessors (from whom your legal tradition derives) nor comprehensive works arranged by chapter."[41] In the introduction to *Tahdhīb al-aḥkām*, al-Shaykh al-Ṭūsī states that he compiled the hadith collection in response to Sunni critics who held that the Shiite legal tradition is flawed because they have too many conflicting traditions. The Sunni critics saw this as particularly damning because the Shiites argue that the wide variety of opinion which exists among the Sunnis shows that they are wrong. In the introduction to his extensive legal compendium, *al-Mabsūṭ*, al-Ṭūsī writes:

39. Ibn al-Jawzī, *al-Muntaẓam*, 15: 194–96. MacDonald erroneously states that this took place at Isfahan (*Development of Muslim Theology*, 193–95).

40. Ibn al-Jawzī, *al-Muntaẓam*, 15: 279.

41. al-Najāshī, *Kitāb al-rijāl*, 2.

> I continually hear groups of our opponents who study law and claim knowledge of legal rulings deprecate and express disdain for the law of our fellows, the Imamis, and claim that the Imamis have few sub-categories of law and few rulings on specific legal questions. They say that (the Shiites) are given over to senseless ranting and contradiction, and that whoever rejects *qiyās* and *ijtihād* is incapable of developing rulings on many legal questions and deriving secondary rulings from fundamental ones.[42]

Statements such as these show that during the Buwayhid period Sunni jurists criticized the Shiites for having an underdeveloped tradition of legal scholarship and inadequate legal methods. The Shiites' need or desire to respond to such criticisms played a critical role in shaping the development of the Shiite legal tradition.

One of the most fundamental issues brought to the fore by Sunni criticisms of the Shiite legal system was the violation of consensus. As mentioned in chapter 2, the concept that it was illicit to go against the consensus (*taḥrīm mukhālafat al-ijmāʿ*) may date back to the time of the Muʿtazilī theologian al-Naẓẓām (d. 220–30/835–45).[43] The Shāfiʿī jurist Ibn al-Qāṣṣ, who died in 335/946, supposedly made the statement, "Whoever denies the consensus of the Community has denied the Prophet."[44] The writings of the Fatimid Shiite jurist al-Qāḍī al-Nuʿmān (d. 363/974) show that such accusations were being directed at Shiites by the mid-tenth century. The Twelver Shiite jurists of the Buwayhid period frequently met with the accusation of violating consensus. Al-Shaykh al-Mufīd's treatise *al-Masāʾil al-ṣāghānīyah* is a response to the accusation on the part of a contemporary Sunni Ḥanafī from Nishapur that a number of Shiite positions on the law, such as the legality of *zawāj al-mutʿah*, or fixed-duration marriage, represent a deviation from consensus (*khurūj ʿan al-ijmāʿ*) and render the Shiites unbelievers. Al-Sharīf al-Murtaḍā wrote his work *al-Intiṣār* specifically in order to counter accusations that Shiite legal positions violated the consensus.[45]

It was primarily such accusations, I believe, that led the Twelver Shiite jurists to develop their own theory of consensus. The recognition of the authority of consensus was the key theoretical step that made the inclusion of the Twelver legal tradition within the *madhhab* system possible. Development of a theory of consensus enabled the Twelvers to counter Sunni accusations of

42. Muḥammad b. al-Ḥasan al-Ṭūsī, *Tahdhīb al-aḥkām*, 10 vols., ed. Sayyid Ḥasan al-Mūsawī al-Kharsān (Beirut: Dār al-aḍwāʾ, 1985), 1: 2; idem, *al-Mabsūṭ fī fiqh al-imāmīyah*, 3 vols., ed. Sayyid Muḥammad Taqī al-Kashfī (Tehran: al-Maṭbaʿah al-ḥaydarīyah, 1967), 1: 1–2.

43. al-Ghazālī, *al-Mustaṣfā*, 1: 173.

44. Cited in al-Khaṭīb al-Baghdādī, *Kitāb al-faqīh waʾl-mutafaqqih*, 2: 19.

45. al-Mufīd, *al-Masāʾil al-ṣāghānīyah*, passim; al-Murtaḍā, *al-Intiṣār*, 1–7.

violating the consensus, with concomitant implications of unbelief or heresy, and to argue that they be allowed to participate fully in legal education and the juridical system. An incident involving al-Sharīf al-Murtaḍā's father, al-Sharīf Abū Aḥmad, shows what was at stake. In 394/1003–4, the Buwayhid *amīr* Bahā' al-Dawlah (379–403/989–1012) decorated Abū Aḥmad in an official ceremony and appointed him Alid *naqīb,* leader of the pilgrimage caravan, supervisor of the grievance council, and chief *qāḍī* of Baghdad. Caliph al-Qādir allowed him to assume all of these positions except that of chief *qāḍī;* he refused to recognize him as such. Messages were exchanged between the caliph and Bahā' al-Dawlah, but al-Qādir refused to give in and Abū Aḥmad did not become the chief *qāḍī.*[46] The sources do not provide specific information regarding these negotiations, but it seems likely that al-Qādir refused to recognize Abū Aḥmad as judge on the grounds that the Twelvers did not have an acceptable legal system and upheld opinions which violated the consensus of the Sunni jurists. An incredible opportunity for the Shiites, the chance to have one of their number serve as chief judge of Baghdad was thus lost and at a time when the Twelvers had made substantial progress in the field of law and could boast accomplished jurists, such as al-Shaykh al-Mufīd and Abū Aḥmad's sons, al-Sharīf al-Murtaḍā and al-Sharīf al-Raḍī, who would probably have served as his deputies had he been appointed. Despite their other social and political successes and despite the backing of the Buwayhid *amīrs*, the Shiites were still subject to systematic discrimination by the Sunni majority, particularly in the field of law.

The leading Shiite jurists al-Shaykh al-Mufīd, al-Sharīf al-Murtaḍā, and al-Shaykh al-Ṭūsī acted as spokesmen for the Shiite community who defended Shiite ideological positions against attack on the part of the Sunnis. Their legal works often answered Sunni accusations that Twelver Shiite legal methodology was inadequate, unreliable, or unfounded. They aimed principally to establish the legitimacy of the Shiite legal tradition, continually pointing out that it fulfilled all the methodological requirements and regulations the Sunnis had set out. They protested at being marginalized, discriminated against, or excluded from public discussion of the sacred law and other religious topics. Although the threat of execution or banishment was remote, considerable social pressure was associated with accusations of heresy. Just as important, however, was what might be termed academic pressure. Al-Murtaḍā's work in particular shows that what was immediately at stake was for the Shiites to be excluded from the process of scholarly disputation on religious legal issues which determined orthodoxy.

With the advent of the Seljuks, who conquered all of Iran and Iraq in the

46. Ibn al-Jawzī, *al-Muntaẓam,* 15: 43; Ibn al-Athīr, *al-Kāmil,* 9: 182.

mid-eleventh century and entered Baghdad in 447/1055, the Sunni traditionalists won their battle against the public presence of Shiism. Sunni political and cultural hegemony was restored. Al-Shaykh al-Ṭūsī, the leading Shiite jurist at the time, fled to Najaf in southern Iraq; his house in al-Karkh was looted and his notebooks burned. Abū ʿAbd Allāh b. al-Jallāb, the head of the cloth-merchants guild, was accused of Shiite heresy (*rafḍ*), executed, and hung above the door of his shop.[47] A period of intellectual activity and exchange crucial for the development of the Shiite legal tradition came to a close. Yet, by then, the Twelvers had acquired the major practical and theoretical foundations necessary to maintain a legal *madhhab* parallel to those of the Sunnis. The tradition was carried on in Najaf and in other cities in Syria and Iran, where Sunni opposition was less severe. It was this historical combination of situations during the Buwayhid period, the high profile of Shiism in the social and political arena coupled with a conservative Sunni traditionalist reaction against religious pluralism, that set the stage for the formation of the Twelver Shiite *madhhab*.

THE BEGINNINGS OF AN ORGANIZED TWELVER *MADHHAB*

As mentioned in chapter 2, Melchert used several criteria to discern the existence of the classical Sunni schools of law as institutions: the recognition of a *raʾīs* or leading jurist, the production of commentaries (*taʿlīqahs*) on standard legal epitomes (*mukhtaṣars*), and the regular transmission of legal knowledge, whereby students were recognized as having completed their legal studies under a particular professor of the law. Adoption of these same criteria allows us to set the establishment of the Twelver Shiite *madhhab* during the time of al-Shaykh al-Mufīd in the late tenth century. Then, probably for the first time, there came into existence a regular system for the education of Twelver jurists, as opposed to theologians and hadith scholars. Al-Shaykh al-Mufīd was recognized as the Twelvers' chief jurist by 377/987–88.[48] Nearly all of the prominent Shiite jurists of the next generation, including al-Sharīf al-Murtaḍā, al-Shaykh al-Ṭūsī, Salār b. ʿAbd al-ʿAzīz al-Daylamī (d. 448/1056), and Abū al-Fatḥ Muḥammad b. ʿAlī al-Karājakī (d. 449/1057), recognized al-Shaykh al-Mufīd as the source of their legal training. After him, al-Sharīf al-Murtaḍā and then al-Shaykh al-Ṭūsī trained equal if not greater numbers of prominent jurists. In contrast, the teachers of al-Shaykh al-Mufīd were primarily theologians and hadith experts; he did not have a recognizable professor of law.[49] In addition, al-Shaykh al-Mufīd authored an epitome of Twelver Shiite law entitled *al-Risālah al-muqniʿah,* which served as a legal reference and textbook. It was in dedication to a ruler (*amīr*) whose name al-Mufīd does not specify, but who

47. Ibn al-Jawzī, *al-Muntaẓam,* 16: 8.

48. Ibn al-Nadīm, *al-Fihrist,* 293.

49. al-Amīn (*Aʿyān al-shīʿah,* 9: 421) provides a list of fifty-six teachers of al-Shaykh al-Mufīd.

may have been the Buwayhid Bahā' al-Dawlah (379–403/ 989–1012) or perhaps the Mazyadid Sanā' al-Dawlah 'Alī b. Mazyad (ca. 350–408/961–1018).[50] The centrality of this text for legal education at the time is demonstrated in that al-Shaykh al-Ṭūsī arranged *Tahdhīb al-aḥkām,* his large compendium of Shiite hadith, according to its chapters, so that it could serve as a sort of companion to or commentary on the work and thereby be a reference for law students. Al-Shaykh al-Ṭūsī, in turn, would write his own epitome of law, entitled *al-Nihāyah fī mujarrad al-fiqh wa'l-fatāwā.*[51] The Twelver Shiite legal tradition adopted the basic formal features of the classical Sunni legal *madhhab*s, and the transmission of legal knowledge took on a regular institutional form which would continue from that time on.

A major indication of the professionalization of Twelver legal education is the regular production of jurists under recognized professors of law. Following are lists of the prominent jurists taught by the three professors al-Shaykh al-Mufīd, al-Sharīf al-Murtaḍā, and al-Shaykh al-Ṭūsī.

Jurists Taught by al-Shaykh al-Mufīd

1. al-Sharīf al-Raḍī (d. 406/1015)
2. al-Sharīf al-Murtaḍā (d. 436/1044)
3. Salār b. 'Abd al-'Azīz al-Daylamī (d. 448/1056)
4. Abū al-Fatḥ Muḥammad b. 'Alī al-Karājakī (d. 449/1057)
5. Aḥmad b. 'Alī al-Najāshī (d. 450/1058)
6. Abū Ja'far Muḥammad b. al-Ḥasan al-Ṭūsī (d. 460/1067)
7. Abū Ya'lā Muḥammad b. al-Ḥasan b. Ḥamzah al-Ja'farī (d. 463/1070–71)[52]
8. Ja'far b. Muḥammad b. Aḥmad al-Rāzī al-Dūryastī (d. ca. 473)[53]
9. Abū al-Faraj al-Muẓaffar b. 'Alī b. al-Ḥusayn al-Ḥamdānī[54]

Jurists Taught by al-Sharīf al-Murtaḍā

1. Abū al-Ṣalāḥ Taqī b. Najm al-Ḥalabī (d. 446/1054)[55]
2. Abū Ya'lā Salār b. 'Abd al-'Azīz al-Daylamī (d. 448/1056 or 463/1071)
3. Abū al-Fatḥ Muḥammad b. 'Alī al-Karājakī (d. 449/1057)

50. al-Shaykh Muḥammad b. Muḥammad b. al-Nu'mān al-Mufīd, *al-Muqni'ah* (Qum: Mu'assasat al-nashr al-islāmī, 1989–90), 27.

51. Al-Ṭūsī (*al-Mabsūṭ,* 1: 2–3) describes *al-Nihāyah* as a *mukhtaṣar,* reporting that he had written the work much earlier *('alā qadīm al-waqt).* He also states that earlier Shiite scholars had written *mukhtaṣar*s on law, though he does not mention any titles.

52. al-Iṣfahānī, *Riyāḍ al-'ulamā',* 4: 16.

53. al-Rāzī, *Fihrist Muntajab al-Dīn,* 37–38; Ibn Shahrāshūb, *Ma'ālim al-'ulamā',* 27; al-Iṣfahānī, *Riyāḍ al-'ulamā',* 1: 110–11; al-Baḥrānī, *Lu'lu'at al-Baḥrayn,* 343–45.

54. al-Rāzī, *Fihrist Muntajab al-Dīn,* 156; al-Iṣfahānī, *Riyāḍ al-'ulamā',* 4: 18–19.

55. Al-Sharīf al-Murtaḍa's students, except for al-Najāshī and al-Ṭūsī, are noted by al-Iṣfahānī (*Riyāḍ al-'ulamā',* 1: 99–100; 2: 445–49; 4: 16–17 [citing a list recorded by al-Shahīd al-Awwal], 34–39; 5: 158) and al-Rāzī (*Fihrist Muntajab al-Dīn,* 35, 47–48, 85–86, 108).

4. Aḥmad b. ʿAlī al-Najāshī (d. 450/1058)
5. al-Shaykh Abū Jaʿfar Muḥammad b. al-Ḥasan al-Ṭūsī (d. 460/1067)
6. Abū Yaʿlā Muḥammad b. al-Ḥasan b. Ḥamzah al-Jaʿfarī (d. 463/1070–71)
7. al-Qāḍī Abū al-Qāsim ʿAbd al-ʿAzīz b. Niḥrīr Ibn al-Barrāj (d. 481/1088)
8. Ibn Rūḥ (d. ?)
9. Hibat Allāh al-Warrāq al-Ṭarābulsī
10. Abū Yaʿlā al-Hāshimī al-ʿAbbāsī
11. Abū al-Ḥasan Sulaymān b. al-Ḥasan al-Ṣihrashtī
12. Abū Muḥammad ʿAbd al-Raḥmān b. Aḥmad b. al-Ḥusayn al-Nīsābūrī al-Khuzāʿī
13. Abū al-Faḍl Thābit b. ʿAbd Allāh al-Yashkurī
14. al-Sayyid Najīb al-Dīn al-Ḥasan b. Muḥammad b. al-Ḥasan al-Mūsawī
15. Abū al-Ḥasan Muḥammad b. Muḥammad al-Buṣrawī

Jurists Taught by al-Shaykh al-Ṭūsī

1. Abū al-Ṣalāḥ Taqī al-Dīn b. Najm al-Dīn al-Ḥalabī (d. 446/1054)[56]
2. Aḥmad b. ʿAlī al-Najāshī (d. 450/1058)
3. al-Qāḍī Abū al-Qāsim ʿAbd al-ʿAzīz b. Niḥrīr Ibn al-Barrāj (d. 481/1088)
4. Abū al-Wafāʾ ʿAbd al-Jabbār b. ʿAbd Allāh b. ʿAlī al-Rāzī (d. after 503/1110)
5. Abū ʿAlī al-Ḥasan b. Muḥammad b. al-Ḥasan al-Ṭūsī (d. after 515/1121)
6. Abū Bakr Aḥmad b. al-Ḥusayn b. Aḥmad al-Nīsābūrī al-Khuzāʿī
7. Ādam b. Yūnus b. al-Muhājir al-Nasafī
8. Abū al-Khayr Barakah b. Muḥammad b. Barakah al-Asadī
9. al-Ḥasan b. al-Ḥusayn b. Bābawayh al-Qummī
10. Muḥyī al-Dīn Abū ʿAbd Allāh al-Ḥusayn b. al-Muẓaffar b. ʿAlī al-Ḥamdānī
11. Abū Muḥammad al-Ḥasan b. ʿAbd al-ʿAzīz b. al-Muḥassin al-Jabhānī
12. al-Sayyid Abū Muḥammad Zayd b. ʿAlī b. al-Ḥusayn al-Ḥasanī
13. Abū al-Ḥasan Sulaymān b. al-Ḥasan al-Ṣihrashtī
14. Ṣāʿid b. Rabīʿah b. Abī Ghānim
15. Abū al-Ṣalt b. ʿAbd al-Qādir b. Muḥammad
16. Abū Muḥammad ʿAbd al-Raḥmān b. Aḥmad b. al-Ḥusayn al-Nīsābūrī al-Khuzāʿī
17. ʿAlī b. ʿAbd al-Ṣamad al-Tamīmī al-Sabzawārī
18. Ghāzī b. Aḥmad b. Abī Manṣūr al-Sāmānī
19. Kurdī b. ʿUkbar b. Kurdī al-Fārisī
20. Abū ʿAbd Allāh Muḥammad b. Hibat Allāh b. Jaʿfar al-Warrāq al-Ṭarābulsī
21. al-Sayyid Abū Ibrāhīm Nāṣir b. al-Riḍā b. Muḥammad al-ʿAlawī al-Ḥusaynī

56. Al-Shaykh al-Ṭūsī's students, except for al-Najāshī, are noted by al-Rāzī, (*Fihrist Muntajab al-Dīn*, 7–8, 9–10, 27, 30, 42–43, 44, 80, 85–86, 99, 107, 108–9, 142, 148, 155, 192), al-Iṣfahānī (*Riyāḍ al-ʿulamāʾ*, 1: 334–38; 3: 66–69), and al-Amīn (*Aʿyān al-Shīʿah*, 5: 244–46; 7: 433–34).

The Twelver Shiite legal tradition had begun to adopt some formal features of the classical Sunni schools of law even before the doctrine of the Greater Occultation was established. Al-Kulaynī wrote his work *al-Kāfī,* the first major compilation of Shiite hadith to be arranged according to the standard chapter-order of Sunni legal works, before the Greater Occultation—he died the year it began. Watt has already suggested that this work represented the adaptation of an essentially Sunni practice to Shiite tradition, a step indicative of the dominance of Sunni conceptions in Islamic thought.[57] We have seen that the scholar Muḥammad b. Aḥmad b. Ibrāhīm b. Yūsuf al-Kātib, born in 281/894–95, had studied both Shiite and Shāfiʿī law. Given that he would have been forty-eight years old at the time the Greater Occultation began, it is most probable that his studies took place before then. Al-Masʿūdī apparently studied both Shiite and Shāfiʿī law in the early tenth century. There had been earlier efforts to establish a regular Twelver Shiite legal system, particularly by the jurist Ibn al-Junayd, but they proved abortive, and it is clear that the subsequent Twelver legal tradition derives quite directly from the work of al-Shaykh al-Mufīd and his successors.

While the sources provide only scattered pieces of information concerning Shiite legal education during this period, a few observations deserve mention. Contemporary Sunni legal education generally took place in a *masjid-khān* complex.[58] For example, Abū Ḥamīd al-Isfarāʾinī (d. 406/1015), the leading Shāfiʿī jurist of Baghdad in his day, taught at the mosque of ʿAbd Allāh b. al-Mubārak, next to Qaṭīʿat al-rabīʿ, where the *khān* or hostel of the law students was located. According to the sources, as many as seven hundred students attended his lessons.[59] The settings in which Shiite jurists taught appear to have been less public than those to which their Sunni contemporaries were accustomed. Al-Shaykh al-Mufīd, al-Sharīf al-Murtaḍā, and al-Shaykh al-Ṭūsī all taught in their own houses or in mosques they had built adjacent to their homes. These top jurists established themselves as law professors—in addition to their other activities and academic commitments—and appointed deputies to teach in their place when they were absent. Al-Shaykh al-Mufīd apparently appointed his son-in-law, Abū Yaʿlā Muḥammad b. al-Ḥasan b. Ḥamzah al-Jaʿfarī (d. 463/1070–71), as his deputy; al-Sharīf al-Murtaḍā appointed Salār b. ʿAbd al-ʿAzīz al-Daylamī (d. 448/1056 or 463/1071) as his deputy.[60] It is not clear where the Shiite law students from outside Baghdad lodged, whether anything like the Sunni law students' hostels existed.

The Twelver law students certainly received stipends. As mentioned earlier, al-Sharīf al-Murtaḍā gave al-Shaykh al-Ṭūsī a stipend of twelve dinars per

57. Watt, *Formative Period,* 278.

58. Makdisi, *Rise of the Colleges,* 27–32.

59. al-Shīrāzī, *Ṭabaqāt al-fuqahāʾ,* 124; Ibn al-Jawzī, *al-Muntaẓam,* 15: 112–13.

60. al-Iṣfahānī, *Riyāḍ al-ʿulamāʾ,* 4: 16, citing al-Shahīd al-Awwal.

month and gave 'Abd al-'Azīz Ibn al-Barrāj (d. 481/1088) a stipend of eight dinars per month. He supposedly granted stipends to all his students.[61] This report implies that the jurists themselves had control over the stipends. It is not clear what the source of the stipends was; there is no mention of *waqf* endowments for this purpose in the sources. The leading jurists may have received pensions from Shiite patrons, such as the Buwayhid *amīrs* or the Mazyadids, who ruled from ca. 350/961 until 545/1150 in southern Iraq and founded the city of Ḥillah, which would become the leading center of Shiite learning in the twelfth and thirteenth centuries, shortly after 397/1007.[62] Al-Shaykh al-Mufīd, at least, enjoyed the patronage of the Mazyadids. Ibn al-Jawzī writes, "He enjoyed special status with the princes of the outlying regions because they tended toward his belief."[63] Ibn al-Jawzī does not specify which princes these were, but the Mazyadids must have been chief among them. When al-Mufīd was exiled from Baghdad in 398/ 1007–8 following Sunni-Shiite riots, he probably took refuge in Karbalā' or Najaf in southern Iraq, for he was able to return to Baghdad when 'Alī b. Mazyad (r. ca. 350–408/961–1018) interceded on his behalf.[64] Al-Sharīf al-Murtaḍā was fabulously wealthy, in addition to having many opportunites for patronage from the Buwayhids, Mazyadids, and others; Yāqūt al-Ḥamawī reports that the yearly income from al-Murtaḍā's properties came to 124,000 dinars.[65] When al-Murtaḍā and al-Raḍī were captured by an Arab chieftain on the way to lead the pilgrimage in 389/999, they paid a ransom of 9,000 dinars.[66] Upon his death, he supposedly left a library of 80,000 volumes. Even after a number of officials had taken many of them, the remaining works were valued at 30,000 dinars.[67] According to another report, he left 30,000 books, over 50,000 dinars and more than that in rugs, vessels, and other belongings.[68] Much of al-Murtaḍā's funds for student stipends probably came

61. al-Iṣfahānī, *Riyāḍ al-'ulamā'*, 3: 142, citing Bahā' al-Dīn al-'Āmilī, citing al-Shahīd al-Awwal; 4: 23, 30.

62. See George Makdisi, "Notes on Ḥilla and the Mazyadids in Medieval Islam," *JAOS* 74 (1954): 249–62.

63. Ibn al-Jawzī, *al-Muntaẓam*, 15: 157.

64. Ibid., 59.

65. al-Ḥamawī, *Mu'jam al-udabā'*, 4: 81, citing a work entitled *al-Mudhayyal* by a certain Tāj al-Islām, who in turn cites a Zaydī contemporary of al-Murtaḍā named al-Kiyā Abū al-Ḥusayn Yaḥyā b. al-Ḥusayn al-'Alawī.

66. al-Khwānsārī, *Rawḍāt al-jannāt*, 4: 286, citing the work *Itḥāf al-warā bi-akhbār Umm al-qurā* by Abū al-Qāsim al-Fahd al-Hāshimī.(d. 835/1431).

67. al-Iṣfahānī, *Riyāḍ al-'ulamā'*, 4: 22, 41, citing al-Shahīd al-Thānī's glosses on al-'Allāmah al-Ḥillī's *Khulāṣat al-aqwāl*, citing al-Tanūkhī (d. 442/1050). Al-Khwānsārī states in *Rawḍāt al-jannāt* (4: 286) that this report derives from al-Tha'ālibī's *Yatīmat al-dahr*, but this is not possible since al-Tha'ālibī died before he did, in 429/1038. Al-Murtaḍā does not appear in *Yatīmat al-dahr*, though he does in the sequel *Tatimmat yatīmat al-dahr*. Of course he was still alive at the time al-Tha'ālibī was writing.

68. Tāj al-Dīn b. Muḥammad Ibn Zuhrah al-Ḥalabī (fl. 753/1352–53), *Ghāyat al-ikhtiṣār fī al-buyūtāt al-'alawīyah al-maḥfūẓah min al-ghubār*, ed. Muḥammad Ṣādiq Baḥr al-'Ulūm (Najaf: al-Maṭba'ah al-ḥaydarīyah, 1962), 76.

from the income on his property—he is supposed to have owned eighty villages between Baghdad and Karbalā'—and it is said that he endowed the income from an entire village to provide paper for his law students.[69]

In addition, the jurists may have been able to expend *khums* funds as stipends for the Shiite law students. The top Shiite jurists in Baghdad controlled a large network of legal consultation that stretched far beyond the immediate region of Baghdad and indeed outside Iraq to Egypt, Syria, and Iran. Al-Shaykh al-Mufīd issued legal *responsa* for Shiites in Egypt, Mosul and Mayyāfāriqīn in Iraq, Ḥarrān in Syria, and Ṣāghān, Dīnawar, Ṭabaristān, Māzandarān, Nūbandajān, and Jurjān in Iran.[70] Al-Sharīf al-Murtaḍā issued *responsa* for followers in Egypt, Ramlah, Sidon, Tripoli, Damascus, Aleppo, Mosul, Wāsiṭ, Daylam, Rayy, Ṭūs, and Jurjān.[71] Al-Shaykh al-Ṭūsī wrote *responsa* for petitioners from Karbalā', Damascus, Aleppo, Rayy, and Qum.[72] Their students served as their representatives in other regions. Al-Sharīf al-Murtaḍā informed his followers in Aleppo that they need not petition him for *fatwā*s when they had Abū al-Ṣalāḥ al-Ḥalabī in their own city.[73] In a similar fashion, al-Qāḍī Ibn al-Barrāj served as al-Ṭūsī's representative in Syria. Such representatives may have relayed *khums* funds from Shiites in their regions to the leading jurists in Baghdad.

EXTANT TWELVER MANUALS OF JURISPRUDENCE

It is in the late tenth and early eleventh centuries that the first extant Twelver Shiite works in the genre of *uṣūl al-fiqh* were produced, nearly two centuries after the appearance of al-Shāfi'ī's *Epistle.* The earliest extant Shiite work in this genre is the manual of al-Shaykh al-Mufīd, which survives in a short abridgment included in the anthology *Kanz al-fawā'id* of Abū al-Fatḥ al-Karājakī (d. 449/1057), one of al-Mufīd's students.[74] The title of al-Mufīd's work is not known. The title prefaced to the abridgment in *Kanz al-fawā'id, Mukhtaṣar al-tadhkirah bi-uṣūl al-fiqh,* "The Abridgment of the Memento on Jurisprudence," appears to be chosen by al-Karājakī himself, rather than indicating he has abridged a work by al-Shaykh al-Mufīd entitled *al-Tadhkirah bi-*

69. al-Iṣfahānī, *Riyāḍ al-'ulamā',* 4: 21, 22, 23, 30.

70. al-Najāshī, *Kitāb al-rijāl,* 312–15; al-Ṭūsī, *Fihrist Kutub al-shī'ah,* 187.

71. al-Najāshī, *Kitāb al-rijāl,* 206–7; al-Ṭūsī, *Fihrist Kutub al-shī'ah,* 125–26; Muḥsin al-Amīn, *A'yān al-Shī'ah,* 8: 219.

72. al-Amīn, *A'yān al-Shī'ah,* 9: 166.

73. al-Iṣfahānī, *Riyāḍ al-'ulamā',* 4: 17.

74. Abū al-Fatḥ Muḥammad b. 'Alī al-Karājakī, *Kanz al-fawā'id,* 2 vols., ed. 'Abd Allāh Ni'mah (Beirut: Dār al-aḍwā', 1985), 2: 15–30. Several scholars report that the text in *Kanz al-fawā'id* is the complete work (Robert Brunschvig, "Les *Uṣūl al-Fiqh* Imāmites à leur stade ancien (Xe et XIe siècles)," in *Études d'Islamologie,* ed. Abdel Magid Turki (Paris: G. P. Maisonneuve et Larose, 1976), 3:326; McDermott, *Theology of al-Shaykh al-Mufīd,* 28; Sezgin, *GAS,* 1: 551. Modarressi correctly notes that the extant text is merely a summary of the original work (see his *Shī'ī Law,* 7). Al-Karājakī states of the text, "I have excerpted it *(istakhrajtuh)* from the book of our Master al-Mufīd." (*Kanz al-fawā'id,* 2: 15).

uṣūl al-fiqh. It seems to reflect al-Karājakī's statement at the beginning of the text regarding the reason he composed the work: "You have requested—may God prolong your glory—that I set down for you a collection of opinions concerning *uṣūl al-fiqh* in abridged form (*mukhtaṣarah*), so that it might serve you as an accessible memento (*tadhkirah*) of our beliefs concerning this topic."[75] The use of the two terms *tadhkirah* and *mukhtaṣar* here suggest that al-Karājakī's title is meant to describe his own abridgment and does not refer to the original title of al-Mufīd's work. Similarly, it is not known how long al-Mufīd's original work was. It must have been a great deal longer than the abridgment, because al-Karājakī informs the reader that he has produced only the basic doctrines, stripping the text of all extraneous material. At the end of the abridgment he writes, "I have set down for you—may God support you—the collection you requested be set forth, and I have presented it without its proofs and derivations, so that it might serve as a memento to you of our beliefs, as you mentioned."[76] In the introduction to his *'Uddat al-uṣūl*, al-Ṭūsī describes al-Mufīd's text—he omits the title as well—as a short work (*mukhtaṣar*). This term may designate a sizable one-volume work; al-Ṭūsī refers to his own *'Uddat al-uṣūl*, just over three hundred pages in the lithograph edition, as a *mukhtaṣar* as well.[77]

Al-Mufīd probably wrote his manual on *uṣūl al-fiqh* before 380/990. In the seventeenth volume of *al-Mughnī*, devoted to jurisprudence, al-Qāḍī 'Abd al-Jabbār addresses a number of Twelver Shiite positions concerning consensus. It seems most likely that these were articulated in al-Mufīd's manual on *uṣūl al-fiqh;* no other alternative source readily suggests itself. Since 'Abd al-Jabbār dictated *al-Mughnī* between 360/970 and 380/990,[78] al-Mufīd must have completed his work before the latter date.

The next two major works on Twelver Shiite *uṣūl al-fiqh* were al-Ṭūsī's *'Uddat al-uṣūl* and al-Murtaḍā's *al-Dharī'ah ilā uṣūl al-sharī'ah*. The younger jurist al-Ṭusī wrote *'Uddat al-uṣūl* before al-Murtaḍā wrote his major manual on the topic, *al-Dharī'ah ilā uṣūl al-sharī'ah*.[79] In the introduction to *'Uddat al-uṣūl*, al-Ṭūsī first mentions al-Shaykh al-Mufīd's work on *uṣūl al-fiqh*, observing that it did not treat the topic fully; al-Mufīd, he writes, missed important

75. al-Karājakī, *Kanz al-fawā'id*, 2: 15. Moussavi states that this was the title of the original work (*Religious Authority*, 24 n. 33, 79).

76. al-Karājakī, *Kanz al-fawā'id*, 2: 30.

77. al-Ṭūsī, *'Uddat al-uṣūl*, 2.

78. Johannes Reiner Theodorus Maria Peters, *God's Created Speech* (Leiden: E. J. Brill, 1976), 14.

79. That al-Ṭūsī wrote *'Uddat al-uṣūl* first has also been pointed out by Aron Zysow (*Economy of Certainty*, 514 n. 30). Nevertheless, the assertion that al-Sharīf al-Murtaḍā's work is the earlier of the two continues to be made. For example, Sachedina states, "*al-Dharī'a* was the first complete work of its kind" (*Just Ruler*, 11). Moussavi's discussion also implies that *al-Dharī'ah* predates *'Uddat al-uṣūl*. (*Religious Authority*, 25–26).

points which deserved treatment, and some of his statements needed to be rectified. Al-Ṭūsī then states that al-Sharīf al-Murtaḍā—whom he calls *sayyidunā al-ajall*—has not yet written a comprehensive work on *uṣūl al-fiqh,* although he has taught the topic for some time. Al-Ṭūsī writes, "Although [*uṣūl al-fiqh*] is discussed extensively in his dictations and the texts which are studied under him, he has not written a work on the topic to serve as a reference and support."[80] Thus, al-Murtaḍā's work *al-Dharī'ah* did not exist when al-Ṭūsī began writing *'Uddat al-uṣūl.*

In the introduction to *al-Dharī'ah,* al-Sharīf al-Murtaḍā praises al-Ṭūsī, but criticizes his work. Although al-Ṭūsī's name does not appear in the text, it is certainly in reference to *'Uddat al-uṣūl* that al-Murtaḍā writes: "I have found that one [scholar] who has devoted an independent work to *uṣūl al-fiqh,* although he presented many of its concepts, topics, and forms correctly, strayed from the definition and method of the genre of *uṣūl al-fiqh* and transgressed it."[81] Al-Murtaḍā criticizes al-Ṭūsī for mixing subjects meant to be dealt with in works on theology or philosophy with his *uṣūl al-fiqh.* He refers to the definition of necessary and acquired knowledge, the means by which philosophical speculation can produce certitude, causality, the relative status of the Koran and prophetic hadith as scripture, and other topics that are found in the introduction to al-Ṭūsī's work.[82] Al-Ṭūsī had prefaced *'Uddat al-uṣūl* with these epistemological and theological postulates because he felt they were logically necessary to support the results of *uṣūl al-fiqh,* but al-Murtaḍa replies that if one takes this stand, one must include all of *uṣūl al-dīn* in *uṣūl al-fiqh,* thus violating the definition of the genre.[83]

Al-Murtaḍā completed *al-Dharī'ah ilā uṣūl al-sharī'ah* in 430/1038–39.[84] At the outset one may therefore say that al-Ṭūsī wrote *'Uddat al-uṣūl* before 430/1038–39, the date of *al-Dharī'ah,* and after 413/1022, when al-Shaykh al-Mufīd died, for al-Ṭūsī refers to him in the text as having passed away. It seems likely, though, that al-Ṭūsī wrote *'Uddat al-uṣūl* after al-Murtaḍā wrote *Jawāb al-masā'il al-tabbānīyāt* and *Jawāb al-masā'il al-mawṣilīyāt al-thālithah,* which date to ca. 420/1029. These are probably al-Murtaḍā's treatises on *uṣūl al-fiqh* topics to which al-Ṭūsī refers in his introduction. In other words, *'Ud-*

80. al-Ṭūsī, *'Uddat al-uṣūl,* 2. Calder ("Structure of Authority," 175), assuming that *'Uddat al-uṣūl* was written after *al-Dharī'ah,* avoids taking this statement literally and asserts that al-Ṭūsī's remark "reflected professional antipathy rather than objective assessment."

81. al-Sharīf al-Murtaḍā, *al-Dharī'ah ilā uṣūl al-sharī'ah,* 2 vols., ed. Abu al-Qāsim Gorjī. Tehran, 1967–69), 1: 2.

82. al-Ṭūsī, *'Uddat al-uṣūl,* 4–25.

83. al-Murtaḍā, *al-Dharī'ah,* 1: 2–3. Al-Murtaḍā's criticisms of al-Ṭūsī here are strikingly similar to al-Baṣrī's criticisms of al-Qāḍī 'Abd al-Jabbār's work on jurisprudence, *al-'Umad,* in the introduction to *al-Mu'tamad* (Al-Baṣrī, *al-Mu'tamad,* 1: 3–4; Makdisi, "Juridical Theology," 15–16).

84. al-Ṭihrānī, *al-Dharī'ah ilā taṣānīf al-shī'ah,* 10: 26.

dat al-uṣūl dates to the 420s/1030s. Nevertheless, al-Shaykh al-Ṭūsī must have subsequently edited *'Uddat al-uṣūl* after al-Sharīf al-Murtaḍā's death in 436/1044. While the introduction to the work and the phrases of blessing that occur after al-Murtaḍā's name in several passages imply he was alive when al-Ṭūsī was writing, the phrases of blessing appearing after his name elsewhere in the work—*qaddasa 'Llāhu rūḥah,* "may God bless his soul," or *raḥimahu 'Llāh,* "may God have mercy on him"—imply he was deceased when those passages were written. Moreover, in one passage of *'Uddat al-uṣūl* al-Ṭūsī mentions his commentary, *Talkhīṣ al-shāfī,* on the theory of the imamate, which he completed in Rajab 432/March 1041, several years after al-Murtaḍā had completed *al-Dharī'ah.*[85] Al-Ṭūsī must therefore have written *'Uddat al-uṣūl* initially during al-Murtaḍā's lifetime, before 430/1038–39, and subsequently redrafted sections of the work after al-Murtaḍā's death, though he left the original introduction intact.

'Uddat al-uṣūl and *al-Dharī'ah* show an acute awareness of the Sunni genre of *uṣūl al-fiqh.* They cite Sunni works in the genre such as the *Risālah* of al-Shāfi'ī and al-Qāḍī 'Abd al-Jabbār's *al-'Umad.* Al-Ṭūsī's introduction reports that he was asked to write a short manual including all the chapters generally found in *uṣūl al-fiqh* works. He refers to these well-known chapters in setting forth the organization of his own work, and adds that while some authors have included the topics of *ijmā', qiyās, ijtihād,* the jurisconsult and the layman, and the question of original licitness or prohibition in the chapter on acts (*af'āl*), he will not do so.[86] As mentioned above, al-Murtaḍā also refers to the standard definition of the genre in criticizing al-Ṭūsī's inclusion of philosophical topics in *al-'Uddah.* It is clear from their individual remarks that they both had clear notions concerning the existing—that is, Sunni—genre of *uṣūl al-fiqh.*

Al-Sharīf al-Murtaḍā also wrote a number of treatises on individual topics generally falling under the rubric of *uṣūl al-fiqh,* including his early work, *Jawāb al-masā'il al-mawṣilīyāt al-ūlā,* which treated *qiyās* and was completed in 382/992–93.[87] His treatise *Jawābāt al-masā'il al-mawṣilīyāt al-thālithah* was completed shortly after Rabī' I 420/March–April 1029, when the questions addressed in it were posed. His *Jawāb al-masā'il al-tabbānīyāt* was written prior to 420/1019, for he mentions that work in *Jawābāt al-masā'il al-mawṣilīyāt al-thālithah,* stating that nothing like it is to be found in any of the Shiites'

85. al-Ṭūsī, *'Uddat al-uṣūl,* 2, 28, 36, 68, 124, 189, 199, 203, 209, 232, 269, 279, 291, 296, 303; idem, *Talkhīṣ al-shāfī,* 3 vols., ed. Sayyid Ḥusayn Baḥr al-'Ulūm (Najaf: Maṭba'at al-ādāb, 1963), 3: 227.

86. al-Ṭūsī, *'Uddat al-uṣūl,* 2–3, 203, 294.

87. al-Murtaḍā, *al-Dharī'ah,* editor's introduction, 1: 2 n. 5. Al-Murtaḍā mentions in his *Jawāb al-masā'il al-mawṣilīyāt al-thālithah* that he wrote this work in the 380s/990s (*Rasā'il al-Sharīf al-Murtaḍā,* 4 vols. [Qum: Maṭba'at al-khayyām, 1985–89], 1: 204).

compiled (*muṣannaf*) works and implying that it provides the most substantial Shiite discussion to date on *uṣūl al-fiqh* topics.[88] It is probably these two works in particular that al-Ṭūsī refers to in the introduction to *'Uddat al-uṣūl* when he remarks that al-Murtaḍā has not written a complete work on *uṣūl al-fiqh* although he deals with a number of *uṣūl al-fiqh* topics in his dictations and the other works studied under him.

EARLIER SHIITE MANUALS OF JURISPRUDENCE

Shiite works on *uṣūl al-fiqh* may have been written before al-Shaykh al-Mufīd wrote his manual, though they have not been preserved. The famous Shiite historian al-Mas'ūdī, who was active in the first half of the tenth century, wrote a number of legal works, including several works on *uṣūl al-fiqh*. It was suggested above that al-Mas'ūdī participated in the Shāfi'ī legal *madhhab*, and his works on jurisprudence may have been written from a Sunni, Shāfi'ī point of view. There is nevertheless some chance that one or more of them was dedicated to Shiite *uṣūl al-fiqh*. Three of his works appear to treat jurisprudence: *Naẓm al-adillah fī uṣūl al-millah*, *Naẓm al-a'lām fī uṣūl al-aḥkām*, and *Kitāb al-masā'il wa'l-'ilal fī al-madhāhib wa'l-milal*.[89] Al-Mas'ūdī mentions all three of these works in the introduction to his later work, *Kitāb al-Tanbīh wa'l-ishrāf*. The introduction to *Murūj al-dhahab* mentions only *Naẓm al-adillah fī uṣūl al-millah*, which must therefore date to before 332/943–44, when he began writing the history. The other two works likely date to between 332/943–44 and ca. 345/956, when al-Mas'ūdī died.

In the introduction to *al-Tanbīh*, al-Mas'ūdī gives a general description of the topics treated in these works without differentiating among the three. He writes that they treat the conflicting opinions jurists have held concerning fundamental religious doctrines. The term he uses is *uṣūl al-dīn*, which later would refer more specifically to philosophical theology but apparently refers here to legal methodology. The only specific school of thought he mentions in this passage is that of the Ẓāhirīs. He rejects the Ẓāhirī position, which includes the rejection of *qiyās*, *ra'y*, and *istiḥsān* in legal issues, claiming that Koranic verses and prophetic hadith specifically warn against adopting blind imitation (*taqlīd*) and the overrestriction of the sense of scriptural texts. He adds that these works treat additional topics related to the principles of arriving at legal opinions (*uṣūl al-fatwā*), including both rational and scriptural methods.[90] His use of the term *uṣūl al-fatwā* here implies that these three works indeed

88. al-Murtaḍā, *Rasā'il*, 1: 201, 206.

89. On these works see al-Mas'ūdī, *Murūj al-dhahab*, 1: 12–13; idem, *Kitāb al-Tanbīh wa'l-ishrāf*, 4–5; Khalidi, *Islamic Historiography*, 159–60, 162; Shboul, *Al-Mas'ūdī*, 56–57.

90. al-Mas'ūdī, *Kitāb al-Tanbīh wa'l-ishrāf*, 4–5.

treat *uṣūl al-fiqh* in particular, as one would expect from the titles *Naẓm al-a'lām fī uṣūl al-aḥkām* and *Naẓm al-adillah fī uṣūl al-millah*, both characteristic of later titles in the genre of *uṣūl al-fiqh*.

In the introduction to *Murūj al-dhahab*, al-Mas'ūdī describes the contents of *Naẓm al-adillah fī uṣūl al-millah* in detail, showing clearly that it was a manual of *uṣūl al-fiqh* which included the topics found in later works in the genre, such as al-Baṣrī's *al-Mu'tamad fī uṣūl al-fiqh*. The topics he cites, in the order they appear in his text, are as follows: legal analogy and *ijtihād*, speculation and *istiḥsān*, abrogating and abrogated scriptural texts, consensus, particular and general scriptural texts, divine commands and prohibitions, the innate prohibition or licitness of acts, oral traditions including a discussion of concurrent and isolated traditions, and the acts of the Prophet (*af'āl al-nabī*). Al-Mas'ūdī, in referring to a polemical context with respect to the work, states that it "rebuts the opinions[91] of the opponents concerning those (questions) on which they have differed with us, but agrees with them concerning some part of these."[92] Al-Mas'ūdī does not specify here who these "opponents" (*al-khuṣūm*) are, but he uses the term in a way which suggests that they constitute a defined group and that their identity should be obvious to the reader. It is certainly possible to read this passage as a Shiite reference to Sunnis. It is also possible, given al-Mas'ūdī's statements against literalist interpretations and *taqlīd* elsewhere, to read it as a reference to strict traditionalists or literalists, whether Sunni or Shiite, who reject the use of rational methods in deriving legal rules. The first interpretation, if correct, would imply that the work was indeed a Shiite manual of *uṣūl al-fiqh*.

The description of the contents of *Naẓm al-adillah fī uṣūl al-millah* in *Murūj al-dhahab* as well as the discussion of all three works in *al-Tanbīh* suggest that the topics of *qiyās, ijtihād, ra'y*, and *istiḥsān* were of polemic concern to al-Mas'ūdī. These terms appear first in the book's list of contents, breaking out of the typical order of chapters in *uṣūl al-fiqh* works. The printed text of *Murūj al-dhahab* implies that the work upheld the use of *qiyās, ijtihād, ra'y*, and *istiḥsān* in deriving legal opinions, holding that the book contains legal methodological principles (*uṣūl al-fatwā wa-qawānīn al-aḥkām*), such as "the certitude of the use of analogy and independent reasoning in deriving legal rules" (*tayaqqun al-qiyās wa-l-ijtihād fī l-aḥkām*) and "the occurrence of speculation and the search for the preferable" (*waq' al-ra'y wa-l-istiḥsān*). Ḥasan al-Amīn, the editor of his father's *A'yān al-shī'ah*, remarks that the published text of *Murūj al-dhahab* is corrupt here; according to him, the noun *tayaqqun*

91. Reading *ārā'*, "opinions," instead of *anbā'*, "reports, accounts," in the text. Pellat translates *anbā'* as "arguments," which seems to stretch the meaning of the word. Abū al-Ḥasan al-Mas'ūdī, *Les Prairies d'or*, 2 vols., trans. Barbier de Meynard et Pavet de Courteille, revue et corrigée par Charles Pellat (Paris: Centre national de la recherche scientifique, 1962), 1: 3.

92. al-Mas'ūdī, *Murūj al-dhahab*, 1: 12–13.

should read *nafy,* "refutation, rejection," and the noun *waq'* should read *raf',* "abolition, removal."[93] The words *tayaqqun* and *waq'* do appear awkward in the text, but it is also true that al-Mas'ūdī expresses disdain for literalist interpretations in the passage cited above in the *al-Tanbīh* in a nearly identical context, implying that he approved of *qiyās, ijtihād, istiḥsān,* and *ra'y.* Al-Amīn's editing of the text apparently intends to bring al-Mas'ūdī's opinions more in line with what is known of early Shiite jurisprudence. The question of the true intent of this text cannot be answered in a satisfactory manner without an extensive examination of the manuscripts of *Murūj al-dhahab,* but it would seem that al-Mas'ūdī must have taken a rationalist approach in his exposition of *uṣūl al-fiqh,* in contrast to al-Shaykh al-Mufīd, al-Sharīf al-Murtaḍā, and al-Shaykh al-Ṭūsī, who rejected *qiyās* emphatically. Appearing before 332/943–44, over a century after al-Shāfi'ī's *al-Risālah, Naẓm al-adillah* was perhaps the first Shiite work of *uṣūl al-fiqh* in Islamic history. It may represent a fascinating stage in the development of Shiite jurisprudence, one which was simply lost and forgotten or rejected on principle by the major architects of Shiite jurisprudence in the Buwayhid period. Al-Mas'ūdī's jurisprudence accepted the principle of *ijmā',* though we cannot tell from his description how he may have reconciled the concept of consensus with the theoretical authority of the imam. It also included *qiyās* and *ijtihād,* which the main jurists of the Buwayhid period would reject.

Abū 'Alī Muḥammad b. Aḥmad b. al-Junayd, also known as Ibn al-Junaydī or al-Kātib al-Iskāfī, was a tenth-century Twelver Shiite scholar who lived in Baghdad, though he traveled and taught in Iran as well.[94] He was from the village of al-Iskāf near Nahrawānāt in southern Iraq. We do not have exact dates for Ibn al-Junayd; the report that he died in Rayy in 981/991, cited in a number of studies, is incorrect.[95] Sayyid Muḥammad Mahdī Baḥr al-'Ulūm holds that this piece of misinformation probably resulted from confusion between Ibn al-Junayd and Ibn Bābawayh al-Qummī, who did die in Rayy in 981/991. It goes back to al-Ardabīlī's biographical work, *Jāmi' al-ruwāt,* which was completed in 1100/1689.[96] Baḥr al-'Ulūm himself does not state when Ibn al-Ju-

93. al-Amīn, *A'yān al-shī'ah,* 8: 223, 223 nn. 1–2.

94. Ibn Nadīm, *al-Fihrist,* 291, 315; al-Ṭūsī, *Fihrist kutub al-shī'ah,* 160; al-Najāshī, *Kitāb al-rijāl,* 299–302; Ibn Shahrāshūb, *Ma'ālim al-'ulamā',* 87–88; Ibn al-Muṭahhar al-Ḥillī, *Rijāl al-'Allāmah al-Ḥillī,* 145; al-Ḥurr al-'Āmilī, *Amal al-āmil,* 2: 236–37; al-Iṣfahānī, *Riyāḍ al-'ulamā',* 5: 19–21; Sayyid Muḥammad Mahdī Baḥr al-'Ulūm, *Rijāl al-Sayyid Baḥr al-'Ulūm,* 4 vols. (Najaf: Maṭba'at al-ādāb, 1965–67), 3: 205–25; al-Amīn, *A'yān al-shī'ah,* 9: 101; Modarressi, *Introduction to Shī'ī Law,* 35–39.

95. For example, Gustav Flügel, editor of Ibn Nadīm, *Kitāb al-fihrist,* 2 vols. (Leipzig: F. C. W. Vogel, 1871–72), 2: 83 n. 3; Zysow, *Economy of Certainty,* 498; Sachedina, *Just Ruler,* 9; Klemm, "Vier sufarā'," 128.

96. Muḥammad b. 'Alī al-Ardabīlī, *Jāmi' al-ruwāt,* 2 vols. (Qum: Maktabat Āyat Allāh al-Mar'ashī, 1983), 2: 59. Al-Ardābīlī clearly makes a mistake here, since he claims to be citing this piece of information from al-Najāshī.

nayd died, but only remarks that his death occurred before 381/991.[97] Ibn al-Junayd is reported to have written *responsa* for the Buwayhid *amīr* Mu'izz al-Dawlah, who entered Baghdad on 13 Jumādā 334/21 December 945 and ruled until his death in 356/967. He also wrote many *responsa (masā'il kathīrah)* for Abū Manṣūr Sebuktegin, who served as governor under the last Sāmānids but was *de facto* ruler from 366/977 until 387/997[98]—which would imply that Ibn al-Junayd died no earlier than 366/977. Ibn al-Naddīm mentions Ibn al-Junayd in *al-Fihrist,* refers to him as a prominent Imami scholar (*min akābir al-shī'ah al-imāmīyah*), and states that he was "of recent times" (*qarīb al-'ahd*), implying that he had died not long before 377/987–88, when Ibn al-Nadīm was writing.[99] Ibn al-Junayd's death date can therefore be set reliably between 366/977 and 377/988.

Ibn al-Junayd was probably born near the beginning of the tenth century. He must have studied as a youth in Baghdad. Already an accomplished scholar, he went to Iran, where he stopped in Nishapur in 340/951–52. He probably returned to Baghdad and spent a number of years there, then returned to Iran and attended the court of Sebuktegin after 366/977. The main evidence for this sketch is to be found in al-Shaykh al-Mufīd's treatise *al-Masā'il al-ṣāghānīyah.* Al-Shaykh al-Mufīd cites a Ḥanafī interlocutor from Nishapur who reports that Ibn al-Junayd arrived there in 340/951–52 and taught law to the local Twelver Shiites. The Ḥanafī scholar accused Ibn al-Junayd of claiming to have correspondence with the twelfth imam and of collecting funds in Nishapur on the imam's behalf, though al-Mufīd rejects these accusations as spurious. Al-Mufīd also notes that Ibn Junayd received money from Iran—"the East"—after his subsequent return to Baghdad, so it appears that he had spent a considerable amount of time in Baghdad before 340/951–52 and returned there after his sojourn in Iran.[100] That al-Shaykh al-Mufīd knew this piece of information and in addition says "we used to rebuke him soundly" for his adoption of *qiyās* implies they knew each other for some time in Baghdad. Ibn al-Nadīm's account in the *al-Fihrist* implies that Ibn al-Junayd was a well-known scholar of some stature in Baghdad in the mid-tenth century.

Ibn al-Junayd was a prolific writer on Shiite law, and his works show evidence of a highly developed system of jurisprudence. They include a twenty-volume compendium of Shiite law entitled *Tahdhīb al-shī'ah li-aḥkām al-sharī'ah;* al-Najāshī records its chapter headings, which show that it was an extensive work covering all of the standard categories of *fiqh.*[101] He also wrote

97. Baḥr al-'Ulūm, *Rijāl al-Sayyid Baḥr al-'Ulūm,* 3: 222.

98. al-Najāshī, *Kitāb al-rijāl,* 301.

99. Ibn al-Nadīm, *al-Fihrist,* 291.

100. al-Mufīd, *al-Masā'il al-ṣāghānīyah,* 17–18.

101. al-Najāshī, *Kitāb al-rijāl,* 299–301.

a short work on Shiite *fiqh*, giving the legal rulings without their derivation (*mujarrad*), entitled *Kitāb al-mukhtaṣar al-aḥmadī li'l-fiqh al-muḥammadī*.[102] This work was an epitome of Twelver law like the later works *al-Muqni'ah* of al-Shaykh al-Mufīd and *al-Nihāyah* of al-Shaykh al-Ṭūsī and was probably intended to serve as a reference work and legal textbook. It was preserved until long after the Buwayhid period. From it, al-'Allāmah al-Ḥillī cites Ibn al-Junayd's legal opinions, many of which agree with Ḥanafī positions, in his *Mukhtalaf al-shī'ah*.[103] Ibn al-Junayd also wrote a work giving his individual legal opinions entitled *Ḥadā'iq al-quds*.[104] He wrote *Kitāb khalāṣ al-mubtadi'īn min ḥayrat al-mujādilīn*, probably a work on dialectic and legal disputation; and as mentioned above, he accepted the concepts of *qiyās* and *ijtihād*, and wrote works entitled *The Removal of Distortion and Deception for Gullible Shiites Concerning Analogical Reasoning* and *Disclosing Traditions from the Imams Concerning Ijtihād that Stubborn Opponents Have Suppressed*.[105]

Ibn al-Junayd's *Kitāb al-ifhām li-uṣūl al-aḥkām* appears, from its title, to be a work on *uṣūl al-fiqh*.[106] Ibn al-Nadīm's text adds the comment "it follows the method of al-Ṭabarī's *Epistles* for its chapters" (*yajrī majrā rasā'il al-Ṭabarī li-kutubih*), and al-Ṭūsī's text adds, "it follows the method of al-Ṭabarī's *Questions*" (*yajrī majrā masā'il al-Ṭabarī*).[107] This reference is possibly to a work by the well-known Shāfi'ī jurist Abū 'Alī al-Ḥusayn b. al-Qāsim al-Ṭabarī (d. 350/961). Al-Subkī reports that Abū 'Alī wrote a work on *uṣūl al-fiqh*, and Ibn al-Nadīm reports that he wrote a work entitled *Kitāb mukhtaṣar masā'il al-khilāf fī al-kalām wa'l-naẓar* on philosophical theology and dialectic.[108] Ibn al-Nadīm's comparison may relate to the method or organization of the work. In any case, it appears very likely that *Kitāb al-ifhām ilā uṣūl al-aḥkām* treated *uṣūl al-fiqh* in particular.

Ibn al-Junayd brought Shiite jurisprudence closer in line with Sunni jurisprudence than contemporary Shiite scholars were willing to allow. He accepted *ijtihād* and *qiyās* as legitimate legal principles and probably wrote a complete work on *uṣūl al-fiqh*. Al-Shaykh al-Mufīd cites a Shiite interlocutor mentioning the differences of opinion to be found between the works of Ibn Bābawayh al-Qummī on hadith and the works of Ibn al-Junayd on points of

102. al-Ṭūsī, *Fihrist kutub al-shī'ah*, 160.

103. Bāqir al-Muḥsinī al-Khurramshahrī has culled the legal opinions of Ibn al-Junayd from earlier sources in *al-Fatāwā li-Ibn al-Junayd al-Iskāfī* (Qum: al-Maṭba'ah al-'ilmīyah, 1991).

104. Ibn al-Nadīm, *al-Fihrist*, 291. This is clearly the first half of a *saj'* title, the second half of which must have been *fī al-aḥkām allatī ikhtārahā li'l-nafs*, or something of that sort.

105. al-Najāshī, *Kitāb al-rijāl*, 301, 302.

106. The title is mentioned in Ibn al-Nadīm, *al-Fihrist*, 291; al-Ṭūsī, *Fihrist kutub al-shī'ah*, 160; Ibn Shahrāshūb, *Ma'ālim al-'ulamā'*, 87.

107. Ibn al-Nadīm, *al-Fihrist*, 291; al-Ṭūsī, *Fihrist kutub al-shī'ah*, 160.

108. al-Subkī, *Ṭabaqāt al-shāfi'iyah al-kubrā*, 3: 280; Ibn al-Nadīm, *al-Fihrist*, 315.

law (*al-masā'il al-fiqhīyah*). Al-Mufīd characterizes Ibn al-Junayd's books as follows: "He filled them with legal rulings which he arrived at through conjecture (*ẓann*) and through adopting the doctrine of our opponents (*madhhab al-mukhālifīn*) and analogy (*qiyās*)." In the work *al-Masā'il al-miṣrīyah,* legal *responsa* to questions sent from Twelver Shiites in Egypt, Ibn al-Junayd claimed that a number of hadiths handed down from the imams were contradictory and on that basis held that the imams accepted the use of *ra'y,* personal opinion or speculation; al-Shaykh al-Mufīd wrote a refutation of this work.[109] According to al-Shaykh al-Mufīd, Shiite scholars rejected Ibn al-Junayd's works and did not pay any attention to them because of his use of *qiyās;* al-Ṭūsī makes a similar statement.[110] As mentioned above, al-Murtaḍā wrote a treatise rejecting the use of *qiyās* entitled *al-Mawṣilīyāt al-ūlā* in 382/992–93. In an attempt to explain Ibn al-Junayd's adoption of *qiyās* as an aberration, later Shiite scholars make the unsupported claim that he eventually repented of his use of *qiyās* and abandoned it.[111]

EARLY SHIITE WORKS ON THE DISPUTED POINTS OF LAW

The writing of works on Sunni-Shiite *khilāf* or disputed legal opinions imply a certain acceptance, at least on the surface or for the sake of argument, of the idea of coordinate schools of law or a plurality of legal traditions belonging to the same Islamic community. For the Twelver Shiites, the major motive behind writing such works was to enable them to debate efficiently with Sunni jurists. Their goal was to get their legal rulings recognized as legitimate dissenting opinions, having the same status as those held in the Sunni *madhhab*s. The first such work on *khilāf* the historical record reveals is al-Mas'ūdī's *Kitāb al-wājib fī al-furūḍ al-lawāzib* (or *al-lawāzim*), which includes such disputed issues as fixed-duration marriage (*mut'ah*) and the wiping of one's boots as part of ablutions (*al-masḥ 'alā al-khuffayn*). Ibn al-Junayd's works *Kitāb al-nuṣrah li-aḥkām al-'itrah, Kitāb al-khāṣim li'l-shī'ah fī nikāḥ al-mut'ah,* and *Kitāb al-intiṣāf li-man rawā al-inḥirāf 'an madhhab al-ashrāf fī mawārīth al-akhlāf* also appear to deal with Sunni-Shiite *khilāf,* the latter two treating temporary marriage and inheritance law in particular.[112] The earliest extant Shiite work on *khilāf* is al-Shaykh al-Mufīd's short treatise on the topic, a compendium of those rulings on which the Shiites differ from the Sunnis.[113] This treatise is probably the work Ibn Shahrāshūb refers to as *al-A'lām mimmā ijtama'at 'alayh al-imāmīyah*

109. al-Mufīd, *al-Masā'il al-sarawīyah,* in his *'Iddat rasā'il li'l-Shaykh al-Mufīd* (Qum: Maktabat al-Mufīd, n.d.), 222–23, 224.

110. al-Shaykh al-Mufīd, *al-Masā'il al-ṣāghānīyah,* 18; al-Ṭūsī, *Fihrist kutub al-shī'ah,* 160.

111. al-Karakī, *Hidāyat al-abrār,* 306; al-Jazā'irī, *Zahr al-rabī',* 573.

112. al-Najāshī, *Kitāb al-rijāl,* 301–2.

113. al-Shaykh al-Mufīd, *'Iddat rasā'il li'al-Shaykh al-Mufīd* (Qum: Maktabat al-Mufīd, n.d.), 318–42.

(min al-aḥkām).[114] It is not dated, but was written after *Awā'il al-maqālāt,* which he mentions in the text. The next such work was *al-Intiṣār,* by al-Sharīf al-Murtaḍā. He completed *al-Intiṣār* after Rabī' I 420/March–April 1029, the date he wrote the treatise *Jawābāt al-masā'il al-mawṣilīyāt al-thālithah,* for in the latter work he mentions that he is currently composing a book on conflicting legal opinions (*kitāb masā'il al-khilāf al-shar'īyah*) and asks for God's help in finishing it. In another passage of the same treatise he refers to *al-Intiṣār* as a work on "legal rulings which the Imami Shiites have adopted uniquely" (*al-masā'il al-fiqhīyah allatī tafarradat bihā al-shī'ah al-imāmīyah*).[115] The next work of this kind is al-Ṭūsī's *al-Khilāf,* a much larger compendium which presents not only those opinions the Shiites hold uniquely but also the conflicting Sunni opinions in much greater detail.[116] In a sense, works on Sunni-Shiite *khilāf* imply a certain acceptance of the coordinate *madhhab* system in which consensus operates.

THE SHIITE ADOPTION OF CONSENSUS

The term consensus (*ijmā'*) appears occasionally in early Shiite sources in reference to the opinions of *al-'iṣābah,* "the loyal band," a group of companions of the later imams. They played a role in evaluating the reliability of earlier transmitters of Shiite hadith, and their unanimous decision concerning which companions of Muḥammad al-Bāqir and Ja'far al-Ṣādiq could be trusted is taken as irrefutable evidence by later scholars.[117] Nevertheless, this early usage seems to have little to do with the Twelver incorporation of the concept of consensus into their legal theory, which dates to the Buwayhid period. Sunni works on *uṣūl al-fiqh* hold that consensus was a *ḥujjah,* literally "proof." This term implies that a ruling held by consensus, although it may not necessarily be based on an explicit scriptural text, is a binding or irrefutable argument. Because of this edict, one cannot contradict or deviate from consensus; to do so is not only incorrect but impermissible, illegal, or tantamount to unbelief. The implication, in the Sunni view, is that since consensus is a binding proof the Shiites either had to retract their opinions or be excluded from the community of opinion which constituted Islamic orthodoxy. The crucial step the first Twelver Shiite works on jurisprudence took was the adoption of the Sunni principle of legal consensus in an attempt to obviate this structural difficulty with the Sunni legal system. The works of al-Shaykh al-Mufīd, al-Sharīf al-

114. Ibn Shahrāshūb, *Ma'ālim al-'ulamā',* 101.

115. al-Murtaḍā, *Rasā'il,* 1: 169, 201, 212.

116. Muḥammad b. al-Ḥasan al-Ṭūsī, *al-Khilāf,* 3 vols. (Tehran: Dār al-ma'ārif al-islāmī, n.d.).

117. Muḥammad b. al-Ḥasan al-Ṭūsī, *Ikhtiyār ma'rifat al-rijāl,* 2 vols. [= *Rijāl al-Kashshī,* printed with the *Ta'līqah* of Mīr-i Dāmād Muḥammad Bāqir al-Ḥusaynī], ed. Sayyid Mahdī al-Rajā'ī (Qum: Mu'assasat Āl al-bayt, 1983–84), 2: 507.

Murtaḍā, and al-Shaykh al-Ṭūsī incorporated consensus into Twelver Shiite legal methodology. Their discussions set the boundaries within which the great majority of later Twelver discussions of legal methodology in general and consensus in particular would be framed. The Twelvers' adoption of consensus was a crucial theoretical step necessary to gain recognition for their tradition as a coordinate *madhhab* on a par with the Sunni *madhhabs*.

A key to understanding the adoption of legal consensus by the Shiites may be sought in the legal theory of Ibrāhīm al-Naẓẓām (d. 220–30/835–45), the great Muʿtazilī theologian. Many works on jurisprudence state that al-Naẓẓām rejected the principle of consensus and claimed that it was not a binding proof, or *ḥujjah*.[118] Al-Ghazālī reports, however, that this was not exactly the case. Al-Naẓẓām at first did not accept consensus, but when reports reached him that to go against consensus was declared unlawful (*taḥrīm mukhālafat al-ijmāʿ*), he then accepted consensus out of necessity. He defined it, however, in such a way that it could fit into his already established legal theory. The result was what seemed to be a circular definition; he defined consensus as "any opinion which has been irrefutably proven" (*kullu qawlin qāmat ḥujjatuh*). That is, when confronted with the charge that it was unlawful to go against consensus, he adopted consensus in such a way that he could agree with his opponents that *ijmāʿ* was an irrefutable proof but not be forced to retract his earlier opinions. While Shiite definitions of consensus are not so obviously circular, their genesis appears to follow the same pattern.

As latecomers to the *madhhab* system, the Shiites were in a difficult position. If they wished to be accepted in the majority system, they had to ensure that they be counted or considered in the consensus. Yet Sunni jurists argued that they should be excluded from legal debate on the very grounds that their traditional positions on a number of legal issues were unacceptable and violated the consensus of the jurists. They therefore had to accept the consensus of the Muslim community as a valid concept, but also prove, retroactively, that they had not deviated from an earlier consensus of recognized Muslim jurists. Consequently, they had to argue that they possessed a sound legal tradition going back to the early generations of the Muslim community and that their legal methodology was valid and equivalent to those followed by Sunni jurists. At the same time, however, the Shiites felt that they had been singled out among the Muslims for divine guidance and had a privileged position with respect to religious truth—a sense of their special status that had been reinforced by their historical persecution at the hands of the Sunni community. Their theory of consensus reflects this tension in Shiite thought.

When the Twelver jurists accepted the legal concept of consensus, they

118. al-Baṣrī, *al-Muʿtamad*, 1: 459.

modified it into a two-tiered system. A comparison with the legal theory of the Zaydī Shiites is informative here. By the late tenth century, Zaydis had also developed a two-tiered theory of consensus. The Zaydis accepted the consensus of the Muslim community (*ijmāʿ al-ummah*) as a valid concept, but also held that another, privileged sort of consensus existed: the consensus of the descendants of the Prophet (*ijmāʿ ahl al-bayt*). Abū Ṭālib Yaḥyā b. al-Ḥusayn b. Hārūn al-Nāṭiq bi'l-Ḥaqq (d. 424/1033) holds in his work *Kitāb al-diʿāmah fī tathbīt al-imāmah*, probably written in Rayy before 385/995, that *ijmāʿ ahl al-bayt* is a binding argument (*ḥujjah*).[119] This assertion implies that the consensus of the Muslim community (*ijmāʿ al-ummah*) is also a binding argument because the community as a whole includes *ahl al-bayt*. This position became standard in Zaydī jurisprudence.[120] Similarly, the Twelvers accepted both *ijmāʿ al-ummah* along with a more restricted consensus of the Twelver Shiite minority (*ijmāʿ al-firqah* or *ijmāʿ al-ṭāʾifah*) as binding arguments.

A chronological sketch of the earliest Shiite legal works that discuss the theory of consensus provides a basis for examination of its historical development. The main works are listed as follows:

Work	Author	Date
1. Book on *uṣūl al-fiqh*	al-Shaykh al-Mufīd	before 380/990
2. *Awāʾil al-maqālāt*	al-Shaykh al-Mufīd	400–6/1009–15
3. *al-Shāfī fī al-imāmah*	al-Sharīf al-Murtaḍā	380–415/990–1024
4. *al-Masāʾil al-tabbānīyāt*	al-Sharīf al-Murtaḍā	417–19/1026–28
5. *al-Mawṣilīyāt al-thālithah*	al-Sharīf al-Murtaḍā	420/1029
6. *al-Intiṣār*	al-Sharīf al-Murtaḍā	ca. 417–20/1026–29
7. *ʿUddat al-uṣūl*	al-Shaykh al-Ṭūsī	after 420/1029
8. *al-Masāʾil al-rassīyah al-ūlā*	al-Sharīf al-Murtaḍā	429/1037
9. *al-Dharīʿah*	al-Sharīf al-Murtaḍā	430/1038–39
10. *Talkhīṣ al-shāfī*	al-Shaykh al-Ṭūsī	432/1040
11. 2d redaction of *al-ʿUddah*	al-Shaykh al-Ṭūsī	after 436/1044

The basic outlines of the Twelver theory of consensus appear already in the works of al-Shaykh al-Mufīd, though his extant discussions of consensus are

119. Erroneously attributed to al-Ṣāḥib Ibn ʿAbbād and published as *Nuṣrat madhāhib al-zaydiyah*, ed. Nājī Ḥasan (Beirut: al-Dār al-muttaḥidah li'l-nashr, 1981), 175–79. See Wilferd Madelung, "Einige Werke des Imams Abū Ṭālib an-Nāṭiq bi l-Ḥaqq," *Der Islam* 63 (1986): 10. The date of the work may be set prior to 385/995 because al-Ṣāḥib Ibn ʿAbbād, who died in that year, is mentioned in the introduction.

120. See, for example, Aḥmad b. Yaḥyā Ibn al-Murtaḍā's *Kitāb miʿyār al-ʿuqūl fī ʿilm al-uṣūl*, in his *al-Baḥr al-zakhkhār al-jāmiʿ li-madhāhib ʿulamāʾ al-amṣār*, 6 vols. (Beirut: Muʾassasat al-risālah, 1975), 1: 185.

quite short.[121] Al-Qāḍī ʿAbd al-Jabbar devotes the seventeenth volume of his monumental twenty-volume work on theology, *al-Mughnī fī abwāb al-tawḥīd wa'l-ʿadl,* which he completed between 360/970 and 380/990, to jurisprudence. In the course of the chapter on consensus he refers several times to Twelver opinions on the topic. He must be referring here to the opinions of al-Shaykh al-Mufīd in particular, for none of al-Sharīf al-Murtaḍā's works treating consensus had yet been written. It seems most likely that he was drawing on al-Shaykh al-Mufīd's now lost manual of *uṣūl al-fiqh.* He claims that the Twelvers had no reason to consider consensus if they were indeed correct in their beliefs concerning the necessity for and existence of an infallible imam whose opinion was a binding argument. In another passage, he counters the Shiites' argument that if each individual considered in the consensus can err, then the group which they constitute can err also.[122] This last argument does not appear in al-Shaykh al-Mufīd's extant statements on consensus; it probably was presented in his manual of *uṣūl al-fiqh* but was edited out by al-Karājakī for his abridgment. These passages allow us to date al-Mufīd's manual on *uṣūl al-fiqh* to before 380/990 since ʿAbd al-Jabbār had completed *al-Mughnī* by that date. Al-Shaykh al-Mufīd wrote *Awāʾil al-maqālāt* at the request of al-Sharīf al-Raḍī while the latter held the office of *naqīb;* this would date the work to between 400/1009 and 406/1015.[123] Al-Shaykh al-Mufīd is also reported to have written an individual treatise on consensus (*Kitāb masʾalah fī al-ijmāʿ*), but it has not come down to us.[124]

Most of the Shiite discussions of consensus that have come down to us from this period are those of al-Sharīf al-Murtaḍā. They treat the topic in great detail, and he clearly expended great effort to develop the concept beyond the work of al-Mufīd. His earliest work to treat consensus is *al-Shāfī fī al-imāmah,* a refutation of the twentieth volume (which is on the imamate) of ʿAbd al-Jabbār's *al-Mughnī.* The repeated references to ʿAbd al-Jabbār and the

121. al-Shaykh Muḥammad b. Muḥammad b. al-Nuʿmān al-Mufīd, *Awāʾil al-maqālāt fī al-madhāhib al-mukhtārāt,* ed. ʿAbbās Qulī Wāʿiẓ Charandābī and Faḍl Allah al-Zanjānī (Tabriz, 1951–52), 99–100.

122. al-Qāḍī ʿAbd al-Jabbār, *al-Mughnī,* 17: 156–59, 204.

123. al-Mufīd, *Awāʾil al-maqālāt,* xxiv–xxv; Dominique Sourdel, "L'Imamisme vu par le Cheikh al-Mufīd," *Revue des Études Islamiques* 40 (1972): 249 n. 2. In the introduction to *Awāʾil al-maqālāt,* al-Shaykh al-Mufīd writes that he authored the work in response to a request by "Sayyidnā al-Sharīf al-Naqīb" (1). At the end of the work is an appendix consisting of extra questions which al-Sharīf al-Raḍī asked al-Shaykh al-Mufīd to answer and add to the work (111-16). It therefore seems likely that the "Sayyidnā al-Sharīf al-Naqīb" mentioned at the beginning of the work is al-Sharīf al-Raḍī. Because he is described as *naqīb* at the time, al-Zanjānī sets the date of the work between 396 A.H. and 406 A.H., the date al-Sharīf al-Raḍī died, and Sourdel sets it between 398 A.H. and 406 A.H. I would set the date between 400/1009–10 and 406/1015. Al-Raḍī's father al-Ḥusayn b. Mūsā died in 400/1009–10, and al-Raḍī assumed the office of *naqīb.* Before that, he would merely have been the deputy *naqīb.*

124. al-Najāshī, *Kitāb al-rijāl,* 314.

comments addressed directly to him in the work suggest that he was alive when al-Murtaḍā was writing, so *al-Shāfī* may be dated to between 380/990, when *al-Mughnī* was completed, and 415/1024. Although *al-Shāfī* deals primarily with the imamate, al-Murtaḍā includes in it a lengthy refutation of 'Abd al-Jabbār's chapter on consensus from the seventeenth volume of *al-Mughnī* on *uṣūl al-fiqh*. Unfortunately, the discussion of consensus there is primarily a refutation of Sunni arguments for the binding authority of consensus and says relatively little about the Shiite concept of consensus. There is nevertheless some reference to the Shiite theory of the consensus of the Muslim community.[125]

Al-Murtaḍā's first major work focusing on consensus is his collection of legal *responsa*, *Jawābāt al-masā'il al-tabbānīyāt*, which cites the earlier work *al-Shāfī*.[126] It was probably written after Sha'bān 417/September–October 1026. On that date, al-Murtaḍā issued an *ijāzah* to Abū al-Ḥasan Muḥammad b. Muḥammad al-Buṣrawī, and the document presents a catalogue of his works written up until that time.[127] While it includes a work entitled *al-Masā'il al-tabbānīyah*, this treatise is described as including *responsa* to three questions, one on *tadhakkur* (?), one on the interpretation of Koranic verse 4: 48, and one on repentance;[128] this text is therefore not the same as the extant treatise, *al-Masā'il al-tabbānīyāt*. The *Jawābāt al-masā'il al-tabbānīyāt* may be dated to 419/1028 at the latest, for the *responsa* were written in answer to questions from theologian Abū 'Abd Allāh Muḥammad b. 'Abd al-Malik al-Tabbān, who died in that year.[129] Al-Murtaḍā cites them in his third set of legal *responsa* to questions from Mawṣil, *Jawābāt al-masā'il al-mawṣilīyāt al-thālithah*, which date to Rabī' I 420/March–April 1029. He cites *Jawābāt al-masā'il al-tabbānīyāt* in his later works and refers to the treatise as an important treatment of topics in jurisprudence and consensus in particular. *Jawābāt al-masā'il al-mawṣilīyāt al-thālithah* also includes a discussion of consensus.[130]

Al-Murtaḍā's most important discussion of consensus appears in his work *al-Intiṣār*, a work of *khilāf* justifying the Shiites' dissenting positions on a number of points of law and arguing against Sunni accusations that the Shi-

125. al-Murtaḍā, *al-Shāfī*, 1: 78, 214–75.

126. al-Murtaḍā, *Rasā'il*, 1: 84, 212.

127. al-Iṣfahānī, *Riyāḍ al-'ulamā'*, 4: 34–39.

128. Ibid., 37. Al-Najāshī (*Kitāb al-rijāl*, 207) mentions a treatise entitled *al-Masā'il al-tabbānīyah* and reports that it is "three questions asked by the Sultan." It would appear to be the same treatise mentioned in al-Buṣrawī's *ijāzah*.

129. Ibn al-Jawzī, *al-Muntaẓam*, 15: 193. Al-Murtaḍā includes the phrase of blessing, *raḥimahu 'Llāh*, after al-Tabbān's name, indicating that he had passed away the year before al-Murtaḍā wrote *Jawābāt al-masā'il al-mawṣilīyah al-thālithah*. See al-Murtaḍā, *Rasā'il*, 1: 206 (reading al-Tabbān for al-Battān).

130. al-Murtaḍā, *al-Intiṣār*, 6; idem, *Rasā'il*, 1: 201, 205–8; 3: 202.

ites violated consensus. He began it before 417/1026 since it is mentioned in the *ijāzah* of al-Buṣrawī.[131] He did not complete it, however, until after 420/1029, the date of *Jawābāt al-masā'il al-mawṣilīyāt al-thālithah,* which he mentions in the introduction. Al-Murtaḍā had been working on *al-Intiṣār* for a number of years, for he mentions it in *Jawābāt al-masā'il al-tabbānīyāt, Jawābāt al-masā'il al-mawṣilīyāt al-thāniyah,* and *Jawābāt al-masā'il al-mawṣilīyāt al-thālithah.* In the latter treatise, he asks for God's assistance in completing *al-Intiṣār,* so it is clear he was still working on it in 420/1029.[132] He wrote it in response to a request by "His Exalted Presence the Vizier al-'Amīd," probably 'Amīd al-Dawlah Abū Sa'd b. 'Abd al-Raḥīm, who served six times as vizier during the reign of the Buwayhid ruler Jalāl al-Dawlah Shīrzīl (416-35/1025–44).[133] He probably finished the work shortly after 420/1029.

After this stage, in which the topic of consensus was treated in specialized treatises and legal *responsa,* al-Ṭūsī's *'Uddat al-uṣūl* and al-Murtaḍā's *al-Dharī'ah ilā uṣūl al-sharī'ah* incorporated the Twelver theory of consensus into general legal theory as expressed in the genre of *uṣūl al-fiqh.* In these works, the doctrine of consensus assumed the form it would maintain, in basic outline, for centuries later in the Shiite legal tradition. Al-Ṭūsī's discussions of consensus generally follow those of al-Murtaḍā, though he disagrees with his teacher on a few subsidiary points. It is therefore safe to say that the main architect of the Shiite theory of legal consensus was al-Sharīf al-Murtaḍā and that his major treatments of the topic clustered around the year 420/1029.

Shiite jurists' works on *uṣūl al-fiqh* per se reveal little direct evidence concerning motives for the adoption of specific points; they only present the Shiite position on these issues. In order to get a better understanding of why the Shiite jurists adopted Sunni methods it will be useful to examine al-Shaykh al-Mufīd's treatise *al-Masā'il al-ṣāghānīyah;* a passage in his work *al-Fuṣūl al-mukhtārah;* and al-Murtaḍā's work *al-Intiṣār.* Al-Mufīd wrote *al-Masā'il al-ṣāghānīyah* as the result of a polemic exchange that had taken place between a Ḥanafī scholar from Nishapur and a Twelver Shiite from the town of Ṣāghān in Iran at some time after 340/951–52. The treatise aims to answer the accusation that Shiite legal positions, particularly the opinion that *mut'ah* marriage is permissible, violate the consensus of Muslim jurists. The method of argument al-Mufīd follows in the polemic shows how such accusations led Shiites to adopt

131. al-Iṣfahānī, *Riyāḍ al-'ulamā',* 4: 38.

132. al-Murtaḍā, *Rasā'il* 1: 169, 212–13.

133. al-Murtaḍā, *al-Intiṣār,* 1. The editor of *al-Intiṣār,* Sayyid Muḥammad Riḍā b. Ḥasan al-Kharsān, identifies this vizier as Abū Naṣr Muḥammad b. Manṣūr, known as 'Amīd al-Mulk al-Kundurī al-Nīsābūrī, who served as vizier for the Seljuk sultans Tughrul Bek and Alp Arslan and was executed on 16 Dhū al-Ḥijjah 456/29 November 1064 in his 40s (*al-Intiṣār,* 1 n. 2). This is very unlikely since the Seljuks were great enemies of the Twelvers and their Buwayhid patrons and since al-Kundurī would have been much too young for al-Murtaḍā to dedicate a work to him ca. 420/1029.

the principle of consensus themselves. The Ḥanafī interlocutor accuses the Twelver Shiites of violating the consensus (*al-khurūj 'an al-ijmā'*); they are therefore unbelievers (*khārijūn 'an al-īmān*). Al-Mufīd answers this accusation by arguing that the consensus referred to here cannot be valid because it does not include the opinions of the Shiites. He asks, concerning the Shiites's position on temporary marriage, "How can this be a rejection of consensus when the descendants of the Prophet and their supporters in the East and West of the Earth uphold this opinion and trace it back reliably to the Bearer of the Sacred Law (the Prophet Muḥammad)?" If the consensus which the Sunnis claim exists were an actual consensus, al-Mufīd holds, it would imply that 'Alī b. Abī Ṭālib had himself violated consensus, held deviant opinions, and was therefore an unbeliever and an apostate.[134]

In this polemic context, al-Mufīd uses the term *ijmā' al-ummah* repeatedly, and in several passages uses the concept of consensus as an argument against his Sunni opponent.[135] Al-Mufīd holds that his opponent's claims of consensus are invalid because they fail to take into account the opinions of the Shiites. He asks, "What consensus does not include the descendants of the Prophet and their followers, if it were not for your obstinacy and chauvinism?"[136] Moreover, the Shiites' contemporary opinions are not groundless innovations; they are based on a reliable legal tradition which goes directly back to the early imams Ja'far al-Ṣādiq and 'Alī b. Abī Ṭālib. Al-Mufīd makes an explicit comparison between Ja'far al-Ṣādiq and Abū Ḥanīfah and cites instances where Abū Ḥanīfah held opinions that were not in agreement with the other *madhhabs*. While al-Mufīd labels Abū Ḥanīfah an unbeliever and accuses him of adopting legal opinions which contradict the Prophet and agree with Satan, he nevertheless puts Ja'far al-Ṣādiq in a position parallel to that of the eponymous founders of the Sunni legal *madhhabs*.[137]

In *al-Fuṣūl al-mukhtārah*, al-Shaykh al-Mufīd records a debate he had with al-Qāḍī 'Abd al-Jabbār (d. 415/1024) during which the issue of consensus arose. 'Abd al-Jabbār criticized one of al-Shaykh al-Mufīd's legal opinions, claiming that it violated legal consensus. Al-Shaykh al-Mufīd asked him what consensus he intended, and 'Abd al-Jabbār replied that he meant the consensus of the Muslim jurists who are well known for granting legal opinions. Al-Mufīd then countered, arguing, among other things, that the descendants of the Prophet, including 'Alī b. Abī Ṭālib, must also be included in the group of jurists whose opinions should be taken into consideration in consensus.[138]

134. al-Mufīd, *al-Masā'il al-ṣāghāniyah*, 2–3, 5, 7, 8–10, 45.

135. Ibid., 10, 32, 33, 38, 44.

136. Ibid., 39. A similar statement occurs on p. 37.

137. Ibid., 15–16, 46–63.

138. al-Mufīd, *al-Fuṣūl al-mukhtārah min al-'uyūn wa'l-maḥāsin* (Qum: Maṭba'at mihr, 1983), 132–35.

Al-Sharīf al-Murtaḍā's work *al-Intiṣār* presents the dissenting opinions on the points of law the Shiites hold with respect to their Sunni opponents. Al-Murtaḍā's purpose in writing *al-Intiṣār* seems to be to remove obstacles between the Shiite jurists and the majority Sunni-controlled, legal system and to gain the acceptance of Twelver Shiite jurisprudence on the part of the majority as a legitimate alternative on a par with that of the established Sunni *madhhabs*. He wrote the book in response to a request that he set forth the dissenting legal opinions for which Shiites have been attacked on the grounds of violating the consensus. The introduction shows that Sunnis argued that Shiites were beyond the pale of orthodoxy because of their violation of consensus. They used this charge as an excuse to bar Shiites from debate on legal topics and, consequently, from the entire system of legal education and scholarship. Al-Murtaḍā states specifically that Sunnis refused to debate with Shiite jurists and to take their opinions into account.[139]

Al-Murtaḍā makes a plea for Shiite legal opinions to be recognized as legitimate, holding that, since the scriptural texts which the Sunnis cite as proofs of the validity of consensus include the Shiites, their opinions should therefore be taken into consideration, whether for the consensus of the Muslim community as a whole or for the consensus of the jurists in particular. He aims to counter Sunni arguments, proving that Shiite opinions are just as authoritative as those of the Sunnis and should therefore be considered in verifying the existence of a legal consensus. His first counter argument is that the legal opinions of the Shiites are not as outlandish as they have been made out to be. Many opinions the Shiites hold are also held, or have been held in the past, by Sunni jurists: "On most of these [questions], the Shiites agree with other recent or ancient scholars and jurists."[140] In the body of *al-Intiṣār,* al-Murtaḍā mentions whenever possible the Sunni jurists who have held the same opinions as those for which the Shiites have been criticized.

Next, al-Murtaḍā points out that the Shiites, when they are in complete disagreement with the Sunnis on a certain matter, have sound evidence to support their views. This evidence includes texts from the Koran or hadith, or reports attributing these opinions to earlier authorities, especially the imams. Because Shiite legal opinions are supported in this fashion, he argues, they are as legitimate as Sunni opinions, and the Sunnis should accept them as such: "For those questions on which they are not in agreement with any of the Sunni jurists, they have clear evidence and apparent proofs which relieve them of the need for a concurring opinion, and which are not impugned by the disagreement of an opponent." Because the Shiite scholars have a sound legal

139. al-Murtaḍā, *al-Intiṣār,* 1, 4.
140. Ibid., 1, 4–5.

methodology, al-Murtaḍā contends, the Sunnis should accept their opinions as valid, and should not reject their opinions on the points of law merely on the basis of their chance failure to coincide with those of the Sunni jurists. He elaborates, drawing a direct comparison between the Shiite legal tradition and the Sunni legal *madhhabs*:

> Then how have vituperous attacks against the Shiites for the opinions which they hold uniquely been allowed, while every other jurist who professed opinions uniquely, so that all the jurists were in disagreement with him, such as Abū Ḥanīfah, al-Shāfiʿī, Mālik, and those who came after them, has not been attacked? What is the difference between the opinions which the Shiites hold uniquely and with which no one else concurs, and those of Abū Ḥanīfah or al-Shāfiʿī with which no one else concurs?[141]

In this section of his argument, al-Murtaḍā implies that there is no essential difference between Shiite and Sunni jurists and that any Muslim jurist is entitled to hold an opinion which goes against those of his colleagues as long as he bases it on acceptable evidence.

The Sunnis claim, however, that the opinions the Shiites hold uniquely are innovations, in contrast to those of the well-known Sunni jurists. They insist that it is not permissible for Shiites to originate a new opinion after a consensus has been established. Sunnis hold that the dissenting opinions of al-Shāfiʿī and Abū Ḥanīfah were not innovations but were based on the transmission of legal opinions also held by the *salaf*, "predecessors," men of the early generations of the Muslim community. They attribute many of Abū Ḥanīfah's opinions to the *salaf* who lived in Kūfah and many of al-Shāfiʿī's opinions to the *salaf* who lived in the Ḥijāz, but, the Sunnis claim, this is not the case with the Shiites. Al-Murtaḍā first answers this argument by insisting that the Shiites' opinions are not innovations, but have been handed down from the imams, so that the Sunnis' accusation is invalid:

> The Shiites also claim and transmit that the opinions which they hold uniquely are the opinions of Jaʿfar b. Muḥammad al-Ṣādiq [the sixth imam], Muḥammad b. ʿAlī al-Bāqir [the fifth imam], and ʿAlī b. al-Ḥusayn Zayn al-ʿĀbidīn [the fourth imam]. They even transmit these opinions from the Commander of the Faithful ʿAlī b. Abī Ṭālib, and trace them back to him. Then grant (the Shiites) what you have granted Abū Ḥanīfah and al-Shāfiʿī and So-and-so and So-and-so, or at the very least put them down to the status of Ibn Ḥanbal and Muḥammad b. Jarīr al-Ṭabarī in that which they profess uniquely. For you allow [Ibn Ḥanbal and

141. Ibid., 1–2.

> Ibn Jarīr] differing opinions in that which they profess uniquely, but do not allow the Shiites to differ in that which they profess uniquely. This is an injustice to the Shiites and a wrong against them.[142]

Islamic schools of thought in general seek to establish the legitimacy of their opinions by projecting them back into early Islamic history, and the legal *madhhabs* were certainly no exception. The claim that the Sunni legal *madhhabs* were actually begun by the jurists whose names they took was already anachronistic, and even then it was somewhat embarrassing that there was a considerable temporal gap between the demise of the Prophet and the activities of Mālik, Abū Ḥanīfah, al-Shāfiʿī, and Ibn Ḥanbal. Just as the Sunni jurists project the opinions of al-Shāfiʿī and Abū Ḥanīfah back to the early years of the Muslim community, al-Sharīf al-Murtaḍā maintains that the Shiite jurists' opinions may be traced back to Imams Zayn al-ʿĀbidīn, Muḥammad al-Bāqir, and Jaʿfar al-Ṣādiq. At the same time, he admits that it is possible to innovate opinions, but his projection of Shiite legal doctrine back to the time of these early imams is important in establishing the historical authority of Shiite opinions. Thus, the Shiite imams are transformed from charismatic leaders of the community and arbiters of revelation into patrons of the Imami legal *madhhab.*

Al-Murtaḍā then questions his accuser's premise, claiming that some of the opinions of al-Shāfiʿī and Abū Ḥanīfah were probably innovations. He goes on to claim that Abū Ḥanīfah arrived at unprecedented opinions through the application of analogy (*qiyās*), which the Shiites do not accept as a valid method of legal reasoning:

> Moreover, the opinions of Abū Ḥanīfah which he reached by analogical reasoning include some for which it may not be claimed that he has any precursors who professed them among the Companions or the Followers [the generation following that of the Prophet's Companions]. If we so desired, we could point to many individual legal opinions of Abū Ḥanīfah which fit this description. Then how have you not attacked him for adopting that which no one before him had ever adopted, when you have attacked the Shiites for the same thing?"[143]

Al-Murtaḍā points to the lack of authoritative sources for some legal opinions of Abū Ḥanīfah and asks how the Sunni jurists differentiate between those opinions and the traditional legal positions of the Shiites. The Shiites indeed claim authoritative sources for their opinions, but, as a secondary argument,

142. Ibid., 2–3.
143. Ibid., 3.

why should the Sunni jurists not accept their opinions anyway, when they accept Abū Ḥanīfah's unsupported opinions?

On historical grounds, al-Murtaḍā maintains that the Sunni jurists' claim of an earlier consensus against the Shiites is invalid. He argues, "Your claim of a preceding consensus against that which the Shiites profess is unfounded, for (our) scholars trace their opinions back to a group among the predecessors. The existence of their opinions and the fact that they were not in agreement with other scholars make it impossible for there to have been a consensus to the exclusion of their opinions."[144] Thus, al-Murtaḍā maintains, the Sunnis' evaluation of the consensus was incomplete because the opinions of the Shiites were not taken into consideration. The consensus claimed by the Sunnis was not actually valid, so the Shiites cannot be said to have violated it.

Consequently, the Shiite jurists' opinions should be considered in the formation of any present consensus. Sunni jurists should honor their opinions and stop refusing to debate with them:

> Even if this were granted to you, despite the possible arguments against it, you would then have to allow the Shiites those dissenting opinions they profess uniquely which go against the opinions Abū Ḥanīfah reached by analogical reasoning, for which he had no precursor and concerning which no consensus preceded him. But we do not see you allowing them conflicting opinions on anything which they profess uniquely, and you do not permit this, as the present discussion on this matter has shown necessary. Moreover, you debate with and honor the dissenting opinions of Dā'ūd, Muḥammad b. Jarīr, and Aḥmad b. Ḥanbal concerning those questions on which they hold unique opinions even though, according to you, a preceding consensus had gone into effect against their opinions. Should you not either cease to honor their conflicting opinions and to debate with them on these issues as you have done with the Shiites, or treat the Shiites as you have treated them with respect to the consideration of dissenting opinions and debate?[145]

This passage reflects al-Murtaḍā's main goal, to have Shiite legal opinions honored as acceptable alternatives within the *madhhab* system. He makes a clear plea for Shiite jurists to be allowed to participate in the process of debate which characterized that system, on the grounds that their legal methodology is just as sound as those of the other *madhhabs*. Inclusion in the system involved the simultaneous acceptance of the concept of consensus and refutation of the accusation of violating consensus. Against this background, the theory of

144. Ibid.
145. Ibid., 3–4.

consensus adopted in the works of the Shiite jurists of the Buwayhid period becomes more comprehensible.

That al-Murtaḍā considered the Shiite legal institution to form a *madhhab* parallel to the Sunni *madhhab*s is shown in *al-Intiṣār* by his repeated comparison of Twelver Shiite jurisprudence with that of the Sunni *madhhab*s. The Shiites form a *madhhab* in the same way that Shāfiʿī or Ḥanafī jurists form a *madhhab*. The patrons of the *madhhab* are the imams who, with regard to the legal system, correspond to al-Shāfiʿī and Abū Ḥanīfah. Al-Murtaḍā does not use the term "Jaʿfarī *madhhab*," which developed at a much later date, nor would he have considered this term appropriate.[146] The patronage of the Shiite *madhhab* is not limited to the figure of Jaʿfar al-Ṣādiq, but is vested in other imams as well. Al-Murtaḍā specifically mentions ʿAlī b. Abī Ṭālib, Zayn al-ʿĀbidīn, and Muḥammad al-Bāqir in addition to Jaʿfar al-Ṣādiq in this regard. In al-Murtaḍā's works and other sources of this period, the Shiite legal tradition is labeled the Imami *madhhab*, the Shiite *madhhab*, or the Imami Shiite *madhhab*.

Al-Murtaḍā does not use the term "the fifth *madhhab*" because he does not see that the Sunni *madhhab*s are limited to four in number. Rather, his discussion implies that there were six in his day: the Ḥanafī, Shāfiʿī, Mālikī, Ḥanbalī, Ẓāhirī, and Jarīrī *madhhab*s. The Imami legal *madhhab* would be one of seven, not one of five. Furthermore, al-Murtaḍā holds that the Twelver Shiite *madhhab* should not be assigned to the last position in the pecking order of the *madhhab*s. For reasons of chronological precedence, he evidently sees that the Shiites merit higher status than the Ḥanbalīs, the Jarīrīs, and the Ẓāhirīs. His arguments imply that Dāʾūd, the founder of the Ẓāhirī guild, Ibn Ḥanbal, and Muḥammad b. Jarīr al-Ṭabarī, who lived much later than Abū Ḥanīfah and al-Shāfiʿī, are not equal in status with the latter two and, furthermore, are innovators, having produced new opinions after a so-called consensus. As a secondary argument, he suggests that the Sunnis should at least grant the Shiites the status of the Ẓāhirīs, Ḥanbalīs, and Jarīrīs if they are not willing to grant them the same status as the Shāfiʿīs and the Ḥanafīs. One notes also that the Mālikīs, whose numbers were limited in the eastern Muslim world, do not figure prominently in al-Murtaḍā's argument.

Al-Murtaḍā recognizes that Shiite legal opinions differ from Sunni opinions, but he maintains that these differences are not so many nor so wide as is claimed by opponents of the Shiites. What is more, the Shiite jurists form and support their opinions in the same way that the Sunni jurists do, and their *madhhab* functions in the same way as the Sunni *madhhab*s. Sunnis should

146. The Shiite jurist al-Qāḍī Nūr Allāh al-Shushtarī used this term in the late sixteenth or early seventeenth century (*Socio-Intellectual History*, 1: 365–67.

therefore recognize Shiite opinions as valid and refrain from barring their entry to the *madhhab* system. This change would allow them the privilege to debate freely with Sunni scholars on legal topics and, presumably, to study and teach law and to serve as legal authorities, in short, to participate fully in the system of Islamic legal study and scholarship.

THE CONSENSUS OF THE MUSLIM COMMUNITY

Al-Shaykh al-Mufid has two extant statements on the concept of consensus, one in *Awāʾil al-maqālāt* and one in his manual of jurisprudence, extant only in al-Karājakī's abridgment. No earlier statements on consensus in Twelver Shiite sources are known. These statements were to form the basis of all later Twelver discussions of *ijmāʿ*. Al-Karājakī's abridgment states succinctly the basic principle adopted by the Shiites concerning legal consensus: "The consensus of the Muslim community (*ijmāʿ al-ummah*) has no authoritative value inasmuch as it is a consensus, but only inasmuch as it includes the opinion of the Imam."[147] Al-Mufid accepted the consensus of the Muslim community as a binding or authoritative argument (*ḥujjah*) but gave a different justification for this authority from that upheld by the Sunni jurists. The Sunnis held that the consensus of the Muslims was valid because of Koranic verses and prophetic hadiths which indicated that the Muslim community was in effect infallible. The Shiites, however, held that consensus was an authoritative argument only because it included the opinion of the Hidden Imam, which was itself infallible. Even if all Muslim jurists except the imam were in agreement, their consensus would have no validity; the imam would be right and everyone else wrong. This interpretation of consensus appears to assign little value to legal consensus per se, but the net result was the acceptance of the principle that consensus constituted an authoritative argument and that Sunnis and Shiites could agree on this fundamental point.

The Shiite understanding of consensus presented by al-Mufid was not exactly parallel to the Sunni concept. Al-Mufid merely points out that the Sunni concept can be valid in certain cases and implies that when Sunnis claim that a consensus exists it is often invalid. Al-Mufid leaves unstated the logical implication that when the Sunnis claim there is a consensus, they usually have not taken into account the opinion of the imam or the opinions of the Shiites themselves. He writes, "When it is demonstrated that the entire community holds one opinion, then there is no doubt that this opinion includes the opinion of the Infallible Imam, for if this were not the case, then the statement that the community was in unanimous agreement would be false. Only in this fashion may consensus be correctly accepted as an authoritative argument."[148]

147. al-Karājakī, *Kanz al-fawāʾid,* 2: 29–30.
148. Ibid., 30.

The modern scholar Brunschvig makes a serious error when analyzing al-Mufīd's argument. He maintains that the Shiite interpretation of consensus was unabashedly different from that of the Sunnis, whereas the truth is that they wanted it to resemble that of the Sunnis as much as possible while remaining logically tied to their accepted beliefs. Brunschvig observes, "Que l'attitude adoptée à l'égard de l'ijmāʿ ou 'consensus' soit typiquement, exclusivement šīʿite, notre auteur [al-Mufīd] ne le cache pas; elle est liée à la conception de l'imamat. . . . Entendons, bien sûr par communauté, la communauté šīʿite, plus spécifiquement, l'imamienne."[149] Brunschvig is mistaken in claiming that the term "community" (*al-ummah*) in al-Mufīd's statement refers exclusively to Twelver Shiites. Al-Mufīd is using the term *al-ummah* in the same sense as are the contemporary Sunni jurists. Twelver Shiite jurists during al-Mufīd's period did not refer to their own sect as *al-ummah;* rather, they called themselves *al-shīʿah, al-imāmīyah, al-ṭāʾifah,* or *al-firqah,* "the sect"; *al-ṭāʾifah al-muḥiqqah* or *al-firqah al-muḥiqqah,* "the sect which upholds the truth"; or *al-khāṣṣah,* "the elite." Brunschvig assumes here that since al-Mufīd's work treats Shiite jurisprudence, this passage must refer to the consensus of the Shiites exclusively, when it actually presents a Shiite view of Muslim consensus. The use of the term *al-ummah* in al-Ṭūsī's *al-Khilāf* clarifies this point. In proving his answer to a legal question, al-Ṭūsī states, "Our evidence is the consensus of the Shiites, and even the consensus of the Muslim community, because this conflicting opinion has ceased be held" (*dalīluna ijmāʿu 'l-firqati bal ijmāʿu 'l-ummati liʾanna hādha 'l-khilāfa 'nqaraḍ*).[150] Since al-Ṭūsī here juxtaposes *ijmāʿ al-firqah* and *ijmāʿ al-ummah* using the adversative particle *bal,* it is clear that they are two different entities. These Shiite jurists accepted Sunnis as part of the Muslim community, at least on a practical level. This is in marked contrast to the use of the term *al-ummah* in the work of the Ismāʿīlī jurist al-Qāḍī al-Nuʿmān, who equates it with *ahl al-ḥaqq,* referring to Ismāʿīlī Shiites exclusively.[151]

Al-Ṭūsī, like al-Mufīd, accepts the principle that the consensus of the Muslim community is an authoritative proof, giving as the reason that a consensus of the entire community necessarily includes the opinion of the imam, who is infallible:

> The opinion which I profess is that it is not permissible for the Muslim community to agree on an error. That upon which the community agrees can only be the correct opinion and an authoritative argument. This is because, according to the Twelver Shiites, no age is free of an infallible Imam

149. Brunschvig, "Les Uṣūl al-Fiqh Imāmites," vol. 3, 327.
150. al-Ṭūsī, *al-Khilāf,* 1: 158. See 1: 242, 302–3 for similar statements.
151. al-Qāḍī al-Nuʿmān, *Ikhtilāf uṣūl al-madhāhib,* 78.

> who upholds the religious law and whose opinion is a binding argument to which one must refer, just as one must refer to the opinion of the Prophet.... Whenever the community has agreed on one opinion, it must be a binding argument because the Imam is included in the whole of the community.[152]

A key idea behind these views supporting the binding authority of the consensus of the Muslim community is that the Sunnis must take the opinion of the imam—and by extension, the opinions of the Shiite jurists—into consideration in evaluating a consensus. This argument is the one described above with which al-Mufīd and al-Murtaḍā countered accusations of violating the consensus.

This line of argument leads the Shiite jurists to redefine the twelfth imam himself as a Muslim scholar or a Twelver Shiite jurist. Al-Murtaḍā states:

> Our statement "consensus" refers either to the entire Muslim community, or to the believers among them, or to the scholars with regard to those issues for which their consensus is taken into account. In each case, the opinion of the Imam must be included in the group, for he is a member of the community, among the most respectable believers and most learned scholars.[153]

It is as if the twelfth imam participated in consensus in his capacity as a scholar rather than in his capacity as imam. Al-Sharīf al-Murtaḍā stresses that the consensus of the Twelver jurists must include the opinion of the imam because he falls under the category of Twelver jurists, which provokes statements that the imam must himself be a Muʿtazilī and a Twelver Shiite in addition to many claims that he is a scholar (*ʿālim*), a term which, in this context, means primarily jurist (*faqīh*). Al-Murtaḍā claims, "The Imam is the master of the Imamis, the most knowledgeable of them, and the most learned." He continues: "Since the Imam—peace be upon him—is one of the scholars, indeed, their master (*sayyidahum*), then his opinion must be within the totality of the opinions of the scholars." He describes the imam as "the master of the scholars and the head of the faith" and claims that "the Infallible Imam is one of [the Twelvers'] scholars, and not one of their laymen or one of the scholars of others besides them."[154] Since the imam is treated here as a jurist, Twelver Shiite law functions like that of any other legal *madhhab*, where the opinions of the living jurists of that *madhhab* are taken into consideration in the formation of consensus.

152. al-Ṭūsī, *ʿUddat al-uṣūl*, 232.

153. al-Murtaḍā, *al-Dharīʿah*, 2: 604–5.

154. al-Murtaḍā, *Rasāʾil*, 1: 15 (reading *ahl al-ʿadl waʾl-tawḥīd* for *ahl al-ʿilm waʾl-tawḥīd*), 18, 205, 208; 2: 366.

A number of modern scholars have expressed the view that the Shiite theory of consensus is simply window dressing and that it has little purpose other than to imitate Sunni legal theory in form: Scarcia refers to Shiism as an "Islam without *ijmāʿ*." Gardet denies that the Shiites accept *ijmāʿ* as one of the fundamental principles of jurisprudence: "Le Shiisme duodécimain, religion officielle de l'Iran, reconnaît les deux premières 'sources,' Coran et Sunna, mais remplace l'*ijmāʿ* par la décision de l'Imam infaillible. . . . L'idée d'*ijmāʿ*, *consensus* des docteurs, n'est pas écartée; mais ne saurait être valide sans l'accord de l'Imam." Goldziher succinctly expresses this idea: "Thus if we wish to characterize in brief the essential difference between Sunni and Shiite Islam, we may say that the former is based on *ijmāʿ*, and the latter on the authoritarian principle." Concerning the Shiite theory of consensus, he adds, "The *ijmāʿ* itself is reduced to a mere formality. In theory, it is true, the influence of *ijmāʿ* on the resolution of religious questions is acknowledged. But Shiite theology sees the significance of consensus only in the fact that it cannot come into existence without the contribution of the Imams. Only this integrating element can give meaning to the principle of *ijmāʿ*." Arjomand remarks of Shiite theory of consensus in general, "This nugatory interpretation disposes of the principle of *ijmāʿ* in reality despite its formal retention." He refers to al-Murtaḍā's theory as the virtual negation of consensus as an independent principle. The twentieth-century Shiite scholar al-Muẓaffar observes of consensus: "[The Shiite jurists] made it one of the sources . . . in a formal and nominal sense only, in order to follow the scholarly method of the Sunnis in [the science of] *uṣūl al-fiqh*." Madelung holds that the Shiites "had no use for the Sunnite principle of consensus since it could not be valid without the inclusion of the imam whose opinion alone counted." He adds that a consensus of the Shiite jurists is of no legal consequence, unlike a consensus of the Sunni jurists.[155] In response to the statements above, one may cite numerous statements by al-Sharīf al-Murtaḍā which hold that consensus is not only a valid source of the law but also perhaps the single most important source, since through it the jurists are able to arrive at most legal rulings. One may also cite statements such as that of Zayn al-Dīn al-ʿĀmilī, who reports that while some Sunni scholars accuse the Shiites of rejecting the authority of consensus, their claims are false. He adds that historically, consensus has been one of the most important principles for the elaboration of Shiite law.[156]

Despite the differences between Sunni and Shiite legal theory on the basis

155. Gianroberto Scarcia, "Intorno alle controversie tra Aḫbārī e Uṣūlī presso gli Imamiti di Persia," *Rivista degli Studi Orientali* 33 (1958): 232–34; Louis Gardet, *L'islam* (Paris: Desclée De Brouwer, 1967), 197–98; Goldziher, *Islamic Theology and Law*, 191; Arjomand, *Shadow of God*, 55, 286 n. 121; al-Muẓaffar, *Uṣūl al-fiqh*, 3: 97; Madelung, "Authority in Twelver Shiism," 164, 169.

156. al-Murtaḍā, *Rasāʾil*, 2: 366; Zayn al-Dīn al-ʿĀmilī, *Tamhīd al-qawāʿid*, 34.

of the authority of consensus, the Shiites' adoption of consensus in the manner they did allowed them to accept as well many of the formal properties of Sunni consensus. This approach, it appears, was the intent behind the adoption of the concept, an idea which the foremost legal theorists hint at if they do not state it outright. In his glossary of technical terms in the Islamic sciences, al-Murtaḍā defines *ijmāʿ* as follows: "The agreement of the scholars of religion in a generation after the Prophet, concerning a legal case, on one legal opinion, one sanction, and one practice." This definition would hold as easily for Sunni legal theory as it would for the Shiites. In *al-Dharīʿah,* he observes, "Thus, our opinion has come to agree with the opinion of those who hold that consensus is a binding authority in issuing legal *responsa.*"[157] Since consensus is infallible, it is therefore an authoritative argument and may be used as legal proof. The consensus of all ages is an authoritative argument; it is not limited to any particular time or place. Consensus is determined, in practical terms, by the absence of *khilāf* or dissenting opinion. The opinions taken into consideration are those of the scholars and not the common people.[158] Originating a new opinion—that is, raising a dissenting opinion after consensus has been established—is not permissible.[159] Going against consensus (*mukhālafat al-ijmāʿ*) is not permissible. It must have been very gratifying for the Shiites to be able to make these statements since they were often accused of the very same error. They were thus able to support the very norm which threatened to exclude them from the legal system. This issue is made poignantly clear by later Shiite statements on violating the consensus that recall the terrible implications of similar Sunni statements. The thirteenth-century Shiite jurist al-Muḥaqqiq al-Ḥillī writes, "He who denies a ruling upon which there is consensus is an unbeliever (*kāfir*), because he is denying something which is known truly to be a part of the sacred law."[160]

THE CONSENSUS OF THE SHIITE MINORITY

In his manual on jurisprudence, al-Mufid does not consider consensus one of the *uṣūl* or fundamental sources of law, though he argues that the consensus of the Muslim community is valid. In his hermeneutic system there are three *uṣūl:* the Koran, the Sunnah of the Prophet, and the sayings (*aqwāl*) of the Imams.[161] Three paths (*ṭuruq*) lead to knowledge of the *uṣūl:* reason (*ʿaql*), lexicography (*lisān*), and hadiths which provide certitude. Neither consensus nor reason, both considered sources of the law in later Twelver jurisprudence,

157. al-Murtaḍā, *Rasāʾil,* 2: 262; idem, *al-Dharīʿah,* 2: 605.
158. al-Ṭūsī, *ʿUddat al-uṣūl,* 248.
159. al-Murtaḍā, *al-Dharīʿah,* 2: 659.
160. Najm al-Dīn Jaʿfar al-Ḥillī, *Maʿārij al-uṣūl,* 129.
161. Arjomand, *Shadow of God,* 55, 186.

appeared as *uṣūl* themselves. Al-Mufīd gives a more detailed statement on consensus in *Awāʾil al-maqālāt:*

> I hold that the consensus of the Muslim community is an authoritative argument because it includes the opinion of the Imam (*al-ḥujjah*). Likewise, the consensus of the Shiites (*ijmāʿ al-shīʿah*) is an authoritative argument for the same reason, and not because of consensus itself. The guiding principle in this topic is that truth is established in consensus by the opinion of the Imam, who stands in place of the Prophet—may God bless him and grant him peace. If he alone were to adopt an opinion and no one else were to agree with him, it would still be enough to serve as an authoritative argument and proof. We have discussed consensus and declared it authoritative argument through the Imam because it is impossible for consensus to occur unless he is included in it, for he has the greatest stature in the community, and he precedes all others in blessings, sound opinions, and good works. This is the doctrine of those who uphold the Imamate (*ahl al-imāmah*) in particular. The Muʿtazilīs, Murjiʾah, Khārijīs, and determinist traditionalists oppose them in this.[162]

This passage is similar to that cited above from his manual on *uṣūl al-fiqh,* but shows that al-Shaykh al-Mufīd developed the concept of the consensus of the Shiites (*ijmāʿ al-shīʿah*) in addition to *ijmāʿ al-ummah.* The concept of the consensus of the Shiites follows from the basis of the authority of consensus. If the consensus of the Muslim community as a whole is valid on the grounds that it includes the opinion of the infallible imam, then the consensus of the Shiites alone is also valid on the same grounds.

Al-Sharīf al-Murtaḍā and al-Shaykh al-Ṭūsī adopted and elaborated the concept of Shiite consensus proposed by al-Shaykh al-Mufīd, though they usually use the term *ijmāʿ al-firqah,* "the consensus of the sect," or *ijmāʿ al-firqah al-muḥiqqah,* "the consensus of the sect which upholds the truth," rather than *ijmāʿ al-shīʿah,* "the consensus of the Shiites," as it appears in al-Mufīd's text. Notwithstanding, the concept was the same. The exact term *ijmāʿ al-firqah* may have already come into use during al-Shaykh al-Mufīd's lifetime, for al-Ṭūsī mentions *ijmāʿ al-muslimīn* and *ijmāʿ al-firqah al-muḥiqqah* in the introduction to *Tahdhīb al-aḥkām.* Based on al-Shaykh al-Mufīd's legal compendium *al-Muqniʿah,* this work was one of al-Ṭūsī's earliest, and the blessing which occurs in the introduction after al-Mufīd's name, *ayyadahu 'Llāh,* "May God support him," indicates that he was alive at the time al-Ṭūsī was writing.[163]

The major step which al-Ṭūsī and al-Murtaḍā made beyond the work of

162. al-Mufīd, *Awāʾil al-maqālāt,* 99–100.
163. al-Ṭūsī, *Tahdhīb al-aḥkām,* 1: 2, 3.

al-Mufīd was that they accepted consensus not only as an authoritative argument (*ḥujjah*) but also as an *aṣl* or *dalīl*, one of the sources from which legal rulings could be derived, thus incorporating consensus into a more developed theory of jurisprudence. One major reason for the development of *ijmāʿ al-firqah*, was, it appears, the need to use it as a supporting proof in arguments against Sunni opponents. Al-Sharīf al-Murtaḍā in *al-Intiṣār* and al-Shaykh al-Ṭūsī in *al-Khilāf* often evoke *ijmāʿ al-firqah* and *ijmāʿ al-ummah* as proof of the validity of particular Shiite legal rulings. This is not to say that consensus appears only in the context of debate with Sunnis. Al-Ṭūsī makes frequent use of consensus as an argument in other works, such as *Tahdhīb al-aḥkām* and *al-Istibṣār*, that are directed primarily at a Shiite audience.

Both al-Murtaḍā and al-Ṭūsī treat the obvious issue of why the Shiites should adopt the concept of consensus even if the principle behind it is not consensus itself but rather the opinion of the imam. Sunni jurists object that the Shiites actually have no need of consensus and should instead merely refer directly to the opinion of the imam as a source of the law. In *Jawābāt al-masāʾil al-tabbānīyāt*, al-Sharīf al-Murtaḍā answers this objection as follows: "When the Prophet or Imam is known and identified, his opinions and doctrines may be known through direct address or through reliable reports. When, however, he is hidden and not identifiable—although it is certain that he exists and mixes with us—his opinions may be known through the consensus of the sect (*ijmāʿ al-ṭāʾifah*), whose opinions, we are certain, include his opinion."[164] Al-Ṭūsī observes similarly that in many cases, it is not possible to ascertain the opinion of the imam, but it is then possible to examine consensus in order to ascertain whether the imam agrees with a certain opinion. As the modern Shiite scholar al-Muẓaffar explains it, *ijmāʿ* in this case is like a hadith expressing the opinion of the imam, except that the *ijmāʿ* does not give the exact words the imam spoke; it is merely an indication of the content of the imam's opinion. For this reason, *ijmāʿ* has been called by modern Shiite jurists a *dalīl lubbī*, "proof in terms of sense, or content" rather than a *dalīl lafẓī*, "verbatim proof" which would be a hadith.[165] Al-Ṭūsī answers this objection:

> There is a well-known benefit to our taking consensus into consideration, and that is that the opinion of the Imam might not be apparent to us on many occasions, so that we must consider consensus in order to know, through the unanimous agreement of the jurists, whether the opinion of the Imam is included. If the opinion of the Infallible Imam, which is an authoritative argument, were apparent to us, we would aver that his opinion was the authoritative argument.[166]

164. al-Murtaḍā, *Rasāʾil*, 1:11.
165. al-Muẓaffar, *Uṣūl al-fiqh*, 3: 105.
166. al-Ṭūsī, *ʿUddat al-uṣūl*, 232–33.

The benefit of consensus is therefore linked to the special situation of the Occultation. During the Greater Occultation, direct access to the imam is impossible and one cannot obtain his opinions directly. The existence of a consensus, whether a consensus of the Shiite jurists alone or a consensus of Muslim jurists, allows the ascertainment of the imam's opinion in an indirect manner.

Two major points have been overlooked by scholars who claim that the Shiite theory of *ijmāʿ* empties it of all value. One is the crucial factor that the Shiite theory of *ijmāʿ* accepts the consensus of the entire Muslim community. Not only is it valid but it is also a *ḥujjah,* or irrefutable proof. The other point has to do with the ability of the Shiites to determine the opinion of the imam. When modern scholars state that an *ijmāʿ* based on the opinion of the imam is a nugatory principle, they ignore the fact that during the Greater Occultation there is no direct access to the opinion of the imam, as al-Ṭūsī points out. One might go so far as to restate the Shiite interpretation of consensus in the following manner: the consensus represents the truth, since it is known by virtue of its being a valid consensus that it must coincide with the opinion of the imam. In other words, the consensus of the Shiite jurists shows what the opinion of the imam is when direct access to him is impossible. This interpretation seems to be the implication of al-Sharīf al-Murtaḍā's and al-Shaykh al-Ṭūsī's discussions of consensus.

Later Shiite legal theorists state even more directly that the consensus of Shiite jurists indicates where the opinion of the imam lies: Al-Muḥaqqiq al-Ḥillī holds that one may know the opinion of the imam in three ways. One may know it from an actual audience with the imam himself or through reliable reports; he then adds, "In the absence of these two methods, if the Imamis agree unanimously on a matter in such a way that all Imami scholars without exception hold this opinion, then one may be certain of the inclusion of the Infallible Imam in the consensus, because it has been proved irrefutably that their opinions are true and that the Infallible Imam cannot commit an injustice." In the Shiite legal tradition, this principle has come to be expressed in the statement that consensus "discovers" or "reveals" the opinion of the imam (*al-ijmāʿu kāshifun ʿan qawli ʾl-imām*).[167] While for Sunni jurists, the consensus "discovers" the will of God concerning a particular legal issue, for the Shiites, the consensus "discovers" the opinion of the imam, which in turn indicates God's will.

The binding authority of the consensus of Shiite jurists, as opposed to all Muslim jurists, embodies the idea that the Shiites have privileged access to the truth. It is as if the jurists of one of the Sunni *madhhabs* were to claim that

167. Najm al-Dīn Jaʿfar al-Ḥillī, *Maʿārij al-uṣūl,* 126, 132; Ḥasan b. Zayn al-Dīn al-ʿĀmilī, *Maʿālim al-dīn wa-malādh al-mujtahidīn* (Tehran, n.d.), 192.

their own consensus, and not just the consensus of the jurists of all the recognized *madhhabs*, determined religious truth for the Muslim community as a whole. It cannot be stated that the Sunnis are always wrong and the Shiites always right, for the two types of consensus overlap; but according to the logic of *ijmāʿ al-firqah*, it may be stated that the Sunnis are sometimes right—when they happen to agree with the Shiites—and that the Shiites are always right. The theory of *ijmāʿ al-firqah* indicates, in a fashion, one possible attitude of the Shiite jurists to the Sunnis: they are often misled, but are not in complete error. The theory of *ijmāʿ al-firqah* has been expressed in many different ways since the eleventh century, and it is difficult to tell how it has functioned in practice. Later jurists complained that al-Murtaḍā and al-Ṭūsī used the concept of consensus carelessly and made many false claims of its existence on particular issues. Nevertheless, the three chief jurists of Buwayhid Baghdad succeeded in their goal of creating a consensus that looked like Sunni consensus outwardly but fit with the fundamental tenets of their sect, and their theory has retained its basic outlines until the present in Twelver jurisprudence.[168]

EARLIER SHIITE THEORIES OF CONSENSUS

The theory of consensus adopted in subsequent Twelver Shiite legal tradition undoubtedly goes back to the work of al-Shaykh al-Mufīd and the elaborations of al-Sharīf al-Murtaḍā and al-Shaykh al-Ṭūsī. There is nevertheless a strong possibility that similar theories were proposed by Shiite jurists prior to al-Shaykh al-Mufīd and that these theories influenced his adoption of consensus. Al-Masʿūdī, as pointed out, wrote several *uṣūl al-fiqh* works in the early tenth century, one or more of which may have set forth a Shiite theory of jurisprudence. His *Naẓm al-adillah fī uṣūl al-millah* in particular included a chapter on consensus along with the other typical topics of *uṣūl al-fiqh*, though it is not clear how he defined it.

Modern scholars have noted the important place in the history of Shiite Islamic law of the tenth-century scholars Ibn al-Junayd and his contemporary Ibn Abī ʿAqīl al-ʿUmānī (fl. 4th/10th c.),[169] known in later Shiite legal tradi-

168. See, for example, Najm al-Dīn Jaʿfar al-Ḥillī, *Maʿārij al-uṣūl*, 126; Ibn al-Muṭahhar b. Yūsuf Ibn al-Muṭahhar al-Ḥillī, *Mabādiʾ al-uṣūl*, 190; idem, *Tahdhīb al-wuṣūl*, 70; idem, "Nihāyat al-wuṣūl," (MS, Princeton University Library, Arabic New Series, 376), fols. 163–64; Ḥasan b. Zayn al-Dīn al-ʿĀmilī, *Maʿālim al-dīn*, 192; Bahāʾ al-Dīn Muḥammad al-ʿĀmilī, *Zubdat al-uṣūl* (Iṣfahān: Dār al-ṭibāʿah, 1899), 75–76; Mirza al-Qummī, *Qawānīn al-uṣūl*, 175. Perhaps the most extensive discussion of consensus in later Twelver theory is that of Asad Allāh al-Tustarī (d. 1234/1818-19) in his *Kashf al-qināʿ*, where he argues that a consensus reported through a single chain of transmission is *not* a binding argument, a position which became generally accepted by Twelver jurists after his time (Asad Allāh b. Ismāʿīl al-Kāẓimī al-Tustarī, *Kashf al-qināʿ ʿan wujūh ḥujjīyat al-ijmāʿ* [Qum: Muʾassasat Āl al-bayt li-iḥyāʾ al-turāth, n.d. Reprint of Bombay, 1899 ed.]).

169. Ḥasan b. ʿAlī (or ʿĪsā) al-Ḥadhdhāʾ, a teacher of Jaʿfar b. Muḥammad b. Qūlawayh (d. 369/979–80). See al-Amīn, *Aʿyān al-shīʿah*, 5: 157–59.

tion as "the Two Ancients" (*al-Qadīmayn*), holding that they were the first scholars to engage in the theoretical elaboration of the law on the basis of rational deduction and speculation. Modarressi considers them "the founders of Shī'ī systematic law, as distinct from the Tradition."[170] Unfortunately, nearly all the works attributed to these scholars have been lost, though some of their opinions survive in later works such as al-Allāmah al-Ḥillī's *Mukhtalaf al-shī'ah*. The truth is, though, that the theoretical elaboration of the law these two scholars achieved was rejected by their immediate successors and did not form a continuous tradition. It was only much later that some of their work was reintroduced into Twelver legal scholarship.

Ibn Abī 'Aqīl wrote a work on Twelver law entitled *al-Mutamassik bi-ḥabl āl al-rasūl* that was popular during the tenth and eleventh centuries. No other works of his are known. Ibn al-Junayd, much more than Ibn Abī 'Aqīl, had a highly developed legal methodology. Within his system of Twelver Shiite jurisprudence, he clearly adopted *ijtihād* and *qiyās* as legitimate principles for the elaboration of the law. It seems probable that his legal theory included a theory of consensus. Though some Muslim jurists limited the definition and purview of consensus—Dā'ūd al-Iṣfahānī and his Ẓāhirī followers limited valid consensus to that of the Companions—it is difficult to conceive of an Islamic theory of jurisprudence which adopts *ijtihād* and *qiyās* but does not recognize the authority of consensus, for consensus is the basis of the system within which *ijtihād* operates. In the absence of the principle of consensus, nothing would limit the proliferation of conflicting opinions, and the process of debate and disputation over specific issues could have only the vaguest of goals. There would be no principle or mechanism whereby the probability, value, or success of a particular opinion could be determined, nor would there be fundamental ground rules binding the Muslim jurists together into a community of interpretation. Ibn al-Junayd, and perhaps al-Mas'ūdī before him, had adopted a legal system even closer to the Sunnis than that espoused by al-Shaykh al-Mufīd and his students, who rejected *qiyās* and *ijtihād* and therefore limited the use of rationalist methods in the elaboration of the law. A Shiite system of jurisprudence that included a concept of *ijtihād* must have included the concept of legal consensus as well.

It is likely that Ibn al-Junayd had developed a two-tiered concept of consensus, espousing the binding authority of *ijmā' al-firqah*—designated by some similar term—and *ijmā' al-ummah* by the mid-tenth century. As with the later Shiite jurists, he must have argued that the binding authority of the consensus exists as such because it includes the opinion of the Imam. Al-Shaykh al-Mufīd and the later scholars al-Sharīf al-Murtaḍā and al-Shaykh al-Ṭūsī must have been aware of his theory of consensus just as they were aware

170. Modarressi, *Shī'ī Law*, 35–39.

of his adoption of *qiyās,* but because they rejected Ibn al-Junayd's legal works, they would not have recognized any debt they may have had to him in the text of their own legal works. That such a scenario is possible seems more likely when we note that al-Mufīd admits that Ibn al-Junayd was a clever and accomplished jurist, albeit misguided.[171]

In only one case in the Buwayhid Twelver jurists's writings is there an explicit indication of a precedent to their theory of Shiite consensus. Al-Sharīf al-Murtaḍā states in the introduction to *al-Intiṣār* that a number of Mu'tazilī scholars have adopted the opinion that the consensus of the descendants of the Prophet (*ijmā' ahl al-bayt*) is a binding argument (*ḥujjah*).[172] Al-Qāḍī 'Abd al-Jabbār likewise reports that some jurists (*ba'ḍuhum*) have held that the consensus of the descendants of the Prophet (*ijmā' 'itrat al-rasūl wa-ahl baytih*) is a binding argument (*ḥujjah*). 'Abd al-Jabbār himself apparently supported this view.[173] In *al-Shāfī fī al-imāmah,* al-Murtaḍā may have been referring primarily to 'Abd al-Jabbār, but he may also have intended the Zaydi scholar Abū Ṭālib Yaḥyā b. al-Ḥusayn b. Hārūn al-Nāṭiq bi'l-Ḥaqq (d. 424/1033), who, by 385/995, had proposed in his *Kitāb al-di'āmah fī tathbīt al-imāmah* a two-tiered definition of consensus, holding that *ijmā' ahl al-bayt* is a binding argument (*ḥujjah*).[174] In any case, al-Murtaḍā seems to admit that the Twelver theory of consensus espoused by al-Shaykh al-Mufīd and himself was influenced by earlier theories.

THE SHIITES' PRIVILEGED ACCESS TO GOD'S LAW

Confidence that the Shiites are the "chosen" sect in Islam and that absolute truth rests with them has not always outweighed their strong desire to be accepted by the majority Sunni community. Their two-tiered theory of consensus embodies this tension within Shiite thought. On the one hand, they were historically persecuted and deprived of their rights by the majority. On the other hand, they often desired to participate in the greater Islamic community. While the Shiites' adoption of the first tier of consensus, *ijmā' al-ummah,* implied their acceptance of the Sunni methodology of jurisprudence and expressed their own desire to be included in that system, their development of the second tier of consensus, *ijmā' al-firqah,* expressed their unwillingness to relinquish their privileged position as a sect blessed, through the imams, with divine guidance the Sunnis did not enjoy.

The theory of *ijmā' al-firqah* holds that the consensus of the Shiites,

171. al-Mufīd, *al-Masā'il al-ṣāghānīyah,* 19.

172. al-Murtaḍā, *al-Intiṣār,* 6.

173. al-Qāḍī 'Abd al-Jabbār, *al-Mughnī,* 17: 205; 20, pt. 1: 192. See also, al-Murtaḍā, *al-Shāfī,* 3: 120–29.

174. al-Murtaḍā, *al-Shāfī,* 3: 120–29; *Kitāb al-di'āma* is erroneously attributed to Ibn 'Abbād and published as *Nuṣrat madhāhib al-zaydīyah,* 175–79. See Madelung, "Einige Werke," 10.

which potentially excludes the Sunnis, is an authoritative argument. Since *ijmāʿ al-firqah* always includes the opinion of the imam, it amounts to a guarantee that the Shiite community can never be wrong. This places the Shiite *madhhab* in sharp contrast to the individual Sunni *madhhab*s, whose jurists do not generally make this claim, though they often oppose each other vociferously. If al-Murtaḍā had hoped the Sunnis would accept the Shiite jurists on equal terms, it seems logical or fair that he would also have accepted them on equal terms. Yet, he did not.

In several passages, al-Murtaḍā implies that Shiite law is inherently superior to Sunni law. His arguments indicate that the Shiites would like to participate with the Sunnis on equal terms, but must debase themselves in order to do so. It is only as a favor to the Sunnis that the Shiites concede to debate with them, for the Shiites know that they are the sole possessors of the truth. This attitude is particularly evident in two areas. One has to do with the role of dogma or basic theology (*uṣūl al-diyānāt*) in the relationship between Shiite and Sunni law. Al-Murtaḍā states that Shiite beliefs do not require them to be considered heretics by the Sunnis, but only sinners. This stance is plausible enough, and one might imagine that he would then state the converse: that according to Shiites, Sunnis are also only sinners, and therefore it should be acceptable that they debate each other. He does not do this. Rather, he states that whereas the Shiites are sinners according to the Sunni system, the Sunnis are somewhat worse off in the Shiite system. He does not say so explicitly, but he implies that because the Sunnis deny the correct doctrine of the imamate, Shiites necessarily regard them as unbelievers. Hence, it seems difficult for the Shiites to justify their intent to debate with the Sunnis other than as a perverse desire to participate in the activities of a corrupt majority or as an attempt to convert the enemy, which was bound to antagonize fellow Muslims and create problems for the Shiites.

The other point has to do with Shiite consensus. According to the theory of Shiite consensus—as represented in the theory of al-Murtaḍā and al-Ṭūsī, and al-Shaykh al-Mufīd before them—the Shiites are always right. Their view of Shiite consensus thus prevents further rapprochement. The Shiites can never be wrong on a point, because their opinions are always safeguarded by the theoretical presence of the opinion of the imam. In practice, Shiite consensus seems to have been used frequently, particularly by al-Murtaḍā and al-Ṭūsī, as an all-purpose argument for their opinions, whether they are arguing against Sunnis or against other Shiites. The Shiites can nearly always claim that their opinion is necessarily true because of the binding authority of Shiite consensus. Al-Murtaḍā makes this point clear in the introduction to *al-Intiṣār.* He states that Shiite consensus, in itself, is enough to prove all the points he will make in the body of the book, and then adds, in a condescending manner, that he will also present other concrete evidence even though it is unnecessary and superfluous. The implication is that he thinks all outcome of debate with the Sunnis is a foregone conclusion. If the Shiites can never be wrong, why debate? His answer would be, one assumes, so that the truth may be revealed and Shiite jurists gain the recognition due them in Islamic society, rather than being marginalized or excluded from legal scholarship. Indeed, he holds that when debating the Sunni jurists on legal questions it is better to avoid recourse to the concept of Shiite consensus, which the Sunnis reject. Using Shiite consensus as evidence will turn the debate away from legal issues to that of the imamate, which is not a legal issue and which Sunni jurists are not qualified to discuss. Instead, the Shiite jurist should use evidence the Sunnis accept (notwithstanding that the Shiites do not accept it themselves), such as legal analogies and hadiths reported through a single chain of transmission. The main reason behind the writing of *al-Intiṣār* was to provide Shiite jurists with such arguments.[175]

The sixteenth-century Shiite jurist al-Shahīd al-Thānī apparently had a more equal view of the relationship between Shiite and Sunni law than did al-Murtaḍā, which is reflected in his theory of consensus. In a forthright manner, he criticizes the theories of previous Shiite scholars on consensus, theories built on the foundations set by al-Shaykh al-Mufīd, al-Sharīf al-Murtaḍā, and al-Shaykh al-Ṭūsī. He wrote a treatise on the instances where al-Shaykh al-Ṭūsī incorrectly claimed the existence of consensus on specific points of law.[176] The most innovative position of al-Shahīd al-Thānī was his criticism of *ijmāʿ al-firqah*. He relinquished this theory of the Shiites' privileged access to the truth, bringing Shiite jurisprudence even closer to that of the Sunni *madhhabs*.

Shiite jurists before al-Shahīd al-Thānī claim that it is possible to determine the presence of the imam's opinion within the collection of opinions held by Shiite jurists although one cannot determine the identity of the imam himself. One method for identifying the imam was established by al-Murtaḍā and al-Ṭūsī. If, within the gamut of conflicting opinions on a certain issue, some opinions are attributable to jurists whose genealogies are known (*maʿrūf al-nasab*), then they are not to be considered and do not invalidate the consensus. If the jurists' genealogies are not known, then their opinions invalidate the

175. al-Murtaḍā, *Rasāʾil*, 2: 119.

176. Zayn al-Dīn al-ʿĀmilī *"Risālah ḥawl ijmāʿāt al-Shaykh al-Ṭūsī,"* in his *al-Dhikrā al-alfiyah li ʾl-Shaykh al-Ṭūsī* (Mashhad: Dānishkadah-yi ilāhiyāt va-maʿarif-i islāmī, 1971), 2: 790–98. Al-ʿĀmilī accuses many Shiite jurists of having made incorrect claims of *ijmāʿ*, but he criticizes al-Sharīf al-Murtaḍā and al-Shaykh al-Ṭūsī most severely.

177. al-Ṭūsī, *ʿUddat al-uṣūl*, 246.

consensus.[177] The reasoning is that a jurist whose genealogy is known cannot himself be the imam. Only jurists whose genealogies are not known might possibly be the imam, and therefore only *their* opinions might represent the necessary and indisputable truth. This rule, a logical consequence of the Shiites' theory of the Occultation and their definition of consensus, creates an important functional difference between Shiite consensus and Sunni legal consensus. In the Sunni legal system, consensus is established by the absence of dissenting opinions expressed by recognized jurists. The system described by al-Ṭūsī seems to work in exactly the opposite manner. The opinions of individual recognized jurists can be eliminated and not taken into account. Consensus is not defined by the absence of dissenting opinion and may exist despite dissent, just as long as the dissenting parties are individual, identifiable jurists. This feature of Shiite theory seems to bring consensus out of its original role as a principle regulating debate between the jurists over unsettled issues as part of a process of search for the truth. At the same time it grants consensus a very wide purview in deciding legal questions by allowing that "consensus" often exists despite dissenting opinions.

Al-Shahīd al-Thānī, going against the mainstream of Shiite scholarship for the previous five hundred years, rejects this interpretation of Shiite consensus outright. Interestingly enough, he uses the same argument one might expect the Sunnis to use. In his treatise on Friday prayer, completed in 962/1555, he criticizes earlier Shiite scholars sternly for claiming the ability to determine where the opinion of the imam lies. He asks, "Where do they get this knowledge concerning such questions, when they have not come upon any news of [the imam's] *person,* let alone his opinion?!" He continues, "How do they arrive at this decisive certainty that [the imam's opinion] coincides with the opinions of the Shiite scholars, despite the complete break and total separation between them, and their utter ignorance of his opinions for a period exceeding six hundred years?!"[178] Al-Shahīd al-Thānī's objections here effectively undermine the theory of *ijmāʿ al-firqah* which al-Murtaḍā and al-Ṭūsī were so keen to establish and which would render debate with the Sunnis futile or inane.

Al-Shahīd al-Thānī also questions the value of *ijmāʿ al-firqah* in *Tamhīd al-qawāʿid,* completed in 958/1551. After explaining the Shiite view concerning the authority of consensus of the Muslim community, he turns to the principle according to which the opinions of jurists with known genealogies do not affect consensus, while the opinions of jurists whose genealogies are not known must be taken into consideration. He protests:

178. Zayn al-Dīn al-ʿĀmilī, *Risālah fī ṣalāt al-jumʿah,* in his *Rasāʾil al-Shahīd* (Qum: Maktabah-yi baṣīratī, 1895–96), 88–89.

> I have strong reservations about all of this, which I have set down precisely in an independent discussion.[179] The disputed questions contained in the law which are based on this—an incalculable number—is clear. Moreover, [Shiite consensus] is one of the most important legal principles upon which subsidiary rulings are based, yet [the Shiite jurists'] discussions of it have not been carefully examined, and their opinions concerning it vary very widely, as one who has read them carefully may attest.[180]

In al-Shahīd al-Thānī's view, the rule Shiite jurists use to determine which opinions to take into consideration for consensus is seriously flawed, and Shiite discussions of the point until his day are inadequate. This glaring error in the Shiite legal system stands out as deserving rectification particularly because it is used so often in the Shiite tradition to justify positions on particular points of law.

Al-Shahīd al-Thānī's conclusion seems to be that the Shiites cannot rely so heavily on Shiite consensus during the Occultation, for it is simply impossible to determine where the imam's opinion lies. They must pay more attention to other evidence:

> When the Infallible Imam is manifest, certitude is reached upon knowing his opinion or establishing that it is included among the opinions of his followers (*shī'ah*). This was the case with his forefathers with regard to many questions on which the opinions of the Shiite scholars concurred with the reports transmitted from [the imams], such as the opinion that it is obligatory to wipe the feet in performing ablutions, the prohibition of wiping the shoes (in performing ablutions), the prohibition of reduction of obligatory shares (*'awl*) and agnatic distribution of excess (*ta'ṣīb*) in inheritance law, and other similar matters. In legal cases which first occurred during the time of the Occultation, and concerning which conflicting opinions have been voiced, one must refer to the dictates of the Koran and the Sunnah and other legally permissible evidence, and not to completely unfounded claims such as these.[181]

It is not possible, al-Shahīd al-Thānī holds, to determine the opinion of the imam during the Occultation. Therefore, one cannot look to Shiite consensus, which has been widely abused, to provide answers to all problems. According

179. Zayn al-Dīn al-'Āmilī is referring here to a treatise devoted exclusively to the issue of consensus, entitled *Risālah fī taḥqīq al-ijmā'*, which is not extant but was in the possession of his great-grandson in the seventeenth century (see 'Alī b. Muḥammad al-'Āmilī, *al-Durr al-manthūr*, 2: 188).

180. Zayn al-Dīn al-'Āmilī, *Tamhīd al-qawā'id*, 34.

181. Zayn al-Dīn al-'Āmilī, *Risālah fī ṣalāt al-jum'ah*, 89.

to his model, the situations of the Shiite and Sunni jurists were for all practical purposes identical. The Shiite jurist could not be certain that truth was restricted to those opinions given by Shiites alone. No theoretical construct, no guarantee that one could determine the opinion of the Hidden Imam, prevented them from falling into error. It is this common ground which allows al-Shahīd al-Thānī to make a more convincing appeal than al-Murtaḍā's for Sunnis to examine Shiite opinions, and vice versa. He did not, like al-Murtaḍā, adopt a defensive or superior attitude; he believed that cooperation and exchange of ideas between Sunnis and Shiite scholars would help overcome the problems they all faced as Muslim jurists and further the fundamental goal of legal scholarship: the search for truth.

In a discussion with his Shāfiʿī teacher Abū al-Ḥasan al-Bakrī in 943/1537, al-Shahīd al-Thānī called upon Sunni scholars to examine the opinions of the Shiites just as al-Murtaḍā had. He did not express al-Murtaḍā's idea that the Shiites enjoyed a monopoly on religious truth, as al-Murtaḍā had, and his theory of Shiite consensus, substantially different from that of al-Murtaḍā, reflects this contrast. His discussion with al-Bakrī shows his concern for the status of Muslim scholarship, which he saw as plagued by insularity of study in the individual *madhhab*s and lack of inquiry into the bases of previous scholarship. Al-Shahīd al-Thānī asked him:

> "What do you say of the matter of those common people and rabble who know nothing of the signs which save us from grave sins? What is their stance before God the Exalted? Does He approve of them despite this ignorance? Let us turn the discussion, rather, to the learned and noble legal scholars, each group of which has hardened in adopting one of the four *madhhab*s, and knows nothing of what has been said in any *madhhab* other than the one they have chosen, despite having the ability to peruse, examine, and understand legal questions. They have resigned themselves to accepting the opinions of their predecessors as authoritative without proof, and have stated categorically that their predecessors have provided them with the necessary basis for that decision. It is well known that Truth is on one side; if one group has said that the Truth is with it, citing So-and-so and So-and-so, then the other group says the same, citing their own great scholars and well-known masters—since no group lacks their own authorities to whom they refer and on whom they depend. For example, the Shāfiʿīs say 'The Imam al-Shāfiʿī and So-and-so and So-and-so have spared us the effort of doing this.' Similarly, the Ḥanafīs rely upon the Imam Abu Ḥanīfah and other great scholars of the *madhhab,* and the Ḥanbalīs rely upon their great masters and scholars. The Shiites also say al-Sayyid al-Murtaḍā, al-Shaykh al-Ṭūsī, al-Khwājah Naṣīr al-Dīn al-Ṭūsī, al-Shaykh

Jamāl al-Dīn [al-ʿAllāmah al-Ḥillī], and others have expended great efforts, enabling us to do without close examination, and we are certain and confident of our position. How, therefore, can such scholars make do with restricting themselves to one of these *madhhab*s and not examine the truth of the other *madhhab*s, nay, not even look at the works of its writers, nor even know their names? The Truth may not lie with all of these groups, and if we say that it is with one of them, we are preferring one group over the others without proof."

Master Abū al-Ḥasan [al-Bakrī] answered him, "As for the question of the common people, we beg the forgiveness of God that He not hold their shortcomings against them. As for the scholars, it is enough that they outwardly adhere to the truth."

Our Master [al-Shahīd al-Thānī] asked him, "How can that be enough for them, given what has been said of their neglect of examination and rigorous proof?"

He answered, "Oh Master, the answer to your question is simple. An example of this is someone who is born circumcised naturally. This circumcision spares him from having to undergo the circumcision required by religious law."

Our Master said, "This naturally circumcised man does not lose the obligation until he knows that his circumcision is itself the circumcision required by law, so that he might be asked and interrogated by men of experience and those who deal with this matter as to whether this naturally present state is sufficient to fulfill the obligation legally or not. But if he, on his own, makes do with what he has found, that is not legally sufficient to relieve him of the obligation."

[Al-Bakrī] replied, "Oh Master, this is not the first bottle to be broken in Islam."[182]

Like al-Murtaḍā, al-Shahīd al-Thānī also sees the Shiites as participating in the *madhhab* system, yet his tone and position are less defensive. He describes the Shiite *madhhab* as functioning exactly as the Sunni *madhhab*s do, which is not surprising from a jurist who spent many years studying as a Shāfiʿī law student and later would teach at a Shāfiʿī *madrasah,* as discussed in chapter 3. Al-Shahīd al-Thānī seems to have put his ideas on this topic into practice. His objections to his Sunni teacher were not idle words describing an ideal, unattainable situation.

Al-Shahīd al-Thānī complains that legal scholars do not examine the

182. ʿAlī al-ʿĀmilī, *al-Durr al-manthūr,* 2: 164–65.

works of other *madhhabs*. This is similar to al-Murtaḍā's complaint that Sunni scholars do not accept Shiite opinions and do not debate with them, but there is an important difference: al-Shahīd al-Thānī's complaint does not appear so one-sided. Rather than accuse the Sunnis of discriminating against the Shiites, he states that Sunnis and Shiites alike are guilty of the same shortcomings. Shāfiʿīs read only Shāfiʿī books, Ḥanafīs read only Ḥanafī books, and Shiites read only Shiite books. This insularity is a problem common to Sunnis and Shiites; they would both benefit by overcoming it. In this argument al-Shahīd al-Thānī does not *a priori* grant his own *madhhab* superiority over its Sunni counterparts, but holds them equally accountable. The truth on a particular legal issue, it appears, may lie with any one of the *madhhabs*. The Shiite *madhhab* is functionally equivalent to the other *madhhabs* and is not necessarily privileged with being any better or closer to the truth than they are. This approach is a far cry from the ideas of al-Murtaḍā, who saw the Shiite *madhhab* as being preserved from nearly all error by the concept of Shiite consensus. Al-Shahīd al-Thānī holds that one cannot assume the truth lies with one of the *madhhabs* in particular without examination, for that would be preferring one possibility over others without any evidence (*tarjīḥ min ghayr murajjiḥ*).

Insularity in legal scholarship, according to al-Shahīd al-Thānī, was linked to a deeper academic problem: the lack of critical examination of previous scholarship. He implies that complacency, lack of intellectual acumen, and an exaggerated reverence for earlier scholars petrified legal scholarship and caused gross errors to be accepted as correct. Again, he portrays Shiites and Sunnis as equal in this regard. The Shiites look to al-Sharīf al-Murtaḍā, al-Shaykh al-Ṭūsī, Naṣīr al-Dīn al-Ṭūsī, and al-ʿAllāmah al-Ḥillī as authorities. Later scholars accept their work without further examination and assume that they have solved major problems in the legal tradition definitively, obviating the need to consider them anew. The Shāfiʿīs look to al-Shāfiʿī in a similar manner, and the Ḥanafīs look to Abū Ḥanīfah in the same way. In his treatise on Friday prayer, al-Shahīd al-Thānī states, "Do not be one of those who know the truth by the man, and so fall into the abyss of error!" (*wa-lā takun mimman yaʿrifu 'l-ḥaqqa bi'r-rijāl * fa-taqaʿa fī mahāwī 'ḍ-ḍalāl **).[183] This blind acceptance of earlier scholarship was reinforced, or made possible, in that jurists felt it unnecessary to examine the works and opinions of other *madhhabs*, practices that would inevitably call their accepted beliefs and opinions into question and force them to reexamine the bases of their assumptions. Limiting oneself to a single *madhhab* rendered serious scholarship nearly impossible because too many ideas were accepted as final and unquestionable.

183. Zayn al-Dīn al-ʿĀmilī, *Risālah fī ṣalāt al-jumʿah*, 89.

CONCLUSION

The Twelver Shiites' attempt to establish their own legal *madhhab* and thereby fit into the Sunni *madhhab* system has been the guiding force behind much of the development of Shiite jurisprudence over the last millennium. The first, crucial step in the pursuit of this strategy was the development of a theory of consensus, which would allow the Shiites to accept the ground rules, as it were, of the Sunni legal system and provide a basis from which to argue for their own inclusion. In the late tenth century, al-Shaykh al-Mufīd developed a theory of consensus, and al-Sharīf al-Murtaḍā and al-Shaykh al-Ṭūsī elaborated on this theory early in the next century. By accepting the concept of consensus, Shiite jurists were opting, at least outwardly, for inclusion within the Sunni community of legal interpretation. The implications of this important historical event run counter to most portrayals of Shiism in scholarship to date. Treatments of Shiism in general works on Islam and in more specialized works focusing on Shiism or Islamic law lead one to believe that the Twelver Shiites reject consensus and the Sunni *madhhab* system categorically. Any number of features attributed to Shiism and seen as characterizing it throughout its history, such as its insistence on the imamate, its authoritarian nature, or its tendency to serve as a vehicle of protest against an oppressive majority, would require that Shiite believers reject the Sunni legal system altogether, yet this has not been the case. While the rejection of consensus has played a significant role in the history of Twelver Shiite jurisprudence, it has been offset and indeed surpassed by the desire to gain the acceptance of the Sunnis and participate in Sunni-dominated society on roughly equal terms. There has always been a significant tension within Shiism concerning its position vis-à-vis that of the majority, which is reflected in the Shiite theory of legal consensus, but the strength of the desire to be included and to be accepted by the majority is demonstrated by the establishment and continued vitality of the Twelver legal *madhhab*.

5

Rejection of Consensus

Twelver Akhbārism as an Anti-*Madhhab* Movement

> "By God, they follow none of that which you have adopted, nor do you follow any of that which they have adopted. So go against them; in no way are they part of the Pure Faith."[1]
>
> Ja'far al-Ṣādiq

Of the possible reactions to Sunni legal consensus, the trend within Shiism to reject it needs the least explanation. The bulk of Orientalist literature on Islam implies that this position would be the only one possible for Shiite doctrine. The Shiites, it is held, are guided in religious matters by an imam at all times, which is the crucial feature of their belief. They therefore have no need for the Sunni legal system or the principles on which it is based. If the Sunnis exclude Shiites from the pale of orthodoxy, it has no effect on them in the religious sense. Since truth lies with the imam beyond all doubt, the Shiites' rewards in the afterlife, as long as they uphold their allegiance to the imam, are not affected by the Sunnis' actions or opinions. By excluding the Shiites from their purported Islamic orthodoxy, the Sunnis merely reinforce their own error in refusing to follow the religious leader with whom the truth lies and thus ensure their own doom in the afterlife.

This chapter focuses on manifestations of Shiite rejection of the type of legal system developed by the Sunnis. While the rejection of Sunni juridical norms is obvious among the Ismā'īlī Shiites, it is not well studied concerning the Twelvers although it is fully expected by most scholars of Sunni Islam. The chapter examines the Twelver Akhbārīs, and in particular the Akhbārī revival of the seventeenth century, showing that the conflict between them and their opponents, the Uṣūlīs or *mujtahids*, was not simply one of rationalism versus

1. al-Ḥurr al-'Āmilī, *al-Fawā'id al-ṭūsīyah*, 364, 415.

traditionalism. Rather, the Akhbārīs were attacking the very conception of religious authority adopted by the Uṣūlīs, the idea that the jurists as a class had in effect assumed the role of religious guidance during the Occultation of the imam. The Akhbārīs held that the Shiite jurists, out of either negligence or misguidedness, had adopted this system from the Sunnis despite its being inconsonant with fundamental Shiite doctrine. Their polemic soundly rejected the concept of legal consensus, which, in their view, had no validity. The consensus of the majority community or, as they put it, the chance coincidence of opinions (*ittifāq al-ārā*) was, moreover, proven wrong both by the history of Islamic doctrines and by the political history of the Muslim community. Instead, the Akhbārīs envisioned a system of religious authority rooted more soundly in scripture and, they claimed, more true to Shiite tradition. The truth was not to be found in the interpretations of jurists but in the texts of Shiite hadith.

THE SHIITE REJECTION OF SUNNI JURISPRUDENCE

Goldziher asserts that, whereas Sunni Islam is based on the concept of consensus, Shiite Islam is based on rigid authority: "Thus if we wish to characterize in brief the essential difference between Sunnī and Shīʿī Islam, we may say that the former is based on the *ijmāʿ* and the latter on the authoritarian principle." He continues by emphasizing the role of the imam as the sole recognized interpreter of the law:

> Only the teaching and the will of the infallible Imām, or of his authorized deputy, carry a sure guarantee of truth and justice. Just as in any age the Imām alone is the legitimate political head of the Islamic community, so the Imām alone has the authority to decide questions that have not already been decided at the outset and for all time by received law, and the Imām alone has the authority to interpret and apply the law.[2]

Recent investigators have repeated this view, contrasting Shiism as a "church of authority" with Sunnism as a "church of consensus."[3] Such statements cannot be taken as accurate characterizations of Shiism at any period since the tenth century, as is clear from the preceding chapter. Nevertheless, the rejection of consensus has played an important role in a number of intellectual movements within Shiism, including Twelver Shiism, since that time.

It appears only logical that the Shiites would reject the Sunni legal *madhhab* system and the principle of consensus on which it is based. This point of view is the implication of current textbooks on Islam, which stress the imamate as the feature of Shiism that renders it schismatic; it is the reaction ex-

2. Goldziher, *Islamic Theology and Law,* 191.

3. See, for example, Makdisi, "Scholasticism and Humanism," 176; idem, *Rise of Humanism,* 29.

pected from the Shiites by scholars, such as Hodgson, who view Shiism as a perennial vehicle of protest and dissent.[4] A number of modern scholars of Islamic law, including Coulson and Eliash, see rejection as the most authentic stance Shiism could take in response to Sunni jurisprudence.[5] It is also the reaction implied in many Shiite treatises on the imamate and countless popular Shiite religious rituals that stress allegiance to the imams as the sole path to salvation and condemn all those who have denied or opposed the imams. While rejection of the Sunni majority has not been the only possible attitude of Shiites in Islamic history, its attraction has been strong. The idea that Shiites, because of their reliance on the imam as a guide in religious matters, have no use for the system of jurisprudence invented by the Sunnis has been present, though not always accepted, throughout the history of Shiite jurisprudence.

Rejection of the Sunni legal system has been the typical response of the branches of Ismāʿīlī Shiism, in which constant contact with the imam, either direct or through an intermediary, has been maintained. The Nizārī branch of Ismāʿīlīs, the followers of the Agha Khan, vest all legal authority in their imam, who is termed "Mawlana Hazar Imam" (*al-imām al-ḥāḍir*), meaning the imam who is present and not in occultation.[6] The Bohras, representing the Mustaʿlī branch of Ismāʿīlīs, including the Dāʾūdī and Sulaymānī subdivisions, maintain contact with their concealed (*mastūr*) imam through a representative similar to the Twelver Shiite *safīr*s of the Lesser Occultation known as *dāʿī muṭlaq* ("the supreme missionary") and addressed as Sayyidna ("Our Master").[7] These groups have no need of a legal system organized around a professional class of jurists like those represented by the Sunni *madhhab*s, for they have regular access, at least theoretically, to a divinely inspired religious authority.

While Ismāʿīlī communities maintained contact with the imam and preserved something like the system of authority found in pre-Occultation Twelver Shiism, there were responses to the Sunni challenge. A document of the Ismāʿīlī rejection of the Sunni science of jurisprudence and the legal system based thereon has come down to us from the mid-tenth century. The well-known Ismāʿīlī scholar al-Qāḍī al-Nuʿmān b. Muḥammad, the founder of Ismāʿīlī law, wrote a work entitled *Ikhtilāf uṣūl al-madhāhib waʾl-radd ʿalā man khālaf al-ḥaqq fīhā* ("Conflict over the Fundamental Doctrines of the Is-

4. Marshall G. S. Hodgson, *The Venture of Islam*. 3 vols. (Chicago: University of Chicago Press, 1974), 2: 39; Mangol Bayat, *Mysticism and Dissent* (Syracuse: Syracuse University Press, 1982), 2–7.

5. Eliash, "*Ithnāʿasharī-Shīʿī* Juristic Theory," 17–30; idem, "Misconceptions," 9–25.

6. On the Nizārī Ismāʿīlīs, see Azim Nanji, *The Nizārī Ismāʿīlī Tradition in the Indo-Pakistan Subcontinent* (Delmar, New York: Caravan Books, 1978); Marshall G. S. Hodgson, *The Order of Assassins* (The Hague: Mouton, 1955).

7. On the Bohras, see Asghar Ali Engineer, *The Bohras* (New Delhi: Vikas Publishing House, 1980).

lamic Sects and a Refutation of Those Who Have Gone against the Truth in These Matters") between 343/954 and 361/971.[8] This work is the first sustained, extant Shiite reaction to the science of *uṣūl al-fiqh*. An early Shiite view of the Sunni system of jurisprudence during its formative period, it states quite directly that the Sunni legal system is incompatible with Shiite, and therefore true Islamic, doctrine.

Some evidence indicates that early Imami or Twelver Shiite scholars were also engaged in refuting Sunni legal methods in what may have been a similar fashion. Rejection of the majority Sunni community in scholarly and legal matters is well documented in Twelver Shiism of the early period. Some hadith reports stress the insularity of the Shiite community and the need to protect it from outside influence: "Teach your children our hadiths before their minds become familiar with that which is in books which do not derive from us."[9] In *'Ilal al-sharā'i'*, Ibn Bābawayh al-Qummī argues that rejection of Sunni law is a natural extension of the Shiite theory of the imamate, explaining that the Shiites are obliged to espouse opinions which oppose those of the Sunnis (*yajibu'l-akhdhu bi-khilāfi mā taqūluhu'l-'āmmah*). He presents four hadiths which support this claim, three attributed to the sixth imam, Ja'far al-Ṣādiq, and one to the eighth imam, 'Alī al-Riḍā. In the first hadith, Ja'far al-Ṣādiq asserts that the Sunnis' desire to undermine 'Alī's authority caused them to adopt opinions opposed to those of 'Alī in the first place. The Sunnis would ask 'Alī about religious matters and, when he gave them his opinion, would create an opposite opinion in order to confuse the believers. The Shiites must therefore reject Sunni opinions outright. The fourth hadith, attributed to al-Riḍā, states that if the Shiite believer does not have access to a Shiite scholar for advice on the religious law, he should consult the local Sunni judge for his opinion, then do the opposite, for that is surely the true opinion.[10] Abū Sahl Ismā'īl b. 'Alī b. Isḥāq al-Nawbakhtī (d. 311/924), an Imami Shiite theologian with strong Mu'tazilī connections, wrote *Kitāb naqḍ Risālat al-Shāfi'ī*, a refutation of al-Shāfi'ī's work on *uṣūl al-fiqh*.[11] While this work is unfortunately not extant, it may have comprised a systematic rejection of Sunni legal principles and methods like that found in al-Qāḍī al-Nu'mān's work.

8. The work must have been written after 28 Rabī' I 343/30 September 954, when the Fāṭimid caliph al-Mu'izz li-Dīn Allāh (341–65/953–75) granted al-Qāḍī al-Nu'mān a letter of appointment (which he includes in *Ikhtilāf uṣūl al-madhāhib*, 24) and before the author's death on 29 Jumādā II 363/27 March 974. Furthermore, the work probably dates to before 361/971, when, following the Fatimid conquest of Egypt, al-Nu'mān accompanied the caliph from al-Mahdīyah in Tunisia to the new capital in Cairo, since this momentous event is not mentioned in the work.

9. al-Astarābādī, *al-Fawā'id al-madanīyah*, 29.

10. Ibn Bābawayh al-Qummī, *'Ilal al-sharā'i'*, 531.

11. Ibn al-Nadīm, *al-Fihrist*, 265. The statement in *A'yān al-shī'ah* that Abū Sahl was born in 337

In *Ikhtilāf uṣūl al-madhāhib* and other works, al-Qāḍī al-Nuʿmān maintains that the Fatimid caliph is the ultimate source of legal authority.[12] He rejects all other sources of authority, and rejects as well Sunni methods of jurisprudence, including *taqlīd, ijmāʿ, naẓar,* "speculation," *qiyās, istiḥsān,* "juristic preference," and *ijtihād.* In a letter of appointment issued to al-Qāḍī al-Nuʿmān in 343/954, Caliph al-Muʿizz li-Dīn Allāh (341–65/953–75) explains the Ismāʿīlī system of legal authority, at least in theory, quite simply and clearly. He instructs the new judge that when confronted with a problem, he should first consult the Koran, then the *sunnah* of the Prophet, then the opinions of earlier imams. If the problem remains unresolved at this point, he should refer directly to al-Muʿizz himself, and the caliph will provide him with the correct answer.[13] Thus, it is the caliph who has ultimate authority on religious matters. Others, like al-Qāḍī al-Nuʿmān himself, are entitled to issue legal opinions and hand down verdicts, but only through the permission of the caliph; their authority is derivative and dependent. Heresy and orthodoxy or religious conformity and deviance are easily defined in such a system. The crucial matter is allegiance and obedience to the caliph. The followers of the Fatimids, whom al-Qāḍī al-Nuʿmān terms *ahl al-ḥaqq,* "the People of the Truth," are true believers because they are guided by the caliph in their religious duties. They are the one true *ummah,* or Muslim community. Those who do not follow the caliph, whom al-Qāḍī al-Nuʿmān terms *al-ʿāmmah,* "the generality," are heretics.

THE AKHBĀRĪ REVIVAL OF THE SEVENTEENTH CENTURY

Rejection of Sunni jurisprudence is not limited to the Ismāʿīlī Shiites but is also found within Twelver Shiism, particularly in the school of Twelver thought known as Akhbārism, the name of which derives from its reliance on the *akhbār* or hadith reports of the twelve imams. While E. G. Browne was one of the first Orientalists to mention the Akhbārī movement within Twelver Shiism, it was Gianroberto Scarcia, in a 1958 study, who made the first significant presentation of Akhbārī thought in Western scholarship.[14] A number of studies published since the early 1980s have given Akhbārism fairly high exposure in scholarship on Shiism.[15] Although the Akhbārī movement maintained a con-

A.H. and died in 411 A.H. is an error (al-Amīn, *Aʿyān al-shīʿah,* 3: 383–88; Madelung, "Abū Sahl al-Nawbakhtī").

12. al-Qāḍī al-Nuʿmān, *Daʿāʾim al-islām wa-dhikr al-ḥalāl waʾl-ḥarām waʾl-qaḍāyā waʾl-aḥkām,* 2 vols., ed. ʿĀrif Tāmir (Beirut: Dār al-aḍwāʾ, 1995), 1: 50–139.

13. al-Qāḍī al-Nuʿmān, *Ikhtilāf uṣūl al-madhāhib,* 21.

14. E. G. Browne, *A Literary History of Persia,* 4 vols. (Cambridge: Cambridge University Press, 1929), 4: 374; Scarcia, "Intorno alle controversie," 211–50.

15. On the Akhbārīs in general, see Arjomand, *Shadow of God,* 13–14, 145–47, 152–53; Juan R. Cole, "Shīʿī Clerics in Iraq and Iran, 1722–1780," *Iranian Studies* 18 (1985): 3–34; idem, *Roots of North Indian Shīʿism,* 17–22, 31–39; Abdoljavad Falaturi, "Die Zwölfer-Schia aus der Sicht eines Schiiten," in *Fest*

tinual though limited presence from the tenth until the sixteenth century,[16] there was a resurgence of the movement in the seventeenth century and it remained very strong for the next one hundred and fifty years or so. During this period the Akhbārī movement claimed substantial support among Shiite scholars and dominated Najaf and other Shiite centers of learning until the second half of the eighteenth century, when Muḥammad Bāqir b. Muḥammad Akmal al-Bihbihānī (d. 1205/1791) successfully refuted the Akhbārīs and re-established the predominance of their opponents, the Uṣūlīs. Prominent scholars of the Akhbārī heyday include Muḥammad Amīn al-Astarābādī (d. 1036/1626–27), Ḥusayn b. Shihāb al-Dīn al-Karakī (d. 1076/1665), Muḥsin al-Fayḍ al-Kāshānī (d. 1091/1680), Muḥammad b. al-Ḥasan al-Ḥurr al-ʿĀmilī (d. 1099/1688), and Niʿmat Allāh al-Jazāʾirī (d. 1112/1701), to name a few. Akhbārism has since died out in Iran and Iraq, but the Akhbārī scholarly tradition has continued on a much smaller scale in Bahrain, eastern Saudi Arabia, and parts of India until the present.[17]

The work credited with inaugurating the Akhbārī revival is *al-Fawaʾid al-madanīyah,* which Muḥammad Amīn al-Astarābādī completed in Mecca in 1031/1622.[18] Al-Astarābādī's birth date is not known, but his *nisbah* indicates that he was a native of Astarābād in northern Iran. During his youth he studied in Shiraz for four years. He studied hadith and *rijāl* in Karbalāʾ with Muḥammad b. ʿAlī b. Abī al-Ḥasan al-ʿĀmilī (d. 1009/1600), receiving an *ijāzah* from him in 1007/1598–99. From 1015/1606 to 1025/1616, he studied in Mecca with the Shiite hadith scholar Mīrzā Muḥammad b. ʿAlī al-Astarābādī (d. 1028/1619).[19] At some point during this ten-year period, his teacher suggested that he write a work "to revive the way of the Akhbārīs." Muḥammad Amīn reports that he wrote *al-Fawāʾid al-madanīyah* in response to the request of a number of students—presumably Shiites—in Mecca that he teach them

schrift Werner Caskel, ed. Erwin Graf (Leiden: E. J. Brill, 1968), 62–95; Etan Kohlberg, "Akbārīya," *Encyclopaedia Iranica,* 716–18; idem, "Aspects of Akhbari Thought in the Seventeenth and Eighteenth Centuries," in *Eighteenth-Century Renewal and Reform in Islam,* ed. Nehemiah Levtzion and John O. Voll (Syracuse: Syracuse University Press, 1987), 133–60; Wilferd Madelung, "al-Akhbāriyya," *EI*², supp., 56–57; Hossein Modarressi, "Rationalism and Traditionalism in Shīʿī Jurisprudence," *Studia Islamica* 59 (1984): 148–58; idem, *Shīʿī Law,* 52–57; Moojan Momen, *An Introduction to Shīʿī Islam* (New Haven: Yale University Press, 1985), 117–18, 222–25; Newman, "Development and Political Significance"; idem, "The Nature of the Akhbārī/Uṣūlī Dispute in Late Ṣafawid Iran, p.1: ʿAbdallāh al-Samāhījī's *Munyat al-mumārisīn,* pt. 2: The Conflict Reassessed," *BSOAS* 15 (1992): 22–51, 250–61; Zysow, *Economy of Certainty,* 501–8.

16. Newman, " Development and Political Significance."

17. Modarressi, *Shīʿī Law,* 52–57.

18. al-Ṭihrānī, *al-Dharīʿah,* 16: 358.

19. al-Astarābādī, *al-Fawāʾid al-madanīyah,* 17–18, 133.

uṣūl al-fiqh.[20] The work was completed in Rabīʿ I 1031/January–February 1622.[21] Al-Astarābādī died in 1036/1626–27.[22]

Modern scholars have recognized the importance of *al-Fawāʾid al-madanīyah* for Shiite intellectual history and have reached several important conclusions concerning it: (1) the work touched off a controversy that dominated Shiite intellectual life for over a century, in which the two opposing groups were called the Akhbārīs, who espoused the opinions presented in *al-Fawāʾid al-madanīyah,* and the Uṣūlīs, who rejected them; (2) the two groups divided along the lines of traditionalists (i.e., the Akhbārīs) versus rationalists (i.e., the Uṣūlīs); (3) this conflict was not completely new, but had existed earlier in Shiite history; and (4) the opinions espoused by the Akhbārīs tended to undermine the authority of the Shiite jurists or *mujtahids*.[23]

Arjomand has voiced several additional interpretations of the Akhbārī movement from a sociopolitical perspective. He suggests that Akhbārism was an attack on the part of the Persian clerical estate, local landed notables in Iran from whose ranks the Safavid and earlier Iranian governments traditionally drew members of the bureaucracy, directed against the authority of the Arab Shiite jurists who had gained tremendous power in Iran during the early Safavid period. This idea seems based primarily on the fact that the author of *al-Fawāʾid al-madanīyah* was an Iranian. Since a number of native Arab scholars, such as Muḥammad b. al-Ḥasan al-Ḥurr al-ʿĀmilī, Ḥusayn b. Shihāb al-Dīn al-Karakī, and Niʿmat Allāh al-Jazāʾirī were prominent Akhbārīs as well, and indeed were among the most important spokesmen for the Akhbārīs in the seventeenth century, this interpretation is suspect. Arjomand also asserts that Akhbārī traditionalism was associated with gnostic philosophy.[24] This view has some credence since Muḥsin al-Fayḍ al-Kāshānī, a well-known Akhbārī who lived two generations after al-Astarābādī, harbored a deep interest in philosophy and wrote a number of important philosophical works. Nevertheless, a

20. al-Khwānsārī, *Rawḍāt al-jannāt,* 1:134; al-Astarābādī, *al-Fawāʾid al-madanīyah,* 2.

21. al-Ṭihrānī, *al-Dharīʿah,* 4: 433.

22. There are conflicting reports regarding his death date. In *Sulāfat al-ʿaṣr* and *Amal al-āmil,* the date 1026/1617 is given (ʿAlī b. Aḥmad al-Madanī Ibn Maʿṣūm, *Sulāfat al-ʿaṣr fī maḥāsin al-shuʿarāʾ bi-kull miṣr* (Cairo, 1905), 499; al-Ḥurr al-ʿĀmilī, *Amal al-āmil,* 2: 246). Al-Khwānsārī gives the date 1033/1623–24 and states that the date 1026 given in *Amal al-āmil* is an error (*Rawḍāt al-jannāt,* 1: 147. Madelung ("al-Akhbāriyya") and Momen (*Shiʿi Islam,* 117) both give 1033 A.H. (1623–24) as the death date. The report of al-Iṣfahānī (*Riyāḍ al-ʿulamāʾ,* 5: 36) that Muḥammad Amīn wrote a treatise discussing the ritual purity of alcoholic beverages *(khamr)* in 1034/1624–25 calls both these dates into question and gives credence to 1036/1626–27, the date he reports. The date of 1026 reported in *Amal al-āmil* may be easily explained as a copyist's error for 1036: the numbers 2 and 3 are easily confused.

23. Arjomand, *Shadow of God,* 13, 145–46; Kohlberg, "Akbārīya," 716–18; Madelung, "al-Akhbāriyya," 56–57; Momen, *Shīʿi Islam,* 117, 118, 186, 222, 302; Modarressi, "Rationalism and Traditionalism,"146–54, 156–57; idem, *Shīʿi Law,* 32–35, 52, 54–55.

24. Arjomand, *Shadow of God,* 145–46, 153.

chapter in *al-Fawā'id al-madanīyah* rejects the methods of the philosophers, which calls this view into question,[25] and a survey of the well-known Akhbārīs of the period shows al-Kāshānī 's involvement with philosophy to be an anomaly. Arjomand also claims that the Akhbārī movement tended to enhance the prestige of *sayyids*, the living descendants of the imams.[26] While this last suggestion might reflect some of the social implications of the Akhbārī movement, it is at best tentative and would require additional documentation.

AKHBĀRISM BEFORE THE REVIVAL

The Akhbārīs constituted a recognized group long before their resurgence in the seventeenth century with the work of Muḥammad Amīn al-Astarābādī and his followers, though the adherents of this trend were not always designated by the same name. The use of the term "Akhbārī" in particular to describe a faction within Twelver Shiism goes back at least to al-Shahrastānī's famous heresiography *al-Milal wa'l-niḥal,* completed in 521/1127. He reports that the Akhbārī and "Kalāmī" factions among the Twelvers killed each other and declared each other unbelievers.[27] Al-'Allāmah al-Ḥillī also uses the terms Akhbārīyūn and Uṣūlīyūn to describe two opposed Twelver factions in *Nihāyat al-wuṣūl ilā 'ilm al-uṣūl,* which dates to 704/1305.[28] The seventeenth-century proponents of Akhbārism presented their theses not as new discoveries but as a revival of traditional Shiite positions. They identify early Twelver scholars, such as Muḥammad b. Ya'qūb al-Kulaynī (d. 329/940) and the "two Ṣadūqs," Ibn Bābawayh al-Qummī (d. 381/991) and his father, as Akhbārīs.[29] This assessment seems historically accurate regarding Ibn Bābawayh, at least, if one judges from his writings. Ibn Bābawayh, whose works deal nearly exclusively with hadith, clearly supported the Akhbārī trend within Shiism. The fact that his most extensive collection of hadith is entitled *Man lā yaḥḍuruh al-faqīh,* "He who does not have a jurist nearby," implies that a Shiite jurist is, for all intents and purposes, an expert in the hadith of the imams and not someone trained in legal methodology.

The Buwayhid jurist al-Sharīf al-Murtaḍā does not use the term *akhbārī,* but designates scholars who ascribed to what was essentially the same school of thought as *aṣḥāb al-ḥadīth.* His statements imply that *aṣḥāb al-ḥadīth* are unqualified to give legal opinions and that their claims to religious authority

25. al-Astarābādī, *al-Fawā'id al-madanīyah,* 242–66

26. Arjomand, *Shadow of God,* 13.

27. Abū al-Fatḥ Muḥammad b. 'Abd al-Karīm al-Shahrastānī, *al-Milal wa'l-niḥal,* 2 vols., ed. Abū 'Abd Allāh al-Sa'īd al-Mandūh (Beirut: Mu'assasat al-kutub al-thaqāfīyah, 1994), 1: 126.

28. Ibn al-Muṭahhar al-Ḥillī, "Nihāyat al-wuṣūl," fol. 201a.

29. al-Astarābādī, *al-Fawā'id al-madanīyah,* 43–44; al-Karakī, *Hidāyat al-abrār,* 51.

are unfounded. In his view, that they relate reports transmitted from their ancestors does not grant them the right to decide legal questions. He suggests that they often base legal opinions on reports of doubtful certitude or adopt an opinion on a particular legal issue simply because they find it attributed to an earlier hadith transmitter in a book. Elsewhere he holds that the layman must resort to a legal scholar for a sound opinion and cannot merely consult one of the Shiites' compiled works (*kitāb muṣannaf*).[30] Already by the eleventh century a strong opposition existed between the rationalist jurists on the one hand and proponents of hadith on the other.

In *Kitāb al-naqḍ*, written ca. 565/1170, 'Abd al-Jalīl al-Qazwīnī refers frequently to the Uṣūlī faction among the Twelver Shiites and opposes it to the Akhbārīyah, the Ḥashwīyah, "Literalists," and the Ghulāt, "Extremists." His presentation makes it clear that these were well-established groups in the Shiite community. According to him, the Uṣūlīs are the only true Shiites. He claims that the Akhbārīs, whom he despises, are Shiites only in the sense that they label themselves as such and adds that they hide their heterodox views from the Uṣūlīs. Akhbārism, he claims, was losing popularity during his era, and not many of its proponents remained.[31] One gathers from his text that the Uṣūlīs are the proponents of a science of legal methodology similar to that of the Sunnis and that the Akhbārīs are altogether opposed to this science. Already in the twelfth century, this conflict seems to be an old one. The *Fihrist* of Muntajab al-Dīn al-Rāzī (d. ca. 600/1203) mentions a work which seems to be directed against Akhbārī Shiites who rejected the methods of the jurists. Nāṣir al-Dīn Abū Ismā'īl Muḥammad b. Ḥamdān al-Ḥamdānī, a twelfth-century figure who was the leading Shiite scholar (*ra'īs*) in Qazvīn, wrote a work entitled *al-Fuṣūl fī dhamm a'dā' al-uṣūl*, "The Chapters on Censure of the Enemies of *Uṣūl (al-Fiqh)*," ostensibly an Uṣūlī critique of contemporary Akhbārism.[32] The early Akhbārī tradition died out, for the most part, and few of the works have been preserved. The main sources for the beliefs and opinions representative of this trend within Twelver Shiism are therefore the works written during the Akhbārī revival in the seventeenth and eighteenth centuries.

30. al-Murtaḍā, *Jawāb al-masā'il al-mawṣilīyāt al-thālithah* in his *Rasā'il*, 1: 211–12; see also 2: 331–33.

31. 'Abd al-Jalīl al-Qazwīnī, *Kitāb al-naqḍ*, ed. Mīr Jalāl al-Dīn Muḥaddith (Tehran, 1980). References to the Akhbārīs are found on pp. 3, 282, 458, 529, 568–69. The editor, Muḥaddith, apparently did not recognize the importance of the term Uṣūlī, for the index cites only five references to them, when they are actually mentioned on pp. 3, 27, 29, 59, 99, 109, 114, 119, 272, 278, 281–82, 286, 295, 318, 322, 394, 407–8, 415–16, 459, 481, 501, 506, 514, 528–30, 561, 568–69, 613. Al-Qazwīnī was an Uṣūlī himself, and frequently holds that the accusations of his Sunni opponent are valid only with regard to the Akhbārīs or Ghulāt.

32. Muntajab al-Dīn al-Rāzī, *Fihrist Muntajab al-Dīn*, 161.

THE AKHBĀRĪ-UṢŪLĪ CONTROVERSY REINTERPRETED

The significance of the conflict between the Akhbārī and Uṣūlī movements in Twelver Shiite juridical and intellectual history remains only partially understood if viewed as a phenomenon internal to Shiism. The Akhbārīs, whose appellation derives from their reliance on the traditions (*akhbār*) attributed to the imams as the basis for elaboration of the law, have usually been styled traditionalists, whereas their Uṣūlī opponents, so called because of their use of the science of legal methodology (*uṣūl al-fiqh*), have been labeled rationalists. From a comparative perspective, however, an examination of the Akhbārī movement within Twelver Shiism leads to the conclusion that the Akhbārīs were not simply Shiite traditionalists opposed to the Uṣūlīs, Shiite rationalists. Another crucial feature of the Akhbārī movement was that it rejected the juridical system of the Sunnis and the conception of religious authority on which it was based. Moreover, it opposed the influence of this system on the Shiite tradition.

Modern scholars are correct in seeing *al-Fawā'id al-madanīyah* as a traditionalist manifesto against rationalist elaboration of the law on the part of Shiite jurists. Many individual passages of the work show al-Astarābādī to be a strict traditionalist opposed to rationalist methods, similar to Sunni Ẓāhirīs, such as Ibn Ḥazm (d. 456/1064).[33] The twelve chapters of *al-Fawā'id al-madanīyah* include one chapter arguing that the use of rational or speculative derivation (*al-istinbāṭāt al-ẓannīyah*) in the interpretation of the sacred law is invalid (chapter one, 90–128); another chapter refuting specific rationalist methods used in the science of jurisprudence, including *istiḥsān, istiṣḥāb,* and so on (chapter six, 133–50); a chapter on the errors of Mu'tazilī and Ash'arī philosophical theology (chapter eleven, 200–242); a chapter on the errors of the philosophers and the inadequacy of Aristotelian logic (chapter twelve, 242–66); a chapter arguing that the sole basis of Shiite jurisprudence should be the traditions of the imams (chapter two, 128–32); and a chapter criticizing rationalist terminology (chapter ten, 194–200). Al-Astarābādī gives a representative statement of his traditionalist position in the following passage:

> The frequent reliance of this group [of later Shiite jurists] on mere reason led them to go against the reports reliably transmitted from the Chaste Descendants of the Prophet on many points of theology and juridisprudence. From these contradictions in jurisprudence resulted many further contradictions in individual legal rulings, yet [the jurists] did not recognize their source. Furthermore, their reliance on these [rationalist meth-

33. See, for example, Ibn Ḥazm, *Mulakhkhaṣ ibṭāl al-qiyās wa'l-ra'y wa'l-istiḥsān wa'l-taqlīd wa'l-ta'līl,* ed. Sa'īd al-Afghānī (Damascus: Maṭba'at jāmi'at dimashq, 1960); Goldziher, *Ẓāhiriten.* See also Ibn Ḥazm, *al-Iḥkām fi uṣūl al-aḥkām* (Cairo: Maktabat 'Āṭif, 1978), 992–1036, 1206–1351, wherein he rejects the use of *ra'y, istiḥsān,* and *qiyās* in the religious law.

> ods] and their lack of recourse to the Speech of the Imams were due either to specious arguments which they mistakenly accepted or to inattention. But God knows best. If, upon writing in these sciences, they had consistently begun chapters, sections, and questions, for example, with the Speech of the Chaste Descendants, then explicated them and supported them with rational arguments, it would have been better for them.[34]

This passage is enough to show that the author is an extreme traditionalist who wishes to restrict severely the use of reason in the interpretation of the sacred law and to grant precedence to scriptural texts in law and legal methodology as well as other fields of religious scholarship.

The author of *al-Fawā'id al-madanīyah* does much more, however, than describe a conflict between rationalists and traditionalists. It is also clear that al-Astarābādī was combating the influence of Sunni jurisprudence on Shiism. Modern scholars have hinted at this aspect of the work, but do not in general identify opposition to Sunni influence as a major feature of the Akhbārī school.[35] The text of *al-Fawā'id al-madanīyah* argues that Shiite jurists have developed a legal *madhhab* modeled on those of the Sunnis. Al-Astarābādī aims to denounce this system, declaring it completely invalid and fundamentally incompatible with the basic tenets of Shiism. Scholars who have examined the history of Shiite jurisprudence have underestimated the importance of this point, that al-Astarābādī is attacking what he sees as an essentially Sunni system. This misconception has occurred because scholars treating the history of Shiite jurisprudence have viewed it, for the most part, as an independent entity rather than one facet of Islamic jurisprudence in general. Such a perspective has led several modern scholars to reproduce lists of the conflicting opinions of the Akhbārīs and Uṣūlīs without analyzing sufficiently the import or bases of these differences of opinion.[36]

A key idea underlying the ideological position of the Akhbārīs is that *khilāf,* the disagreements or differences of opinion which characterize the Sunni legal system, are a defect or an evil. The absence of unanimous agreement among the believers, ensured through reference to a single imam designated to guide the believers in religious matters, indicates to many Shiites that the Muslim community has strayed from the truth. Duncan MacDonald holds that the Shiites "utterly reject the idea of co-ordinate schools of law; to the

34. al-Astarābādī, *al-Fawā'id al-madanīyah,* 29–30.

35. Madelung, "Authority in Twelver Shiism," 173 n. 25; Arjomand, *Shadow of God,* 145; Kohlberg, "Aspects of Akhbari Thought," 134. An exception to these authors' writings is the recent work of Ahmad Kazemi Moussavi, which identifies the repudiation of Shiite involvement with Sunni legal methods as a major feature of the movement (*Religious Authority,* 91–93).

36. Falaturi, "Zwölfer-Schia," 81 ff.; Momen, *Shī'ī Islam,* 223–25; Newman, "Development and Political Significance," 24–38; Scarcia, "Intorno alle controversie," 225–46.

doctrine of the varying (*ikhtilāf*) as it is called, and the liberty of diversity which lies in it, they oppose the authority of the Imam. There can be only one truth and there can be no trifling with it even in details."[37] Coulson stresses that the Shiite system of authority necessarily rejects the principles of consensus and dissent found in Sunni jurisprudence:

> It follows that consensus (*ijmā'*), whether as a spontaneous source of law or as a criterion regulating the authority of human reasoning, has no place in such a scheme of jurisprudence, where the authority of the Imam supersedes that of agreed practice and his infallibility is diametrically opposed to the concept of probable rules of law (*ẓann*) and equally authoritative variants (*khilāf*).[38]

While these statements can in no way be taken to characterize Shiite jurisprudence in general, they do accurately describe the views of the Akhbārīs. According to them, there is only one truth and only one possible correct answer to religious questions. The Sunnis' legal methods depend on probability rather than certainty when certainty is required.

The remedy for conflicting opinions is reliance on the imams—all other methods of arriving at sound religious opinions are inadequate. Al-Astarābādī states, "every path except holding to the speech of the Imams leads to conflicting legal opinions (*ikhtilāf al-fatāwā*) and blasphemy (*al-kadhib 'alā 'Llāh*)."[39] Here he equates difference of legal opinion with the adoption of heretical beliefs. In another passage, he argues, "Every path which leads to variant legal rulings (*ikhtilāf al-fatāwā*) except in cases where dissimulation (*taqīyah*) is required is rejected and unacceptable to God inasmuch as it leads to disagreement (*ikhtilāf*)."[40] Al-Astarābādī and many other Shiite scholars, including al-Qāḍī al-Nu'mān, felt that the fundamental purpose of religion itself was to avoid conflict and difference of opinion:

> Reason and revelation both demonstrate that the benefit of sending prophets and revealing scripture is to remove disagreement and disputes among the believers so that their lives in this world and the next might be in order. But if speculation is considered a permissible method of interpretation with regard to God's rules of law, then this benefit is lost through the occurrence of disagreement and disputes, as is plainly observable.[41]

There are no authoritative variant opinions in a system based on recourse to the imams; unanimity is theoretically guaranteed by a single authority. Ac-

37. MacDonald, *Development of Muslim Theology*, 116.
38. Coulson, *History of Islamic Law*, 107.
39. al-Astarābādī, *al-Fawā'id al-madanīyah*, 128.
40. Ibid., 94. Shihāb al-Dīn al-Karakī makes a similar argument in *Hidāyat al-abrār*, 215–19.
41. al-Astarābādī, *al-Fawā'id al-madanīyah*, 129.

cording to reason alone, al-Astarābādī asserts, difference of opinion is not good. He asks how two Muslim jurists faced with exactly the same case can give contradictory opinions without questioning the validity of the juridical system, when they are both supposed to believe in the same God, the same Prophet, and the same Book.[42]

To the Akhbārīs, that the Sunni legal system was characterized by variant opinions indicates its fundamental flaws and shows that Sunni jurists' opinions did not derive from an authoritative source. This view of disagreement over religious matters is succinctly captured by a tradition attributed to ʿAlī where he scolds judges for following their personal opinions "when their God is *one*, and their Book is *one*, and their Prophet is *one!* Did they follow [the Prophet] after he commanded them to disagree, or did they disobey him after he forbade them to disagree?!"[43] The Ismāʿīlī jurist al-Qāḍī al-Nuʿmān stresses the arbitrary, personal nature of the opinions that constituted *khilāf.* He relates that Sunni jurists "increased in number and their various whims led them to uphold conflicting opinions, going against the fundamental nature of the Sacred Law." He holds further that they neglected to refer religious questions to the imams out of obstinacy and concern for their own status:

> When they were incapable of understanding the Koran or the Sunnah, they disagreed, and derived rulings for the Muslim community according to their own fancy. They did this to such a degree that they were reluctant to refer the matters which they disputed to those to whom God had commanded them to consult, out of covetousness for their dominant position (*riʾāsah*) and so that those over whom they claimed to have authority (*man tarāʾasū ʿalayh*) might not view them as incapable and subsequently cease to follow them.[44]

Here al-Qāḍī al-Nuʿmān asserts that the Sunni jurists have made unfounded claims to exclusive religious authority and thus usurped the authority of the imams. Differences of opinion on legal matters result from refusal to consult the imams, whose authority is uniquely valid and who may settle disputed questions definitively. Conflicting views therefore do not arise naturally in the course of the search for religious truth, which is singular. Rather, the persistence of such opinions indicates that the most basic function of the religion, referral to a valid religious authority, has been disrupted or abandoned altogether.

The natural consequence of this view is that legal consensus is inherently

42. al-Astarābādī, *al-Fawāʾid al-madanīyah,* 94.

43. Muḥsin al-Fayḍ al-Kāshānī, *Tashīl al-sabīl bi-l-ḥujjah fī intikhāb Kashf al-maḥajjah li-thamrat al-muhjah* (Tehran: Muʾassasat al-buḥūth waʾl-taḥqīqāt, 1987), 26.

44. al-Qāḍī al-Nuʿmān, *Ikhtilāf uṣūl al-madhāhib,* 5, 6.

invalid, since it allows for difference of opinion. Al-Astarābādī states unequivocally, "The consensus of the Muslim community is not incontestable; rather, it is known to be invalid" (*ijmāʿu 'l-ummati ghayru musallamin bal maʿlūmu 'l-buṭlān*). He insists that it is a groundless, Sunni invention: "The authority of consensus is one of the contrivances and inventions of the Sunnis" (*inna ḥujjīyata 'l-ijmāʿi min tadābīri 'l-ʿāmmati waʾkhtirāʿātihim*).[45] Similarly, al-Ḥurr al-ʿĀmilī holds that the authority of consensus is a Sunni invention: "The truth is that consensus actually comes from the Sunnis, and not from the Shiites, so how could there be any authority in it? The Akhbārīs and all of the early Shiite scholars (*jamīʿ aṣḥābinā al-mutaqaddimīn*) are opposed to it." He goes on to argue that the concept of equally valid competing opinions must be unsound, since the Sunnis use this as an excuse for the wars which took place among the Companions during ʿAlī's caliphate.[46] Ḥusayn b. Shihāb al-Dīn al-Karakī also holds that consensus is a Sunni invention. He rejects several elements of Sunni legal theory, adding, "especially consensus, for it is the most widely known of their proofs—indeed, it is the basis of their miscreance (*bal huwa asāsu ḍalālihim*)." He explains that the Sunnis "made the chance agreement of their prominent leaders in miscreance on a particular matter a binding proof (*ḥujjah*) and called it consensus."[47] Al-Kāshānī holds that the consensus of the Muslims is obviously invalid since it was used to justify the caliphate of Abū Bakr.[48] Al-Ḥurr al-ʿĀmilī claims that the Sunnis invented consensus in order to usurp the caliphate and then to justify any other falsehood they wished.[49] Consensus should be categorically rejected by the Shiites.

By rejecting the concept of consensus, the Akhbārī Shiites accepted and admitted that they violated it. They even made a point of going against the consensus, which they knew to be wrong. They accepted deviant status, separating themselves, at least theoretically, from the remainder of the Muslim community. They might, in order to survive in a Sunni society, pretend to accept the majority's norms out of *taqīyah,* but this pretence was a completely external phenomenon unmatched by any inner acceptance of or accommodation to the Sunni legal system. Their attitude toward the Sunni community was theoretically one of complete rejection. Thus, al-Ḥurr al-ʿĀmilī refers to Sunnis as *aʿdāʾ al-dīn,* "the enemies of the faith." He explains that the Shiites have been expressly commanded in scriptural texts transmitted reliably from the imams to avoid the adoption of Sunni methods and conformance with their beliefs and practices. He cites a hadith attributed to Jaʿfar al-Ṣādiq that

45. al-Astarābādī, *al-Fawāʾid al-madanīyah,* 13, 112.
46. al-Ḥurr al-ʿĀmilī, *al-Fawāʾid al-ṭūsīyah,* 403, 405.
47. al-Karakī, *Hidāyat al-abrār,* 152, 261, 263.
48. al-Kashānī, *Tashīl al-sabīl,* 26.
49. al-Ḥurr al-ʿĀmilī, *al-Fawāʾid al-ṭūsīyah,* 434.

reads, "By God, they follow none of that which you have adopted, nor do you follow any of that which they have adopted. So go against them (*fa-khālifūhum*); in no way are they part of the Pure Faith (*al-Ḥanīfiyah*)." He interprets another hadith attributed to Ja'far al-Ṣādiq as implying that the only element of Islam to which the Sunnis still adhere is prayer toward the Ka'bah.[50] In other words, they are only outward believers (*ahl al-qiblah*), Muslims in name only. Al-Ḥurr al-'Āmilī cites with approval the hadith report which urges the believer who does not have access to a Shiite jurist to consult the local Sunni judge then do the opposite of what the judge advises. He elevates this behavior to a general principle, holding that whatever ruling is opposite that adopted by the Sunnis is correct and should be followed. Similarly, Ḥusayn b. Shihāb al-Dīn al-Karakī holds that Shiites should scrupulously oppose the Sunnis where faith is concerned: "going against (the Sunnis) has become a general principle on which one should rely concerning matters of religion" (*ṣāra khilāfuhum qā'idatan yurja'u ilayhā fi umūri'd-dīn*).[51]

THE SUNNI ORIGINS OF SHIITE LEGAL METHODS

Al-Astarābādī singles out specific elements of Shiite jurisprudence and legal methodology for criticism, not only because they are rationalist but also because they derive from the Sunni legal tradition. He asserts that *ijmā', istiḥsān, istiṣḥāb,* "presumed continuity of *status quo ante,*" and *qiyās* are all basic Sunni legal concepts alien to Shiite jurisprudence. The Sunnis needed to develop these methods in the first place only because they denied the necessity of an imam to serve as a guide in religious matters. The later Akhbārī scholar Muḥsin al-Fayḍ al-Kāshānī states that *ijmā'* and *ijtihād* were originally Sunni concepts. Al-Ḥurr al-'Āmilī holds that *ijmā', qiyās, barā'ah aṣlīyah,* "original licitness," and *istiṣḥāb* are all invalid Sunni proofs.[52]

The Akhbārīs went to great lengths to argue that the legal system which had developed within Twelver Shiism was at heart a Sunni system incompatible with Shiite beliefs. Al-Astarābādī asserts that the science of *uṣūl al-fiqh* in its entirety was invented by the Sunnis. He cites a number of Sunni works on *uṣūl al-fiqh* to argue that *ijtihād* was also a Sunni concept.[53] Sunni jurisprudence, following the methodology of *uṣūl al-fiqh,* relies on probability (*ẓann*), when

50. Ibid., 252, 364, 370, 415, 416.

51. al-Karakī, *Hidāyat al-abrār,* 170, 174, 175.

52. al-Astarābādī, *al-Fawā'id al-madanīyah,* 45–47; Muḥsin al-Fayḍ al-Kāshānī, *Safīnat al-najāt,* ed. Muḥammad Riḍā al-Naqūsānī (Tehran, 1960), 9–10; al-Ḥurr al-'Āmilī, *al-Fawā'id al-ṭūsīyah,* 410, 414.

53. al-Karakī, *Hidāyat al-abrār,* 182, 234; al-Astarābādī, *al-Fawā'id al-madanīyah,* 18–29. The works he cites include *al-Iḥkām* by al-Āmidī, *Sharḥ al-mukhtaṣar* by 'Aḍud al-Dīn al-Ījī, and *al-Talwīḥ* by al-Taftazānī.

what is required is certitude (*qaṭ'*). The early Shiites did not have works on *uṣūl al-fiqh* because they were simply not necessary.[54] Al-Astarābādī elaborates:

> Some jurisprudential rules put forth by the Sunni *uṣūlīs* only follow logically because they deny that the Prophet left for every age an entrusted infallible [guide], a recourse for all men, knowing, through divine inspiration (*waḥy*) rather than personal opinion (*ra'y*), everything the Muslim community would require until the Day of Resurrection, and because they denied the binding authority (*ḥujjīyah*) of the hadiths transmitted from the Chaste Descendants.[55]

It was only the Sunnis' refusal to accept the authority of the imams and their hadith that led them to concoct their legal methods in the first place. For Shiites, therefore, these methods were completely unnecessary.

Al-Astarābādī then argues that later Shiite jurists adopted principles from Sunni *uṣūl al-fiqh,* including *ijtihād,* even though these concepts contradicted the hadith of the imams. Muḥsin al-Fayḍ al-Kāshānī also holds that Shiite jurists took the concepts of *ijmā'* and *ijtihād* from the Sunnis. Ḥusayn b. Shihāb al-Dīn al-Karakī claims that *uṣūl al-fiqh* was contrived by the Sunnis, adding, "In no other science has there arisen so much confusion and disagreement; for the most part, it resembles pure ranting and raving."[56] Al-Ḥurr al-'Āmilī asserts that the methods of legal proof which Shiite Uṣūlī jurists have adopted are clearly Sunni in origin:

> You should be aware that these types of proof all concur with the proofs and methods of the Sunnis; indeed, they are the very same proofs on which the Sunnis rely in their books, and are their inventions and innovations. This fact in itself should suffice as evidence that they are invalid and proof that they are flawed. If they were correct, then the opinions of the Sunnis would be correct, yet both the premise and the consequence are known to be false. We have been commanded in a text related from our Imams through many chains of authority to distance ourselves from the ways of the Sunnis, to abandon the methods they follow, and to avoid resembling them (*mushākalatihim*) in their beliefs and their actions. One must not neglect this point.[57]

The Akhbārīs thus rejected not only rationalist methods per se but also all tendencies on the part of Shiite jurists to adopt Sunni methods and to develop a Shiite legal system which resembled that of the Sunnis.

54. al-Karakī, *Hidāyat al-abrār,* 182, 233.

55. al-Astarābādī, *al-Fawā'id al-madanīyah,* 28–29.

56. al-Astarābādī, *al-Fawā'id al-madanīyah,* 29, 47; al-Kāshānī, *Safīnat al-najāt,* 9–10; al-Karakī, *Hidāyat al-abrār,* 182, 234.

57. al-Ḥurr al-'Āmilī, *al-Fawā'id al-ṭūsīyah,* 370–71.

THE ROLE OF AL-'ALLĀMAH AL-ḤILLĪ

In assessing the history of Shiite jurisprudence, al-Astarābādī focuses blame on al-'Allāmah al-Ḥillī and attacks him for innovations that resulted from Sunni influence. He holds al-'Allāmah especially responsible because of the great influence his work exerted on later Shiite jurists. Many later Shiite jurists, he reports, adopted the opinions of this "Sea of Knowledge" (*Baḥr al-'ulūm*) because of his enormous prestige in the Shiite scholarly tradition.[58] Al-Astarābādī singles al-Ḥillī out for the most severe criticism, although other Shiite jurists held similar views, on the grounds that he was the main innovator, responsible for introducing the most fundamental Sunni concepts into Shiite jurisprudence and thereby doing the greatest damage. He claims that al-Ḥillī

> admired many of the jurisprudential principles and derivations of the points of law recorded in the books of the Sunnis, so he included them in his own works, not paying attention to the fact that they were based on rules which go against essential doctrinal tenets of the Rightful Sect (*ḍarūrīyāt aṭ-ṭā'ifah al-muḥiqqah*).[59]

Al-Astarābādī also claims that al-Ḥillī's *Tahdhīb al-wuṣūl ilā 'ilm al-uṣūl,* for several centuries a standard textbook of Shiite *uṣūl al-fiqh,* was actually based on Sunni works:

> It has become well known among the scholars that the *Tahdhīb* of al-'Allāmah al-Ḥillī is an abridgment of the *Mukhtaṣar* of Ibn al-Ḥājib, which is an abridgment of the *Muntahā* of Ibn al-Ḥājib, which is an abridgment of the *Iḥkām* of al-Āmidī, which is an abridgment of the *Maḥṣūl* of Fakhr al-Dīn al-Rāzī, which is an abridgment of the *Mu'tamad* of Abū 'l-Ḥusayn al-Baṣrī.[60]

With these assertions al-Astarābādī means to imply that al-'Allāmah al-Ḥillī actually worked in the heart of Sunni tradition, when he should have been paying more attention to the Shiite tradition. As we have seen, this statement has some basis in fact, for al-Ḥillī indeed wrote a commentary on a famous Sunni *uṣūl al-fiqh* text, the *Mukhtaṣar* of Ibn al-Ḥājib, which al-Astarābādī claims served as the basis for *Tahdhīb al-wuṣūl.*

Al-Astarābādī focuses on two particularly destructive innovations he attributes to al-'Allāmah al-Ḥillī. One has to do with the application of Sunni methods of hadith criticism to Shiite hadith, a project al-Astarābādī felt detracted from the authority of the collections of Shiite hadith that had been accepted in the Shiite community for many centuries. The introduction of the categories

58. al-Astarābādī, *al-Fawā'id al-madanīyah,* 30.
59. Ibid., 278.
60. Ibid., 277–78.

the Sunnis used to describe the reliability of individual hadiths—*ḍaʿīf*, "weak," *ḥasan*, "good," *ṣaḥīḥ*, "sound," etc.—called into question the authenticity of many hadiths included in the standard Shiite compilations: al-Kulaynī's *al-Kāfī*, Ibn Bābawayh's *Man lā yaḥḍuruh al-faqīh*, and al-Shaykh al-Ṭūsī's *Tahdhīb al-aḥkām* and *al-Istibṣār*. This doubt created a grave problem for the Shiite legal tradition, since many of the Shiites' legal positions were based on these texts. The second innovation was, in effect, the adoption of the *madhhab* system of Sunni jurisprudence. The key element of this system, in al-Astarābādī's view, was the formation of an exclusive group of legal scholars, termed *mujtahids*, who claimed sole authority to elaborate and interpret the sacred law. The term al-Astarābādī uses to refer to the establishment of this system is the "division" (*taqsīm*) of the Muslim community into two groups: *mujtahid* and *muqallid*. He writes:

> It has become widespread opinion, in the works of some recent learned and accomplished scholars such as al-ʿAllāmah al-Ḥillī and those who have agreed with him, that during the time of Occultation the populace is divided into *mujtahid* and *muqallid*, that the *muqallid* must have recourse to the conjecture of the *mujtahid* concerning those matters of the religious law which are not fundamental aspects of the religion or the sect (*madhhab*), and that the absolute *mujtahid* is the only one who is able to deduce a ruling for disputed, subsidiary, and speculative points of the religious law. They claim that this ability is achieved when one masters the means for discerning all rulings of the religious law, and this mastery is obtained through knowledge of all six propaedeutic sciences—philosophical theology, dogma, syntax, morphology, lexicography, and the methods of proof—as well as the four sources, namely the Koran, tradition, consensus, and rational argument (*dalīl al-ʿaql*).[61]

Al-Astarābādī attacks this system, claiming that the creation of an exclusive, privileged group entrusted with legal authority for the Shiite community which this division entails goes against the basic tenets of Shiism. Other Akhbārīs similarly criticize the position held by al-ʿAllāmah and later Shiite jurists that only a *mujtahid* may grant legal opinions.[62] Rather, as al-Astarābādī holds in the seventh chapter of *al-Fawāʾid al-madanīyah*, anyone

61. al-Astarābādī, *al-Fawāʾid al-madanīyah*, 4. In another passage, al-Astarābādī uses the term *ḥaṣr*, "limitation," "confinement," or "restriction," rather than *taqsīm* to describe the monopoly over legal authority claimed by the *mujtahids*. He mentions the "restriction of the populace to [membership in one of the two groups] *mujtahid* and *muqallid*" (*ḥaṣr al-raʿīyah fī al-mujtahid waʾl-muqallid*) (3). Similar statements are made by later Akhbārī scholars. Shihāb al-Dīn al-Karakī reports the Uṣūlīs claim that the populace is divided into two groups *(qism)*, *mujtahid* and *muqallid*, and that the *muqallid* is under an obligation to follow the opinions of the *mujtahid* (*Hidāyat al-abrār*, 182).

62. al-Ḥurr al-ʿĀmilī, *al-Fawāʾid al-ṭūsīyah*, 330–31.

learned in the hadith of the imams may act as a jurisconsult (*muftī*) or judge (*qāḍī*).[63] There is no reason to restrict these functions to a specific class of people trained in rational derivation, many of whom lack adequate background in hadith, or, worse yet, rule against the purport of a scriptural text on the basis of rational argument.

AKHBĀRISM AS AN ANTI-*MADHHAB* MOVEMENT

Al-Astarābādī's attacks highlight the existence of a legal *madhhab* within Shiism during his time. To al-Astarābādī, the *madhhab* was based on the dichotomy between *ijtihād* and *taqlīd*. It makes little sense to describe Shiism—or Sunnism, for that matter—in terms of *ijtihād* alone or *taqlīd* alone, for these are two aspects of the same system and both aspects are necessary to create the legal *madhhab*. The *mujtahid* must have an exclusive right to interpret the sacred law and the layman must be obligated to refer to a recognized *mujtahid* in order for the legal *madhhab* to establish its monopoly over the granting of legal opinions. Al-Astarābādī shows that this type of legal system was in favor in his own time and implies that it had been in place since the time of al-'Allāmah al-Ḥillī, that is, since the beginning of the fourteenth century. Most important, the origin of the system is to be found with the Sunnis. He asserts:

> This division (*taqsīm*), that is, the division of the populace into *mujtahid* and *muqallid*, and [the application of] its related stipulations and rules have occurred in imitation of the Sunni jurisprudents, inasmuch as they divided the people after the Prophet into two groups, *mujtahid* and *muqallid*. . . The truth is that these premises hold only for those who do not confess the necessity of adherence to the Chaste Descendants [i.e., the Twelver Shiite Imams] and do not render them a means toward the understanding of the Book of God and the Sunnah of His Prophet. An Imami could only hold such an opinion out of ignorance of this important point.[64]

The Akhbārīs thus make a fundamental claim about the history of Islam, namely, that the Twelver Shiites modeled their legal *madhhab* on the Sunni *madhhabs*. The legal *madhhabs* originated in Sunni Islam, and this system was subsequently and gradually adopted by the Twelver Shiites. According to al-Astarābādī, by the fourteenth century Twelver Shiite law became a fully established *madhhab*, parallel to the Sunni *madhhabs*, with the innovations of al-'Allāmah al-Ḥillī. According to al-Ḥurr al-'Āmilī, the process of imitation and borrowing went so far that the methods of the later Shiite jurists rarely

63. al-Astarābādī, *al-Fawā'id al-madanīyah*, 150–53.
64. al-Astarābādī, *al-Fawā'id al-madanīyah*, 18.

differ from those of the Sunnis. The Uṣūlī jurists even use *qiyās,* which is explicitly denounced in the hadiths of the imams, though they do so unwittingly and do not label their methods of reasoning *qiyās* explicitly.[65]

While al-Astarābādī claims it was with al-ʿAllāmah al-Ḥillī that the Shiite legal *madhhab* was firmly established, he asserts that Sunni influence had been important much earlier in history. He gives the following synopsis of the history of Sunni influence on Shiite jurisprudence. The first to rely on the Sunni science of legal methodology, according to al-Astarābādī, was Muḥammad b. Aḥmad b. al-Junayd, who adopted legal proof by analogy (*qiyās*). Al-Shaykh al-Mufīd approved of Ibn al-Junayd's writings, and his students al-Sharīf al-Murtaḍā and al-Shaykh al-Ṭūsī adopted some Sunni methods in the eleventh century. Thereafter, the influence of Sunni law was well established, but it was al-ʿAllāmah al-Ḥillī who adopted in his own works an even greater portion of Sunni legal methodology. Al-ʿAllāmah was followed by al-Shahīd al-Awwal in the late fourteenth century and by ʿAlī b. ʿAbd al-ʿĀlī al-Karakī and al-Shahīd al-Thānī in the sixteenth century.[66] These scholars are the latest al-Astarābādī criticizes as proponents of the pseudo-Sunni legal *madhhab,* but his remarks show that this system was current in his day and implicate contemporary Shiite jurists. He was of course aware of this, and was sensitive to the danger to himself, for he envisages being subject to attack in the introduction to *al-Fawāʾid,* where he states, "It became necessary that I reveal this, and no one's censure prevented me from fulfilling my obligation to God. So I have revealed it, and God will protect me from the people."[67]

The rejection of the legal *madhhab* developed by the Twelver Shiites was a—perhaps *the*—crucial feature of the Akhbbārī movement. Akhbārī writings not only show that Shiite scholars conceived of the Twelver or Imāmī *madhhab* as a professional organization based on the exclusive authority of jurists in the seventeenth century and earlier but also argue plainly and bluntly that the Shiites adopted this system from the Sunnis.[68] Akhbārīs and Uṣūlīs are therefore not, as has been suggested, two *madhhab*s within Shiism parallel to, for example, the Shāfiʿī and Mālikī *madhhab*s in Sunni Islam.[69] Rather, the Uṣūlīs are the proponents of the Imami professional legal *madhhab,* and Akhbārism is an anti-*madhhab* movement. It is thus comparable with the Jewish Karaite movement, which began in Iraq in the ninth century, had its hey-

65. al-Ḥurr al-ʿĀmilī, *al-Fawāʾid al-ṭūsīyah,* 193; al-Karakī, *Hidāyat al-abrār,* 308–9.

66. al-Astarābādī, *al-Fawāʾid al-madanīyah,* 30.

67. Ibid., 3. The last phrase is probably a reference to Qurʾān 5:67, which reads, "O Messenger! Make known that which hath been revealed unto thee from thy Lord, for if thou do it not, thou wilt not have conveyed His message. God will protect thee from mankind."

68. From the preceding it should be clear that Moojan Momen's assessment of the relation of the Akhbārī movement to Sunnism, according to which the Akhbārī tendency is actually closer to Sunnism than the Uṣūlī tendency, is untenable (*Shīʿī Islam,* 222).

69. Scarcia, "Intorno alle controversie," 218. Similar is Moussavi's report that al-Astarābādī turned Akhbārism into a "juridical school" (*Religious Authority,* 91).

day in the the Middle Ages, and survives to this day in small communities. The Karaites rejected the Oral Law together with the authority of the rabbis and insisted on a more strict reliance on scripture. Like the Akhbārīs, the Karaites held that the establishment of a legal institution controlled by a professional class of jurists who held a monopoly over religious interpretation was a heretical innovation which went against fundamental Jewish principles. Like the Akhbārīs, the Karaites sought to locate all religious authority in the scriptural text itself.[70]

The Akhbārīs uphold a completely different sort of religious authority from that of the Twelver Shiite jurists, given that religious authority after the Greater Occultation of the twelfth imam is in the hands of *muḥaddithūn* or hadith experts rather than *fuqahā'* or jurists. It is not through expertise in jurisprudence, with its rationalist methods which are inimical to Shiism and derive from the Shiites' enemies and oppressors, that one attains authority in the community and serves as a reference for others, but rather through knowledge of the recorded statements of the imams and expertise in their interpretation. That the conflict was essentially between these two conceptions of authority, embodied in two authoritative groups of scholars, may be seen in the works from the period of the conflict that come increasingly to term the factions involved *muḥaddithūn* and *mujtahidūn* in addition to Akhbārīs and Uṣūlīs. The conflict between these two groups was similar to the conflict between hadith experts and jurists prominent earlier in Sunni Islam—particularly between the ninth and the eleventh centuries—which was resolved, by and large, to the benefit of the jurists.[71]

The Akhbārīs' fundamental claim was that the authority embodied in hadith was the only legitimate extension of the authority of the imams available during the time of the Occultation, in contradistinction to the authority claimed by the jurists. They held that authority lies in the hadith of the imams as it is recorded in reliable Shiite sources,[72] adopting a tenet similar to Martin Luther's slogan *sola scriptura,* locating authority in the Biblical text alone. Al-Kāshānī even makes the statement that the hadith books themselves serve as reliable guides for believers and stand in place of the imams (*qā'imah maqāmahum*) with regard to this function.[73] This stance would seem to deny the authority of the hadith experts, and indeed, the Akhbārīs argued that the

70. See Zvi Cahn, *The Rise of the Karaite Sect* (New York: M. Tausner, 1937); Leon Nemoy, "The Karaites," *Encyclopaedia Judaica;* idem, ed. and trans., *Karaite Anthology* (New Haven: Yale University Press, 1952); Ya'qūb al-Qirqisānī, *Kitāb al-Anwār wal-Marāqib,* 5 vols., ed. Leon Nemoy (New York: Alexander Kohut Foundation, 1939–45).

71. For the Sunni hadith experts' conception of their authority, see al-Ḥākim al-Nīsābūrī, *Ma'rifat 'ulūm al-ḥadīth* (Beirut: Dār maktabat al-hilāl, 1989), 11–14, 16; al-Khaṭīb al-Baghdādī, *Kitāb al-faqīh wa'l-mutafaqqih,* 1: 138–54; 2: 71–86.

72. al-Ḥurr al-'Āmilī, *al-Fawā'id al-ṭūsīyah,* 316–17.

73. al-Kāshānī, *Tashīl al-sabīl,* 23.

Shiites should accept no subauthorities under the Hidden Imam.[74] It is clear, though, that if religious knowledge is embodied in the hadith, he who knows the hadith best and consults it before turning to any rational considerations would necessarily assume a modicum of religious authority. Thus, the Akhbārīs interpret the *maqbūlah* of Ibn Ḥanẓalah, in which Ja'far al-Ṣādiq commands the believers to consult someone who knows the traditions of the imams for guidance, as referring to hadith experts in particular rather than to the jurists (while the Uṣūlī jurists interpret this tradition as referring to themselves). They stress the need to consult transmitters of the traditions of the imams concerning legal cases which arise during the Occultation and hold that an explicit command to do so was given in a rescript by the twelfth imam issued through his representative al-'Amrī. The rescript includes the statement, "As for the legal cases which arise, consult concerning them the transmitters of our hadith, for they are my proof (*ḥujjah*) over you, and I am God's proof over them."[75]

The Akhbārīs deny any authority outside the sacred text itself, for, as al-Ḥurr al-'Āmilī puts it, the Shiite believers must consult the transmitters of tradition concerning only the legal rulings they transmit and not their personal opinions.[76] They hold that the scholar or hadith expert merely relates the legal opinions of *ahl al-bayt* and does not give his own opinions. The layman cannot perform *taqlīd;* he must not merely follow what the transmitter relates to him, but must also understand the text and the opinion it expresses.[77] Nevertheless, it is clear from their discussions that religious authority—the ability to serve as a reliable reference for believers—is based on specific method and expertise and that the expertise which they are asserting as uniquely valid, as opposed to the expertise of the jurists, is that of the traditionists. Al-Ḥurr al-'Āmilī reports that throughout Shiite history, transmitters of the hadith of the imams have served as references for the inhabitants of their regions (*kānū marji'an li-ahli bilādihim*) although they were not trained in the rational, legal sciences. The authoritative position of such hadith experts is clear from the use of the term *marji'*, "reference." Moreover, the Shiite layman has an obligation to consult such scholars.[78]

74. al-Karakī, *Hidāyat al-abrār,* 211.

75. Ibid., 142, 208–14; al-Ḥurr al-'Āmilī, *al-Fawā'id al-ṭūsīyah,* 413. In analyzing such Akhbārī arguments, Moussavi fails to grasp the import of the distinction the Akhbārīs make between jurists and hadith experts. He notes that al-Astarābādī allows the "scholars" *('ulamā')* to administer justice and give legal *responsa* and even cites the hadith of Ibn Ḥanẓalah to support the authority of the scholars. Characterizing these statements as Uṣūlī arguments, Moussavi writes, "Astarābādī's vigorous attack on the office of *mujtahid* should not be taken as a denial of any juristic authority for jurists during the absence of the Imam of the age" (*Religious Authority,* 93–94). This statement is wrong, because the Akhbārīs interpret *'ulamā'* here to mean hadith experts rather than jurists.

76. al-Ḥurr al-'Āmilī, *al-Fawā'id al-ṭūsīyah,* 413.

77. al-Karakī, *Hidāyat al-abrār,* 204.

78. al-Ḥurr al-'Āmilī, *al-Fawā'id al-ṭūsīyah,* 413, 440.

From a comparative perspective, an examination of the Akhbārī agenda as espoused in *al-Fawā'id al-madanīyah* and subsequent Akhbārī works provides several insightful interpretations of the history of Twelver Shiite jurisprudence. The Akhbārīs attacked what they saw as a Sunni system of jurisprudence. The conflict between Akhbārīs and Uṣūlīs was not simply one of traditionalism versus rationalism, but was also, and perhaps more importantly, one of separatist Shiite principles versus assimilation to the majority community. The Akhbārīs rejected the Sunni legal system and the concept of consensus on which it was based. They saw the Shiite school of law espoused by the Uṣūlīs as a legal *madhhab* parallel to and modeled on those of the Sunnis. Furthermore, they felt that the establishment of the Twelver Shiite legal *madhhab* had resulted directly from Sunni influence. It was created in large part by a reprehensible tendency on the part of Shiite scholars to imitate Sunni jurisprudence, a strategy that did injustice to the basic tenets of Shiism and the traditional Shiite system of authority and derivation of the law. The Akhbārīs' agenda consisted of alerting their coreligionists to this historical process, which had led dangerously close to assimilation, and of calling for a return to fundamental Shiite principles. In place of the current legal system based on the exclusive authority of qualified jurists, they urged a return to scripture, particularly the traditions of the imams, which entailed an emphasis on the knowledge of Shiite hadith in particular, though the Akhbārīs themselves denied the exclusive authority of traditionists as a group, ascribing religious authority to the text itself instead.

CAUSES OF SUNNI INFLUENCE ON THE SHIITE LEGAL TRADITION

Akhbārī scholars point to some of the main structural features which allowed the Shiite Uṣūlīs to adopt their juridical system from the Sunnis. They stress the fact that the Occultation created an authority vacuum, or so it seemed, during which communication with the imam was cut off, with the result that many Shiites looked for religious guidance in the wrong places. In this situation, Sunni dominance of society and especially religious scholarship played a major role in promoting the adoption of Sunni legal methods on the part of Shiite scholars. Al-Kāshānī writes:

> When the epoch of the infallible Imams came to an end and the intermediaries (*sufarā'*) between them and their supporters (*shī'atihim*) had been cut off, their absence became difficult to endure and the reign of the usurpers had gone on for a long time. The Shiites mixed with the Sunnis and became familiar with their books as youths, since these were the books commonly taught in the colleges, mosques, and elsewhere—for the kings and government officials were Sunnis, and subjects always follow the lead of their kings and government officials. The Shiites studied the religious sciences together with the Sunnis and read the *uṣūl al-fiqh* works which the

> Sunnis had written in their aim to facilitate the speculations upon which their legal rulings were based. They approved of some of what the Sunnis had written and disapproved of some. This led them to write books on this science, either corroborating it or detracting from it. They discussed matters which neither the Prophet nor the infallible Imams had brought forth, but which the Sunnis had discussed. They increased the number of questions concerning these topics and confounded the jurists with regard to the methods of legal proof.[79]

Al-Kāshānī, unlike al-Astarābādī, refrains from singling out well-known Shiite scholars as culprits. He emphasizes the extenuating circumstances, including the lack of communication with the imam and Sunni control of governments and the institutions of learning (al-Kāshānī ignores here the Shiite regimes that had existed in Islamic history). He avoids stating that the Shiite jurists were incompetent, stupid, or malicious and asserts only that they were confused, inattentive, and overly influenced by the majority:

> When the works of our fellows on [*ijmā*ʿ and *ijtihād*] increased in number, and they discussed *uṣūl al-fiqh* and its branches using the Sunnis' terminology, the juridical methodology and terminology of the two sects (*ṭāʾifatān*) came to resemble one another. This brought about the effect that some [Shiite jurists] became thoroughly confused, to such an extent that they claimed it was permissible to perform *ijtihād*, give legal rulings on the basis of personal opinion, set down rules and stipulations for such matters, and interpret ambiguous passages [in the Sacred texts] through conjecture, estimation, and the adoption of opinions merely because they are widely accepted (*al-akhdh bi-ʾttifāqi ʾl-ārāʾ*).[80]

These circumstances allowed Shiite jurisprudence to grow more and more like Sunni jurisprudence and caused some Shiite jurists to lose sight of the fundamental principles of their sect and to adopt Sunni principles inconsonant with true Shiite doctrine. It was the relative authority vacuum caused by the Occultation of the imam and not any other specific agent that brought about this deplorable situation.

The suggestion that the Occultation forced the Shiites to rely on a specific legal method is tantamount to stating that Islamic law developed because the Prophet Muḥammad died. Twelver Shiite law would probably not have evolved as it did in the presence of the imams, just as Sunni jurisprudence would not have developed as it did in the presence of the Prophet. Once the

79. al-Kāshānī, *Safīnat al-najāt*, 9–10. Al-Karakī makes a similar statement in which he mentions that the Shiites studied Sunni books on *kalām* and *uṣūl al-fiqh* in particular (*Hidāyat al-abrār*, 219).

80. al-Kāshānī, *Safīnat al-najāt*, 11.

system of religious authority which these charismatic leaders represented had lapsed, some other system had to replace it. Nevertheless, the lapse of the old system did not per se determine the form the new system would take, so one cannot claim that the Occultation of the imam *caused* Shiites to develop a particular legal system. The most one can say is that the Occultation facilitated or set the stage for the development of a particular legal system; other factors determined its characteristics.

Similarly, Sunni dominance in society, while certainly a structural feature affecting Shiite religious and intellectual history, is not in itself a sufficient cause of the specific developments found in Shiite jurisprudence. The claim that the great Shiite jurists of the past became confused or unwittingly adopted Sunni methods avoids setting blame squarely on them or attributing reprehensible motives to them, but it also ascribes to them an unlikely naiveté and ignores their actual motives. Al-Kāshānī's claim that the Sunnis controlled education comes closer to explaining the forces which shaped the Shiite legal tradition and influenced the Shiites' motives. He and other Akhbārī scholars comment frequently that Shiite scholars "mixed" with Sunnis and studied their books, suggesting that this process led to the adoption of Sunni methods. Ḥusayn b. Shihāb al-Dīn al-Karakī remarks, for example, that the use of rational rules of legal derivation by Shiite Uṣūlīs is "an innovated method (*ṭarīq muḥdath*) which arose from mixing with the Sunnis." Al-Astarābādī argues that the Shiites studied with Sunnis out of dissimulation. In order to fit into Sunni society, Shiites kept company with Sunnis, studied hadith with them, and pretended to be Sunnis. They created this illusion out of fear of the Sunnis' power (*shawkah*), for the rulers were all Sunnis.[81] This statement implies that the Shiites did not actually want to study with the Sunnis but did so only for the sake of appearances, something which is not very likely. Shiites studied subjects such as law and theology under Sunni teachers because, in many environments and in many fields, it was the only, or at least the most convenient, way they could get an education, particularly if they aspired to scholarly excellence. In many regions and periods, Shiite teachers were limited in number and had limited resources. Al-Astarābādī states that the later Shiite jurists, al-'Allāmah al-Ḥillī and those who came after him, "studied the books of the Sunnis out of their desire to excel in all the sciences (*li-irādatihimu 't-tabaḥḥura fī 'l-'ulūm*)."[82] Once having associated with the Sunnis for some time, the Akhbārīs claim, Shiites adopted their methods as a result of confusion. Al-Karakī explains:

> When the Greater Occultation occurred and the greater part of *taqīyah* became unnecessary, the Shiites mixed with the Sunnis. They discussed legal

81. al-Karakī, *Hidāyat al-abrār*, 198; al-Astarābādī, *al-Fawā'id al-madanīyah*, 69.
82. al-Astarābādī, *al-Fawā'id al-madanīyah*, 56.

> methodology and the points of law with them, read their books, and followed their method of debate and dialectic. They would base their religious acts only on hadiths, as we have mentioned above, but since association occasionally has an effect, some of them erred unwittingly concerning some questions.[83]

It was nearly impossible for the Shiites to avoid mixing with Sunnis in the academic realm because Sunnis controlled the governments and the *madrasahs*. The professors in the *madrasahs* were Sunnis and the common texts were Sunni works. Shiites studied and taught these Sunni texts, particularly in *kalām* and *uṣūl al-fiqh*.[84] Both al-Kāshānī and al-Karakī stress, however, that the Shiite jurists' adoption of Sunni methods was unintentional, holding that it occurred out of "lack of awareness" or "inattention" (*ghaflah*) or because they became confused or confounded (*iltabasa 'alayhimu 'l-amr*).

Nevertheless, knowing that Shiites studied Sunni books does not explain why exactly they adopted Sunni methods in their own law. It merely reveals a probable conduit of Sunni influence. The suggestion that Shiite jurists mixed Sunni with Shiite principles out of confusion is too simplistic and portrays the jurists in too passive a light. One reason the Akhbārīs suggest why the Shiites adopted Sunni methods was that they were intellectually attracted to them. Al-Karakī reports that al-'Allāmah al-Ḥillī studied the works of the Sunnis and wrote similar works because he was impressed with their detailed discussions. He states that al-'Allāmah and later Shiite jurists who adopted his methods constantly referred to Sunni works on the points of law and legal methodology because of the detailed arguments and precise definitions they contained. He holds that most scholars are innately attracted to such texts and that one may see this phenomenon in the behavior of law students in his own day. These jurists then fell into errors because of their excessive familiarity with Sunni works on legal methodology (*li-ulfat adhhānihim bi-kutub uṣūl al-'āmmah*). Having read the works of Shāfi'ī authors such as al-Juwaynī, al-Ghazālī, al-Rāfi'ī, and al-Rāzī, Shiite jurists were impressed with their detailed discussions and developed a desire to write similar texts.[85] Al-Ḥurr al-'Āmilī observes that the Uṣūlīs' involvement with Sunni scholarship on doctrinally marked subjects—hadith, Koranic exegesis, theology, and legal methodology—exceeded proper bounds. Shiite scholars came to think extremely highly of Sunni works and approved of their contents to such a degree that they thought it wrong to go against them. Al-Ḥurr al-'Āmilī reports that in his own day some Shiite scholars consider it a communal religious obligation (*farḍ kifāyah*) for the Shi-

83. al-Karakī, *Hidāyat al-abrār*, 306.
84. Ibid., 219.
85. Ibid., 10, 68, 95–96, 152–53.

ites to be versed in Sunni works and that many of his contemporaries even favor Sunni arguments over those of the Shiites.[86]

The Akhbārīs disapproved of the organized study of Sunni works, even for the purpose of defending Shiite positions. Al-Astarābādī cites traditions of the imams to argue that it is wrong to derive knowledge from Sunni texts, even if they do contain some truth. These texts include the reports: "Teach your children our hadiths before their minds become familiar with the contents of books which do not derive from us" and "The truth which men possess has come from the descendants of the Prophet (*ahl al-bayt*), and the falsehood which they possess has come from themselves."[87] The Akhbārīs cite such scriptural texts to counter arguments by Uṣūlī scholars that it is necessary to study Sunni works for religious purposes, particularly in order to refute them. One such argument is made by ʿAlī b. ʿAbd al-ʿĀlī al-Karakī, who, as seen in chapter 3, studied under Sunni teachers in Damascus and Cairo. He states in an *ijāzah* dated 9 Ramaḍān, 937/26 April 1531:

> With regard to the books of the Sunnis, the Twelver Shiites have continued to relate and transmit them, expending their efforts and valuable time in doing so, for a sound religious purpose. These works contain proofs of the truth and the means to discover the many cases of [the Sunnis'] concoction of false statements. When your opponent in disputation provides your proof, it has a tremendous effect on the hearts of men, and is more persuasive in silencing and refuting the arguments of the adversaries who deny the truth. Moreover, there are other important benefits gained from knowledge of [these texts].[88]

Yusūf al-Baḥrānī, an eighteenth-century Shiite scholar from Bahrain, makes a similar comment in his *ijāzah* to his nephews: "It is necessary that we mention the paths of transmission known to us of the books of Sunni *akhbār* and *tafsīr*, so that one may cite them as needed in order to refute the Sunnis."[89] These statements show one of the possible stances of the Shiites toward Sunni legal scholarship, which might be characterized as a defensive attitude. While these legal theorists do not shun Sunni learning altogether, they state that the main purpose of study with Sunnis is to use Sunni evidence in support of the Shiite cause. They felt it necessary to justify their own concern with Sunni learning to a Shiite audience who might be inimical to Sunnis or concerned about excessive familiarity with Sunni scholarship. Al-Ḥurr al-ʿĀmilī responds to this type

86. al-Ḥurr al-ʿĀmilī, *al-Fawāʾid al-ṭūsīyah*, 252.

87. al-Astarābādī, *al-Fawāʾid al-madanīyah*, 29. Al-Ḥurr al-ʿĀmilī interprets a number of hadiths in the same manner (*al-Fawāʾid al-ṭūsīyah*, 249–53).

88. al-Majlisī, *Biḥār al-anwār*, 108: 79.

89. al-Baḥrānī, *Luʾluʾat al-Baḥrayn*, 430.

of argument by saying that the Shiites should examine Sunni works only with the aim of refuting them or obtaining specific information about their Sunni doctrines. They should not think well of Sunni books or read them in their entirety in order to learn from them. He concludes, "the evils of studying their works are many and obvious; the least of them is approval of them concerning points which are not known to be in agreement with the Imamis or are in opposition to them."[90] Rather than benefiting Shiite tradition and increasing the sophistication of the Shiites' legal arguments, the study of Sunni works represents a grave danger.

Al-Ḥurr al-ʿĀmilī gives a negative assessment of the Shiite jurists' historical tradition of study under Sunni teachers. Concerning the studies of al-ʿAllāmah al-Ḥillī, al-Shahīd al-Awwal, and al-Shahīd al-Thānī, he states, "There is no doubt that their intentions were sound. Nevertheless, the results of [their studies with Sunnis] are apparent to anyone who has examined and assiduously perused the books of legal methodology, legal derivation, and hadith."[91] He means to imply that as a result of these scholars' studies under Sunni teachers, a great deal of Sunni material or methodology has crept into Shiite scholarship on law and hadith. As an Akhbārī, he was opposed to this process of influence and borrowing, and saw it as an unfortunate quirk of Shiite intellectual history, a dangerous step toward assimilation to an oppressive and misguided majority. The Akhbārīs felt that it was wrong to trust the views of the Shiites' doctrinal enemies on any topic, but especially on the law and the religious sciences. Furthermore, they felt that studying with Sunnis threatened to allow the entrance of corrupt ideas into Shiite scholarship, something which could be avoided only by rigid separation.

THE AKHBĀRĪS AS HISTORIANS OF ISLAMIC LAW AND THE TWELVER *MADHHAB*

Colored by their virulent, anti-Sunni polemical agenda, many of the Akhbārīs' assessments of Islamic legal history cannot be accepted at face value. Particularly egregious are some of their statements concerning the rise of the Sunni legal system, which are outlandish and demonstrably false. The four Sunni *madhhab*s were created at the instigation of the Abbasid caliph al-Manṣūr (136–58/754–75), one Akhbārī author alleges, to counter the influence of Jaʿfar al-Ṣādiq and the four thousand scholars who transmitted hadith from him.[92] Ḥusayn b. Shihāb al-Dīn al-Karakī reports that the Sunnis resorted to rational, probabilistic methods because their hadith did not deal extensively

90. al-Ḥurr al-ʿĀmilī, *al-Fawāʾid al-ṭūsīyah*, 341.
91. al-Ḥurr al-ʿĀmilī, *Amal al-āmil*, 1: 89.
92. al-Ḥurr al-ʿĀmilī, *al-Fawāʾid al-ṭūsīyah*, 341.

with legal questions and they had a dearth of scriptural source material on which to base their law. Their need to adopt rational derivation was particularly pressing because power was in their hands and they were the ones serving as judges. Neither of these statements can be taken to reflect the actual history of Islamic law. The Akhbārīs were correct, however, in reporting one crucial aspect of the *madhhab* system as it developed in the medieval period. It had long been established that there were only four recognized *madhhab*s and that anyone who went against the legal rulings of these *madhhab*s was treated as a heretic.[93] They recognized that this feature of the Sunni legal system put enormous pressure on the Shiites to conform.

The Akhbārīs' reading of Twelver Shiite legal history is also skewed by their polemic goals, but nevertheless includes several major points that fit the historical data. The scholars al-Astarābādī attacks most in *al-Fawā'id al-madanīyah* include many of those jurists who were in fact influenced heavily by Sunni scholarship. Al-Astarābādī repeatedly states that he is supporting the views of early Shiite scholars (*qudamā' aṣḥābinā*) against a group of later Shiite scholars (*jam' min muta'akhkhirī aṣḥābinā*) who adopted Sunni methods. This latter group includes al-'Allāmah al-Ḥillī, al-Shahīd al-Awwal, 'Alī b. 'Abd al-'Ālī al-Karakī, and al-Shahīd al-Thānī. All of them had studied the legal sciences with Sunni scholars and used Sunni legal methodology extensively in their work.

In addition to pointing out the Sunni origin of general concepts and methods used by Shiite jurists, the Akhbārīs occasionally claimed specific instances of borrowing and influence from Sunni sources. As mentioned above, al-Astarābādī remarks that al-Ḥillī's *Tahdhīb al-wuṣūl* was an abridgment of the *Mukhtaṣar* of Ibn al-Ḥājib and derived from the tradition of Shāfi'ī *uṣūl al-fiqh* works represented by *Iḥkām al-aḥkām* of al-Āmidī (d. 631/1234), *al-Maḥṣūl* of Fakhr al-Dīn al-Rāzī (d. 606/1209), and *al-Mu'tamad* of Abū 'l-Ḥusayn al-Baṣrī (d. 436/1044). According to a statement by al-Shahīd al-Thānī in *Sharḥ al-sharā'i'*, al-Ṭūsī's work *al-Mabsūṭ* is a distillation of Shāfi'ī legal works.[94] Al-Ḥurr al-'Āmilī complains that the only dissenting Shiite opinions al-Ḥillī mentions in *Tahdhīb al-wuṣūl* are those of al-Sharīf al-Murtaḍā and al-Shaykh al-Ṭūsī, while he cites the opinions of a large number of Sunni jurists.[95] Ḥusayn b. Shihāb al-Dīn al-Karakī notes that Shiite jurists including al-'Allāmah, al-Shahīd al-Awwal, 'Alī al-Karakī, and al-Shahīd al-Thānī were influenced a great deal by reading such Sunni works on *fiqh* and *uṣūl al-fiqh* as *al-Sharḥ al-'Aḍudī*, the *Qawā'id* of Ibn al-Ṣalāḥ al-Shahrazūrī (d. 643/1245), and *al-Qawā'id al-'alā'ī* by the Shāfi'ī jurist 'Alā' al-Dīn Abū Sa'īd

93. al-Karakī, *Hidāyat al-abrār*, 9, 134, 182–83.

94. al-Astarābādī, *al-Fawā'id al-madanīyah*, 277–78; al-Karakī, *Hidāyat al-abrār*, 136, 234.

95. al-Ḥurr al-'Āmilī, *al-Fawā'id al-ṭūsīyah*, 235.

Khalīl b. Kaykaldī al-Dimashqī (d. 761/1359).[96] He reports that Shiite jurists read the works of such Shāfiʿī authors as al-Juwaynī, al-Ghazālī, al-Rāfiʿī, and al-Rāzī and then decided to write similar works. He remarks that al-ʿAllāmah's works, especially *Nihāyat al-wuṣūl* and *Qawāʿid al-aḥkām,* are written according to Sunni methods and that *Qawāʿid al-aḥkām* is abridged from the Shāfiʿī legal work *al-ʿAzīz* by ʿAbd al-Karīm b. Muḥammad al-Qazwīnī al-Rāfiʿī (d. 623/1226).[97] He also claims that al-Shahīd al-Thānī's work *Tamhīd al-qawāʿid* is an abridgment of *al-Qawāʿid al-ʿalāʾīyah* and that many passages in his work *Sharḥ al-sharāʾiʿ*—probably *Masālik al-afhām*—are lifted from Shāfiʿī legal works, such as *al-ʿAzīz.*[98] While one cannot evaluate such specific claims without much further study, their general import, that Shiite jurisprudence, and especially the legal scholarship of these particular jurists, developed in extensive contact with Sunni jurisprudence and with the Shāfiʿī legal tradition in particular, is not farfetched.

An examination of the general development of Shiite law shows that there was a high correlation between legal study under Sunni teachers and the advancement of Shiite legal scholarship along Sunni lines. Al-ʿAllāmah al-Ḥillī, al-Shahīd al-Awwal, al-Karakī, and al-Shahīd al-Thānī all made innovative contributions to Shiite legal scholarship based on their adaptations of Sunni legal concepts and academic practices. These contributions have yet to be studied in detail, but they have had an enormous impact on the history of Twelver Shiite jurisprudence. It thus appears that participation in the Shāfiʿī legal *madhhab,* discussed in chapter 3, was an important means toward the development of the Twelver legal *madhhab* itself. The legal expertise gained through familiarity with Shāfiʿī legal scholarship helped the Shiites in their endeavors to establish and refine a legal *madhhab* of their own on a par with those of the Sunnis.

The significance of Sunni legal studies for the Shiite legal system may be seen in the career of al-Shahīd al-Thānī. As discussed above, during the years 942–43/1535–37 he studied extensively under prominent professors of Shāfiʿī law in Cairo and read the major texts of Shāfiʿī law and legal methodology current in his day. These studies were a crucial part of his formation as a

96. al-Karakī, *Hidāyat al-abrār,* 10. The printed text has *al-Qawāʿid al-ʿalānīyah* consistently for the correct title, *al-ʿalāʾīyah,* which derives from the name of the author, ʿAlāʾ al-Dīn. The original title of the work is *al-Majmūʿ al-mudhahhab fī qawāʿid al-madhhab.* On the author, see al-Subkī, *Ṭabaqāt al-shāfiʿīyah al-kubrā,* 10: 35–38. I have not been able to locate a work by Ibn al-Ṣalāḥ entitled *al-Qawāʿid* in the sources.

97. al-Karakī, *Hidāyat al-abrār,* 95–96, 152–53, 221. On al-Rāfiʿī, see al-Subkī, *Ṭabaqāt al-shāfiʿīyah al-kubrā,* 8: 281–93. His work *al-Fatḥ al-ʿazīz fī sharḥ al-wajīz* is a long commentary on al-Ghazālī's epitome of Shāfiʿī law *al-Wajīz,* and was commonly known in the Shāfiʿī tradition as *al-ʿAzīz.*

98. al-Karakī, *Hidāyat al-abrār,* 10–11.

scholar and jurist, and it cannot be a coincidence that he reached the level of *ijtihād* in 944/1537–38, the year he returned from Cairo to Jabal ʿĀmil. It must have been largely al-Shahīd al-Thānī's studies of Sunni legal theory which convinced him to claim the rank of *mujtahid*, as a Shiite jurist. He did not study with any Shiite teachers during or after his stay in Cairo, and he had not studied with any Shiite teachers for a number of years beforehand. For al-Shahīd al-Thānī, Sunni and Shiite legal methods were quite similar if not identical. His familiarity with Sunni law and legal theory fed directly into his scholarship on Shiite law, and little separated the two fields of inquiry. In his legal commentary *al-Rawḍah al-bahīyah*, for example, he reports that the student of law need not consult specialized works on logic or dialectic in order to learn the methods of proof (*sharāʾiṭ al-dalīl*), since most of such information is contained in the shorter manuals of *uṣūl al-fiqh*, such as al-ʿAllāmah al-Ḥillī's work *Tahdhīb al-wuṣūl* or the *Mukhtaṣar* of Ibn al-Ḥājib.[99] This statement, juxtaposing a Shiite *uṣūl al-fiqh* text with a Sunni work, implies that Islamic legal theory, whether Shiite or Sunni, works on the same assumptions and uses the same methods. The transfer of scholarship from one field to the other is therefore perfectly natural and is based on the conception, which other Uṣūlī jurists apparently shared with al-Shahīd al-Thānī, that Shiite jurisprudence is in essence functionally equivalent to Sunni jurisprudence.

While the Akhbārīs' portrayal of the history of Shiite legal theory may be judged roughly accurate in its assessment of the work of al-ʿAllāmah al-Ḥillī and later jurists, it is less convincing in assessing the legacy of the Shiites who preceded al-ʿAllāmah. Al-Astarābādī tends to identify the work of al-ʿAllāmah as the crucial point of departure from authentic Shiite tradition, when the most dangerous Sunni methods and concepts in jurisprudence were adopted. In general, the Akhbārīs designated later jurists as mere imitators of al-Ḥillī,[100] and endeavored to fit earlier jurists into an Akhbārī mold. While the reasons for this dialectic tactic are many, it is clear that the Akhbārīs, in presenting their view of religious authority within Shiism as more authentic to the faith, desired to reclaim the jurists of the early period for their own camp. They therefore hold that scholars such as al-Shaykh al-Mufīd, al-Sharīf al-Murtaḍā, and al-Shaykh al-Ṭūsī were essentially Akhbārīs. Their main evidence for this claim is that these jurists rejected the use of *qiyās* and *ijtihād*, in keeping with early Shiite tradition, and thus avoided al-Ḥillī's greatest sin, his adoption of *ijtihād* and the introduction of probability and speculation into Shiite legal interpretation.

The Akhbārīs resort to some questionable arguments in order to explain how the three main jurists of the Buwayhid period wrote on legal methodol-

99. Ali al-ʿĀmilī, *al-Durr al-manthūr*, 2: 183; Zayn al-Dīn al-ʿĀmilī, *al-Rawḍah al-bahīyah*, 3: 65.
100. al-Karakī, *Hidāyat al-abrār*, 10.

ogy and adopted a number of Sunni legal concepts, yet were indeed Akhbārīs. They emphasize that while these jurists engaged in debate with the Sunnis on legal topics, they used rational methods only for the sake of argument with their opponents. According to the Akhbārīs, the prominent jurists of Buwayhid Baghdad followed the principle that the most effective means of debate is to use the opponent's own assumptions to prove him wrong—in this way he is forced to admit defeat—while they did not accept these proofs as valid themselves.[101] Al-Ḥurr al-ʿĀmilī claims that al-Sharīf al-Murtaḍā and al-Shaykh al-Ṭūsī actually wrote their works—he mentions *ʿUddat al-uṣūl* specifically—to refute *uṣūl al-fiqh* rather than to validate it. Similarly, the Akhbārīs interpret the adoption of the legal principle of consensus by the Shiite jurists of the Buwayhid period as mere window-dressing. Of course, the Akhbārīs themselves reject both the consensus of the Muslims and the consensus of the Shiites as invalid principles. Neither is an authoritative argument, and neither is possible to ascertain. They hold that al-Murtaḍā and al-Ṭūsī did not actually accept these principles themselves but adopted them only for use in debate against the Sunnis. These two jurists supposedly cited *ijmāʿ al-ṭāʾifah* as a proof frequently in their works simply because they were continually arguing against Sunni opponents, and not because it was a valid principle in itself.[102]

This assessment of the Buwayhid jurists ignores several important aspects. Al-Shaykh al-Mufīd, al-Sharīf al-Murtaḍā, and al-Shaykh al-Ṭūsī were clearly *uṣūlīs* in the basic sense that they wrote works on *uṣūl al-fiqh*, outlining a method of legal interpretation. They rejected *qiyās* and *ijtihād*, but they were using the term *ijtihād* in the narrow sense of mere speculation or personal opinion, while nevertheless upholding the ability of the jurist to arrive at a legal ruling from sacred texts through rational methods of derivation. Al-Ṭūsī even lists the four *dalīl*s or types of evidence used for legal argument as the Koran (*al-kitāb*), tradition (*al-sunnah*), consensus (*al-ijmāʿ*), and reason (*dalīl al-ʿaql*), which of course goes against the Akhbārīs' claims by including consensus and reason as sources of law. They termed themselves *fuqahāʾ* and *uṣūlīyūn* and differentiated between themselves and *aṣḥāb al-ḥadīth*, the equivalent of the later Akhbārīs.[103] They supported the authority of the jurists in particular to act as authorities for the Shiite believer, and, in clear contrast with the Akhbārīs, denied this right to hadith experts, whom they considered mere copyists.

While it is true that the principle of consensus adopted by the Buwayhid jurists was used extensively in and was shaped by debate with the Sunnis, it is

101. al-Karakī, *Hidāyat al-abrār*, 151, 233; al-Ḥurr al-ʿĀmilī, *al-Fawāʾid al-ṭūsīyah*, 235–36, 339–40.

102. al-Ḥurr al-ʿĀmilī, *al-Fawāʾid al-ṭūsīyah*, 235–36, 433, 439; al-Jazāʾirī, *Zahr al-rabīʿ*, 571; al-Karakī, *Hidāyat al-abrār*, 99, 150, 261.

103. al-Ṭūsī, *ʿUddat al-uṣūl*, 120–21 See also 52, 254.

unlikely that these jurists held consensus—as they explained it—to be invalid. They used the concept of consensus quite often in arguing not only against Sunnis but also against Shiite opponents; on this basis, they differentiated between a variety of opinions held by the Shiites themselves.[104] The later Akhbārīs' claim that consensus was not an integral part of Shiite jurisprudence at this time ignores the importance al-Sharīf al-Murtaḍā and al-Shaykh al-Ṭūsī in particular assign to it. The theory that the consensus of the jurists indicates where the opinion of the imam lies conflicts with the Akhbārīs' statement that the consensus was of no consequence. The Akhbārīs also ignored the crucial implication of the adoption of consensus, which places the Shiite legal tradition within the Sunni *madhhab* system and allows it to claim status as an authentic legal *madhhab* parallel to those of the Sunnis. The Akhbārīs would place the main step in this development much later, with the adoption of *ijtihād* by al-ʿAllāmah al-Ḥillī.

In holding that the Twelver Shiite legal *madhhab* took recognizable, pseudo-Sunni form only with the theories of al-ʿAllāmah al-Ḥillī, the Akhbārīs are wrong in an important sense. As mentioned above, al-Astarābādī located the crucial feature of the pseudo-Sunni legal *madhhab* in the division of the Shiite populace into *mujtahid*s and *muqallid*s. While it is true that al-Ḥillī was the first major figure in the Shiite tradition to use this particular language, the division of the Shiite populace into laymen and qualified jurists whom the laymen are required to consult existed long before the time of al-Ḥillī. As will be mentioned in the next chapter, al-Sharīf al-Murtaḍā claims that the Shiites agree on the obligation of the layman to consult the jurisconsult (*wujūb rujūʿ al-ʿāmmī ilā al-muftī*).[105] If this point is the pivotal feature of the legal *madhhab* as established along Sunni lines, then it already existed in the eleventh century.

CONCLUSION

It would make no sense to express an opinion here concerning the main argument of the Akhbārīs, that is, to decide whether the religious authority of traditionists or the religious authority of jurists is actually more authentic to Shiism. Even in monotheistic religious traditions that make strong arguments for monovalent authority, a plurality of competing authorities has often existed. In the case of the Twelver Shiites, there is little solid ground for arguing which system of authority is most authentic to pre-Occultation Shiism, for all the historically possible types those of *sufarā'* or representatives of the Imam, theologians, mystics, monarchs, traditionists, or jurists—involve a sig-

104. For many examples, see Muḥammad b. al-Ḥasan al-Ṭūsī, *al-Istibṣār fīmā ikhtalaf min al-akhbār,* 4 vols, ed. Sayyid Ḥasan al-Kharsān (Beirut: Dār al-aḍwā', 1985).

105. al-Murtaḍā, *al-Dharīʿah,* 2: 796–97.

nificant change from the system of authority based on recourse to the imams themselves, and no one system can be held *a priori* to follow logically from that which they represented. Historically, however, it is clear that the jurists have won the competition for authority between the various groups. Their ascendancy has been challenged seriously by the traditionists several times, but the latter were soundly defeated, first in the twelfth and then again in the eighteenth century.

The Akhbārī thinkers of the seventeenth century were not only competitors in the struggle for religious authority within Twelver Shiism but also revisionist historians of the Twelver Shiite legal tradition. They examined the history of Twelver Shiite jurisprudence with reference to that of Sunni jurisprudence and concluded that there had been enormous Sunni influence on the Shiite tradition. They noted the close historical connection between the Twelver Shiite and Shāfiʿī legal *madhhab*s and posited Sunni influence on the development of Twelver Shiite law. They identified some of the major figures in the Shiite tradition who incorporated Sunni legal concepts and methods into Shiite jurisprudence, including al-ʿAllāmah al-Ḥillī, al-Shahīd al-Awwal, and al-Shahīd al-Thānī. In some cases, they identified specific works of these jurists as deriving from Sunni legal scholarship. They recognized that the Shiites were latecomers to the Islamic system of legal *madhhab*s and that the Twelver *madhhab* as it existed in their time had developed in large part as a result of prolonged contact and debate with the Sunnis. Their polemical goals notwithstanding, the Akhbārīs' analysis of Twelver Shiite legal history is fairly accurate on these important points.

6

A Comparison of the Sunni and the Twelver Shiite *Madhhabs*

"The jurisconsult, in the Muslim community, stands in the place of the Prophet."

Ibrāhīm b. Mūsā al-Shāṭibī (d. 790/1388)

"The jurists...are the successors of the Chosen Messenger...and custodians of the way of the saved sect among the Muslim community."[1]

Muḥammad Bāqir al-Bihbihānī (d. 1205/1791)

Although the degree of acceptance the Twelver Shiite legal *madhhab* has encountered in Sunni circles has varied widely, it is evident that the Twelvers have produced and maintained a vigorous Islamic legal tradition in a form largely compatible with the legal system of the Sunni majority. Modern scholarship, however, has not brought out fully the fundamental similarities between the Sunni and Shiite *madhhabs*, and tends rather to emphasize the qualities or features of the Shiite legal system which purportedly set it apart from that of the Sunnis. Points of similarity include such major constituent elements of the *madhhab* as the conception and justification of the jurists' religious authority, the curriculum a scholar follows in order to gain recognition as a competent jurist, and the license he receives recognizing his competence and authority. The claim to *ijtihād*, commonly believed to distinguish modern Twelver Shiite jurists from their Sunni counterparts, cannot be said to characterize the Shiite legal system alone. Nor can the hierarchy evident in modern Twelver Shiite legal institutions be labeled an exclusively Shiite phenomenon. Taken with a broad historical perspective, the following remarks look beyond differences in termi-

1. al-Bihbihānī, *Risālat al-akhbār wa'l-ijtihād*, 9.

nology and attempt to show the fundamental theoretical and structural similarities between the Twelver Shiite and the premodern Sunni legal *madhhabs*.

THE AUTHORITY OF THE JURISTS

A prevalent misconception concerning the Shiite legal system is that the exclusive authority of the Shiite jurists was not established until quite recently, even as late as the nineteenth century. Denis MacEoin claims that the location of charismatic authority in the senior Shiite jurists dates back to the work of Muḥammad Bāqir al-Bihbihānī and his students in the late eighteenth century.[2] Arjomand's characterization of the rise of juristic authority in Twelver Shiism reflects a more thorough grasp of the development of Shiite legal theory, but still places the crucial development of a clearly defined split between the jurist and layman in the nineteenth century:

> the Shi'ite norms of the juristic authority of the specialist in religious learning. . . emerge with the rise of the Shi'ite science of jurisprudence (*Uṣūl al-fiqh*) in the eleventh century and assumes its final form in the division of the Shi'ite community into *mujtahid* (jurist) and *muqallid* (follower) in the nineteenth century.[3]

While it may be true that the institution of *marji' al-taqlīd*—see the discussion below—did not take recognizable shape until the nineteenth century, the location of religious authority among senior jurists and the division of the Shiite community into jurists and laymen is nearly as old as the Twelver Shiite legal *madhhab* itself. Al-Astarābādī's *al-Fawā'id al-madanīyah* shows that the division of the Shiite community into *mujtahid* and *muqallid* was well established by his own time, the early seventeenth century, and his claim that the division was instituted by al-'Allāmah al-Ḥillī would date its beginning to the fourteenth century. The Akhbārī challenge of the authority of the *mujtahids* in the seventeenth and eighteenth centuries does not negate the evidence that their authority had been established long before. Already in the sixth/twelfth century, Ibn Zuhrah al-Ḥalabī (d. 585/1189–90) argues against an unnamed Shiite opponent who claims that the Shiite layman *must* consult a *muftī* and perform his religious obligations according to the *muftī*'s opinion (*wujūb rujū' al-'āmmī ilā 'l-muftī wa 'l-'amal bi-qawlih*) and that this is the unanimous consensus of Shiite jurists (*ijmā' al-ṭā'ifah*).[4]

Since the late tenth century, it was generally held by prominent Shiite ju-

2. Denis MacEoin, "Orthodoxy and Heterodoxy in Nineteenth-Century Shī'ism," *JAOS*, 110 (1990): 323–29, esp. 326; see also idem, "Changes in Charismatic Authority in Qajar Shī'ism," in *Qajar Iran*, ed. E. Bosworth and C. Hillenbrand (Edinburgh: Edinburgh University Press, 1983), 148–76.

3. Arjomand, *Shadow of God*, 14.

4. Ibn Zuhrah al-Ḥalabī Ḥamzah b. 'Alī, *Ghunyat al-nuzū'*, 486.

rists—if not accepted by all Shiites—that scholars, and jurists in particular, should be the ones to take over the essential functions of the imam during the Occultation. Muḥammad b. Masʿūd al-ʿAyyāshī al-Samarqandī, author of a famous commentary on the Koran, lived during the tenth century and wrote a work entitled *Kitāb farḍ ṭāʿat al-ʿulamāʾ* ("The Book on the Obligation of Obedience to the Scholars").[5] The title does not specify which particular group of scholars al-ʿAyyāshī intends, whether jurists, theologians, or hadith experts, but it nevertheless implies that religious authority once located specifically in the imam had been delegated to the scholars as a group. Many modern investigators, convinced that the power of the Shiite jurists in modern Iranian history is a recent phenomenon, imagine that such claims did not arise until quite recently in Shiism. They also draw support from the Shiite rejection of the term *ijtihād* before the thirteenth century. Nevertheless, important evidence sets the establishment of the Shiite jurists as a dominant if not exclusive authoritative group within the community at a date contemporary with the rise of the Shiite science of jurisprudence in the Buwayhid period.

With the works of al-Sharīf al-Murtaḍā and al-Shaykh al-Ṭūsī, an important change entered into the system of legal authority. Al-Ṭūsī makes it clear that Shiite jurists are exclusively responsible for performing legal functions in the absence of the imam. He states in *al-Nihāyah* concerning the position of judge: "judging between litigants is only permissible for someone to whom the legitimate ruler [i.e., the imam] has granted permission to do so. The Imams have entrusted this task to the jurists among their followers during such time as they are not able to exercise it in person." Furthermore, the expertise of the jurist derives from his study of jurisprudence and not from his knowledge of hadith. In the introduction to *ʿUddat al-uṣūl,* al-Ṭūsī reports that it was especially necessary to write on the science of jurisprudence, "because the religious law in its entirety is based on it" (*liʾanna ʾsh-sharīʿata kullahā mabnīyatun ʿalayh*).[6] If the discipline of *uṣūl al-fiqh* is the exclusive basis of the *sharīʿah,* then religious authority belongs to those skilled in jurisprudence.

Al-Ṭūsī provides a clear picture of juristic authority in the section on the jurisconsult (*muftī*) and the layman (*mustaftī*) in *ʿUddat al-uṣūl.* It is legal expertise which gives the scholar the right to issue legal *responsa;* without that specific expertise, one cannot answer legal questions with authority. The requirements he lists for the qualified legal scholar essentially recapitulate the contents of his work on *uṣūl al-fiqh*—and therefore, roughly, that of Sunni works in the same field. In addition to basic theology, the jurist must know the Arabic language, syntax, and semantics. He must understand the text of the

5. al-Najāshī, *Kitāb al-rijāl,* 272; Ibn Shahrāshūb, *Maʿālim al-ʿulamāʾ,* 89.

6. Muḥammad b. al-Ḥasan al-Ṭūsī, *al-Nihāyah fī mujarrad al-fiqh waʾl-fatāwā* (Tehran, 1963), 304; idem, *ʿUddat al-uṣūl,* 2.

Koran, its literal and figurative meanings, abrogating and abrogated passages, general and specific passages, and unrestricted and restricted passages.[7] Al-Sharīf al-Murtaḍā's similar discussion, though not as explicitly linked to the standard chapters of *uṣūl al-fiqh* works, holds that the jurist must know fundamental theology, the Koran, hadith, and Arabic grammar and lexicography to that extent which enables him to arrive at answers for cases coming to his attention.[8] Both scholars hold that one does not need to have expertise in legal analogy (*qiyās*) and speculative opinion (*ijtihād*), as most Sunni jurists claim. They use *ijtihād* here, though, not to refer to legal expertise—those tools the knowledge of which enables one to grant legal opinions—but rather to a specific mode of analysis—speculation—which they reject as ineffective and impermissible as a method for discovery of the law. Conversely, it is clear that they believe the acquisition of legal expertise, also termed *ijtihād* in contemporary Sunni legal texts, grants the scholar in question religious authority which he may exercise in practical terms by granting opinions to laymen. Al-Muḥaqqiq al-Ḥillī makes this point in his work *Ma'ārij al-uṣūl*, where he states that *ijtihād*, "in the customary usage of the jurists, is the expense of effort to derive legal rules. . . . If one were to state, 'In this case, then Imāmī [jurists] are *mujtahids (min ahl al-ijtihād)*,' I would respond, 'This is true, but it risks giving a false impression, in view of the fact that *qiyās* is one of the parts of *ijtihād*. If *qiyās* is ruled out, then we are *mujtahids*, expending effort to derive legal rules through speculative methods which do not include *qiyās*.'"[9]

The authority to grant legal opinions is not portrayed as completely exclusive in al-Ṭūsī's text, though it becomes so in later Shiite texts on legal methodology, which may be seen in al-Ṭūsī's statement that laymen fall into two separate categories, those who are able to perform the legal reasoning necessary for the case at hand and those who are not. Those who are capable of legal deduction cannot adopt the opinion of a jurist, while those who are incapable may do so.[10] This distinction tends to blur the division between jurists and laymen, in contrast with later Shiite jurists such as al-'Allāmah al-Ḥillī who assert, in agreement with many Sunni jurists, that one is either *muqallid*, a layman obligated to consult a jurist, or *muqallad*, a legal authority–there is no third option.

Al-Ṭūsī also appears to soften the claim of authority for the jurists in his presentation by granting that it is *permissible (yajūz)* rather than *obligatory* for the layman to resort to the jurist for a legal opinion. This statement, however, does not necessarily imply rejection of the exclusive authority of the jurists. A

7. al-Ṭūsī, *'Uddat al-uṣūl*, 292–93.
8. al-Murtaḍā, *al-Dharī'ah*, 2: 800.
9. Najm al-Dīn Ja'far al-Ḥillī, *Ma'ārij al-uṣūl*, 179–80.
10. al-Ṭūsī, *'Uddat al-uṣūl*, 293.

major concern behind treatment of this particular question in both Sunni and Shiite texts on jurisprudence was to argue against the view that no responsible believer could ever perform *taqlīd* or adopt the opinions of others in matters of religion. Many philosophical theologians claimed that the layman has to know and understand the reasoning behind all his essential opinions on the faith and cannot simply adopt the opinion of a scholar, just as one cannot accept others' opinions blindly on matters of rational inquiry. This issue is clearly important in al-Ṭūsī's text, for he attributes the strict prohibition of *taqlīd* to the Baghdādī Mu'tazilī theologians in the same passage. In contrast, he records that the Baṣrī Mu'tazilī theologians and all Muslim jurists (*al-fuqahā' bi-asri-him*) assert that it is permissible to consult qualified jurists and adopt their opinions on matters of the law, though not on matters of fundamental theological doctrine. Many Sunni texts on jurisprudence use the same language, asserting that it is *permissible* for the layman to adopt a jurist's opinions on the points of law, in contradistinction to basic theology (*uṣūl al-dīn*), where it is not permissible to adopt anyone else's opinion.[11] Al-'Allāmah al-Ḥillī, who clearly upholds the exclusive authority of the jurists, states in one passage of his *Tahdhīb al-wuṣūl*, "The truth is that it is *permissible* for the layman to follow (a jurist's opinion) concerning the points of law, against the Mu'tazilah of Baghdad." In another passage, however, he states quite clearly, "The layman *must* follow (a jurist's opinion) if he is not able to perform *ijtihād*."[12] Such passages are not intended to contradict one another. It is therefore entirely possible that al-Ṭūsī supported the exclusive authority of the jurists despite his saying it is permissible—not obligatory—for the layman to consult a legal expert.

Al-Sharīf al-Murtaḍā makes a stronger statement in the section on jurisconsult and the layman in *al-Dharī'ah ilā uṣūl al-sharī'ah*, implying that the authority of the jurists was indeed exclusive. He asserts that there is no disagreement within the Muslim community concerning the necessity of the layman's consultation of the jurisconsult (*wujūb rujū' al-'āmmī ilā 'l-muftī*). Similarly, in *Jawābāt al-masā'il al-rassīyah al-ūlā*, he reports that the layman is obligated to petition for legal opinions.[13] There is no room for doubt concerning his intention and probably that of al-Ṭūsī as well. The dichotomy between the jurist and the layman that Arjomand places in the nineteenth century and al-Astarābādī considers an innovation on the part of al-'Allāmah al-Ḥillī existed already in the early eleventh century. Al-Sharīf al-Murtaḍā and al-Ṭūsī clearly assign the Shiite layman a position with respect to the Shiite jurist quite similar to that of the Sunni layman with respect to the Sunni jurist. By stress-

11. al-Baṣrī, *al-Mu'tamad*, 2: 360–63; al-Khaṭīb al-Baghdādī, *Kitāb al-faqīh wa'l-mutafaqqih*, 2: 66–68.

12. Ibn al-Muṭahhar al-Ḥillī, *Tahdhīb al-wuṣūl*, 103, 105.

13. al-Murtaḍā, *al-Dharī'ah*, 2: 796–97; idem, *Rasā'il*, 2: 322.

ing the requirements for the granting of legal opinions, they make a claim of authority for the Shiite jurists parallel to those made by the Sunni jurists. As far as extant sources indicate, this idea was introduced by al-Sharīf al-Murtaḍā and al-Shaykh al-Ṭūsī. The extant abridgment of al-Shaykh al-Mufīd's work on jurisprudence, for example, does not include a section on the jurisconsult and the layman or any other statements justifying the authority of the jurists.

The institution of the legal *madhhab* is based on the conception that the jurists, a distinct class of religious professionals, enjoy an exclusive right to engage in the elaboration of Islamic law, thereby exerting a dominant influence on the interpretation of religion and sacred text. Both Sunnis and Shiites agree on this point, despite the implications of some modern studies. It is often claimed that the extensive authority of the jurists is primarily a Shiite phenomenon which reflects the authoritarian nature of Shiism, in constradistinction to Sunni Islam. Many statements in Sunni legal texts upholding the exclusive right of jurists to serve as religious guides for laymen show that it is not the case: Al-Khaṭīb al-Baghdādī reports that he who is incapable of *ijtihād* is obligated to adopt the opinion of a jurist, just as a blind man must consult someone who can see in order to pray in the right direction. Al-Ghazālī holds that the layman is obligated to seek out legal opinions and to follow the dictates of the scholars. According to al-Āmidī, the layman and all those who do not have the full ability to perform *ijtihād,* even though they might be accomplished scholars in some legal and ancillary fields, must follow the legal opinions of a *mujtahid.* Al-Shāṭibī goes so far as to claim that with respect to the contemporary Muslim community, the jurisconsult stands in place of the Prophet (*al-muftī qā'imun fī 'l-ummati maqāma'n-nabī*).[14] These Sunni theorists clearly support the exclusive authority of fully qualified jurists; such claims are not characteristic of Shiism alone.

SCRIPTURAL JUSTIFICATION OF THE JURISTS' AUTHORITY

By the sixteenth century, the authority of the Shiite jurists had become enshrined in the theory of general delegation, according to which the prerogative to decide legal issues was delegated to a "general representative" (*nā'ib 'āmm*) of the imam. As the theory developed, this "general representative" had to be a *mujtahid.* According to Calder, the first scholar to use this specific term was al-Shahīd al-Thānī, although it was prefigured in the work of 'Alī b. 'Abd al-'Ālī al-Karakī (d. 940/1534).[15] Both jurists based this theory on a scriptural text, the hadith termed the *maqbūlah,* "acceptable tradition," of 'Umar b.

14. al-Khaṭīb al-Baghdādī, *Kitāb al-faqīh wa'l-mutafaqqih,* 2: 68; al-Ghazālī, *al-Mustaṣfā,* 2: 389; al-Āmidī, *al-Iḥkām,* 4: 198; Ibrāhīm b. Mūsā al-Shāṭibī, *al-Muwāfaqāt fī uṣūl al-sharī'ah,* 4 vols. (Beirut: Dār al-Kutub al-'ilmiyah, 1991), 4: 178–79.

15. Calder, "Structure of Authority," esp. chapter 4, "The Judicial Delegation," 66–107.

Ḥanẓalah, recorded in al-Kulaynī's *al-Kāfī,* which states on the authority of Ja'far al-Ṣādiq, "Look to someone among you who has transmitted our traditions and studied our rulings, distinguishing what we declare lawful from what we declare forbidden, and accept him as a judge, for I have appointed him a judge."[16] Jurists since al-Shahīd al-Thānī have interpreted this hadith as granting legal authority to the *mujtahid* alone, making him the general representative of the imam during the Occultation. Though this authority is theoretically derivative, it gives the jurists a de facto monopoly over religious authority in the Shiite community during the Occultation, when ordinary means of communication with the imam are cut off.

Sunni jurists argue for their exclusive authority using similar interpretations of scriptural texts. One of the most common of these authority texts is *āyat al-umarā'* (Q 4:59), the Koranic text *aṭī'ū 'Llāha wa-aṭī'ū 'r-rasūla wa-ūlī 'l-amri minkum,* "Obey God, and obey the Prophet and those of you who have authority," which has been used to justify the authority of a variety of groups, including the Sunni caliphs, the Shiite imams, monarchs, and mystics, in addition to the jurists. Al-Khaṭīb al-Baghdādī (d. 463/1071) asserts that the term *ūlū al-amr minkum,* "those of you who have authority" or "those of you who are in charge," in this verse designates the jurists (*fuqahā'*) in particular. Al-Shāṭibī claims that *ūlū al-amr* refers to *muftīs*.[17] Another common authority text is the well-known hadith *al-'ulamā'u warathatu 'l-anbiyā',* "The scholars are the heirs of the prophets"; jurists claim that the term *'ulamā',* "scholars," here refers to them in particular.[18] Ibn al-Ḥājib cites the Koranic verse *fa-s'alū ahla 'dh-dhikri in kuntum lā ta'lamūn,* "Then ask the people of knowledge, if you do not know" (Q 16:43, 21:7), to support the legal authority of the *mujtahids*, and interprets *ahl al-dhikr,* "the people of knowledge," as referring to *mujtahids* in particular. Al-Āmidī cites the same verse in reference to jurists.[19] The Sunni jurists used these texts to claim and legitimate their exclusive religious authority.

Both Sunnis and Shiites cite scriptural authority texts as theoretical justifications for the exclusive authority of the jurists, interpreting them in closely parallel fashion. The main difference is that whereas the Sunnis present their exclusive authority as deriving directly from prophetic authority, the Shiite jurists present their exclusive authority as deriving from prophetic authority through the intermediate authority of the imams. Historically, Shiites have in-

16. al-Kulaynī, *al-Kāfī,* 7: 412.

17. al-Khaṭīb al-Baghdādī, *Kitāb al-faqīh wa'l-mutafaqqih,* 1: 27–28; al-Shāṭibī, *al-Muwāfaqāt,* 4: 179.

18. al-Khaṭīb al-Baghdādī, *Kitāb al-faqīh wa'l-mutafaqqih,* 1: 17.

19. Ibn al-Ḥājib, *Mukhtaṣar muntahā al-sūl,* 2 vols. (Cairo: Maktabat al-kullīyāt al-azharīyah, 1983), 2: 306; al-Āmidī, *al-Iḥkām,* 4: 198.

terpreted the specific authority texts cited by Sunni jurists as arguments for their own authority as proofs of the authority of the imams or *ahl al-bayt.* Shiite exegeses of *āyat al-umarā'* (Q 4:59) and *fa-s'alū ahla dh-dhikri in kuntum lā ta'lamūn* (Q 16:43) consistently maintain that *ūlū al-amr* and *ahl al-dhikr* are the Shiite imams. Writing in the mid-tenth century, the Twelver Shiite Ibn Abī Zaynab al-Nu'mānī cites both these verses as referring to the imams specifically. Al-Qāḍī al-Nu'mān holds that the Fatimid caliphs represent both *ūlū al-amr* and *ahl al-dhikr,* although according to Sunnis, they are either jurists (*fuqahā'*) or commanders of military detachments (*umarā' al-sarāyā*), taken to refer to princes (*umarā'*) or kings (*salāṭīn*). Al-Shaykh al-Ṭūsī and al-Faḍl al-Ṭabrisī (d. 548/1153) report in their Koranic exegeses that *ūlū al-amr* are the imams and that the opinions that this term refers to rulers (*umarā'*) or scholars (*'ulamā'*) are incorrect.[20] These interpretations establish that the authority of the imams derives from the Prophet's authority. The hadith of Ibn Ḥanẓalah serves, in the view of Shiite jurists since the sixteenth century at the latest, to show that the authority of Shiite jurists derives in turn from the authority of the imams.

Nevertheless, some extreme expressions of the jurists' authority within Shiism seem to bypass the authority of the imams. Al-Muḥaqqiq al-Ḥillī declares that jurists are the heirs of the prophets.[21] The sixteenth-century jurist Ḥusayn b. al-Ḥasan al-Karakī (d. 1001/1592–93) refers to himself as heir of the prophets.[22] Writing in the eighteenth century, Sayyid Dildār 'Alī b. Muḥammad al-Laknawī (d. 1235/1820) claims that Shiite jurists are the heirs of the prophets.[23] Muḥammad Bāqir al-Bihbihānī even refers to the jurists as the caliphs or successors (*khulafā'*) of the Prophet and describes their authority in the following manner: "The jurists...are the successors of the Chosen Messenger, guardians of the Chaste Ones' orphans, cut off from them by occultation and concealment, treasurers of the precious faith after the Prophet and the Imams, and custodians of the way of the saved sect among the Muslim community."[24] The modern Iranian scholar al-Muntaẓirī interprets a number of well-known authority texts, including the hadith *al-'ulamā'u warathatu 'l-anbiyā'* and *āyat al-umarā'* (Q 4:59), as referring specifically to the jurists, even though, as we have just seen, in the Shiite tradition they have regularly been

20. Ibn Abī Zaynab Muḥammad b. Ibrāhīm b. Ja'far al-Nu'mānī, *al-Ghaybah* (Beirut: Mu'assasat al-a'lamī li 'l-maṭbū'āt, 1983), 29; al-Qāḍī al-Nu'mān, *Ikhtilāf uṣūl al-madhāhib,* 26–27; Muḥammad b. al-Ḥasan al-Ṭūsī, *al-Tibyān fī tafsīr al-qur'ān,* 10 vols. (Beirut and Najaf, 1972), 3: 236–37; Abū 'Alī al-Faḍl b. al-Ḥasan al-Ṭabrisī, *Majma' al-bayān,* 10 vols. (Beirut: Dār al-ma'rifah, 1986), 3: 100.

21. Najm al-Dīn al-Ḥillī, *al-Mu'tabar,* cited in Calder, "Structure of Authority," 186.

22. Iskandar Beg Munshī, *Tārīkh-i 'ālam-ārā-yi 'abbāsī,* 1: 123, 145, 213–15.

23. Sayyid Dildār 'Alī b. Muḥammad al-Laknawī, *Asās al-uṣūl* (Bombay: Maṭba'ah-yi muḥammadiyah, 1848), 3.

24. al-Bihbihānī, *Risālat al-akhbār wa'l-ijtihād,* 9.

taken to refer to the imams.[25] Even ignoring such claims as these last ones, the system justified by the Shiite jurists' claims of authority is parallel, in practical terms, to the Sunni system, given the twelfth imam's Occultation. The difference between the two is that an additional theoretical step is necessary in order to connect the will of God with the normative pronouncements of an exclusive body of religious specialists. For Sunnis, religious authority is transmitted from the realm of the supernatural to the jurists through the Prophet; for the Shiites, religious authority is transmitted from the realm of the supernatural through the Prophet to the imams and through them to the jurists.

THE CURRICULUM OF LEGAL STUDY

Modern Shiite scholars acquire recognition as competent jurists through completion of a highly structured legal education at one of the main Shiite centers of learning—in modern terminology, *ḥawzah 'ilmīyah.* The most important of these centers in our own time are at Najaf in Iraq and Qum in Iran. Muḥsin al-Amīn (d. 1371/1952), a Shiite scholar from Jabal 'Āmil who studied in Najaf between 1308/1890–91 and 1319/1901, gives one of the most detailed available descriptions of the course of study followed in this traditional system.[26] As it developed over the centuries and was instituted in Najaf and Qum, the curriculum has three main stages. The first is called the *muqaddimāt* or "propaedeutic sciences," and includes the study of Arabic syntax and morphology, rhetoric, and logic. The second stage, called *dars al-suṭūḥ* or *al-dars al-saṭḥī,* "study of legal texts," consists of a graded course of standard *fiqh* and *uṣūl al-fiqh* textbooks. According to Muḥsin al-Amīn, it takes about seven and a half years of continuous study to complete the first two stages of the curriculum. The third and final stage, termed *dars al-khārij,* "extra-textual study," or *al-dars al-istidlālī,* "study of the derivation of legal rules," involves the study of *fiqh* and *uṣūl al-fiqh,* concentrating on the process by which rulings on individual points of law are derived. Study at this level follows the lectures of a leading law professor rather than set texts. According to Muḥsin al-Amīn, this stage takes about five years. The complete course of study therefore takes

25. Āyat Allāh al-'Uẓmā al-Muntaẓirī, *Dirāsāt fī wilāyat al-faqīh wa-fiqh al-dawlah al-islāmīyah,* 2 vols. (Qum: Maktab al-i'lām al-islāmī, 1988), 1: 425–92.

26. al-Amīn, *Khiṭaṭ Jabal 'Āmil,* 186–89; idem, *A'yān al-Shī'ah,* 10: 352. I have chosen to present Muḥsin al-Amīn's account of the curriculum rather than more recent accounts because his is presumably closer to the system as it existed in the preceding centuries. The curriculum at the center of learning in Qum follows the same outlines as that used in Najaf, for when 'Abd al-Karīm al-Ḥā'irī founded the center there in 1922, he consciously based the curriculum on that of Najaf. This approach was only logical, for Najaf was the unquestioned world center of Shiite legal study at the time, and al-Ḥā'irī and the other leading Iranian jurists of his day had all studied there. For other descriptions, see Muḥammad Sharīf Rāzī, *Ganjīnah-yi dānishmandān,* 7 vols. (Tehran, 1973), 1: 154–97; Fischer, *Iran,* 247–51; Roy Mottahedeh, *Mantle of the Prophet,* passim.

about twelve and a half years, though, al-Amīn observes, the time required to complete it depends on the ability and application of the student.[27]

I. The Propaedeutic Sciences (*al-Muqaddimāt*)

After memorizing the Koran and learning how to write, the student begins the first stage of the standard curriculum, that of the *muqaddimāt,* which includes Arabic syntax and morphology, rhetoric, and logic.

A. Arabic Grammar, including Syntax and Morphology

First, the student studies a graded series of works on Arabic grammar.

1. *al-Ajrūmīyah* (or *al-Ajurrūmīyah*), a short text on syntax by Ibn Ajurrūm (d. 723/1323). The student must memorize the text of this work and memorize the explication of its examples.
2. *Qaṭr al-nadā wa-ball al-ṣadā* and its commentary, both by Ibn Hishām al-Anṣārī (d. 761/1360)
   At the same time, the student begins to study Sa'd al-Dīn al-Taftazānī's (d. 792/1390) commentary on *Kitāb al-taṣrīf,* by 'Izz al-Dīn al-Zanjānī (fl. 625/1257), on morphology.
3. The *Alfiyah* of Ibn Mālik (d. 672/1274), with the commentary of his son Badr al-Dīn (d. 686/1287), is read for syntax only and not morphology.
   For morphology, the student reads concurrently the commentary of al-Jāribirdī (d. 746/1345) or al-Niẓām al-Nīsābūrī (d. ca. 710/1310) on *al-Shāfiyah* by Ibn al-Ḥājib (d. 646/1249).
4. *Mughnī al-labīb* by Ibn Hishām al-Anṣārī. The student reads only the *mufradāt,* the first section of the work, which treats the Arabic particles in alphabetical order.

B. Rhetoric and Logic

1. On rhetoric, the student reads *al-Muṭawwal* by Sa'd al-Dīn al-Taftazānī, which is his longer commentary on the abridgment, *al-Talkhīṣ,* by al-Khaṭīb al-Qazwīnī (d. 739/1338) of *Miftāḥ al-'ulūm,* by al-Sakkākī (d. 626/1229). Some students read *al-Mukhtaṣar,* al-Taftazānī's shorter commentary on the same work, rather than *al-Muṭawwal.*
2. The student begins to study logic along with rhetoric. He reads the *ḥāshiyah,* gloss or marginal commentary, of Mullā 'Abd Allāh b. Ḥusayn al-Yazdī (d. 981/1573–74) on *Tahdhīb al-manṭiq* by Sa'd al-Dīn al-Taftazānī.
3. The student also reads *Sharḥ al-shamsīyah,* a commentary by Quṭb al-Dīn al-Rāzī (d. 766/1365) on the treatise on logic of 'Alī b. 'Umar al-Kātibī al-Qazwīnī (d. 693/1274). Rarely, *Sharḥ al-maṭāli',* a commentary on the work of 'Aḍud al-Dīn al-Ījī (d. 756/1355), is read in addition.

27. al-Amīn, *Khiṭaṭ Jabal 'Āmil,* 191.

II. Standard Legal Texts (*Dars al-Suṭūḥ*)

The student is now ready to begin the study of law. He studies *fiqh* and *uṣūl al-fiqh* simultaneously, both by gradations. The emphasis, if one judges by Muḥsin al-Amīn's presentation, is on *uṣūl al-fiqh,* just as the emphasis in the study of grammar is on syntax rather than morphology.

1. The student first reads *Ma'ālim al-uṣūl* by Ḥasan b. Zayn al-Dīn al-'Āmilī (d. 1011/1602). At the same time, the student reads some *fiqh* in *Sharā'i' al-islām* by al-Muḥaqqiq al-Ḥillī (d. 676/1276), but does not study the derivation of the legal rulings given therein.
2. Next, the student reads *al-Qawānīn* on *uṣūl al-fiqh,* by Mīrzā Abū al-Qāsim al-Qummī (d. 1231/1816). During Muḥsin al-Amīn's lifetime, *Kifāyat al-uṣūl* by Mullā Kāẓim al-Khurāsānī (d. 1329/1911) began to replace *al-Qawānīn.* Along with *al-Qawānīn,* the student reads *Sharḥ al-lum'ah* by al-Shahīd al-Thānī (d. 965/1558) on *fiqh.*
3. The last *uṣūl al-fiqh* text read before continuing on to *dars al-khārij* is *al-Rasā'il,* also known as *Farā'id al-uṣūl,* by al-Shaykh Murtaḍā al-Anṣārī (d. 1281/1864). At the same time, Murtaḍā al-Anṣārī's work *Riyāḍ al-masā'il* on *fiqh* or his books on *ṭahārah* and *ṣalāt* are also read.

III. The Open Lecture Course (*Dars al-Khārij*)

After completing the second level, the prospective scholar continues to study *fiqh* and *uṣūl al-fiqh* in depth, attending the lectures of the top scholars at the center of learning. The lectures are not based on specific textbooks, hence the term *khārij,* meaning "outside" of books, or extra-textual,[28] though the students use a number of standard legal works as supplementary reference material. In al-Amīn's presentation, there are two regular lectures the student attends, one on *fiqh* and the other on *uṣūl al-fiqh.* (Al-Amīn studied *fiqh* under Āghā Riḍā b. Muḥammad Hādī al-Hamadhānī (d. 1322/1904) and *uṣūl al-fiqh* under Mullā Kāẓim al-Khurasānī (d. 1329/ 1911), author of *Kifāyat al-uṣūl.*) In this stage, the professor lectures from his notes, presenting the opinions of earlier scholars on each subsequent question of law and discussing their arguments. He then presents his own opinion, explaining its derivation and giving evidence for his position. The students then present objections, and he answers them, entering into open debate. It usually takes several years of lectures for the professor to go through the standard order of legal topics. The purpose of this level of study is to teach the students to do legal research, to arrive at an independent legal ruling, and to establish its soundness with adequate proofs.

28. See al-Amīn, *A'yān al-shī'ah,* 10: 352.

While a detailed historical study of the Shiite legal curriculum has not been undertaken, it is clear that the system of education just described goes back a number of centuries within the Shiite tradition. For example, commentaries and anecdotes concerning education in the Safavid period indicate that a curriculum quite similar to the one described existed. An idea of the educational curriculum followed in the seventeenth century can be gained from the description of the works studied by Ḥusayn b. ʿAlī al-ʿĀmilī (d. 1078/1668), a great-great-grandson of al-Shahīd al-Thānī who lived in Isfahan, the Safavid capital. His father and teacher, ʿAlī b. Muḥammad al-ʿĀmilī (d. 1103/1692), recorded the works he studied before he died in 1078/1668 at the young age of twenty-one. This description may be dated precisely, and clearly represents the curriculum followed by a young law student as opposed to a catalogue of works studied at different periods over the course of a lifetime by a mature scholar. On grammar, Ḥusayn studied the commentary on *al-Ajrūmīyah*, the commentary on *Qaṭr al-nadā*, and the commentary on the *Thousand Verses* of Ibn Mālik, all with his father. He studied *Mughnī al-labīb* with another teacher. On rhetoric, he studied the *Mukhtaṣar al-talkhīṣ* and most of *al-Muṭawwal*, both by al-Taftazānī. On logic, he studied the commentary on *al-Shamsīyah* and the commentary on *al-Tajrīd* by Naṣīr al-Dīn al-Ṭūsī. On law, he studied the *Mukhtaṣar al-Nāfiʿ* and *al-Sharāʾiʿ* by al-Muḥaqqiq al-Ḥillī, al-Shahīd al-Thānī's commentary on *al-Lumʿah*, and *al-Alfiyah* by al-Shahīd al-Awwal on ritual prayer. On legal methodology, he studied the *Maʿālim al-dīn* of his great-grandfather Ḥasan b. Zayn al-Dīn al-ʿĀmilī. He also studied a smattering of mathematics, astronomy, hadith, *tafsīr*, and biographies of hadith transmitters.[29] This curriculum of study, truncated by the youth's untimely death, is strikingly similar to the curriculum described by Muḥsin al-Amīn above. The only major difference between the two is the absence from the earlier account of the works of al-Qummī and al-Anṣārī, which became part of the curriculum in the nineteenth century.

In its basic outlines, the contemporary Shiite legal curriculum probably dates back as early as the fourteenth century. As Muḥsin al-Amīn points out, the *uṣūl al-fiqh* text *Maʿālim al-dīn* became part of the curriculum relatively late; it took the place of al-ʿAllāmah al-Ḥillī's *Tahdhīb al-wuṣūl*—read with the commentary *Munyat al-labīb* of his nephew ʿAmīd al-Dīn al-Aʿrajī—and the *Mukhtaṣar* of Ibn al-Ḥājib, read with the famous commentary of ʿAḍud al-Dīn al-Ījī.[30] Niʿmat Allāh al-Jazāʾirī, for example, studied al-ʿAmīdī's commentary on *Tahdhīb al-wuṣūl* in a regular class at the Manṣūrīyah *madrasah* in Shiraz in the 1650s.[31] The list presented in chapter 3 of supercommentaries on

29. ʿAlī al-ʿĀmilī, *al-Durr al-manthūr*, 2: 246–47.
30. al-Amīn, *Khiṭaṭ Jabal ʿĀmil*, 188.
31. Niʿmat Allāh al-Jazāʾirī, *al-Anwār al-nuʿmānīyah* 4 vols. (Tabriz, 1954–59), 4: 309.

al-'Aḍudī's commentary shows the extent to which it served as a standard textbook in Shiite circles until throughout the seventeenth and eighteenth centuries. Similarly, al-Shahīd al-Thānī's commentary on al-Shahīd al-Awwal's *al-Lum'ah al-dimashqīyah* presumably replaced one of al-'Allāmah al-Ḥillī's legal works in the curriculum in the late sixteenth or early seventeenth century.

The Shiite legal curriculum closely resembles that followed by Sunni legal scholars in the late medieval period. It is obvious that the main works studied by the Shiites on the propaedeutic sciences—Arabic grammar, rhetoric, and logic—are all standard Sunni texts which date back to the thirteenth and fourteenth centuries.[32] A blending of traditional Shiite legal studies with the Sunni Iranian scholarly tradition during the Safavid period may have played some role in fixing the Shiite legal curriculum in its present form, particularly with regard to the science of logic. The pre-Safavid and largely Sunni scholarly tradition in Iran was very strong in mathematics, astronomy, logic, and philosophy and boasted such great figures in these fields as 'Aḍud al-Dīn al-Ījī (d. 756/1355), Sa'd al-Dīn al-Taftazānī (d. 791/1390), al-Sharīf al-Jurjānī (d. 816/1413), and Jalāl al-Dīn al-Dawwānī (d. 907/1501). Ibn Khaldun (d. 808/1406) makes the point that during his own period, the study of the rational sciences was most highly developed in Iran and Transoxania, and he mentions al-Taftazānī in particular as excelling in this field.[33] In contrast, the more traditionalist scholars in Arab regions, including Ibn Taymīyah (d. 728/1328) and Jalāl al-Dīn al-Suyūṭī (d. 909/1505), did not think highly of the science of logic, holding that it was unnecessary for religious purposes and even going so far as to state that it was forbidden.[34] Moreover, the rational sciences were underrepresented in pre-Safavid Shiite scholarship, which tended to concentrate on hadith and law. The Sunni Iranian role in promoting the study of logic in the Shiite curriculum is suggested by the place assigned in it to the *ḥāshiyah* of Mullā 'Abd Allāh al-Yazdī on Quṭb al-Dīn al-Rāzī's famous treatise on logic. Al-Yazdī was a sixteenth-century Iranian scholar who came directly out of the tradition of al-Dawwānī and al-Taftazānī. In any case, these Sunni works on the *muqaddimāt* were standard works in the late medieval Sunni legal curricula and had been incorporated into the Shiite curriculum by the sixteenth century at the latest.

32. Cf. the suggestion above in chapter 3 that Quṭb al-Dīn al-Rāzī, the author of *Sharḥ al-shamsīyah* on logic, was a Twelver Shiite passing as a Shāfi'ī.

33. Ibn Khaldūn, *The Muqaddimah*, 3 vols., trans. Franz Rosenthal (New York: Pantheon Books, 1958), 3: 117.

34. See Taqī al-Dīn Aḥmad Ibn Taymīyah's works *Naqḍ al-manṭiq* ("The Destruction of Logic"), ed. Muḥammad b. 'Abd al-Razzāq Ḥamzah, Sulaymān b. 'Abd al-Raḥmān al-Ṣani', and Muḥammad Ḥāmid al-Fiqī (Cairo: Maṭba'at al-sunnah al-muḥammadīyah, 1951) and *al-Radd 'alā al-manṭiqīyīn* ("The Refutation of the Logicians"), ed. 'Abd al-Ṣamad Sharaf al-Dīn al-Kutubī (Bombay: Maṭba'at al-qayyimah, 1949). Al-Suyūṭī wrote a work entitled *Ṣawn al-manṭiq wa'l-kalām 'an fann al-manṭiq wa'l-kalām* ("Defending Discourse and Speech from the Disciplines of Logic and Philosophical Theology") (in his *Kitāb al-taḥadduth bi-ni'mat Allāh*, 2: 106).

A detailed historical study of Sunni legal curricula has yet to be completed. Makdisi has pointed out the existence of three stages of legal study for the classical Islamic period, roughly between the tenth and the thirteenth centuries. The first level included the study of the literary arts, which served as preparation for the study of law and other fields. In the second level, the student concentrated on *madhhab* law, the accepted legal doctrines of a particular school. Makdisi likens this level to undergraduate studies and finds that it generally entailed a regular four-year program of study. In the third level of study, the student, now a *ṣāḥib* or "fellow" of a law professor, concentrated on *khilāf*, the disputed questions of the law. Makdisi likens this level to graduate studies.[35] It is undoubtedly this *madhhab/khilāf* mode of organization of the legal curriculum in the early medieval period that prompted Shiite jurists to write works on the law of the *madhhab* and *khilāf*, such as al-Shaykh al-Ṭūsī's *al-Nihāyah* and *al-Khilāf* and al-'Allāmah al-Ḥillī's *Muntahā al-maṭlab fī taḥqīq al-madhhab* and *Mukhtalaf al-shī'ah*. This system differs markedly, however, from that represented by the modern Shiite curriculum, particularly in its emphasis on the disputed points of law.

Sunni sources, such as al-Sakhāwī's biographical work *al-Ḍaw' al-lāmi'*, show that a Shāfi'ī or Ḥanafī law student in Cairo or Damascus in the fifteenth century would have followed a course of study quite similar to the Shiite curriculum outlined above. The system still entailed three basic stages of study. After memorizing the Koran, the student read a number of standard texts, memorizing and presenting them in order to obtain a certificate in an oral exam. Both the exam itself and the certificate received were termed *'arḍ*, "presentation." He studied the introductory sciences, reading a number of the works still used in the Shiite curriculum such as *al-Ajrūmīyah*, Ibn Mālik's *Alfiyah*, Ibn Hishām's *Mughnī al-labīb*, al-Taftazānī's *Mukhtaṣar*, and so on. At the next stage, that of concentration on the law itself, the student first studied the standard texts, such as al-Nawawī's *Minhāj al-ṭālibīn* on Shāfi'ī law and al-Juwaynī's *Waraqāt* and the *Mukhtaṣar* of Ibn al-Ḥājib on *uṣūl al-fiqh*. As an advanced student or "fellow" (*ṣāḥib*) of a prominent law professor, the student usually studied the professor's own commentary on one of the standard works of law, such as al-Rāfi'ī's *al-Fatḥ al-'azīz*, al-Qazwīnī's *al-Ḥāwī al-ṣaghīr*, or al-Nawawī's *Minhāj al-ṭālibīn* or *al-Rawḍah*. It is reported, for example, that Zakarīyā al-Anṣārī (d. 926/1520) taught his legal commentary *Sharḥ al-bahjah* fifty-seven times.[36] He must have done so as part of a regular, cyclical course

35. Makdisi, *Rise of Colleges*, 84, 96, 114.

36. al-Sha'rānī, *al-Ṭabaqāt al-ṣughrā*, 37; al-Ghazzī, *al-Kawākib al-sā'irah*, 1: 196–207. The work in question is al-Anṣārī's *al-Ghurar al-bahīyah*, a commentary on *al-Bahjah al-wardīyah* by Abū Ḥafṣ 'Umar b. Muẓaffar al-Wardī (d. 749/1348), itself a commentary on the standard Shāfi'ī legal text *al-Ḥāwī al-saghīr fī al-fatāwī* by Najm al-Dīn 'Abd al-Ghaffār b. 'Abd al-Karīm al-Qazwīnī (d. 665/1266) (Brockelmann, *GAL*, 1: 393).

for advanced students which was intended to explicate all topics of the law. It used a standard text as a basis, in this case *al-Ḥāwī al-ṣaghīr,* but presented the professor's own views and readings of particular points in the law. This system would appear to parallel the modern Shiite curriculum quite closely.

THE ADVANCED STUDENT'S LEGAL REPORT

In the modern Shiite legal curriculum, the aspiring jurist completes a work termed a *taqrīrah* in the course of the *khārij* level. This work is a report presenting and commenting on the professor's legal opinions and method based on his lectures. For example, Muḥsin al-Amīn records that his teacher Āghā Riḍā al-Hamadhānī wrote two *taqrīrahs* based on the lectures of Mīrzā Ḥasan al-Shīrāzī (d. 1312/1895), one on *uṣūl al-fiqh* and the other on the law of sales, in *fiqh.*[37] Āghā Buzurg al-Ṭihrānī reports that works of this type were first written in Shiite circles in the late eighteenth century and have remained popular ever since. The number of such works extant is extremely large, he adds, since professors such as Mīrzā Ḥasan al-Shīrāzī had over five hundred advanced law students and Muḥammad Kāẓim al-Khurāsānī had over twelve hundred. Nevertheless, Āghā Buzurg lists a number of *taqrīrahs* cited in his catalogue of Shiite works.[38] If the professor approves of the *taqrīrah,* the student is eligible to receive a license recognizing him as a fully competent legal scholar. The label of the genre derives from *taqrīr,* "determination," a medieval technical term referring to the settling of a question at the end of a disputation.[39] The *taqrīrah* appears to be functionally parallel to the Sunni *ta'līqah,* a similar type of work prepared by advanced students in law and other fields in the classical Islamic period. Makdisi argues that the *ta'līqah* arose out of the scholastic method and the teaching of disputation, and defines it as a report on the law professor's method of dealing with the disputed questions of the law. Some famous *ta'līqahs* include that of Ibn Abī Hurayrah (d. 345/956), which consisted of a commentary on the *Epitome* of al-Muzanī (d. 264/878), *al-Ta'līqah al-kubrā* of Abū Ḥamīd al-Isfarā'inī, which also included a commentary on al-Muzanī's work, and al-Ghazālī's *al-Mankhūl min ta'līqāt al-uṣūl,* which he prepared under his professor, Imām al-Ḥaramayn al-Juwaynī.[40] Despite the difference in time, the two types of work show remarkable similarities.

THE DOCTORATE OF LAW

Al-Astarābādī's discussions in *al-Fawā'id al-madanīyah* imply that between the fourteenth and seventeenth centuries, membership in the *mujtahid* class was

37. al-Amīn, *A'yān al-Shī'ah,* 7: 23.
38. al-Ṭihrānī, *al-Dharī'ah,* 4: 366–87.
39. Makdisi, *Rise of Colleges,* 111, 152, 250.
40. Ibid., 114–28.

accorded Shiite jurists who had developed the ability to derive independent legal rulings, which was gained through a regular program of legal study. He does not explain how such membership was established in practical terms. On the contrary, he states that it is impossible to determine such an elusive, internal ability in an objective way and claims that there are constant disputes among the scholars, both Sunni and Shiite, concerning the definition of a *mujtahid* and the requirements for *ijtihād*.[41] In the twentieth century, accession to the rank of a *mujtahid* is determined by receipt of a license, the *ijāzat al-ijtihād*, the granting of which is standard practice in the centers of Shiite learning in Najaf and Qum. Muḥsin al-Amīn gives the following definition of the *ijāzah:*

> The *ijāzat al-ijtihād*...certifies that the recipient has acquired the ability to derive the points of law from fundamental principles, and that he is a trustworthy and upright man whom one may properly consult for legal rulings. This is known through personal contact, especially when the recipient is a student of the scholar who issues the *ijāzah*.[42]

The *ijāzah* is granted by *mujtahids* to students who have completed the three levels of legal studies described above, and certifies the student's ability to derive and issue legal opinions. The twentieth-century Iranian author Mīrzā Muḥammad 'Alī Mudarris Tabrīzī includes in the introduction to his biographical dictionary *Rayḥānat al-adab* several facsimiles of this type of *ijāzah* granted to him by leading jurists of his day.[43]

It is not clear how far back this practice goes. The *ijāzat al-ijtihād* had certainly become prevalent by the mid-nineteenth century, for Muḥammad Ḥasan Najafī (d. 1266/1849–50) is known to have been quite permissive in licensing *mujtahids*; he taught about sixty in the course of his career.[44] The granting of this license may have become a regular practice in the late eighteenth century as the result of an effort to regularize the system of legal education in reaction to Akhbārī attacks on the jurists. Modarressi reports of Muḥammad Bāqir al-Bihbihānī (d. 1205/1791), the scholar held responsible for the ultimate defeat of the Akhbārī movement and the triumph of the Uṣūlīs, that "The legal system of his school was the first to be constructed entirely in accord with the rules and principles of *uṣūl al-fiqh*."[45] Because of the prominent role the term *ijtihād* played in the Akhbārī-Uṣūlī controversy, by the eighteenth century the term "*mujtahids*" came to designate the Uṣūlīs. The

41. al-Astarābādī, *al-Fawā'id al-madanīyah*, 45.

42. al-Amīn, *A'yān al-shī'ah*, 10: 352.

43. Mīrzā Muḥammad 'Alī Mudarris, *Rayḥānat al-adab fī tarājim al-ma'rūfīn bi'l-kunyah wa'l-laqab*, 2d ed., 8 vols. (Tabriz: Chāp-khānah-yi shafaq, 1967–70), 8: 18–19, 25, 27, 29, 30–31.

44. al-Amīn, *A'yān al-Shī'ah*, 9: 149.

45. Modarressi, *Shī'ī Law*, 56.

Akhbārī challenge led to a reassertion, on the part of the Uṣūlīs, of the right to use *ijtihād*, which resulted in a more general use of the term. The emphasis on the term *ijtihād* during this period explains al-Bihbihānī's choice of a title for his refutation of the Akhbārīs, *Risālat al-ijtihād wa'l-akhbār*, which he completed on 13 Rajab 1155/13 September 1742.[46] The fact that the term *ijtihād* figures prominently in the modern Shiite license's designation, in contrast with the *ijāzat al-iftā'* or *ijāzat al-tadrīs wa'l-iftā'* of the Sunnis, suggests that it too developed during the late eighteenth or early nineteenth century as part of the Uṣūlī jurists' reassertion of their authority.

Makdisi has identified the *ijāzat al-tadrīs wa 'l-iftā'*, "license to teach law and grant legal opinions," as the Islamic doctorate of law, an integral part of the system of legal education since the classical period. This license is said to go back to the eighth century. The Meccan jurist Muslim b. Khālid (d. 180/796) supposedly granted al-Shāfi'ī permission to issue legal opinions at the age of fifteen. His contemporary Mālik b. Anas was supposedly authorized to give legal opinions by seventy jurists. Makdisi's presentation implies that the *ijāzat al-tadrīs wa 'l-iftā'* had become a standard feature of Islamic legal education by the eleventh century. Beyond the early examples of Mālik and al-Shāfi'ī, however, the reports he cites depicting jurists granting students permission to issue legal opinions and teach law date from the fourteenth and fifteenth centuries.[47] Other texts show that the license was well established by the thirteenth century and continued to be issued until modern times: al-Udfuwī (d. 748/1347) mentions a license to teach law granted to Muḥammad b. 'Alī al-Qūṣī in Upper Egypt, dated 15 Sha'bān 650/21 October 1252 and signed by two witnesses, and he provides the text of a license to teach Shāfi'ī law and issue legal opinions granted to Shams al-Dīn al-Manfalūṭī (d. 667/1268). Al-Qalqashandī (d. 821/ 1418) provides the text of a license to teach Shāfi'ī law and grant legal *responsa* he received in Alexandria in 778/1376–77 at the age of twenty-one. Al-Sakhāwī (d. 902/1497) cites passages from the texts of several such documents dating from the fifteenth century. 'Abd al-Wahhāb al-Sha'rānī (d. 973/1565) tells of thirty-seven contemporary scholars in sixteenth-century Cairo who received the *ijāzat al-tadrīs wa'l-iftā'*. Al-Murādī (d. 1206/ 1791) reports numerous instances when jurists obtained the *ijāzah bi-l-iftā' wa-l-tadrīs* in Cairo and Damascus in the eighteenth century.[48] This traditional license was granted at al-Azhar in Cairo until the first Azhar reform law created

46. al-Bihbihānī, *Risālat al-ijtihād wa'l-akhbār*, 1, 94.

47. Makdisi, *Rise of Colleges*, 148–52; idem, *Rise of Humanism*, 26–29.

48. Ja'far b. Tha'lab al-Udfuwī, *al-Ṭāli' al-sa'īd al-jāmi' li-asmā' al-ruwāt bi-a'lā al-ṣa'īd* (Cairo: Maṭba'at al-Jamāliyyah, 1914), 235–36, 309; Aḥmad b. 'Alī al-Qalqashandī, *Ṣubḥ al-a'shā fī ṣinā'at al-inshā*, 17 vols. (Cairo: al-Mu'assasah al-miṣrīyah al-'āmmah, 1964), 14: 322–27; al-Sakhāwī, *al-Ḍaw' al-lāmi'*, 9: 44, for example; al-Sha'rānī, *al-Ṭabaqāt al-ṣughrā*, 50, 82–84, 86, 88, 94, 96–100, 102, 104–6, 108–9, 112–13, 115, 118–20, 126, 128–29, 131–32, 135–40; Muḥammad Khalil al-Murādī, *Silk al-durar fī a'yān al-qarn al-thānī 'ashar*, 4 vols. (Bulaq, 1874), 1: 14, 52, and passim.

a new degree, termed *shahādat al-ʿālimīyah,* "the degree of scholarly status," in 1872.[49]

The Shiite *ijāzat al-ijtihād* and the Sunni *ijāzat al-tadrīs wa'l-iftā'* are functionally equivalent licenses that confer the status of a fully competent jurist upon the recipient. Both may be issued only by a recognized jurist and both serve a restrictive purpose, limiting the number of qualified jurists. It appears, though, that the granting of this certificate did not become standard practice among the Shiites until the late eighteenth or early nineteenth century. Little is known of the practices adopted by Shiite scholars in earlier periods to establish competence as a jurist. Nevertheless, the existence of these parallel licenses shows that there is no essential difference between the Sunni and the Twelver Shiite legal systems in this regard. Given the fundamental similarities between the *ijāzat al-ijtihād* and the *ijāzat al-tadrīs wa'l-iftā',* the relatively recent institution of the former by the Shiites raises the possibility that the practice was borrowed from Sunni circles, but scholarship to date does not support any definite statements on this hypothesis, which must remain at the level of conjecture.

IJTIHĀD

It has long been common to view *ijtihād* as a major point of differentiation between the Shiite and Sunni systems of jurisprudence. Shiite jurists, it is held, are still allowed to practice *ijtihād,* while for Sunnis the gate of *ijtihād* has been closed since the ninth century. For example, Strothmann claims, "Shīʿīs are also to be differentiated from Sunnīs in that the gate of *ijtihād* is not closed."[50] Gardet holds that while Shiites term any doctor of the law a *mujtahid,* Sunnis restrict this term to the very early jurists and the founders of the *madhhabs*.[51] Similarly, MacDonald contrasts the Shiite jurists with their Sunni counterparts:

> True legal authority lies, rather, with the learned doctors of religion and law. As a consequence of this, the Shiʿites still have *Mujtahids,* divines and legists who have a right to form opinions of their own, can expound the original sources at first hand, and can claim the unquestioning assent of their disciples. Such men have not existed among the Sunnites since the middle of the third century of the Hijra; from that time on all Sunnites have been compelled to swear to the words of some master or other, long dead.[52]

49. Muḥammad al-Bahī, *al-Azhar tārikhuh wa-taṭawwuruh* (Cairo: Wizārat al-awqāf, 1964), 303, 305.

50. Rudolf Strothmann, "Shīʿa," *EI*[1], 7: 355.

51. Gardet, *L'Islam,* 187.

52. MacDonald, *Development of Muslim Theology,* 38–39.

He intimates that Sunni legal scholarship is moribund because of an excessive reliance on ancient authorities, while Shiite jurists, permitted a greater degree of independent thinking, maintain a more vigorous intellectual tradition. The twentieth-century Shiite scholar Muḥammad al-Ḥusayn Kāshif al-Ghiṭā' writes that the question of *ijtihād* is one of the lines of demarcation between Sunnis and Shiites, though he adds that he does not understand how the Sunnis can claim that the gate of *ijtihād* is closed:

> Among [the points of difference between Sunnis and Shiites] is that the gate of *ijtihād,* as you have seen, is still open according to the Imamis, as opposed to the majority of Muslims. For, according to the latter, this gate has been closed and locked to the intelligent scholars. I do not know at what time, by what evidence, or in what manner this closure occurred, nor have I found any Muslim scholar who has treated this subject adequately. . . . The burden of explaining this lies with [the Sunnis].[53]

The common opinion that Shiites now accept *ijtihād* while Sunnis do not is somewhat surprising, especially given the view, commonly expressed in textbooks and studies on Islam, that religious authority in Shiism is based solely on recourse to the imam.

In a more detailed discussion, Madelung attempts to explain how the Shiites and Sunnis came to differ on the issue of *ijtihād,* identifying two main reasons for the supposed differences in approach. First, he claims that a consensus of Shiite jurists is of no legal consequence. (As pointed out in chapter 4, consensus in Shiite jurisprudence is actually of legal consequence during the Greater Occultation, so that this argument does not hold.) Madelung then claims that the Shiites' preoccupation with the notion of certitude sets their notion of *ijtihād* apart from that of the Sunnis. He then describes Shiite *ijtihād* as a process of probabilistic approximation to the truth concerning the law; this holds as much for Sunni jurisprudence as it does for Shiite jurisprudence.[54] Recent scholarship has shown the idea that the gate of *ijtihād* was closed in the ninth century untenable. *Ijtihād,* defined as the process of arriving at a legal opinion on a particular case through analysis and research, was exercised in the Sunni system until a much later date.[55]

The first step toward making a useful comparison of the Sunni and Shiite systems is the realization that the term *ijtihād* has a long and complex seman-

53. Muḥammad al-Ḥusayn Kāshif al-Ghiṭā', *Aṣl al-shī'ah wa-uṣūluhā,* 9th ed. (Beirut: Dār al-biḥār, 1960), 120–21.

54. Madelung, "Authority in Twelver Shiism," 169.

55. Makdisi, *Rise of Colleges,* 281–91; Wael B. Hallaq, "Was the Gate of Ijtihad Closed?" *IJMES* 16 (1984): 3–41; idem, "On the Origins of the Controversy about the Existence of Mujtahids and the Gate of Ijtihad," *Studia Islamica* 63 (1986): 129–41.

tic history within both Sunni and Shiite circles. When Muslim or Orientalist scholars state that the gate of *ijtihād* has been closed or that absolute *ijtihād* is no longer possible, they are defining *ijtihād* as the ability to form another *madhhab*, and this meaning is only one of many possibilities. *Ijtihād* may denote (1) a *method* of legal research, (2) the *competence* required to undertake such scholarly inquiry on legal questions, (3) the recognized *rank* of mastery within the legal *madhhab*, or (4) the *establishment* of a new *madhhab*. With the proliferation of subcategories of *ijtihād* beginning as early as the time of al-Ghazālī, the semantic situation becomes even more complicated. Given the semantic complexity of the term *ijtihād*, it is easy for the investigator to fall into the trap of comparing apples and oranges.

If discussion is limited to *ijtihād* defined as the rank held by the master jurist, it becomes clear that the Sunni and Shiite systems are not poles apart. The question is not whether the Sunnis or the Shiites term their jurists *mujtahids* or even whether they use the specific terms *ijtihād* or *taqlīd;* the question is whether their legal systems function in the same way and have similar structures. As seen in the previous chapter, the Akhbārīs treat *ijtihād* and *taqlīd* as two sides of the same coin. The essential feature of the legal system is the dichotomy established between the master jurist, the only one authorized to issue opinions, and the layman, who must have recourse to the master jurist to fulfill his religious obligations. On a fundamental structural level, the Sunni and Shiite systems are nearly identical except for differences in terminology, and have been so, at least in theory, since the time of al-Sharīf al-Murtaḍā and al-Shaykh al-Ṭūsī. In both the Sunni system and the modern Shiite system, the rank of master jurist in the legal *madhhab* is exclusive. It may be established only by completing a set course of legal study and receiving a license to teach law and issue legal *responsa*. In terms of establishing restricted access to the rank of master jurist, the Sunni and Shiite systems are completely parallel. The only difference is one of terminology and not of basic structure.

Similarly, if *ijtihād* is understood to denote the process of legal interpretation undertaken by the *muftī*, then the Sunni and Shiite systems are clearly parallel. From the time of al-Murtaḍā and al-Ṭūsī it is clear that the Shiite layman should consult an expert concerning legal problems which befall him. The scholar consulted, furthermore, should be well versed in the law, and is under the obligation to examine the scriptural sources and previous legal scholarship independently and to come up with his own legal ruling. As explained above, the Shiites rejected the use of the term *ijtihād* to describe this process of legal derivation, for they equated it with arbitrary, personal opinion. Nevertheless, according to al-Sharīf al-Murtaḍā they did recognize independent derivation of legal rulings from scriptural texts (*istinbāṭ*) as the legitimate function of the jurist. He severely criticized those scholars who did not or could not perform this function yet still gave opinions to laymen, holding that expertise in legal derivation was unnecessary. He terms such scholars *ahl al-taqlīd*, "the People of Unquestioning Acceptance," and forbids them merely to report the contents of earlier books of law and hadith to questioners.[56] Similarly, Sunni jurists throughout the medieval and premodern periods—whether they claimed the title *mujtahid* or not—performed the functions of legal research and derivation of the law that is termed *ijtihād* in works on jurisprudence and legal theory.

JURIDICAL HIERARCHIES

It is generally supposed that the Shiite legal system is inherently hierarchical whereas the Sunni system is inherently egalitarian.[57] The continued prevalence of this view is due largely to the role Shiite jurists have played in recent Iranian history and the prominence of the modern Shiite position of *marji' al-taqlīd*, a top Shiite jurist who serves as a reference for laymen.[58] Such views are also justified by inaccurate and anachronistic appeals to the Shiite theory of the imamate, seen as authoritarian in comparison with more "democratic" Sunni doctrines. However, both Sunni and Shiite legal systems have exhibited strong hierarchical tendencies throughout Islamic history, and the two are not nearly so opposed to one another in this regard as commonly supposed. Theoretical works on jurisprudence and historical sources concerning the lives and activities of jurists provide abundant evidence of hierarchies in premodern Sunni and Shiite legal establishments in various historical periods and regions of the Muslim world.

At the centers of learning in the Shiite world, a limited number of top jurists gain wide recognition for their learning and come to serve as authorities for Shiite laymen, who must choose to follow the opinions of one of them in order to fulfill their religious obligations properly. A jurist who is recognized as such an authority is termed *marji' al-taqlīd*. Recent scholarship on Shiism has suggested that the position of *marji' al-taqlīd* is uniquely Shiite and developed fairly recently, perhaps not until the nineteenth century. It is further held that one of the main theoretical underpinnings of the position of *marji' al-taqlīd* is *a'lamīyah*, the doctrine that the layman (*muqallid* or *mustaftī*) must follow the opinions of not just any qualified *mujtahid*, but of the one *mu-*

56. al-Sharīf al-Murtaḍā, *Rasā'il*, 2: 262, 331–33.

57. For a more detailed discussion, see Devin J. Stewart, "Islamic Juridical Hierarchies and the Office of Marj' al-Taqlīd" (paper from Shī'ī Islam: Faith, Experience and Worldview conference, Temple University-University of Pennsylvania, September, 1993) (forthcoming).

58. On the *marji' al-taqlīd* in general, see Anne K. S. Lambton, "A Reconsideration of the Position of *Marja' al-Taqlīd* and the Religious Institution," *Studia Islamica* 20 (1964): 115–35; Cole, "Imami Jurisprudence," 33–46; Ahmad Kazemi Moussavi, "The Establishment of the Position of Marja-'iyyat-i Taqlid in the Twelver-Shi'i Community," *Iranian Studies* 18 (1985): 35–51; Jean Calmard, "Mardja'-i Taḳlīd," *EI*², 6: 548–56.

jtahid recognized as the most learned. This doctrine is also held to have developed relatively recently.[59] The concept of *a'lamīyah,* however, dates back to the beginnings of the Twelver legal *madhhab.* Al-Sharīf al-Murtaḍā states in *al-Dharī'ah* that, according to the more reliable opinion, the layman must consult the jurist who is most learned (*a'lam*) and most pious and observant (*awra' wa-adyan*). This position has been upheld regularly in Shiite legal theory ever since.[60] The condition of *a'lamīyah* is not a recent phenomenon that has arisen in the last few centuries in Twelver Shiite law, but rather a standard feature of Shiite legal theory found in works of jurisprudence from the early eleventh century until the present.

There has been considerable debate in Sunni jurisprudence between the view that the layman may choose to practice according to the opinion of any qualified jurist and the view that he should follow the opinion of the most learned jurist. The latter opinion, though not upheld as regularly as in the Shiite tradition, has been important for many centuries in the Sunni legal system. According to al-Shīrāzī, the prominent Shāfi'ī jurists Ibn Surayj (d. 306/918) and al-Qaffāl al-Shāshī (d. 365/976) held that the layman should follow the most learned (*a'lam*) and most pious (*awra'*) jurist if more than one were available. Al-Āmidī cites Aḥmad b. Ḥanbal, in addition to Ibn Surayj and al-Qaffāl, as holding this opinion. According to Ibn Qudāmah al-Maqdisī, the early Ḥanbalī 'Umar b. al-Ḥusayn al-Khiraqī (d. 334/945) held that when faced with two conflicting opinions, the layman should follow that of the most learned and pious jurist (*al-afḍal fī 'ilmih wa-dīnih*). In *al-Mu'tamad,* Abū al-Ḥusayn al-Baṣrī states that if the opinions given by two jurisconsults differ, the layman must follow that of the most learned (*a'lam*) and most pious (*adyan*) jurist. Al-Khaṭīb al-Baghdādī writes that the layman should consult the most learned (*a'lam*) and most qualified (*amthal*) jurist when seeking an opinion. According to al-Shawkānī, Abū Isḥāq al-Isfarā'inī (d. 418/1027) and 'Alī b. Muḥammad al-Kiyā al-Harāsī (d. 504/1110) both hold it is necessary to consult the most learned (*a'lam*) jurist. The Ḥanbalī Ibn Qayyim al-Jawzīyah (d. 751/1350) holds that the layman must consult the most learned (*a'lam*) jurist. The fourteenth-century Egyptian Shāfi'ī jurisconsult al-Isnawī requires that the layman follow the opinion of the most learned (*a'lam*) and most pious (*awra'*) jurisconsult; if two jurisconsults are equal in learning, he must follow the opinion of the most pious (*adyan*); if one has greater learning but the other is more pious, then he must follow the opinion of the most pious. Though he does not accept it, al-Qarāfī reports the argument for *taqlīd* of the most

59. Moussavi, "Establishment of the Position of Marja'iyyat-i Taqlid," 35, 39; Calmard, "Mardja'-i Taḳlīd," 6: 552. Moussavi corrects this view in *Religious Authority,* 177–83.

60. al-Murtaḍā, *al-Dharī'ah,* 2: 317; see, for example, Najm al-Dīn Ja'far al-Ḥillī, *Ma'ārij al-uṣūl,* 201.

learned scholar as follows. For every matter concerning the religion one should rely on that person most qualified for the job. Just as one should consult an expert in warfare on military matters, one should consult the most learned legal scholar on law in the same fashion. The Mālikī jurist al-Shāṭibī writes that the layman is obliged to consult the most learned jurist, but warns that the process of determining which scholar is actually the most learned, which he terms *tarjīḥ*, "giving preference," should be undertaken by citing the jurists' relative merits and positive qualities of scholars rather than through mean-spirited criticism harping on their defects.[61]

A number of Sunni jurists, however, hold that it is not necessary for the layman to follow the opinions of the most learned scholar. Al-Bāqillānī (d. 403/ 1013) maintains that the layman is free to choose among jurists even if one is more learned than the rest.[62] The Ḥanbalī jurist al-Qāḍī Abū Ya'lā (d. 458/ 1065) reports that the layman may choose any legal authority (*muqallad*) he wishes, because, just as he is not expected to figure out the answer to a particular legal problem himself, he is not expected to distinguish the most learned jurist. The famous Shāfi'ī scholar Abū Isḥāq al-Shīrāzī allows that it is not necessary for the layman to follow the opinions of the most learned jurist and that it is the most correct (*aṣaḥḥ*) opinion. The Andalusian Mālikī jurist Abū al-Walīd al-Bājī (d. 474/1071) observes that many authors on *uṣūl al-fiqh* have held that the layman is obliged to consult the most learned *(afḍal) muftī*, but that this opinion is not correct; he may consult any *muftī* he chooses. Ibn al-Ḥājib (d. 646/1249) permits the layman to adopt the opinion of a scholar who is not the most learned (*taqlīd al-mafḍūl*). Ibn Qudāmah (d. 620/1223) records that the layman is free to choose among the available *mujtahids*, and further claims that Aḥmad b. Ḥanbal most likely held that it was permissible to consult a jurist who was not the most learned (*al-mafḍūl*). Al-Āmidī states that this opinion is the one he prefers (*al-mukhtār*). Al-Qarāfī writes that it is not necessary to refer to the most learned jurist according to the prevalent (*mashhūr*) opinion, and al-Shawkānī (d. 1250/1832) reports that this is the opinion of most Shāfi'īs.[63] The stipulation of *a'lamīyah* is thus not exclusively Shiite.

61. al-Shīrāzī al-Fayrūzābādī, *Kitāb al-luma'*, 121; al-Āmidī, *al-Iḥkām*, 4: 204; Ibn Qudāmah al-Maqdisī, *Rawḍat al-nāẓir*, 207; al-Baṣrī, *al-Mu'tamad*, 2: 364; al-Khaṭīb al-Baghdādī, *Kitāb al-faqīh wa'l-mutafaqqih*, 2: 177; al-Shawkānī, *Irshād al-fuḥūl*, 252; Ibn Qayyim al-Jazīyah, *I'lām al-muwaqqi'īn 'an rabb al-'ālamīn*, 4: 196, 201; Jalāl al-Dīn 'Abd al-Raḥmān al-Isnawī, *Nihāyat al-sūl fī sharḥ minhāj al-uṣūl ilā 'ilm al-uṣūl*, 3 vols. (Cairo: Maṭba'at Muḥammad 'Alī Ṣubayḥ, 1969), 3: 217; al-Qarāfī, *Sharḥ tanqīḥ al-fuṣūl*, 443; al-Shāṭibī, *al-Muwāfaqāt*, 4: 193–99.

62. al-Āmidī, *al-Iḥkām*, 4: 204.

63. Abū Ya'lā, *al-'Uddah*, 4: 1226; Abū Isḥāq al-Shīrāzī al-Fayrūzābāī, *al-Tabṣirah fī uṣūl al-fiqh* (Damascus: Dār al-fikr, 1980), 415; idem, *Kitāb al-luma'*, 121; al-Bājī, *Iḥkām al-fuṣūl*, 729–30; Ibn al-Ḥājib, *Mukhtaṣar muntahā al-sūl*, 2: 307; Ibn Qudāmah al-Maqdisī, *Rawḍat al-nāẓir*, 207; al-Āmidī, *al-Iḥkām*, 4: 204; al-Qarāfī, *Sharḥ tanqīḥ al-fuṣūl*, 443; al-Shawkānī, *Irshād al-fuḥūl*, 452.

Twelver Shiite works on *uṣūl al-fiqh* stress this point more consistently than do Sunni works, but a number of prominent Sunni jurists of various *madhhab*s support the same view.

Sunni texts of jurisprudence beginning with al-Ghazālī's *al-Mustaṣfā min ʿilm uṣūl al-fiqh* define a number of subcategories of *ijtihād.* Many such lists have been examined, and it is not necessary to repeat the typology of each author here. It is sufficient to note that Sunni legal theorists between the eleventh and the sixteenth centuries identify from two to seven distinct categories of jurists based on levels of juridical competence.[64] While some of the theorists claim that one or several of the top categories may be empty or unattainable in their own time—reflecting, in part, a common social tendency to bemoan the decadence of the present—they clearly suppose that the remaining categories are adequately represented by contemporary scholars. Furthermore, one suspects that they have firm convictions concerning the proper places of their contemporaries—not to mention themselves—within the graded schemes they propose. While these theoretical typologies of jurists may be interpreted in a variety of ways, they seem to indicate the existence of recognized relative ranks within the legal profession. They may even be read as an attempt to justify the existence of practical ranks within Sunni legal establishments and to describe them in theoretical terms. These categories of jurists are more detailed versions of the division expressed by Ibn al-Humām (d. 861/1456), who sees qualified jurists as falling into two fundamental categories, *akābir,* "master jurists," who speak out on pressing issues, and *aṣāghir,* "lesser jurists," who remain silent out of deference.[65]

Significant evidence for the existence of a recognized relational hierarchy[66] in a medieval Sunni legal establishment is found in al-Qarāfī's work on the duties of *muftī*s and *qāḍī*s.[67] The elaborate protocol al-Qarāfī sets forth for a *muftī* answering a question that has already been answered by another *muftī* demonstrates a highly developed sense of rank within the Sunni legal establishment in thirteenth-century Cairo. The wording of the second *muftī*'s response as well as the position where he chooses to write it on the petition sheet (*ruqʿah*) are determined, according to al-Qarāfī, by the second *muftī*'s rank relative to that of the first. Al-Qarāfī's statements presuppose, of course, that each *muftī* in the city is able to determine approximately where he stands in the pecking order of qualified jurists and that it is common knowledge in the pro-

64. Hallaq, "Gate of Ijtihād," 29–30.

65. Sherman Jackson, "In Defense of Two-Tiered Orthodoxy" (Ph.D. diss., University of Pennsylvania, 1991), 50–52.

66. I am indebted to Professor Roy Mottahedeh (*Loyalty and Leadership,* 178) for this term, which so aptly describes Islamic juridical hierarchies.

67. Jackson, "Two-Tiered Orthodoxy," 50–52.

fession. Both the detail in which al-Qarāfī describes this process and the terms he uses show the sort of negotiation in which the *muftī* was engaging when answering a legal question already posed to other jurists. The key terms in his discussion are *tawāḍu'* or *ittiḍā'*, "considering oneself lower in rank," and *taraffu'*, "considering oneself higher in rank." He instructs the would-be *muftī*,

> If the second *muftī* considers himself lower in rank than the first *muftī*, he should write his response under the first response, but if he considers himself higher in rank than the first *muftī* he should write alongside the first response, either to the right or to the left of it.[68]

These remarks show that the *muftī* is making a conscious claim as to his rank within the legal establishment by writing his *fatwā*s in a certain manner. It is possible to see how, as a result of repeated claims like this one and repeated responses by other *muftī*s, a publicly recognized ranking of the jurists would be established.

Abundant evidence, in addition to these theoretical discussions, points to the existence of actual hierarchical structures within both Shiite and Sunni legal establishments during various historical periods. Certainly the leading Shiite jurists of Buwayhid Baghdad, identified as *ra'īs*, "chief" or "head man," led a hierarchy of sorts. In the Safavid Empire, the *shaykh al-islām* of the capital city and later the *mullā-bāshī* functioned as the head of a hierarchy of Shiite jurists and exerted significant control over those under him.[69] Perhaps the most obvious example of a hierarchical structure in a Sunni setting is the Ottoman juridical hierarchy, headed by the *shaykh al-islām* or *muftī* of Istanbul.[70] Other less formal hierarchies existed in other Sunni centers of learning such as Fez, Cairo, and Damascus throughout the medieval period and into modern times. 'Abd al-Wahhāb al-Sha'rānī's biographical work *al-Ṭabaqāt al-ṣughrā*, for example, portrays an established legal hierarchy in sixteenth-century Cairo in which each scholar was well aware of his own position in the pecking order of jurists within his *madhhab*.[71] While theoretical discussions in Shiite legal texts stress hierarchical principles more consistently than similar Sunni discussions, this difference has had little effect in terms of practice. Strong hierarchies often developed in both Sunni and Shiite historical legal establishments.

68. Shihāb al-Dīn Aḥmad b. Idrīs al-Qarāfī, *al-Iḥkām fī tamyīz al-fatāwā 'an al-aḥkām wa-taṣarrufāt al-qāḍī wa'l-imām* (Cairo: al-Maktab al-thaqāfī, 1989), 122–23.

69. Said Amir Arjomand, "The Mujtahid of the Age and the Mullā-bāshī," in *Authority and Political Culture in Shi'ism*, ed. Said Amir Arjomand (Albany: State University of New York Press, 1988), 80–97; idem, *Shadow of God*, 137; Stewart, "Biographical Notice," 571; idem, "First *Shaykh al-Islām*."

70. See R. C. Repp, *The Müfti of Istanbul* (London: Ithaca Press, 1986).

71. See Stewart, "Islamic Juridical Hierarchies."

THE QUESTION OF LEGAL GUILDS

In a 1984 article, Makdisi first put forward the opinion that the Sunni *madhhabs* or "schools of law" are indeed professional legal guilds. He argues that the *madhhab* satisfies the fundamental criteria of a guild as discussed by Massignon and Cahen and as outlined in Gabriel Baer's study on guilds in Middle Eastern history. Specifically, the legal *madhhab* includes all the people occupied in a branch of learning and constitutes a defined unit located within a defined area. It performs restrictive practices, limiting legal studies to members of the *madhhab* and recognizing as competent jurists only those who have completed their legal studies to the satisfaction of a master jurist. The attainment of mastership in the Sunni *madhhabs* is officially recognized through the granting of the *ijāzat al-tadrīs wa'l-iftā'*. The *madhhab* includes a framework of officers chosen from among the members, such as the professor of law, the repetitor of law, and other positions in the traditional *madrasah,* and is headed by *ra'īs al-madhhab,* the head of the *madhhab* in a given locality. Focusing on the restrictive practices just mentioned, Makdisi has also suggested that the Sunni *madhhabs* exhibit the most basic features of a guild: namely, autonomy and monopoly. That is, in classical Islam, no one outside the *madhhabs*, whether the caliph or the ruler, had control over the opinions of the doctors of law. Furthermore, the *madhhabs* held a monopoly over legal education and the issuing of legal opinions. No outside authority or scholar in another field could have any say in who attained the rank of master jurist.[72] Following Makdisi, Sherman Jackson has also characterized the *madhhab* as a professional guild, suggesting in addition that, at least in the theory of the thirteenth-century Mālikī jurist al-Qarāfī, the *madhhab* showed some features of corporate status, particularly with respect to the privileges of its members vis-à-vis the state.[73]

An examination of the modern Twelver Shiite legal system, called the *Imāmī, Ithnā-'asharī,* or *Ja'farī madhhab,* shows that, like the Sunni *madhhabs*, it satisfies all the above requirements of a guild. With a few differences in terminology, the basic structure of the Shiite *madhhab* is identical to that of the classical Sunni *madhhabs*. The master in this *madhhab* acquires his rank through completion of a highly structured legal education at one of the main Shiite centers of learning. When the student has developed the ability to derive legal rulings from the sources independently, a master jurist may grant him a license recognizing his competence and authority as a jurist. He is then permitted to teach law and issue legal opinions to laymen. This license has been termed *ijāzat al-ijtihād* in the Shiite system in recent centuries rather than *ijāzat al-tadrīs wa'l-iftā'*, as in the Sunni system, but the nature and function of the documents are parallel. The "headman" of the Shiite *madhhab* is termed "the reference for adoption of legal opinions" (*marji' al-taqlīd*) in

72. Makdisi, "Guilds of Law," 233–52; idem, *Rise of Humanism,* 24–38.

73. Jackson, "Two-Tiered Orthodoxy," 42–52, 79–80.

modern times and "the seal of the *mujtahids*" *(khātam al-mujtahidīn)*[74] in the Safavid period, for example, rather than *ra'īs* or *shaykh al-madhhab.* Though scholars of Shiism have not applied the term "guild" to the Twelver Shiite juridical organization, Arjomand has taken these structural features into account, referring to the Twelver Shiite *madhhab* from the Safavid period as an "autonomous hierocracy" or "professionalized hierocracy."[75]

CONCLUSION

The Twelver Shiite legal *madhhab* has developed along lines quite similar to those of the Sunni *madhhabs*, yet differences in terminology and other political and historical factors have obscured this similarity. Perhaps the main terminological difference at present is the widespread use among contemporary Shiites of the terms *mujtahid* and *ijtihād* to designate any qualified jurist, which resulted primarily from the Uṣūlī reaction against the Akhbārīs' attacks on the legal system and constrasts markedly with modern Sunni usage. By the sixteenth century, this usage had become unusual in Sunni circles; Jalāl al-Dīn al-Suyūṭī was subject to severe criticism by contemporaries for claiming to be a full *mujtahid.*[76] Though this term is used continually in Sunni texts of legal theory, in the late medieval and early modern periods it came to designate not merely a competent legal scholar but also either the founder of a new *madhhab* or a legal scholar of extremely high caliber who was particularly innovative. The ordinary qualified jurist was simply called *muftī.* All in all, though, the systems are closely parallel. Each institution provides a standard course of legal education, a regular means for creating an exclusive class of jurists who claim a monopoly of sorts over religious authority. The perceived authoritarian nature of Shiite Islam and the equally perceived egalitarian nature of Sunni Islam create little difference between the two systems. Relational hierarchies of jurists, often informal but nevertheless important, have existed among both groups.

Historical and ideological factors have brought about a few differences between the Twelver Shiite *madhhab* and the *madhhabs* of the Sunnis, which, though they do not obscure their basic structural and functional similarities, are nevertheless significant. Perhaps the most important of these has to do with the jurists' main sources of income. As Makdisi has shown, the Sunni *madrasahs* and Sunni legal education in general were supported mainly by funds derived from pious endowments (*waqf*).[77] Shiite *waqfs* certainly exist, and have played a particularly important role in Shiite legal education in Iran since the establishment of the Safavid Empire. Their importance in the history of the Shiite legal system pales, however, in comparison with their tremendous

74. On the term *khātam al-mujtahidīn* in general, see Arjomand, *Shadow of God,* 133–35.

75. Ibid., 14, 187.

76. Jalāl al-Dīn al-Suyūṭī, *al-Radd 'alā man akhlada ilā al-arḍ wa-jahila anna al-ijtihād fī kull 'aṣr farḍ,* ed. Khalīl al-Mays (Beirut: Dār al-kutub al-'ilmīyah, 1983).

77. Makdisi, *Rise of Colleges,* 35–74.

impact in Sunni circles. Shiites less often benefited from the patronage of the rulers and the ruling military classes, who were the major founders of *waqf* endowments. In societies dominated by the Sunni majority, they often could not count on the political and social stability that would ensure the continued viability of a Shiite *waqf*. For these and other reasons, Shiite legal education in most areas has been less structured, and has generally depended much more heavily on *khums* funds.

The *khums*, literally "fifth," is a religious tax incumbent on Shiite believers, and paid to the top legal authorities in Najaf or Qum, their local representatives, or independent, local legal authorities. Income from the *khums* funds has given the Shiite jurists a greater degree of independence and power than that enjoyed by their Sunni counterparts. The *khums* is paid and collected without any interference from government authorities, who could easily control administration of endowment funds. In most areas of the Islamic world endowed property has either been confiscated or had its administration put under some type of government supervision. Government control of *waqf* has put an end to the independence of the Sunni jurists. During the Mamlūk and Ottoman periods, the extensive involvement of government officials with the appointment and dismissal of jurists from positions at endowed institutions is striking. In modern Egypt, all endowment property is controlled by a government ministry, and the leading jurists, including the rector of al-Azhar and the Grand Muftī (*muftī al-diyār al-miṣrīyah*) are government employees. The Shiite jurists have been able, for the most part, to avoid this fate because they have not relied so heavily on endowment funds. In addition, the use of *khums* funds is not as strictly regulated as endowment income and therefore gives the jurists who collect it greater ability to adjust to new economic circumstances. They have thus not suffered as extensively from the mismanagement of *waqf* property, an endemic problem throughout the Islamic world. In recent times, the top religious authorities have gained in power because improved communication and transportation have centralized the administration of *khums* funds to a greater degree. These factors have worked to grant the Shiite jurists greater economic independence, academic freedom, and political influence than their Sunni counterparts. The *khums* funds have clearly been of great significance for the Twelver Shiite legal system throughout the history of the Occultation. Unfortunately, information concerning the collection, distribution, and use of *khums* funds in the premodern period is scarce, and the topic awaits further detailed study.[78]

78. Scholarship on the *khums* to date includes Calder, "Structure of Authority," 108–46; idem, "Zakāt in Imāmī Shīʿī Jurisprudence, from the Tenth to the Sixteenth Century, A.D.," *BSOAS* 44 (1981): 468–80; idem, "Khums in Imāmī Shīʿī Jurisprudence, from the Tenth to the Sixteenth Century, A.D.," *BSOAS* 45 (1982): 39–47; Sachedina, *Just Ruler*, 237–45; idem, "Al-khums," *JNES* 39 (1980): 275–89; Moussavi, *Religious Authority*, 218–26; Maḥmūd Hāshimī, *Buḥūth fī al-fiqh*, 2 vols. (Qum: Maktabat al-Sayyid Muḥammad al-Hāshimī, 1989).

As a consequence of the relative lack of reliance on endowment funds, the institution of the permanent *madrasah* has played a much more restricted role in the history of Twelver Shiite legal education than it has in Sunni circles. Many of the most prominent professors of law in the Twelver tradition have taught in what may be termed "personal *madrasahs*," which center on the professor himself and disperse on his death or retirement. Al-Shaykh al-Mufīd taught in the mosque he had built next to his house in Darb al-Riyāḥ. Similarly, al-Sharīf al-Murtaḍā and al-Shaykh al-Ṭūsī taught in their houses in al-Karkh. Al-'Allāmah al-Ḥillī and his son Fakhr al-Muḥaqqiqīn both taught in their house in al-Ḥillah. After returning from Jubā' to his studies in Cairo in 944/1537, al-Shahīd al-Thānī built a new house with an adjacent mosque. The mosque, completed the next year, was clearly meant to serve as a *madrasah*. His student Ibn al-'Awdī reports that he would perform the morning prayer in the mosque and then teach for the remainder of the day.[79] Muḥsin al-Amīn describes the continuation of this practice in Jabal 'Āmil into the late nineteenth century. In the village of Bint Jubayl in southern Lebanon, for example, he attended the personal *madrasah* of Mūsā Sharārah (d. 1304/1887), who founded it when he returned there from Najaf in 1297/1880.[80]

To be sure, Shiite *madrasahs* have existed in many periods and regions, particularly in Iran. 'Abd al-Jalīl al-Qazwīnī, writing in the 1160s, lists a number of contemporary Shiite *madrasahs*, including two in Āvah (Ābah), four in Kāshān, and nine in Qum.[81] Shiite *madrasahs* assumed a much more important role following the rise of the Safavid dynasty in Iran. Many Sunni *madrasahs* such as the Manṣūrīyah in Shiraz were converted into Shiite institutions, and many more Shiite *madrasahs* were built in Isfahan, Mashhad, Qum, and other centers of learning under Safavid control. The Fayḍīyah *madrasah* in Qum, built during the Safavid, has become famous as one of the leading institutions of Shiite legal education in the world after 'Abd al-Karīm Ḥā'irī revived the center of learning there in 1922. The increased presence of *madrasahs* in the Shiite system over the last four centuries notwithstanding, their role in the overall history of Shiite jurisprudence is not comparable with their role in Sunni legal education.

Another difference between the Sunni and Shiite *madhhabs* has to do with the jurists' historical relationship with rulers and the theoretical treatment of political sovereignty. Like the Christian kings of medieval Europe, Sunni rulers have traditionally held significant religious authority. Despite statements contrasting the rule of caliphs, or at least the first four caliphs, with

79. 'Alī al-'Āmilī, *al-Durr al-manthūr*, 2: 155, 168.

80. al-Amīn, *Khiṭaṭ Jabal 'Āmil*, 182–86: idem, *A'yān al-shī'ah*, 10: 342.

81. See Jean Calmard, "Le Chiisme Imamite en Iran à l'époque seldjoukide d'après le *Kitāb al-naqḍ*," in *Le Monde Iranien et l'Islam: Sociétés et Cultures*, vol. 1 (Paris: Librairie Droz, 1971), 43–67, esp. 60–61.

temporal kings (*salāṭīn*), this position has had a great deal of support in Sunni doctrine. For example, Ibn Taymīyah states, "Rulers are God's representatives over His worshippers" (*wa'l-wulātu nuwwābu 'Llāhi 'alā 'ibādih*).[82] The authority of Muslim kings is clear in many of the interpretations of *āyat al-umarā'* (Q 4:59) which identify *ūlū al-amr* as rulers.[83] While Sunni jurists, as we have seen, made claims to a virtual monopoly of religious authority, there has been a strong tendency within Sunni Islam from the ninth century until the present to work out a compromise between monarchical and juridical authorities, dividing public law (taxation, public order, defense, and so on) as the domain of the rulers, from private law (marriage, inheritance, contracts, and so on) as the domain of the jurists. This practical compromise may be seen in many features of the judicial system as it developed under Muslim regimes in the Middle Ages, and seems to be reflected as well in treatments of *āyat al-umarā'* which interpret *ūlū al-amr* as both rulers and jurists.[84] Similar in intent is al-Khaṭīb al-Baghdādī's statement that God singled out two classes (*firqahs*) of Muslims as particularly important for the religion: *mujāhidūn,* "fighters," responsible for the defense of Muslim territory, and *muta'allimūn,* "scholars," responsible for preservation of Islamic law.[85] It seems clear from the context that al-Baghdādī is referring not simply to groups within the nascent Muslim community during the time of the Prophet but also to the rulers and legal scholars of his own day.

In Shiite Islam there has been a tendency to see the monarch's rule as a usurpation of the rights of the imam, and this has impeded the working out of a historical compromise between the authority of rulers and jurists. Moves toward compromise have been made when Shiites lived under Shiite sovereigns, particularly during the Safavid period in Iran, where the top jurists often supported the religious authority of the shahs. Many of the treatises written during this period on the obligatory Friday prayer, for example, confirm or imply acceptance of the shahs' authority.[86] These theoretical compromises, however, did not become a standard part of Shiite legal doctrine, in contrast to the law of the Sunnis. As a result the Shiite jurists have often claimed some of the political prerogatives of the imam, while these prerogatives, both in practice and in theory, devolved upon the political rulers in Sunni Islam. Now described

82. Ibn Taymīyah, *al-Siyāsah al-shar'īyah,* 14.

83. Muḥammad b. Jarīr al-Ṭabarī, *Tafsīr al-Ṭabarī,* 14 vols., ed. Maḥmūd Muḥammad Shākir (Cairo: Dār al-ma'ārif, 1961–69), 8: 502.

84. al-Qāḍī al-Nu'mān, *Ikhtilāf uṣūl al-madhāhib,* 26–27 (on prevalent Sunni opinions); Muḥammad b. Aḥmad al-Qurṭubī, *al-Jāmi' li-aḥkām al-Qur'ān,* 20 vols. (Beirut: Dār iḥyā' al-turāth al-'arabī, 1985), 5: 259–61.

85. al-Khaṭīb al-Baghdādī, *Kitāb al-faqīh wa'l-mutafaqqih,* 1: 1.

86. Ḥusayn b. 'Abd al-Ṣamad al-Ḥārithī al-'Āmilī, *al-'Iqd al-ḥusaynī,* ed. al-Sayyid Jawād al-Mudarrisī al-Yazdī (Yazd: Chāp-i gulbahārī, n.d.).

under the rubric of *wilāyat al-faqīh* or *al-wilāyah al-ʿāmmah,* these rights include the right to collect and dispose of alms and *khums* taxes, the right to hold Friday prayer, and even, according to some jurists, the right to declare *jihād* and to govern.[87] In recent years, Shiite jurists have made more forceful claims to exercise exclusive control over these prerogatives during the Occultation. The same arguments that are used to establish the Shiite jurists' exclusive authority over legal matters are also used to establish their authority in these other areas. Until recently, though, this aspect of Shiite law has assumed relatively little importance and remained a theoretical possibility not often voiced in specific, unambiguous terms. Even the imams, when present, had been unable to exercise most of their political prerogatives.

87. Calder has discussed this topic in some detail in the chapter of his thesis entitled "The General Delegation," as has Sachedina in his study of the development of the concept of *wilāyat al-faqīh* (Calder, "Structure of Authority," 147–70; Sachedina, *Just Ruler*).

7
Conclusion

By the end of the eleventh century, in what Makdisi has termed "the triumph of traditionalism," Sunni jurists succeeded in establishing themselves as the foremost religious authorities in Islam and in founding institutions which would ensure their continued dominance of Islamic religious discourse. The system they devised was intended to exclude other claimants to religious authority, particularly the caliphs and the philosophical theologians. According to his analysis, the Ḥanbalī *madhhab* played a particularly prominent role in this historical process, not only heading the traditionalist movement but also achieving the most perfect fusion of law and traditionalism among the Sunni schools of law. It thus epitomized the Sunni legal system, which was essentially traditionalist and had its roots in a concerted battle against the rationalist excesses of philosophical theology. The rise of the *madhhab* system put immense pressure on the theologians, who were forced to join one of the legal *madhhabs* in order to establish their legitimacy as scholars of the religion. The Mu'tazilīs infiltrated the Ḥanafī *madhhab* and the Ash'arīs infiltrated the Shāfi'ī *madhhab,* swelling their ranks and introducing the methods of speculative theology into their legal traditions. These philosophical and theological inroads into legal theory may be seen in the works of *uṣūl al-fiqh* from the late tenth century on. Nevertheless, the Sunni *madhhabs* remained essentially traditionalist.[1]

This analysis of the Sunni legal *madhhabs*' role in Islamic history omits a large and important facet of their dynamics. The rise of the Sunni *madhhabs* presented a challenge not only to those Islamic groups defined by theological

1. See in particular Makdisi, "Ash'arī"; idem, "Juridical Theology"; idem, "The Significance of the Sunni Schools of Law in Islamic Religious History," *IJMES* 10 (1979): 1–8.

differences, such as the Mu'tazilīs and the Ash'arīs, but also to those groups defined by the historical conflict over the imamate, including the Shiites—Twelvers, Zaydīs, and Ismā'īlīs—and Khārijīs. The same forces which worked to exclude the philosophical theologians from participating fully in Islamic religious discourse worked to exclude the Shiites and Khārijīs, and, with the consolidation of the Sunni *madhhabs*, this pressure became a standard feature of Islamic societies that has continued until the present day. The Twelver Shiites serve as an example of this latter category of Islamic groups; their experience reveals the pressures they faced as a result of the rise of the Sunni juridical *madhhabs* and the strategies they adopted in response.

Pressure on the Shiite community from the Sunni *madhhabs* became acute in the tenth century, and the first major Shiite attempts to respond to this system may be dated to that time. The Sunni jurists had by then established a system of legal institutions which defined a community of interpretation and endeavored to restrict Islamic religious discourse to scholars who belonged to one of the recognized *madhhabs* and had completed a standard legal education. All other scholars were excluded from this system. Their voices were not taken into account for the verification of consensus; their variant opinions were not considered valid. Shiite legal opinions that differed from those of the Sunnis were deemed heretical and were even taken as evidence of the Shiites' outright unbelief. Over the centuries, Shiite responses to the accusation of violating the consensus of the Sunni jurists have had a profound effect on the history of Shiite law, legal theory, and legal institutions. The Shiites did not merely import the institution of the *madhhab* as it existed among the Sunnis, nor did the Sunnis merely force the Shiites to conform to their system. It is nevertheless clear that the parameters set by the Sunni legal *madhhabs* guided the Shiites' formulation and implementation of their views concerning the elaboration of Islamic law during the Occultation.

Violation of consensus was not the only accusation directed against the Shiites and not the only means used in attempts to exclude them from Islamic communal and academic life. The plurality of definitions of heresy used against them throughout the premodern period resulted from the simultaneous existence of several paradigms of Islamic religious authority. The legal system often predominated religious discourse, and it certainly influenced the development of Shiite law most directly. Though the jurists claimed to have done so often enough, they did not completely succeed in establishing a monopoly over Islamic religious authority. Other systems continued to exist alongside the legal system, and various sorts of compromises were worked out between them. Law and legal methodology were not the only areas contested between the various Islamic groups.

After the fall of Baghdad to the Mongols and the execution of the caliph in 658/1256, the imamate ceased to be a pressing political issue, but its importance as a bone of contention between the Sunnis and Twelvers had already fallen off with the Occultation of the twelfth imam in 260/874. There was little threat, in the tenth and eleventh centuries, of the Twelver Shiites' rallying around a living revolutionary religious leader against the Abbasid caliphs or other Sunni rulers, even if they harbored qualms concerning their legitimacy.[2] The imamate remained, however, a contested theological issue, having been incorporated by the philosophical theologians into their compendia of Islamic religious doctrine, and as such it continued to be the basis for continual heated polemics between Sunnis and Shiites. Elaborate analyses of historical events during the early years of the Muslim community were undertaken by each side to support their position on the historical imamate. Yet the historical imamate often had little relevance to contemporary political situations. Directly related to the theological issue of the imamate, the most frequent charge of heresy directed at Shiites throughout the premodern period was not that of *mukhālafat al-ijmā'* but rather that of *rafḍ*, generally understood as blasphemy against the Companions, especially Abū Bakr and 'Umar— "the two Shaykhs"—and 'Ā'ishah, the wife of the Prophet who dared to take up arms against 'Alī.[3] In addition, the Shiites were accused of holding heretical opinions on issues in philosophical theology, such as God's justice, because their theology from the Buwayhid period on tended to follow largely Mu'tazilī lines, and the Sunni community by and large had rejected Mu'tazilī positions by the eleventh century.

The existence of parallel systems of religious authority and definitions of orthodoxy and heresy may be seen in several documents depicting debates between Sunni and Shiite scholars. In 951/1545, the Shiite jurist Ḥusayn b. 'Abd al-Ṣamad al-'Āmilī held a private debate with a friend of his, a Ḥanafī jurist in Aleppo. In the course of this debate, he claims he converted his Ḥanafī opponent to Shiism, and in so doing had to prove that Shiite positions on a number of issues were not heretical. He begins the debate by arguing that the Imami *madhhab* is a legitimate legal *madhhab*, showing that Ja'far al-Ṣādiq is at least as acceptable a leader of a legal *madhhab* as Abū Ḥanīfah. The Twelvers' legal tradition goes back to the imams, he argues, and was then carried on by prominent qualified jurists, including Ibn Bābawayh, al-Shaykh al-

2. The Shiites seem to have paid little attention to the Abbasid puppet caliphs in Mamluk Egypt.

3. The Shiites criticize many other Companions in addition to these three, including 'Uthmān, the third caliph; Ḥafṣah, 'Umar's daughter and a wife of the Prophet; Ṭalḥah and al-Zubayr, 'Ā'ishah's allies against 'Alī; Mu'āwiyah, the first Umayyad caliph; and others. Particularly on the popular level, though, Abū Bakr, 'Umar, and 'Ā'ishah bear the brunt of Shiite criticism. See al-Shīrāzī, "al-Nawāqiḍ," passim; Muḥammad Bāqir Majlisī, *Biḥār al-anwār*, 26 vols. (Tehran, 1884–97), 8: 253–389; Etan Kohlberg, "Some Imāmī Shī'ī Views on the Ṣaḥāba," *Jerusalem Studies in Arabic and Islam* 5 (1984): 143–75; Devin J. Stewart, "Popular Shiism in Medieval Egypt: Vestiges of Islamic Sectarian Polemics in Egyptian Arabic," *Studia Islamica* 84 (1996): 35–66.

Mufīd, al-Sharīf al-Murtaḍā, al-Sharīf al-Raḍī, al-Shaykh al-Ṭūsī, Jamāl al-Dīn Ibn Ṭāwūs, Raḍī al-Dīn Ibn Ṭāwūs, Naṣīr al-Dīn al-Ṭūsī, Maytham al-Baḥrānī, al-Muḥaqqiq al-Ḥillī, and al-ʿAllāmah al-Ḥillī. He then addresses the status of the Companions, which takes up the bulk of the text. At the end of the account, he merely mentions that he also discussed theological issues such as predestination (*al-qaḍā' wa'l-qadar*) and the vision of God, and points of law, such as the issue of wiping one's inner boots in performing ablutions (*al-masḥ*), and temporary marriage.[4]

A similar structure is seen in the record of the debate arranged by Nādir Shah in Najaf on 25 Shawwāl 1156/12 December 1743 between Sunni and Shiite scholars of his realm with the aim of getting Twelver Shiism recognized as an orthodox Sunni *madhhab*.[5] In attendance were about seventy Iranian scholars—one Sunni, the Shhāfiʿī *muftī* of Ardalān in Kurdistan, and the rest Shiites—as well as seven Transoxanian scholars, all Ḥanafīs from Bukhārā, and seven Afghani scholars, also all Ḥanafīs. Al-Suwaydī gives a short summary of the debate between ʿAlī Akbar, Mullā Bāshī of the chief muftī of the Iranian Empire, and Baḥr al-ʿIlm Hādī Khōjah, the leader of the Transoxanian delegation. In the account, the Mullā Bāshī asks the Sunni jurists on what grounds they declare Shiites unbelievers and then recants or denies the objectionable positions. He claims that the Shiite scholars present have never blasphemed the Companions and that they recant the opinions that some Companions were unbelievers or miscreants. He also recants the opinion that ʿAlī was superior to Abū Bakr. He then claims that the Shiites present all follow Ashʿarī theology. In addition, he claims that the Shiites do not violate the consensus and that they hold temporary marriage as forbidden.[6] These blatant misrepresentations of standard Shiite doctrine lend credence to the hypothesis that Nādir Shāh had instructed him to reach a reconciliation at all costs. Nevertheless, these two debates—one from the sixteenth century and one from the eighteenth—are telling in that they include three separate definitions of orthodoxy/heresy, based on three different systems of religious authority—those defined by the imamate, theology, and law—simultaneously. The legal system has therefore not been the only factor in defining the relationship of Shiism to Sunni Islam, but it has played an extremely important role in defining Shiism's status vis-à-vis the majority.

The Twelver Shiite legal tradition responded to the challenge of the Sunni

4. Ḥusayn al-ʿĀmilī, *Munāẓarat al-ʿĀmilī maʿa baʿḍ ʿulamā' Ḥalab* (MS, Maktabat al-Marʿashī, Qum, *majmūʿah* 1161, fols. 1–3), fols. 1, fols. 1b–3a.

5. The section of al-Suwaydī's work which treats the events surrounding the debate as well as the debate itself has been printed as *Muʾtamar al-Najaf* (Cairo: al-Maṭbaʿah al-salafīyah, 1973). It was first printed under the title *al-Ḥujaj al-qāṭiʿah liʾttifāq al-firaq al-islāmīyah* (Cairo: Maṭbaʿat al-saʿādah, 1905).

6. al-Suwaydī, *Muʾtamar al-Najaf*, 39–42.

legal *madhhabs* in three main ways, each defined by a particular strategy with respect to the concept of consensus. In the first type of response, Shiites conformed, at least outwardly, to the requirements of the *madhhab* system established by the Sunni jurists. In order to participate in the legal system, they, like the Muʿtazilī and Ashʿarī theologians, affiliated with one of the existing Sunni *madhhabs*. The Twelvers created a Shiite tradition of legal study within the Shāfiʿī *madhhab* which began in the early tenth century and lasted throughout the premodern period. The choice to affiliate with the Shāfiʿī *madhhab* remained quite constant despite the differences in time and geographical region involved, and seems to have stemmed primarily from the semirationalist positions of the jurists who initiated the tradition in the tenth century. They were much more comfortable with the Shāfiʿīs than with the Ḥanafīs, in their view extreme rationalists who blatantly ignored scriptural texts and contradicted them on the basis of analogy. The adoption of this strategy of affiliation with the Shāfiʿī *madhhab* often involved the extensive performance of *taqīyah*, or dissimulation. This allowed Twelver scholars to pass as Sunni students and professors and to minimize the dangers of being accused of heresy while studying, teaching, and granting legal opinions in Sunni environments. The Twelvers' involvement with the Shāfiʿī *madhhab* was not a temporary, ad hoc, measure; for many of the participants in the tradition it involved years of study, teaching, and writing as Shāfiʿīs.

The second type of response was to argue that the consensus used by the Sunni jurists to exclude the Shiites actually included them, for the Twelver jurists constituted a *madhhab* coordinate with, and equivalent to, the other Sunni *madhhabs*. This strategy led to the adoption of a Twelver Shiite theory of consensus in order to establish the legitimacy of the Shiite legal tradition. The Twelver Shiites agreed that the consensus of the Muslim jurists (*ijmāʿ al-ummah*) was an authoritative argument (*ḥujjah*). They claimed, though, that the basis of consensus cited by the Sunnis was incorrect and that the consensus was rendered valid by its inclusion of the imam's opinion. The consensus of the Shiite jurists (*ijmāʿ al-firqah* or *ijmāʿ al-firqah al-muḥiqqah*) was therefore also an authoritative argument. This introduction of a two-tiered theory of consensus allowed the Shiites to engage in debate with the Sunni jurists and argue for their own inclusion within the legal *madhhab* system, yet at the same time retain their theoretical reliance on the opinion of the imam and the guarantee of guidance to the religious truth that went along with it. Al-Shaykh al-Mufīd probably proposed this theory by 380/990, but similar theories may have existed in the work of Ibn al-Junayd and al-Masʿūdī earlier in the tenth century. Al-Mufīd's students al-Sharīf al-Murtaḍā and al-Shaykh al-Ṭūsī elaborated his theory of consensus and established it as a standard feature of Twelver jurisprudence.

The acceptance of the legal principle of consensus occurred concomitantly with the establishment of a regular system for the transmission of legal knowledge following the methodology of the Sunni legal *madhhabs*. It is with the work of al-Shaykh al-Mufīd in the late tenth century in particular that the Twelver or Imami *madhhab,* as a school of law parallel with the Sunni legal *madhhabs*, came into existence. The Twelvers had in al-Mufīd a recognized *ra'īs* or top legal scholar. Al-Mufīd's legal epitome *al-Muqni'ah* served as the basis for a regular law course. The following generation of Twelver jurists recognized him as the source of its expertise in the law. By 380/990, he had authored a manual on jurisprudence, presenting Twelver legal methodology in a form sanctioned by the Sunni *madhhabs*. In addition, al-Mufīd wrote works on the disputed questions of the law. These basic elements of a standard Twelver legal *madhhab* had been in place in the mid-tenth century in the activities of al-Mufīd's older contemporary Ibn al-Junayd al-Iskāfī, but the tradition he established was truncated, since al-Mufīd, al-Sharīf al-Murtaḍā, and al-Shaykh al-Ṭūsī rejected his works. One cannot claim that he inaugurated the Twelver *madhhab* that has continued until the present.

The third type of response involved rejection of consensus and the Sunni legal system of which it was part. Early Akhbārī scholars, termed *aṣḥāb al-ḥadīth,* argued for the severe restriction of rational methods in the law and closer adherence to the literal texts of scripture. Rejecting Sunni and rationalist legal methods, they upheld instead a religious system based on reliance on hadith reports, which embodied the teachings of the imams. This system, they held, was a more authentic extension of the authority of the imams. All religious authority resided in the scripture itself, though the system naturally tended to boost the authority of hadith experts. Active in the tenth and eleventh centuries, the Akhbārīs lost support in the twelfth century, and the Uṣūlīs, the proponents of the Twelver legal *madhhab,* established their dominance of Shiite religious scholarship. The Uṣūlīs consistently upheld and increasingly emphasized the exclusive religious authority of the jurists, particularly with the development in the sixteenth century of the theory of "general agency" (*al-niyābah al-'āmmah*), whereby the jurists claimed designation as general representatives of the Hidden Imam during the Greater Occultation.

Reacting to what they saw as the excessive adoption of rationalist and specifically Sunni methods, the Akhbārī revival of the seventeenth century aimed to reestablish a religious system which relied closely on the hadith of the imams. This wave of Akhbārism was couched specifically as an anti-Sunni, anti-*madhhab* movement. Muḥammad al-Amīn al-Astarābādī, Muḥsin al-Fayḍ al-Kāshānī, and other prominent leaders of the movement rejected the authority of the jurists and saw that a Shiite scholar's utility to the community lay in his ability to relate the hadith of the imams to the believers. They attached no value to consensus, which was, in their view, an illegitimate innovation used by the Sunni jurists to justify and reinforce the historical oppression of the Shiites within the Islamic community. They rejected the institution of the Twelver Shiite legal *madhhab* as inauthentic to Shiism and inconsonant with fundamental Shiite doctrines and accused earlier Shiite jurists of adopting Sunni legal methods, either on purpose or unwittingly. By the nineteenth century, their program had failed in all but a few isolated circles.

Participation in the Shāfiʿī *madhhab* served as an important means for the Twelver jurists to advance Twelver legal theory and strengthen the institution of the Twelver *madhhab* itself. It is no coincidence that the jurists who engaged most actively in the Shāfiʿī *madhhab* also contributed most to the advancement of Twelver legal scholarship. Even if al-Shaykh al-Ṭūsī is left out of consideration on the grounds that we do not have solid evidence of his Shāfiʿī legal studies, al-ʿAllāmah al-Ḥillī, al-Shahīd al-Awwal, and al-Shahīd al-Thānī, all of whom studied Shāfiʿī law and jurisprudence, stand out as giants in the Twelver legal tradition. Many of their great innovations involved the adoption and incorporation of Sunni methods and concepts into Twelver legal scholarship. Thorough examination of their work on both jurisprudence and the points of law is bound to show, as the Akhbārīs intimated, their debt to Shāfiʿī studies. Al-Ḥillī's *Nihāyat al-wuṣūl, Tahdhīb al-wuṣūl,* and *Qawāʿid al-aḥkām,* al-Shahīd al-Awwal's *al-Qawāʿid waʾl-fawāʾid;* and al-Shahīd al-Thānī's *Tamhīd al-qawāʿid* and *Masālik al-afhām* give ample evidence of their intense involvement with the Shāfiʿī legal tradition in particular.

These three strategies, and the interactions between them, have shaped much of the historical development of Twelver law and legal institutions since the tenth century. The question arises whether the Shiites wished to subvert the Shāfiʿī *madhhab,* to turn it to their own purposes once having established their own participation in it. Makdisi has argued that the Ashʿarīs introduced their own agenda into the Shāfiʿī *madhhab,* just as the Muʿtazilīs found the Ḥanafī *madhhab* fertile ground for the propagation of rationalist, philosophical methods.[7] Did Shiites endeavor to do the same? Scholarship to date does not provide any concrete evidence of such goals, yet to answer this question with any certitude would require a careful comparative analysis of the history of Shāfiʿī and Twelver Shiites scholarship on the points of law, a formidable task. That there has been extensive Shāfiʿī influence on the development of Twelver Shiite law and legal theory seems fairly clear, though the topic has yet to be examined in detail. Given the level of contact between the two systems, it is certainly possible that influence occurred in the other direction as well.

The efforts of the Twelver jurists involved in Shāfiʿī legal scholarship brought Twelver jurisprudence closer and closer to Sunni jurisprudence. Beginning with the work of al-Shaykh al-Mufīd, one discerns in Twelver ju-

7. Makdisi, "Significance of the Sunni Schools of Law," 7–8.

risprudence an obvious progression toward assimilation with Sunni legal theory, which culminated, in a sense, in the work of al-Shahīd al-Thānī. Modarressi has suggested that the work of al-Shahīd al-Thānī, Ḥusayn b. ʿAbd al-Ṣamad al-ʿĀmilī, and other sixteenth-century figures set the stage for the revival of Akhbārism in the next century by calling for more freedom in the interpretation of Shiite law and adopting a critical approach to earlier Shiite legal scholarship. While al-Shahīd al-Thānī's work played an important role in provoking the Akhbārī revival, it is not as a forerunner or part of the vanguard of the Akhbārī school. In attacking the theories of Uṣūlī jurists al-Astarābādī was most likely reacting to the work of al-Shahīd al-Thānī in particular, though he preferred to lay blame on the earlier jurist al-ʿAllāmah al-Ḥillī. Al-Shahīd al-Thānī not only had called into question the authenticity of many traditions contained in the four standard Shiite hadith collections but also had espoused positions on legal theory which brought Shiite jurisprudence dangerously close to that of the Sunnis, as his remarks on consensus show. Al-Shahīd al-Thānī and the Akhbārīs certainly shared an interest in earlier works of hadith, but their intentions were poles apart; the Akhbārīs aimed to bolster the authority of the standard hadith compilations and to gather as much "scriptural" material as possible, while al-Shahīd al-Thānī and Ḥusayn b. ʿAbd al-Ṣamad sought, drawing on the methods of historical criticism, to limit the material accepted as probative to that which could be proved authentic according to rationalist standards. Similarly, their criticisms of earlier Shiite legal scholarship were diametrically opposed. While Akhbārīs criticized Shiite jurists for following what they saw as Sunni methods, al-Shahīd al-Thānī criticized them for not applying these same methods consistently or correctly.

One of the chief historical effects of the Akhbārī revival was to strengthen the Twelver legal *madhhab,* for the Uṣūlīs or *mujtahids* adopted a hard line in their efforts to refute the Akhbārīs, upholding many positions that tended to strengthen the position of the jurists and enhance their authority. The insistence on *ijtihād* in the modern Shiite system of legal education almost certainly results from the Akhbārī-Uṣūlī controversy. The position of *taqlīd al-mayyit,* the permissibility of the layman's following the opinions of a deceased jurist, was championed by a number of Akhbārīs, such as Niʿmat Allāh al-Jazāʾirī, but was soundly defeated by the Uṣūlīs.[8] The requirement to practice according to the opinions of a *living mujtahid* has obviously worked to increase the power of the modern Shiite jurists. The Uṣūlī reaction to the Akhbārīs, led by such thinkers as al-Bihbihānī, brought Twelver jurisprudence, once again, closer to Sunni jurisprudence. It reestablished the monopoly of the

8. Niʿmat Allāh al-Jazāʾirī, *Kitāb manbaʿ al-ḥayāt wa-ḥujjīyat qawl al-mujtahid min al-amwāt,* printed with Muḥammad Muḥsin al-Fayḍ al-Kāshānī, *al-Shihāb al-thāqib fī wujūb ṣalāt al-jumʿah al-ʿaynī* (Beirut: Muʾassasat al-aʿlamī li'l-maṭbūʿāt, 1981.

jurists over religious authority as providing the only legitimate extension of the imam's authority during the Occultation. It stressed the prerogative of the jurists to use rational methods in the derivation of the law and maintained the duty of the jurists to profess legal opinions on the basis of their personal research. Actually, the Shiites appear to have preserved features of the classical Sunni system that have since fallen by the wayside in Sunni environments. Certainly the modern Twelver legal curriculum more closely resembles that followed in late medieval Islamic centers of legal scholarship than does that of al-Azhar in terms of both content and method. The *ijāzat al-ijtihād* seems, too, to preserve the practice of granting the *ijāzat al-tadrīs wa'l-iftā'*, which has been lost at Sunni institutions, such as al-Azhar.

Scholarship on Twelver Shiite law has tended to portray the rise of the legal system and the concomitant authority of the jurists as a logical result of the Occultation of the imam or as a stopgap measure instituted to deal with the authority vacuum brought about by the Occultation. This explanation is severely flawed. It is clear that the legal *madhhab*s were first developed by the Sunnis. They were formed, as institutions for the regular transmission of legal knowledge, not in the eighth century when their eponymous founders lived, but in the late ninth and early tenth centuries. Similarly, it cannot be argued that Ja'far al-Ṣādiq founded the Twelver Shiite legal *madhhab* as an organized institution. The early Shiites did not need such a system, and many saw it as illegitimate in its conception; but when the Sunni legal *madhhab*s threatened to exclude them from the pale of orthodoxy, a number of Shiite scholars, primarily those living in a mixed environment, began to form their own organized institution of legal education and practice, the Imami or Twelver *madhhab*. This process took place in the time of al-Shaykh al-Mufīd in the late tenth century.

Among the most vocal representatives of the Sunni legal *madhhab* system were the Ḥanbalīs. The Ḥanbalīs and their traditionalist allies played a major role in opposing the Twelver Shiites, just as they played a pivotal role in the struggle against the Mu'tazilīs. The Shiites' greatest enemies in Baghdad, they put the greatest amount of social pressure on the Shiite minority in al-Karkh; the two groups were in nearly constant conflict. When, in the early eleventh century, the traditionalists succeeded in gaining the support of al-Qādir, pressure on the Shiites increased markedly. Al-Qādir's declarations forbade the public teaching of Shiite and Mu'tazilī doctrines, and those scholars who wished to retain official positions were required to disavow their suspect views. Sunni traditionalists refused to debate the leading Twelver scholars on the grounds that they were heretics whose opinions were invalid. While the Ḥanbalī role in exerting pressure on the Shiites is undeniable, it would nevertheless be wrong to claim that it was only they and other traditionalists who provoked the Twelvers' foundation and justification of a juridical *madhhab*. The theoretical elaboration of Twelver jurisprudence owed as much to the Mu'tazilīs as it did to the Ḥanbalīs and other traditionalists. The contemporary Sunni theorist with whom the legal works of al-Shaykh al-Mufīd, al-Sharīf al-Murtaḍā, and al-Shaykh al-Ṭūsī engaged most directly was undoubtedly the Mu'tazilī theologian and Shāfi'ī jurist al-Qāḍī 'Abd al-Jabbār. Equally subject to traditionalist attacks and threatened with exclusion from public religious discourse, the Mu'tazilīs and the Twelvers were quite willing to debate each other and partake in scholarly exchanges. Thus, while the early works of Twelver Shiite jurisprudence were clearly formulated in response to a traditionalist threat, they bore a heavy imprint of Mu'tazilī thought, despite the Twelvers' aversion to the extreme rationalism of the Ḥanafīs.

The significance of the Sunni legal *madhhabs* in Islamic religious history therefore is also evident in that they brought about the rise of parallel institutions among the Twelver Shiites, the Zaydi Shiites, and perhaps among the Khārijīs as well. Examination of the religious history of the tenth and eleventh centuries shows that not only four *madhhabs* were created and survived the period of consolidation but rather six, including the Imami and Zaydi *madhhabs*. While the Jarīrī and Ẓāhirī *madhhabs* died out in the course of the eleventh century and the Mālikī *madhhab* virtually died out in the east, the Imami legal *madhhab* was quite successful in Iraq, Iran, Syria, and, before the advent of the Ayyūbids, in Egypt. In the sixteenth century, Ḥusayn b. 'Abd al-Ṣamad al-'Āmilī could claim that the Imami jurists far outnumbered the Ḥanbalīs and the Mālikīs, for example.[9]

A cursory analysis of the history of Zaydī jurisprudence allows one to draw a number of parallels between the Twelver and the Zaydī experience, suggesting that Zaydī responses to the Sunni *madhhab* system closely match the Twelvers' historical responses. The field of Zaydī jurisprudence is considerably more obscure than that of the Twelvers, but its outlines are becoming clearer as important primary sources are published.[10] Like the Twelvers, the Zaydīs participated in the Sunni *madhhabs* beginning in the tenth century. In the early period, they affiliated most often with the Ḥanafī *madhhab*. As mentioned in chapter 3, the Zaydī Imam Abū 'Abd Allāh al-Dā'ī Muḥammad b. al-Ḥasan b. al-Qāsim (d. 360/970–71) studied law with the famous Ḥanafī jurist Abū al-Ḥasan al-Karkhī in Baghdad.[11] The eleventh-century Zaydī scholar Abū al-Sa'd al-Muḥassin b. Muḥammad al-Ḥākim al-Jashmī al-Bayhaqī (d. 494/1100–1101) was also an adept of Mu'tazilī theology and Ḥanafī law. In the late

9. Ḥusayn al-'Āmilī, "Munāẓarat al-'Āmilī," fol. 1b.

10. See, for example, Ibn al-Murtaḍā, *al-Baḥr al-zakhkhār;* Muḥammad b. Ismā'īl al-Amīr al-Ṣan'ānī *Uṣūl al-fiqh al-musammā bi-Ijābat al-sā'il sharḥ Bughyat al-āmil,* ed. Ḥusayn b. Aḥmad al-Sayāghī and Muḥammad Ḥasan Maqbūlī al-Ahdal (Beirut: Mu'assasat al-risālah, 1988).

11. Ibn al-Murtaḍā, *Kitāb Ṭabaqāt al-mu'tazilah,* 113–14.

medieval period, when Zaydism was restricted to Yemen and Zaydī contact with the Ḥanafīs diminished, some Zaydī scholars participated in the Shāfiʿī *madhhab*. The jurist Muḥammad b. Ibrāhīm Ibn al-Wazīr (d. 840/1436–37) studied Shāfiʿī law in Mecca under the Shāfiʿī *qāḍī* Muḥammad b. ʿAbd Allāh b. Abī Ẓahīrah. Muḥammad b. Ismāʿīl Ibn al-Amīr (d. 1182/1768–69) studied the Shāfiʿī legal work *Sharḥ al-ʿumdah* by Ibn Daqīq al-ʿĪd al-Manfalūṭī (d. 702/1302), also in Mecca, under Muḥammad b. Aḥmad al-Asadī.[12] Also like the Twelvers, the Zaydīs probably established a legal *madhhab* before the end of the tenth century. The Zaydī *madhhab* may have begun already with the activities of the Imam Abū ʿAbd Allāh al-Dāʿī, who had studied under al-Karkhī. By the late tenth century, the Zaydīs, like the Twelvers, developed a two-tiered theory of consensus. Before 385/995, Abū Ṭālib Yaḥyā b. al-Ḥusayn b. Hārūn al-Nāṭiq bi'l-Ḥaqq (d. 424/1033) proposed the theory that *ijmāʿ ahl al-bayt* was a binding argument (*ḥujjah*). At the present state of research, it is not clear whether the Zaydī tradition boasted an anti-*madhhab* movement parallel with that of the Twelver Akhbārīs. The scholar Ḥamīdān b. Yaḥyā b. Ḥamīdān (d. 656/1258) certainly criticized his Zaydī fellows for their adoption of Muʿtazilī theology,[13] and he and others may have denounced the adoption of the legal *madhhab* along Sunni lines as well.

The Twelver Shiite legal *madhhab* was not the only possible system available to fill the authority vacuum caused by the Occultation of the twelfth imam. It can therefore not be seen as a logical development within the structure of Twelver Shiism resulting from the Occultation. The rise and continued development of the Twelver Shiite legal *madhhab* can be explained primarily as the result of pressure from the Sunni majority. A number of other systems of religious authority were possible and were tried, either by the Twelvers themselves or by other Shiite groups. A system where theoretical contact with the imam was maintained through the medium of a representative existed within Twelver Shiism for nearly seventy years, and is currently followed by the Bohra Ismāʿīlī sects (Dā'ūdī and Sulaymānī), each of which recognizes a *dāʿī muṭlaq*, "supreme propagandist," who represents the hidden Imam. The Nizārī Ismāʿīlīs rediscovered their line of imams in the twelfth century, after it had been cut off following the conflicts over succession to the Fatimid caliph al-Mustanṣir (d. 497/1094). A system of religious authority controlled by philosophical theologians was also conceivable, and steps were taken to institute such a system during the Muʿtazilī-led inquisition of the first half of the ninth century. A system based on the authority of hadith experts was proposed and established by the Akhbārīs during certain periods of Twelver history, and,

12. Aḥmad Muḥammad Ṣubḥī, *al-Zaydīyah* (Alexandria: al-Zahrā' li'l-iʿlām al-ʿarabī, 1984), 228–54, 435–500, esp. 438, 501–38, esp. 502.

13. Ibid., 395–434.

according to them, was more authentic to Shiite tradition. The success and strength of the Twelver Shiite legal *madhhab* is due, in large part, to the importance of the Sunni legal *madhhab*s in Islamic society at large and not the result of, or a strange quirk brought about by, the Occultation of the twelfth imam. Corroboration of this assessment may be found in the Zaydi tradition, where a Zaydi legal *madhhab* was established, roughly simultaneously with the Twelver legal *madhhab,* in the tenth century. It too has lasted until the present day, and it too has made strong claims for the religious authority of the jurists, even though the Zaydi theory of the imamate differs significantly from that of the Twelvers and given that living imams were present throughout most of the historical development of the *madhhab.*

This study provides some indication of the extent to which the consolidation of the Sunni *madhhab*s controlled the subsequent history of Islamic religious doctrine and institutions, not only within the Sunni community but also within the main marginal or minority Islamic groups of the Shiites and the Khārijīs. Examination of the Twelver Shiite tradition shows that the hegemonic influence of the legal system functioned over the long run to create a large degree of similarity between what had begun as disparate Islamic groups. The Sunni legal system and the theory of consensus on which it was based set the ground rules for marginal sects' negotiation of their identity and place with respect to Islamic legal orthodoxy and the system of legal education. Within this framework, the Twelver Shiite jurists have developed a legal institution which differs in a few minor points from the four Sunni *madhhab*s. The conceptualization of this *madhhab* reached a high point, in terms of similarity to and compatibility with the Sunni *madhhab*s, in the sixteenth century in the thought of Zayn al-Dīn al-ʿĀmilī and then again in the thought of al-Bihbihānī in the eighteenth century. While the Shiite doctors of the law do not renounce belief in the imamate as a fundamental tenet of Islam and must therefore hold Sunnis to be misguided heretics or unbelievers, they nevertheless follow Sunni methods and principles quite closely, and in some cases seem to have preserved aspects of the classical Sunni legal system that have since passed out of existence in Sunni environments. The proponents of the fifth *madhhab* represent those scholars who most regularly tended to espouse the integration—at least formally—of Shiism into the majority community. The extent of integration proposed in the theories of these individual Shiite scholars varied, as did Sunni jurists' willingness to accept these proposals. There was always a tension between the Shiites' desire to participate in the majority community and their belief that they were the chosen sect of Islam, *al-firqah al-nājiyah,* alone blessed with divine guidance to true faith.

Arnold Toynbee has claimed that all history is a response to a challenge. The threat which faced the Shiites, that of exclusion from the community by the Sunni juridical *madhhab*s, presented one of the most formidable challenges within the intellectual history of Islam. It is this challenge, more than any other, which brought about the formation of the Twelver Shiite *madhhab* and the establishment of a legal system based on the authority of the jurists. The Twelvers succeeded in creating a *madhhab* that is essentially functionally equivalent to the Sunni *madhhab*s that has persevered from the tenth until the present century with remarkable intellectual vigor. It has never been fully integrated into the Sunni *madhhab* system, but every so often there appears an indication that it has gained a large degree of acceptance on the part of Sunni jurists. In the comparative legal work *'Umdat al-ṭālib fī ma'rifat al-madhāhib,* the Ḥanafī jurist Muḥammad b. 'Abd al-Raḥmān al-Samarqandī (d. 721/1321) recorded the law of the Twelver Shiite and Ẓāhirī *madhhab*s in addition to that of the four standard Sunni *madhhab*s.[14] The 1959 *fatwā* of Shaykh Maḥmūd Shaltūt, the rector of al-Azhar, recognizing the Twelver and Zaydi legal traditions as legitimate *madhhab*s coordinate with the Sunni *madhhab*s is but one recent tribute to the efforts Shiite jurists have made to participate in the greater Islamic legal system.

14. Ibn Quṭlūbughā, *Tāj al-tarājim,* 57.

Acknowledgments

This is a substantially revised version of a dissertation completed in 1991 at the University of Pennsylvania entitled "Twelver Shīʿī Jurisprudence and Its Struggle with Sunni Consensus." Itself a study of educational institutions, it is in large measure a product of the two institutions where I received my training, the Near Eastern Studies Department at Princeton University and the Oriental Studies Department (now Asian and Middle Eastern Studies) at the University of Pennsylvania. I express my gratitude to my professors in both departments for their guidance and encouragement. The book owes a special debt to three mentors in particular. The late Professor Martin Dickson first sparked my interest in Shiism; it was his inspiration that led me to investigate the lives and works of Twelver Shiite scholars. Professor George Makdisi introduced me to the study of Islamic law and continually imparted, through advice and example, what it means to live the life of a scholar. Professor Adel Allouche taught me to approach problems critically and challenged me to deepen my knowledge of Shiism and medieval Islamic history. For his steady encouragement, generous assistance, and constructive criticism I am especially grateful.

In the intervening years, a grant from the University Research Committee of Emory University in 1993 enabled me to carry out extensive revisions and incorporate new materials into the manuscript. Drs. Hossein Modarressi, Roy Mottahedeh, Paul Walker, and Kevin Reinhart were kind enough to read drafts of the entire work or various sections, and I thank them for their valuable comments and suggestions. Needless to say, errors and shortcomings are entirely my own.

I am most grateful to the editors of *Islamic Law and Society* and E. J. Brill for their kind permission to use material from the following study: Devin J. Stewart, "Ḥusayn b. ʿAbd al-Ṣamad al-ʿĀmilī's Treatise for Sultan Suleiman and the Shīʿī Shāfiʿī Legal Tradition," *Islamic Law and Society* 4 (1997): 156–99.

Finally, I am indebted to many individuals for their support during the years I have spent working on this project. To my parents, Douglas and Dorothy, my brother Daniel and sister Gina, and my exceptional friends Farimah Partovi and Emad Younan go special thanks for their enduring support through trying times. Thanks are also due to the members of RRALL and Peggy Guinan and Diane Moderski of the Oriental Studies Department, without whose help, wit, and cheer this work would not have been possible.

References

UNPUBLISHED WORKS

al-'Āmilī, Ḥusayn b. 'Abd al-Ṣamad al-Ḥārithī. "Munāẓarat al-'Āmilī ma'a ba'ḍ 'ulamā' Ḥalab." MS. Maktabat al-Mar'ashī, Qum, *majmū'ah* 1161, fols. 1–3.

———. *Nūr al-ḥaqīqah wa-nawr al-ḥadīqah.* MS. Leiden University Library, Oriental Collection 979.

Beeson, Caroline J. "The Origins of Conflict in the Ṣafawī Religious Institution." Ph.D. diss., Princeton University, 1982.

Calder, Norman. "The Structure of Authority in Imāmī Shī'ī Jurisprudence." Doctoral diss., School of Oriental and African Studies, University of London, 1980.

Dickson, Martin B. "Shah Tahmasp and the Uzbeks." Ph.D. diss., Princeton University, 1958.

al-Ḥillī, Jamāl al-Dīn al-Ḥasan b. Yūsuf Ibn al-Muṭahhar (al-'Allāmah al-Ḥillī). "Nihāyat al-wuṣūl ilā 'ilm al-uṣūl." MS. Princeton University Library, Arabic New Series, 376.

Jackson, Sherman. "In Defense of Two-Tiered Orthodoxy: A Study of Shihāb al-Dīn al-Qarāfī's *Kitāb al-iḥkām fī tamyīz al-fatāwā 'an al-aḥkām wa taṣarrufāt al-qāḍī wa al-imām.*" Ph.D. diss., University of Pennsylvania, 1991.

Makdisi, George. "Professionalized Higher Learning: Past and Present." Paper presented at Symposium on Occidentalism, University of Pennsylvania, Philadelphia, March 23–24, 1990.

Melchert, Christopher. "The Formsation of the Sunni Schools of Law, Ninth-Tenth Centuries C.E." Ph.D. diss., University of Pennsylvania, 1992.

Newman, Andrew. "The Development and Political Significance of the Rationalist (Uṣūlī) and Traditionalist (Akhbārī) Schools in Imāmī Shī'ī History from the Third/Ninth to the Tenth/Sixteenth Century." Ph.D. diss., University of California, Los Angeles, 1986.

Reinhart, A. Kevin. "Guilding the *Madhhab:* The 'Schools' of Islamic Law and Their Significance." Paper presented at the American Oriental Society, Miami, March 1997.

al-Shīrāzī, Mīrzā Makhdūm. *"al-Nawāqiḍ fī al-radd 'alā al-rawāfiḍ."* MS. Princeton University Library, Garrett Collection, 2629.

Stewart, Devin J. "Islamic Juridical Hierarchies and the Office of Marji' al-Taqlīd." Paper from *Shī'ī Islam: Faith, Experience and Worldview,* Temple University-University of Pennsylvania, Philadelphia, September 1993.

Zysow, Aron. "The Economy of Certainty: An Introduction to the Typology of Islamic Legal Theory." Ph.D. diss., Harvard University, 1984.

PUBLISHED WORKS

al-'Abbādī, Muḥammad b. Aḥmad. *Kitāb ṭabaqāt al-fuqahā' al-shāfi'īyah.* Ed. Gösta Vitestam. Leiden: E. J. Brill, 1964.

Abū Ya'lā, al-Qāḍī. *al-'Uddah fī uṣūl al-fiqh.* 5 vols. Ed. Aḥmad b. 'Alī Sayr al-Mubārakī. Riyāḍ, 1990.

Afsaruddin, Asma. "An Insight into the Ḥadīth Methodology of Jamāl al-Dīn Aḥmad b. Ṭāwūs." *Der Islam* 72 (1995): 25–46

Algar, Hamid. *Religion and State in Iran: The Role of the Ulama in the Qajar Period.* Berkeley: University of California Press, 1969.

al-'Allāmah al-Ḥillī. See al-Ḥillī, Jamāl al-Dīn al-Ḥasan b. Yūsuf Ibn al-Muṭahhar.

Allouche, Adel. Review of Patricia Crone and Martin Hinds, *God's Caliph. Muslim World* 79 (1989): 71–74.

al-Āmidī, Sayf al-Dīn. *al-Iḥkām fī uṣūl al-aḥkām.* 4 vols. Cairo, n.d.

al-'Āmilī, 'Alī b. Muḥammad. *al-Durr al-manthūr min al-ma'thūr wa-ghayr al-ma'thūr.* 2 vols. Qum: Maṭba'at mihr, 1978.

al-'Āmilī, Bahā' al-Dīn Muḥammad. *Ḥurmat dhabā'iḥ ahl al-kitāb.* Ed. Zuhayr al-A'rajī. Beirut: Mu'assasat al-a'lamī li'l-maṭbū'āt, 1990.

———. *al-Wajīzah.* Ed. Muḥammad al-Mishkāt. Tehran: Maṭba'at al-majlis al-shūrī, 1937.

———. *Zubdat al-uṣūl.* Iṣfahān: Dār al-ṭibā'ah, 1899.

al-'Āmilī, Ḥasan b. Zayn al-Dīn. *Ma'ālim al-dīn wa-malādh al-mujtahidīn.* Tehran, n.d.

al-'Āmilī, Ḥusayn b. 'Abd al-Ṣamad al-Ḥārithī. *Arba'ūn ḥadīth.* Ed. Ḥusayn 'Alī Maḥfūz. Tehran: Maṭba'at al-ḥaydarī, 1957.

———. *al-'Iqd al-ḥusaynī.* Ed. al-Sayyid Jawād al-Mudarrisī al-Yazdī. Yazd: Chāp-i gulbahārī, n.d.

———. *Wuṣūl al-akhyār ilā uṣūl al-akhbār.* Ed. 'Abd al-Laṭīf al-Kūhkamarī. Qum: Maṭba'at al-khayyām, 1981.

al-'Āmilī, Nūr al-Dīn. *al-Shawāhid al-makkīyah fī madāḥid ḥujaj al-khayālāt al-madanīyah,* on the margin of the lithograph edition of *al-Fawā'id al-madanīyah.* Tehran, 1902.

al-'Āmilī, Zayn al-Dīn (al-Shahīd al-Thānī). *Munyat al-murīd fī ādāb al-mufīd wa'l-mustafīd.* Najaf: Maṭba'at al-gharī, 1950–51.

———. *al-Rawḍah al-bahīyah fī sharḥ al-lum'ah al-dimashqīyah.* 10 vols. Najaf: Maṭba'at al-ādāb, 1967.

———. *Risālah fī ṣalāt al-jum'ah.* In his *Rasā'il al-Shahīd,* 50–101. Qum: Maktabah-yi baṣīratī, 1895–96.

———. *Risālah ḥawl ijmā'āt al-Shaykh al-Ṭūsī.* In *al-Dhikrā al-alfīyah li'l-Shaykh al-Ṭūsī,* 2: 790–98. Mashhad: Dānishkadah-yi ilāhīyāt va-ma'ārif-i islāmī, 1971.

———. *Sharḥ al-bidāyah fī 'ilm al-dirāyah.* N.p., 1891–92.

———. *Tamhīd al-qawā'id al-uṣūlīyah wa'l-'arabīyah li-tafrī' fawā'id al-aḥkām al-shar'īyah.* Tehran, 1855.

al-Amīn, Muḥsin. *A'yān al-shī'ah.* 10 vols. Beirut: Dār al-ta'āruf li'l-maṭbū'āt, 1984.

———. *Khiṭaṭ Jabal 'Āmil.* Ed. Ḥasan al-Amīn. Beirut: al-Dār al-'ālamīyah, 1983.

al-A'rajī al-Ḥusaynī, 'Amīd al-Dīn b. 'Abd al-Muṭṭalib. *Munyat al-labīb fī sharḥ al-tahdhīb.* Lucknow: Maṭba' Ḍiyā' al-Riḍā, 1898–99.

al-Ardabīlī, Muḥammad b. 'Alī. *Jāmi' al-ruwāt.* 2 vols. Qum: Maktabat Āyat Allāh al-

Mar'ashi, 1983.

Arjomand, Said Amir. "The Consolation of Theology: The Shi'ite Doctrine of Occultation and the Transition from Chiliasm to Law." *Journal of Religion* 76 (1996).

———. "The Crisis of the Imamate and the Institution of Occultation in Twelver Shi'ism: A Sociohistorical Perspective." *IJMES* 28 (1996): 491–515.

———. "Imam *Absconditus* and the Beginnings of a Theology of Occultation: Imami Shi'ism *circa* 280–90 A.H./900 A.D." *JAOS* 117 (1997): 1–12.

———. "The Mujtahid of the Age and the Mullā-bāshī: An Intermediate Stage in the Institutionalization of Religious Authority in Shi'ite Iran." In *Authority and Political Culture in Shi'ism,* 80–97. Ed. Said Amir Arjomand. Albany: State University of New York Press, 1988.

———. *The Shadow of God and the Hidden Imam: Religion, Political Order, and Societal Change in Shi'ite Iran from the Beginning to 1890.* Chicago: University of Chicago Press, 1984.

———. Trans. "Two Decrees of Shah Ṭahmāsp Concerning Statecraft and the Authority of Shaykh 'Alī Al-Karakī." In *Authority and Political Culture in Shi'ism,* 250–62. Ed. Said Amir Arjomand. Albany: State University of New York Press, 1988.

al-Ash'arī, Abū al-Ḥasan. *Maqālāt al-islāmīyīn wa'khtilāf al-muṣallīn.* Ed. Helmut Ritter. Wiesbaden: Franz Steiner Verlag, 1963.

al-Astarābādī, Muḥammad Amīn. *al-Fawā'id al-madanīyah.* Tehran, 1904.

Baer, Gabriel. "Guilds in Middle Eastern History." In *Studies in the Economic History of the Middle East.* Ed. M. A. Cook. London: Oxford University Press, 1970.

Bagley, F. R. G. "The Azhar and Shī'ism." *Muslim World* 50 (1960): 122–29.

al-Bahī, Muḥammad. *al-Azhar tārīkhuh wa-taṭawwuruh.* Cairo: Wizārat al-awqāf, 1964.

Baḥr al-'Ulūm, Sayyid Muḥammad Mahdī. *Rijāl al-Sayyid Baḥr al-'Ulūm.* 4 vols. Najaf: Maṭba'at al-ādāb, 1965–67.

al-Baḥrānī, Yūsuf. *Lu'lu'at al-Baḥrayn.* Ed. Muḥammad Ṣādiq Baḥr al-'Ulūm. Najaf: Maṭba'at nu'mān, 1966.

al-Bājī, Abū al-Walīd. *Iḥkām al-fuṣūl fī aḥkām al-uṣūl.* Ed. Abdel-Magid Turki. Beirut: Dār al-gharb al-islāmī, 1986.

al-Baṣrī, Abū al-Ḥusayn Muḥammad b. 'Alī. *al-Mu'tamad fī uṣūl al-fiqh.* 2 vols. Ed. Khalīl al-Mays. Beirut: Dār al-kutub al-'ilmīyah, 1983.

———. *Sharḥ al-'Umad.* 2 vols. Ed. 'Abd al-Ḥakīm b. 'Alī Abū Zunayd. Medina: Maktabat al-'ulūm wa'l-ḥikam, 1989–90.

Bayat, Mangol. *Mysticism and Dissent: Socioreligious Thought in Qajar Iran.* Syracuse, New York: Syracuse University Press, 1982.

Bernand, Marie. *L'accord unanime de la communauté comme fondement des statuts légaux de l'islam.* Paris, 1970.

———. "Ḥanafī *Uṣūl al-Fiqh* through a Manuscript of al-Ǧaṣṣāṣ." *JAOS* 105 (1985): 623–35.

———. art. "Idjmā'." *EI*².

———. "L'Iǧmā' chez 'Abd al-Ǧabbār et l'objection d'an-Naẓẓām." *Studia Islamica* 30 (1969): 27–38.

al-Bihbihānī, Muḥammad al-Bāqir. *Risālat al-akhbār wa'l-ijtihād.* Tehran, n.d.

Binder, Leonard. "The Proofs of Islam: Religion and Politics in Iran." In *Arabic and Islamic Studies in Honor of Hamilton A. R. Gibb.* Ed. George Makdisi. Leiden: E. J. Brill, 1965.

Brinner, W. M. art. "Ibn Ṭūlūn." *EI*².

Brockelmann, Carl. *GAL.* 2d ed. 2 vols. Leiden: E. J. Brill, 1943–49, 3 supp., 1937–42.

Browne, E. G. *A Literary History of Persia.* 4 vols. Cambridge: Cambridge University Press, 1924.

Brunschvig, Robert. "Les Uṣūl al-fiqh Imāmites à leur stade ancien (Xe et XIe siècles)." In *Ètudes d'Islamologie,* 3: 323–34. Ed. Abdel Magid Turki. Paris: G. P. Maisonneuve et Larose, 1976.

———. "———." In *Le Shī'isme Imamite,* 201–13. Ed. Tawfiq Fahd. Paris: Presses universitaires françaises, 1970.

Burton, Sir Richard Francis. "Terminal Essay." In *The Book of the Thousand Nights and a Night,* 10: 63–302. Trans. Richard Burton. London: Burton Club, n.d.

Busse, Heribert. *Chalif und Grosskönig: Die Buyiden im Iraq (945–1055).* Wiesbaden: Franz Steiner, 1969.

Cahen, Claude. art. "Buwayhids." *EI*².

Cahn, Zvi. *The Rise of the Karaite Sect.* New York: M. Tausner, 1937.

Calder, Norman. "Doubt and Prerogative: The emergence of an Imāmī Shī'ī theory of *Ijtihād.*" *Studia Islamica* 70 (1989): 57–78.

———. "*Ikhtilāf* and *Ijmā'* in Shāfi'ī's *Risāla.*" *Studia Islamica* 58 (1984): 55–81.

———. "Judicial Authority in Imāmī Shī'ī Jurisprudence." *BRISMES* 6 (1979): 104–8.

———. "Khums in Imāmī Shī'ī Jurisprudence from the Tenth to the Sixteenth Century, A.D." *BSOAS* 45 (1982): 39–47.

———. *Studies in Early Muslim Jurisprudence.* Oxford: Clarendon Press, 1993.

———. "Zakāt in Imāmī Shī'ī Jurisprudence from the Tenth to the Sixteenth Century, A.D." *BSOAS* 46 (1981): 468–80.

Calmard, Jean. "Le Chiisme Imamite en Iran à l'époque seldjoukide d'après le *Kitāb al-naqḍ.*" In *Le Monde Iranien et l'Islam: Sociétés et Cultures,* vol. 1. Geneva: Librairie Droz, 1971.

———. art. "Ḳum." *EI*².

———. art. "Marja'-i taḳlīd." *EI*².

Chaumont, Eric. "Bāqillānī, théologien ash'arite et usūliste mālikite, contre les légistes à propos de l'ijtihād et de l'accord unanime de la communauté." *Studia Islamica* 79 (1994): 79–102.

Cole, Juan R. "Imami Jurisprudence and the Role of the Ulama: Mortaza Ansari on Emulating the Supreme Exemplar." In *Religion and Politics in Iran: Shī'ism from Quietism to Revolution,* 33–46. Ed. Nikki R. Keddie. New Haven: Yale University Press, 1983.

———. *Roots of North Indian Shī'ism in Iran and Iraq: Religion and State in Awadh, 1722–1859.* Berkeley: University of California Press, 1988.

———. "Shī'ī Clerics in Iraq and Iran, 1722–1780: The Akhbārī-Uṣūlī Controversy Reconsidered." *Iranian Studies* 18 (1985): 3–34.

Crone, Patricia, and Martin Hinds. *God's Caliph: Authority in the First Centuries of Islam.* Cambridge: Cambridge University Press, 1986.

Coulson, Noel J. *A History of Islamic Law.* Edinburgh: Edinburgh University Press, 1964.

Dabashi, Hamid. *Authority in Islam.* New Brunswick, New Jersey: Transaction Publishers, 1989.

al-Dabūsī, 'Ubayd b. 'Īsā. *Ta'sīs al-naẓar.* See al-Karkhī, al-Ḥasan.

Donaldson, Dwight M. *The Shi'ite Religion: A History of Islam in Persia and Iraḳ.* London: Luzac & Co., 1933.

Eberhard, Elke. *Osmanische Polemik gegen die Safawiden im 16. Jahrhundert nach arabischen Handschriften.* Freiburg: Klaus Schwarz Verlag, 1970.

Eickelmann, Dale. *The Middle East: An Anthropological Approach.* Englewood Cliffs, New Jersey: Prentice Hall, 1981.

Eliash, Joseph. "Ithnā'asharī-Shī'ī Juristic Theory of Political and Legal Authority." *Studia Islamica,* 29 (1969): 17–30.

———. "Misconceptions Regarding the Juridical Status of the Iranian 'Ulamā'." *IJMES* 10 (1979): 9–25.

Elisséeff, Nikita. "Les Monuments de Nūr ad-Dīn: Inventaire, notes archéologiques et bibliographiques." *Bulletin d'études orientales* 13 (1949–51): 5–49.

———. *Nūr al-Dīn: Un grand prince musulman de Syrie au temps des croisades 511–569/1118–1174.* 3 vols. Damascus: Institut français de Damas, 1967.

Encyclopaedia Iranica. London: Routledge and Kegan Paul, 1983–present.

EI[1]. Leiden: E. J. Brill, 1913–38.

EI[2]. Leiden: E. J. Brill, 1954–present.

Engineer, Asghar Ali. *The Bohras.* New Delhi: Vikas Publishing House, 1980.

Esposito, John L. *Islam: The Straight Path.* New York: Oxford University Press, 1988.

Falaturi, Abdoljavad. "Die Zwölfer-Schia aus der Sicht eines Schiiten: Probleme ihrer Untersuchung." In *Festschrift Werner Caskel,* 62–95. Ed. Erwin Graf. Leiden: E. J. Brill, 1968.

Faqīhī, 'Alī Aṣghar. *Āl-i Būyah va-awḍā'-i zamān-i īshān.* Tehran: Intishārāt-i ṣabā, 1986.

Faruqi, Ismā'īl. *Islam.* Brentwood, Maryland: International Graphics, 1984.

Fischer, Michael M. J. *Iran: From Religious Dispute to Revolution.* Cambridge: Harvard University Press, 1980.

Friedlander, I. "The Heterodoxies of the Shiites in the Presentation of Ibn Ḥazm." *JAOS* 28 (1907): 1–80; 29 (1908): 1–183.

Gardet, Louis. *L'Islam: Religion et communauté.* Paris: Desclée De Brouwer, 1967.

———, and M. M. Anawati. *Introduction à la théologie musulmane: Essai de théologie comparée.* 3d ed. Paris: Librairie philosophique J. Vrin, 1981.

al-Ghazālī, Abū Ḥāmid Muḥammad. *Fayṣal al-tafriqah bayn al-islām wa'l-zandaqah.* Cairo: Maṭba'at al-sa'ādah, 1907.

———. *al-Mankhūl min ta'līqāt al-uṣūl.* Damascus: Dār al-fikr, 1980.

———. *al-Mustaṣfā min 'ilm al-uṣūl.* 2 vols. Cairo, 1906.

al-Ghazzī, Najm al-Dīn. *al-Kawākib al-sā'irah bi-a'yān al-mi'ah al-'āshirah.* 3 vols. Beirut: al-Maṭba'ah al-amīrkānīyah, 1945–58.

Glassen, Erika. "Schah Ismā'īl I. und die Theologen seiner Zeit." *Der Islam,* 48 (1972): 254–68.

Goffman, Erving. *Stigma: Notes on the Management of Spoiled Identity.* New York: Simon and Schuster, 1986.

Goldziher, Ignaz. *Introduction to Islamic Theology and Law.* Trans. Andras Hamori and Ruth Hamori. Princeton: Princeton University Press, 1980.

———. "Das Prinzip der *takijja* im Islam." In *Gesammelte Schriften,* 5: 59–72. Ed. Joseph Desomogyi. Hildesheim: Georg Olms Verlagsbuchhandlung, 1970.

———. *Die Ẓâhiriten, ihr Lehrsystem und ihre Geschichte.* Leipzig: O. Schulze, 1884.

———. *The Ẓāhirīs: Their Doctrine and Their History.* Trans. Wolfgang Behn. Leiden: E. J. Brill, 1971.

Hafsi, Ibrahim. "Recherches sur le genre 'Tabaqat' dans la litterature arabe." *Arabica* 23 (1976):227–65; 24 (1977): 1–41, 150–86.

Ḥājjī Khalīfah. *Kashf al-ẓunūn fī asāmī al-kutub wa'l-funūn.* 7 vols. Ed. Gustav Flügel.

Leipzig and London, 1835–58.

Hallaq, Wael B. "On the Authoritativeness of Sunni Consensus." *IJMES* 18 (1986): 427–54.

———. "On the Origins of the Controversy about the Existence of Mujtahids and the Gate of Ijtihad." *Studia Islamica* 63 (1986): 129–41.

———. "Was al-Shāfiʿī the Master Architect of Islamic Jurisprudence?" *IJMES* 25 (1993): 587–605.

———. "Was the Gate of Ijtihad Closed?" *IJMES* 16 (1984): 3–41.

Halm, Heinz. *Die Ausbreitung der šāfiʿitischen Rechtsschule von den Anfangen bis zum 8./14. Jahrhundert.* Wiesbaden: L. Reichert, 1974.

———. *Shiism.* Edinburgh: Edinburgh University Press, 1991.

al-Ḥamawī, Yāqūt. *Irshād al-arīb ilā maʿrifat al-adīb.* 7 vols. Ed. D. S. Margoliouth. London: Luzac, 1907.

———. *Muʿjam al-udabāʾ aw Irshād al-arīb ilā maʿrifat al-adīb.* 6 vols. Beirut: Dār al-kutub al-ʿilmīyah, 1991–93.

———. *Muʿjam al-buldān.* 7 vols. Beirut: Dār al-kutub al-ʿilmīyah, 1990.

Hasan, Ahmed. *The Doctrine of Ijmaʿ in Islam: A Study of the Juridical Principle of Consensus.* Islamabad: Islamic Research Institute, 1984.

Hāshimī, Maḥmūd. *Buḥūth fī al-fiqh: Kitāb al-khums.* 2 vols. Qum: Maktabat al-Sayyid Muḥammad al-Hāshimī, 1989.

al-Ḥillī, Ibn Dāʾūd Taqī al-Dīn al-Ḥasan b. ʿAlī. *Kitāb al-rijāl.* Najaf: al-Maṭbaʿah al-ḥaydarīyah, 1972.

al-Ḥillī, Jamāl al-Dīn al-Ḥasan b. Yūsuf Ibn al-Muṭahhar (al-ʿAllāmah al-Ḥillī). *Mabādiʾ al-wuṣūl.* Najaf: Maṭbaʿat al-ādāb, 1970.

———. *Rijāl al-ʿAllāmah al-Ḥillī (Khulāṣat al-aqwāl fī ʿilm al-rijāl).* Najaf: al-Maṭbaʿah al-ḥaydarīyah, 1961.

———. *Tahdhīb al-wuṣūl.* Tehran, 1890.

al-Ḥillī, Najm al-Dīn Jaʿfar b. al-Ḥasan (al-Muḥaqqiq al-Ḥillī). *Maʿārij al-uṣūl.* Ed. Muḥammad Ḥusayn al-Riḍawī. Qum: Maṭbaʿat Sayyid al-shuhadāʾ, 1983.

Hitti, Philip K. *History of the Arabs.* 10th ed. New York: St. Marten's Press, 1970.

Hodgson, Marshal G. S. *The Venture of Islam.* 3 vols. Chicago: University of Chicago Press, 1974.

———. "How Did the Shīʿa Become Sectarian?" *JAOS* 75 (1955): 1–13.

———. *The Order of Assassins: The Struggle of the Early Nizārī Ismāʿīlīs against the Islamic World.* The Hague: Mouton, 1955.

Hourani, Georges F. "The Basis of Authority of Consensus in Sunnite Islam." *Studia Islamica* 21 (1964): 13–60.

al-Ḥurr al-ʿĀmilī, Muḥammad b. al-Ḥasan. *Amal al-āmil fī ʿulamāʾ Jabal ʿĀmil.* 2 vols. Baghdad: Maktabat al-andalus, 1965–66.

———. *al-Fawāʾid al-ṭūsīyah.* Ed. Mahdī al-Lājiwardī al-Ḥusaynī and Muḥammad Durūdī. Qum: al-Maṭbaʿah al-ʿilmīyah, 1983.

[pseudo-] Ibn ʿAbbād, al-Ṣāḥib. *Nuṣrat madhāhib al-zaydīyah.* Ed. Nājī Ḥasan. Beirut: al-Dār al-muttaḥidah li'l-nashr, 1981.

Ibn Abī Yaʿlā, Muḥammad. *Ṭabaqāt al-ḥanābilah.* 2 vols. Ed. Muḥammad Ḥāmid al-Fiqī. Cairo: Maṭbaʿat al-sunnah al-muḥammadīyah, 1952.

Ibn al-Athīr, ʿIzz al-Dīn ʿAlī b. Muḥammad. *al-Kāmil fī al-tārīkh.* 13 vols. Beirut: Dār ṣādir and Dār bayrūt, 1965–66.

Ibn Bābawayh al-Qummī. *ʿIlal al-sharāʾiʿ.* Ed. Muḥammad Ṣādiq Baḥr al-ʿUlūm. Najaf: al-Maṭbaʿah al-ḥaydarīyah, 1963.

Ibn al-Fuwaṭī, ʿAbd al-Razzāq. *al-Ḥawādith al-jāmiʿah waʾl-tajārib al-nāfiʿah fī al-miʾah al-sābiʿah*. Baghdad: Maṭbaʿat al-Furāt, 1932.

Ibn Ḥajar al-ʿAsqalānī. *al-Durar al-kāminah fī aʿyān al-miʾah al-thāminah*. 4 vols. Ḥaydarābād: Maṭbaʿat majlis al-maʿārif al-ʿuthmānīyah, 1930.

———. *Lisān al-mīzān*. 7 vols. Ḥaydarābād: Maṭbaʿat majlis dāʾirat al-maʿārif al-niẓāmīyah, 1971.

Ibn al-Ḥājib. *Mukhtaṣar al-muntahā*. 2 vols. Cairo: Maktabat al-kullīyāt al-azharīyah, 1983.

Ibn Ḥazm. *al-Fiṣal fī al-milal waʾl-ahwāʾ waʾl-niḥal*. 5 vols. Cairo: Maṭbaʿat al-Khānjī, 1903.

———. *al-Iḥkām fī uṣūl al-aḥkām*. Cairo: Maktabat ʿĀṭif, 1978.

———. *Marātib al-ijmāʿ fīʾl-ʿibādāt waʾl-muʿāmalāt waʾl-muʿtaqadāt*. Beirut: Dār al-āfāq al-jadīdah, 1978.

———. *Mulakhkhaṣ ibṭāl al-qiyās waʾl-raʾy waʾl-istiḥsān waʾl-taqlīd waʾl-taʿlīl*. Ed. Saʿīd al-Afghānī. Damascus: Maṭbaʿat jāmiʿat dimashq, 1960.

Ibn al-ʿImād al-Ḥanbalī, ʿAbd al-Ḥayy. *Shadharāt al-dhahab fī akhbār man dhahab*. 8 vols. Cairo: Maktabat al-qudsī, 1932–33.

Ibn al-Jawzī. *al-Muntaẓam fī tārīkh al-mulūk waʾl-umam*. 18 vols. Ed. Muḥammad ʿAbd al-Qādir ʿAṭā and Muṣṭafā ʿAbd al-Qādir ʿAṭā. Beirut: Dār al-kutub al-ʿilmīyah, 1992.

Ibn Kathīr, ʿImād al-Dīn Ismāʿīl b. ʿUmar. *al-Bidāyah waʾl-nihāyah fī al-tārīkh*. 14 vols. Cairo: Maṭbaʿat al-saʿādah, 1939.

———. *Ṭabaqāt al-fuqahāʾ al-shāfiʿīyīn*. 3 vols. Ed. Aḥmad ʿUmar Hāshim and Muḥammad Zaynhum Muḥammad Gharb. Cairo: Maktabat al-thaqāfah al-dīnīyah, 1993.

Ibn Khaldūn. *The Muqaddimah: An Introduction to History*. 3 vols. Trans. Franz Rosenthal. New York: Pantheon Books, 1958.

Ibn Miskawayh. *Tajārib al-umam*. 2 vols. Tehran: Intishārāt-i zarrīn, 1987.

Ibn al-Mundhir. *al-Ijmāʿ*. Ed. Fuʾād ʿAbd al-Munʿim Aḥmad and ʿAbd Allāh b. Zayd Āl Maḥmūd. Al-Dawḥah, Qaṭar: Dār al-thaqāfah, 1987.

Ibn al-Murtaḍā, Aḥmad b. Yaḥyā. *al-Baḥr al-zakhkhār al-jāmiʿ li-madhāhib ʿulamāʾ al-amṣār*. 6 vols. Beirut: Muʾassasat al-risālah, 1975.

———. *Kitāb ṭabaqāt al-muʿtazilah*. Ed. Susanna Diwald-Wagner. Beirut: Dār al-muntaẓar, 1988.

Ibn al-Nadīm. *al-Fihrist*. Cairo: Maṭbaʿat al-istiqāmah, 1957.

———. *Kitāb al-fihrist*. 2 vols. Ed. Gustav Flügel. Leipzig: F. C. W. Vogel, 1871–72.

Ibn Qāḍī Shuhbah al-Asadī al-Dimashqī, Taqī al-Dīn Abū Bakr b. Aḥmad. *Tārīkh Ibn Qāḍī Shuhbah*. Vol. 1. Ed. ʿAdnān Darwīsh. Damascus: al-Maʿhad al-ʿilmī al-faransī liʾl-dirāsāt al-ʿarabīyah, 1977.

Ibn Qayyim al-Jawzīyah. *Iʿlām al-muwaqqiʿīn ʿan rabb al-ʿālamīn*. 4 vols. Beirut: Dār al-kutub al-ʿilmīyah, 1991.

Ibn Qudāmah al-Maqdisī, Muwaffaq al-Dīn ʿAbd Allāh. *Rawḍat al-nāẓir wa-jannat al-munāẓir*. Cairo: al-Maṭbaʿah al-salafīyah, 1965.

Ibn Quṭlūbughā, Zayn al-Dīn Qāsim. *Tāj al-tarājim fī ṭabaqāt al-ḥanafīyah*. Baghdad: Maṭbaʿat al-ʿĀnī, 1962.

Ibn Rajab ʿAbd al-Raḥman b. Aḥmad al-Baghdādī. *Kitāb al-dhayl ʿalā ṭabaqāt al-ḥanābilah*. 2 vols. Ed. Muḥammad Ḥāmid al-Fiqī. Cairo: Maṭbaʿat al-sunnah al-muḥammadīyah, 1953.

Ibn Shahrāshūb. *Maʿālim al-ʿulamāʾ*. Tehran, 1934.

Ibn Taymīyah, Taqī al-Dīn Aḥmad. *Kitāb minhāj al-sunnah al-nabawīyah fī naqḍ kalām al-shīʿah waʾl-qadarīyah*. 4 vols. Beirut: Dār al-kutub al-ʿilmīyah, 1973.

———. *al-Musawwadah fī uṣūl al-fiqh*. Ed. Muḥammad Muḥyī al-Dīn ʿAbd al-Ḥamīd.

Cairo: Maṭba'at al-madanī, 1964.

———. *Naqḍ al-manṭiq*. Ed. Muḥammad b. 'Abd al-Razzāq Ḥamzah, Sulaymān b. 'Abd al-Raḥmān al-Ṣanī', and Muḥammad Ḥāmid al-Fiqī. Cairo: Maṭba'at al-sunnah al-muḥammadīyah, 1951.

———. *Naqḍ marātib al-ijmā'*. Printed with Ibn Ḥazm. *Marātib al-ijmā' fī al-'ibādāt wa'l-mu'āmalāt wa'l-mu'taqadāt*. Beirut: Dār al-āfāq al-jadīdah, 1978.

———. *al-Radd 'alā al-manṭiqīyīn*. Ed. 'Abd al-Ṣamad Sharaf al-Dīn al-Kutubī. Bombay: Maṭba'at al-qayyimah, 1949.

———. *al-Siyāsah al-shar'īyah fī iṣlāḥ al-ra'īyah*. Beirut: Dār al-āfāq al-jadīdah, 1983.

Ibn Ṭūlūn, Muḥammad. *al-A'immah al-ithnā-'ashar*. Ed. Ṣalāḥ al-Dīn al-Munajjid. Beirut, 1958.

———. *al-Fulk al-mashḥūn fī aḥwāl Muḥammad ibn Ṭūlūn*. Damascus: Maṭba'at al-taraqqī, 1929.

Ibn Zuhrah al-Ḥalabī, Ḥamzah b. 'Alī. *Ghunyat al-nuzū'*. In *al-Jawāmi' al-fiqhīyah*, 461–565. Qum: Maktabat al-Mar'ashī al-Najafī, 1983–84.

Ibn Zuhrah al-Ḥalabī, Tāj al-Dīn b. Muḥammad. *Ghāyat al-ikhtiṣār fī al-buyūtāt al-'alawīyah al-maḥfūẓah min al-ghubār*. Ed. Muḥammad Ṣādiq Baḥr al-'Ulūm. Najaf: al-Maṭba'ah al-ḥaydarīyah, 1962.

al-Ījī, 'Aḍud al-Dīn. *al-Ilāhīyāt wa'l-sam'īyāt min kitāb al-Mawāqif* (Statio Quinta et Sexta et Appendix Libri Mevakif). Ed. Th. Soerensen. Leipzig, 1848.

al-Iṣfahānī, Mīrzā 'Abd Allāh Afandī. *Riyāḍ al-'ulamā' wa-ḥiyāḍ al-fuḍalā'*. 6 vols. Ed. Aḥmad al-Ḥusaynī. Qum: Maṭba'at al-khayyām, 1980.

al-Isfarā'inī, Abū al-Muẓaffar. *al-Tabṣīr fī al-dīn wa-tamyīz al-firqah al-nājiyah 'an al-firaq al-hālikīn*. Ed. Muḥammad Zāhid b. al-Ḥasan al-Kawtharī. Cairo: Maktabat al-Khānjī, 1955.

al-Isnawī, Jalāl al-Dīn 'Abd al-Raḥmān. *Nihāyat al-sūl fī sharḥ Minhāj al-wuṣūl ilā 'ilm al-uṣūl*. 3 vols. Cairo: Maṭba'at Muḥammad 'Alī Ṣubayḥ, 1969.

———. *Ṭabaqāt al-shāfi'īyah*. 2 vols. Ed. Kamāl Yūsuf al-Ḥūt. Beirut: Dār al-kutub al-'ilmīyah, 1987.

Jafri, S. H. M. art. "al-Ḥillī." *EI*².

al-Jāḥiẓ. *Kitāb al-ḥayawān*. 7 vols. Cairo, 1905–7.

al-Jaṣṣāṣ. *al-Fuṣūl fī al-uṣūl*. 4 vols. Ed. 'Ujayl Jāsin al-Nashmī. Kuwait: Wizārat al-awqāf wa'l-shu'ūn al-islāmīyah, 1985–93.

———. *al-Fuṣūl fī al-uṣūl (abwāb al-ijtihād wa'l-qiyās)*. Ed. Saeedullah Qazi. Lahore: al-Maktabah al-'ilmīyah, 1981.

———. *al-Ijmā'*. Ed. Zuhayr Shafīq Kabbī. Beirut: Dār al-muntakhab al-'arabī, 1993.

al-Jazā'irī, Ni'mat Allāh. *al-Anwār al-nu'mānīyah*. 4 vols. Tabriz, 1954–59.

———. *Kitāb manba' al-ḥayāt wa-ḥujjīyat qawl al-mujtahid min al-amwāt*. Printed with Muḥammad Muḥsin al-Fayḍ al-Kāshānī. *al-Shihāb al-thāqib fī wujūb ṣalāt al-jum'ah al-'aynī*. Beirut: Mu'assasat al-a'lamī li'l-maṭbū'āt, 1981.

———. *Zahr al-rabī'*. Beirut: Mu'assasat al-balāgh, 1990.

al-Jazarī, Muḥammad b. Muḥammad. *Ghāyat al-nihāyah fī ṭabaqāt al-qurrā'*. 3 vols. Ed. G. Bergstrasser. Cairo: Maṭba'at al-sa'ādah, 1933.

al-Jizzīnī, Muḥammad b. Makkī (al-Shahīd al-Awwal). *Arba'ūn ḥadīth*. Tehran: n. pub., 1900–1901.

———. *Dhikrā al-shī'ah*. Tehran, 1854–55.

———. *al-Qawā'id wa'l-fawā'id* (Tehran, 1890–91). 2d ed. 2 vols. Ed. al-Sayyid 'Abd al-Hādī al-Ḥakīm. Qum: Maktabat al-Mufīd, 1980.

al-Jubūrī, Ḥusayn Khalaf. *al-Aqwāl al-uṣūlīyah li'l-Imām Abī al-Ḥasan al-Karkhī* Medina: al-Jubūrī, 1989.

al-Juwaynī, Imām al-Ḥaramayn. *al-Burhān fī uṣūl al-fiqh*. 2 vols. Cairo, 1980.

———. *Kitāb al-ijtihād min kitāb al-talkhīṣ*. Damascus: Dār al-qalam, 1987.

———. *al-Waraqāt*. Cairo: Maṭba'at al-Madanī, n.d.

al-Karājakī, Abū al-Fatḥ Muḥammad b. 'Alī. *Kanz al-fawā'id*. Tabrīz, 1904–5.

———. *Kanz al-fawā'id*. 2 vols. Ed. 'Abd Allāh Ni'mah. Beirut: Dār al-aḍwā', 1985.

al-Karakī, Ḥusayn b. Shihāb al-Dīn. *Hidāyat al-abrār ilā ṭarīq al-a'immah al-aṭhār*. Ed. Ra'ūf Jamāl al-Dīn. Najaf, 1977.

al-Karkhī, al-Ḥasan. *al-Uṣūl allatī 'alayhā madār furū' al-ḥanafiyah*. Printed with 'Ubayd b. 'Īsā al-Dabūsī. *Ta'sīs al-naẓar*. Ed. Muṣṭafā Muḥammad al-Qabbānī al-Dimashqī. Beirut: Dār Ibn Zaydūn, n.d.

al-Kāshānī, Muḥsin al-Fayḍ. *Safīnat al-najāt*. Ed. Muḥammad Riḍā al-Naqūsānī. Tehran, 1960.

———. *Tashīl al-sabīl bi'l-ḥujjah fī intikhāb Kashf al-maḥajjah li-thamrat al-muhjah*.Tehran: Mu'assasat al-buḥūth wa'l-taḥqīqāt, 1987.

Kāshif al-Ghiṭā', Muḥammad al-Ḥusayn. *Aṣl al-shī'ah wa-uṣūluhā*. 9th ed. Beirut: Dār al-biḥār, 1960.

al-Kashshī, Muḥammad b. 'Umar. *Kitāb al-rijāl*. Karbalā': Mu'assasat al-a'lamī li'l-maṭbū'āt, 1961.

Khalidi, Tarif. *Islamic Historiography: The Histories of Mas'ūdī*. Albany: State University of New York Press, 1975.

al-Khaṭīb al-Baghdādī. *Kitāb al-faqīh wa'l-mutafaqqih*. 2 vols. Ed. Ismā'īl al-Anṣārī. Beirut: Dār al-kutub al-'ilmīyah, 1980.

———. *Tārīkh Baghdād aw Madīnat al-salām*. 14 vols. Cairo: Maktabat al-Khānjī, 1931.

al-Khurramshahrī, Bāqir al-Muḥsinī. *al-Fatāwā li-Ibn al-Junayd al-Iskāfī*. Qum: al-Maṭba'ah al-'ilmīyah, 1991.

al-Khwānsārī, Muḥammad Bāqir. *Rawḍāt al-jannāt fī aḥwāl al-'ulamā' wa'l-sādāt*. 8 vols. Beirut: al-Dār al-islāmīyah, 1991.

Klemm, Verena. "Die vier sufarā' des Zwölften Imāms." *Die Welt des Orients* 15 (1984): 126–43.

Kohlberg, Etan. art. "Akbārīya," *Encyclopaedia Iranica*.

———. "Aspects of Akhbari Thought in the Seventeenth and Eighteenth Centuries." In *Eighteenth-Century Renewal and Reform in Islam*, 133–60. Ed. Nehemiah Levtzion and John O. Voll. Syracuse: Syracuse University Press, 1987.

———. art. "Bahā' al-Dīn 'Āmelī." *Encyclopaedia Iranica*.

———. "From Imāmiyya to Ithnā-'ashariyya." *BSOAS* 39 (1976): 521–34.

———. "Imām and Community in the Pre-Ghayba Period." In *Authority and Political Culture in Shi'ism*, 25–53. Ed. Said Amir Arjomand. Albany: State University of New York Press, 1988.

———. *A Medieval Muslim Scholar at Work: Ibn Ṭāwūs and His Library*. Leiden: E. J. Brill, 1992.

———. "Some Imāmī Shī'i Views on the *Ṣaḥāba*." *Jerusalem Studies in Arabic and Islam* 5 (1984): 143–75.

———. "Some Imāmī Shī'i Views on Taqiyya." *JAOS* 95 (1975): 395–402.

———. "Some Notes on the Imāmite Attitude to the Qur'ān." In *Islamic Philosophy and the Classical Tradition: Essays Presented by his Friends and Pupils to Richard Walzer on his Seventieth Birthday*, 209–24. Ed. S. M. Stern et al. Oxford: Cassirer Press, 1972.

———. "The Term Rāfiḍa in Imāmī Shīʿī Usage." *JAOS* 99 (1979): 39–47.

———. "Western Studies of Shi'a Islam." In *Shi'ism, Resistance, and Revolution,* 31–44. Ed. Martin Kraemer. Boulder: Westview Press, 1987.

Kraemer, Joel L. *Humanism in the Renaissance of Islam: The Cultural Revival during the Buyid Age.* 2d revised ed. Leiden: E. J. Brill, 1992.

al-Kulaynī, Muḥammad b. Yaʿqūb. *al-Kāfī.* 8 vols. Beirut: Dār al-aḍwāʾ, 1985.

al-Laknawī, Sayyid Dildār ʿAlī b. Muḥammad. *Asās al-uṣūl.* Bombay: Maṭbaʿah-yi muḥammadīyah, 1848.

Lambton, Anne K. S. "A Reconsideration of the Position of *Marjaʿ al-Taqlīd* and the Religious Institution." *Studia Islamica* 20 (1964): 115–35.

Lammens, Henri. *Islam: Beliefs and Institutions.* Trans. Sir E. Dennison Ross. London: Frank Cass and Co., 1968.

Lane, Edward. *Arabic English Lexicon.* 2 vols. Cambridge: Islamic Texts Society, 1984.

Laoust, Henri. art. "al-Barbahārī." *EI*².

———. "La Classification des Sectes dans le *Farq* d'al-Baghdādī." *Revue des études islamiques* 29 (1961): 19–59.

———. "Comment définir le sunnisme et le chiisme." *Révue des études islamiques* 47 (1979): 3–17.

———. *Essai sur les doctrines sociales et politiques de Takī-d-Dīn Aḥmad b. Taimīya.* Cairo, 1939.

———. *Les Schismes dans l'islam: Introduction à une étude de la religion musulmane.* Paris: Payot, 1965.

Lapidus, Ira M. "The Separation of State and Religion." *IJMES* 6 (1975): 363–85.

———. *A History of Islamic Societies.* Cambridge: Cambridge University Press, 1988.

Layish, Aharon. "*Taqiyya* among the Druzes." *Asian and African Studies* 19 (1985): 245–81.

Levi della Vida, G. art. "Salmān al-Fārisī." *EI*¹.

Lewis, Bernard. "The Shīʿa in Islamic History." In *Shi'ism, Resistance, and Revolution,* 21–30. Ed. Martin Kraemer. Boulder: Westview Press, 1987.

———. "Some Observations on the Significance of Heresy in the History of Islam." *Studia Islamica* 1 (1953): 43–63.

Lockhart, Laurence. *Nadir Shah: A Critical Study Based Mainly upon Contemporary Sources.* London: Luzac & Co., 1938.

Löschner, Harald. *Die dogmatischen Grundlagen des šīʿitischen Rechts: Eine Untersuchungen zur modernen imamitischen Rechtsquellenlehre.* Cologne: Carl Heymanns Verlag, 1971.

McDermott, Martin J. *The Theology of al-Shaikh al-Mufīd (d. 413/1022).* Beirut: Dār al-mashriq, 1978.

MacDonald, Duncan Black. *Development of Muslim Theology, Jurisprudence and Constitutional Theory.* New York: Charles Scribner's Sons, 1903.

MacEoin, Denis. "Orthodoxy and Heterodoxy in Nineteenth-Century Shī'ism: The Cases of Shaykhism and Babism." *JAOS* 110 (1990): 323–29.

———. "Changes in Charismatic Authority in Qajar Shīʿism." In *Qajar Iran: Political, Social, and Cultural Change 1800–1925,* 148–76. Ed. E. Bosworth and C. Hillenbrand. Edinburgh: Edinburgh University Press, 1983.

Madelung, Wilferd. art. "Abū Sahl Nawbakhtī." *Encyclopaedia Iranica.*

———. art. "Akhbāriyya." *EI*², Supplement.

———. "Authority in Twelver Shiism in the Absence of the Imam." In *La Notion d'authorité au Moyen-Age: Islam, Byzance, Occident,* 163–73. Ed. George Makdisi, Dominique

Sourdel, and Janine Sourdel-Thomine. Colloques internationaux de la Napoule, 1978. Paris: Presses universitaires de France, 1982.

———. "Einige Werke des Imams Abū Ṭālib an-Nāṭiq bi l-Ḥaqq." *Der Islam* 63 (1986): 1–10.

———. art. "Hishām b. al-Ḥakam." *EI*².

———. art. "Imāma." *EI*².

———. "Imamism and Mu'tazilite Theology." In *Le Shī'isme Imāmite*, 15–30. Ed. Tawfiq Fahd. Paris: Presses universitaires françaises, 1970.

———. art. "'Iṣma." *EI*².

———. art. "al-Karakī." *EI*².

———. "The Sources of Ismā'īlī Law." *JNES* 35 (1976): 29–40.

———. *The Succession to Muḥammad: A Study of the Early Caliphate.* Cambridge: Cambridge University Press, 1997.

Maghniyah, Aḥmad. *Imām Ja'far al-Ṣādiq: 'Arḍ wa-dirāsah.* Beirut: Maktabat al-andalus, 1958.

Majlisī, Muḥammad Bāqir. *Biḥār al-anwār.* 26 vols. Tehran, 1884–97.

———. ———. 110 vols. Tehran: al-Maktabah al-islāmīyah, 1956–72.

Makdisi, George. "Ash'arī and the Ash'arites in Islamic Religious History." *Studia Islamica* 17(1962): 37–80; 18 (1963): 19–39.

———. "La Corporation à l'époque classique de l'Islam." In *Présence de Louis Massignon: Hommages et témoignages,* 35–49. Ed. Daniel Massignon. Paris: Maisonneuve et Larose, 1987.

———. "The Guilds of Law in Medieval Legal History: An Inquiry into the Origins of the Inns of Court." *Zeitschrift für Geshichte der Arabisch-Islamischen Wissenschaften* 1 (1984): 233–52.

———. *Ibn 'Aqīl et la résurgence de l'Islam traditionalist au XIe siècle (Ve siècle de l'Hégire).* Damascus: Institut français de Damas, 1963.

———. "L'Islam Hanbalisant." *Revue des Ètudes Islamiques* 42 (1974): 211–44; 43 (1975): 45–76.

———. "The Juridical Theology of Shāfi'ī: Origins and Significance of Uṣūl al-fiqh." *Studia Islamica* 59 (1984): 5–47.

———. "Muslim Institutions of Learning in Eleventh-Century Baghdad." *BSOAS* 24 (1961): 1–56.

———. "Notes on Ḥilla and the Mazyadids in Medieval Islam." *JAOS* 74 (1954): 249–62.

———. *The Rise of Colleges: Institutions of Learning in Islam and the West.* Edinburgh: Edinburgh University Press, 1981.

———. *The Rise of Humanism in Classical Islam and the Christian West with Special Reference to Scholasticism.* Edinburgh: Edinburgh University Press, 1990.

———. "Scholasticism and Humanism in Classical Islam and the Christian West." *JAOS* 109 (1989): 175–82.

———. "The Significance of the Sunni Schools of Law in Islamic Religious History." *IJMES* 10 (1979): 1–8.

———. "*Ṭabaqāt*-Biography: Law and Orthodoxy in Classical Islam." *Islamic Studies* 32 (1993): 371–96.

Mānakdīm Aḥmad al-Ḥusaynī, Sayyid. *Sharḥ al-uṣūl al-khamsah.* Ed. 'Abd al-Karīm 'Uthmān. Cairo: Maṭba'at wahbah, 1965.

al-Maqrīzī, Taqī al-Dīn Ahmad b. 'Alī. *al-Mawā'iẓ wa'l-i'tibār bi-dhikr al-khiṭaṭ wa'l-āthār.* 2 vols. Cairo: Bulaq, 1854.

Massignon, Louis. "Cadis et Naqībs bagdadiens." *Wiener Zeitschrift für die Kunde des Morgenlandes* 51 (1948): 106–15. Reprinted in his *Opera Minora*, vol.1, 259–65 . Ed. Y. Moubarac. Beirut: Dār al-ma'ārif, 1963.

al-Mas'ūdī, Abū al-Ḥasan. *Kitāb al-Tanbīh wa'l-ishrāf.* Bibliotheca Geographorum Arabicorum, 8. Ed. M. J. de Goeje. Leiden: E. J. Brill, 1894.

———. *Murūj al-dhahab wa-ma'ādin al-jawhar.* 4 vols. Ed. Qāsim al-Shammā'ī al-Rifā'ī. Beirut: Dār al-qalam, 1989.

———. *Les Prairies d'or.* 2 vols. Trans. Barbier de Maynard et Pavet de Courteille, revue et corrigée par Charles Pellat. Paris: Centre national de la recherche scientifique, 1962.

al-Māwardī, 'Alī b. Muḥammad. *Adab al-qāḍī.* 2 vols. Baghdad: Maṭba'at al-irshād, 1971.

Mazzaoui, Michel M. *The Origins of the Ṣafawids: Shī'ism, Ṣūfism, and the Ġulāt.* Wiesbaden: Franz Steiner, 1972.

Melchert, Cristopher. "Sectaries in the Six Books: Evidence for their Exclusion from the Sunni Community." *The Muslim World* 82 (1992): 287–95.

Miquel, André. *La Géographie humaine du monde musulman jusqu'au milieu du XIe siècle.* Paris: Mouton, 1967.

Modarressi, Hossein. *Crisis and Consolidation in the Formative Period of Shi'ite Islam.* Princeton: Darwin Press, 1993.

———. *An Introduction to Shī'ī Law: A Biographical Study.* London: Ithaca Press, 1984.

———. "Rationalism and Traditionalism in Shī'ī Jurisprudence: A Preliminary Survey." *Studia Islamica* 59 (1984): 141–58.

Mohaghegh, M. art. "al-Kātibī." *EI*².

Momen, Moojan. *An Introduction to Shi'i Islam: The History and Doctrines of Twelver Shi'ism.* New Haven: Yale University Press, 1985.

Mottahedeh, Roy. *Loyalty and Leadership in an Early Islamic Society.* Princeton: Princeton University Press, 1980.

———. *The Mantle of the Prophet: Religion and Politics in Iran.* New York: Simon and Schuster, 1985.

Moussavi, Ahmad Kazemi. "The Establishment of Marja'iyyat-i Taqlid in the Twelver-Shi'i Community." *Iranian Studies* 18 (1985): 35–51.

———. *Religious Authority in Shi'ite Islam: From the Office of Mufti to the Institution of Marja'.* Kuala Lumpur: International Institute of Islamic Thought and Civilization, 1996.

Mudarris, Mīrzā Muḥammad 'Alī. *Rayḥānat al-adab fī tarājim al-ma'rūfīn bi'l-kunyah wa'l-laqab.* 2d ed. 8 vols. Tabriz: Chāp-khānah-yi shafaq, 1967–70.

al-Mufīd, al-Shaykh (Muḥammad b. Muḥammad b. al-Nu'mān). *Awā'il al-maqālāt fī al-madhāhib al-mukhtārāt.* Ed. 'Abbās Qulī Wā'iẓ Charandābī and Faḍl Allāh al-Zanjānī. Tabriz: Maktabah-yi ḥaqīqat, 1951.

———. *al-Fuṣūl al-mukhtārah min al-'uyūn wa'l-maḥāsin.* Qum: Maṭba'at mihr, 1983.

———. *'Iddat rasā'il li'l-Shaykh al-Mufīd.* Qum: Maktabat al-Mufīd, n.d.

———. *al-Masā'il al-ṣāghānīyah fī al-radd 'alā Abī Ḥanīfah.* Najaf: al-'Adl al-islāmī, n.d.

———. *al-Masā'il al-sarawīyah.* In his *'Iddat rasā'il li'l-Shaykh al-Mufīd,* 207–32. Qum: Maktabat al-Mufīd, n.d.

———. *al-Muqni'ah.* Qum: Mu'assasat al-nashr al-islāmī, 1989–90.

al-Muhājir, Ja'far. *al-Hijrah al-'Āmilīyah ilā Īrān fī al-'aṣr al-ṣafawī: Asbābuhā al-tārīkhīyah wa-natā'ijuhā al-thaqāfīyah wa'l-siyāsīyah.* Beirut: Dār al-rawḍah, 1989.

———. *Sittat fuqahā' abṭāl.* Beirut: al-Majlis al-islāmī al-shī'ī al-a'lā, 1994.

al-Muḥaqqiq al-Ḥillī. See al-Ḥillī, Najm al-Dīn Ja'far b. al-Ḥasan.

Munshī, Iskandar Beg. *Tārīkh-i 'ālam-ārā-yi 'abbāsī.* 2 vols. Tehran: Chāpkhānah-yi gulshan, 1971.

al-Muntaẓirī, Āyat Allāh al-'Uẓmā. *Dirāsāt fī wilāyat al-faqīh wa-fiqh al-dawlah al-islāmīyah.* 2 vols. Qum: Maktab al-i'lām al-islāmī, 1988.

al-Murādī, Muḥammad Khalīl. *Silk al-durar fī a'yān al-qarn al-thānī 'ashar.* 4 vols. Bulaq, 1874.

al-Murtaḍā, al-Sharīf ('Alī b. al-Ḥusayn al-Mūsawī). *al-Dharī'ah ilā uṣūl al-sharī'ah.* 2 vols. Ed. Abū al-Qāsim Gorjī. Tehran: Intishārāt-i dānishgāh-i Tehran, 1967–69.

———. *al-Intiṣār.* Ed. Sayyid Muḥammad Riḍā b. Ḥasan al-Kharsān. Beirut: Dār al-aḍwā', 1985.

———. *Rasā'il al-Sharīf al-Murtaḍā.* 4 vols. Qum: Maṭba'at al-khayyām, 1985–89.

———. *al-Shāfī fī al-imāmah.* 4 vols. Ed. Sayyid 'Abd al-Zahrā' al-Ḥusaynī al-Khaṭīb. Tehran: Mu'assasat al-Ṣādiq, 1986–87.

al-Muẓaffar, Muḥammad Riḍā. *Uṣūl al-fiqh.* 4 vols. Najaf: Dār al-nu'mān, 1966–67.

al-Najāshī, Abū al-'Abbās Aḥmad b. 'Alī. *Kitāb al-rijāl.* Qum: Markaz-i nashr-i kitāb, n.d.

Nanji, Azim. *The Nizārī Ismā'īlī Tradition in the Indo-Pakistan Subcontinent.* Delmar, New York: Caravan Books, 1978.

al-Nāṭiq bi-l-Ḥaqq, Abū Ṭālib Yaḥyā b. al-Ḥusayn b. Hārūn. *al-Di'āmah fī tathbīt al-imāmah.* Erroneously attributed to al-Ṣāḥib Ibn 'Abbād and published as *Nuṣrat madhāhib al-zaydīyah.* Ed. Nājī Ḥasan. Beirut: al-Dār al-muttaḥidah li'l-nashr, 1981.

Nemoy, Leon, ed. and trans. *Karaite Anthology.* New Haven: Yale University Press, 1952.

———. art. "The Karaites." *Encyclopaedia Judaica.*

Newman, Andrew. "The Myth of Clerical Migration to Safawid Iran: Arab Shiite Opposition to 'Alī al-Karakī and Safawid Shiism." *Die Welt des Islams* 33 (1993): 66–112.

———. "The Nature of the Akhbārī/Uṣūlī Dispute in Late Ṣafawid Iran. Pt. 1: 'Abdallāh al-Samāhijī's *Munyat al-mumārisīn.* Pt. 2: The Conflict Reassessed." *BSOAS* 15 (1992): 22–51, 250–61.

———. "Towards a Reconsideration of the 'Isfahan School of Philosophy': Shaykh Bahā'ī and the Role of the Safawid 'Ulamā'." *Studia Iranica,* 15 (1986): 165–98.

al-Nīsābūrī, al-Ḥākim. *Ma'rifat 'ulūm al-ḥadīth.* Beirut: Dār maktabat al-hilāl, 1989.

al-Nu'aymī, 'Abd al-Qādir b. Muḥammad. *al-Dāris fī tārīkh al-madāris,* 2 vols. Ed. Ja'far al-Ḥanafī. Cairo: Maktabat al-thaqāfah al-dīnīyah, 1988.

al-Nu'mānī, Ibn Abī Zaynab Muḥammad b. Ibrāhīm b. Ja'far. *al-Ghaybah.* Beirut: Mu'assasat al-a'lamī li'l-maṭbū'āt, 1983.

Pellat, Charles. art. "al-Mas'ūdī." *EI*[2].

Peters, Johannes Reiner Theodorus Maria. *God's Created Speech: A Study in the Speculative Theology of the Mu'tazilī Qāḍī al-Quḍāt Abū l-Ḥasan 'Abd al-Jabbār Ibn Aḥmad al-Hamaḍānī.* Leiden: E. J. Brill, 1976.

al-Qāḍī 'Abd al-Jabbār, al-Asadābādī. *al-Mughnī fī abwāb al-tawḥīd wa'l-'adl.* Vol. 17, *al-Shar'īyāt.* Ed. Ṭāhā Ḥusayn and Amīn al-Khōlī. Cairo: Wizārat al-thaqāfah, 1961.

al-Qāḍī al-Nu'mān. *Da'ā'im al-islām wa-dhikr al-ḥalāl wa'l-ḥarām wa'l-qaḍāyā wa'l-aḥkām.* 2 vols. Ed. 'Ārif Tāmir. Beirut: Dār al-aḍwā', 1995.

———. *Ikhtilāf uṣūl al-madhāhib.* Ed. S. T. Lokhandwalla. Simla, India: Indian Institute of Advanced Study, 1972.

al-Qalqashandī, Aḥmad b. 'Alī. *Ṣubḥ al-a'shā fī ṣinā'at al-inshā.* 17 vols. Cairo: al-Mu'assasah al-'āmmah, 1964.

al-Qarāfī, Shihāb al-Dīn Aḥmad b. Idrīs. *al-Furūq.* 4 vols. Beirut: 'Ālam al-kitāb, n.d.

———. *al-Iḥkām fī tamyīz al-fatāwā 'an al-aḥkām wa-taṣarrufāt al-qāḍī wa'l-imām.* Cairo: al-Maktab al-thaqāfī, 1989.

———. *Sharḥ tanqīḥ al-fuṣūl fī ikhtiṣār al-Maḥṣūl fī al-uṣūl.* Cairo: al-Maktabah al-azharīyah li'l-turāth, 1973.

Qazwīnī, 'Abd al-Jalīl. *Kitāb al-Naqḍ*. Ed. Mīr Jalāl al-Dīn Muḥaddith. Tehran, 1980.

al-Qirqisānī, Ya'qūb. *Kitāb al-anwār wa'l-marāqib*. 5 vols. Ed. Leon Nemoy. New York: Alexander Kohut Foundation, 1939–45.

al-Qummī, Mīrzā Abū al-Qāsim. *Qawānīn al-uṣūl*. Tehran, 1858–59.

al-Qummī, Muḥammad Taqī. "Qiṣṣat al-taqrīb." *Risālat al-islām* 11 (1959): 348–59.

al-Qurṭubī, Muḥammad b. Aḥmad. *al-Jāmi' li-aḥkām al-Qur'ān*. 20 vols. Beirut: Dār iḥyā' al-turāth al-'arabī, 1985.

Rahman, Fazlur. *Islam*. 2d ed. Chicago: University of Chicago Press, 1979.

al-Rāzī, Fakhr al-Dīn. *I'tiqādāt firaq al-muslimīn wa'l-mushrikīn*. Ed. 'Alī Sāmī al-Nashshār. Cairo: Maktabat al-nahḍah al-miṣrīyah, 1938.

Rāzī, Muḥammad Sharif. *Ganjīnah-yi dānishmandān*. 7 vols. Tehran, 1973.

al-Rāzī, Muntajab al-Dīn 'Alī b. 'Ubayd Allāh b. Bābawayh. *Fihrist asmā' 'ulamā' al-shī'ah wa-muṣannifīhim (Fihrist Muntajab al-Dīn)*. Ed. 'Abd al-'Azīz al-Ṭabāṭabā'ī. Beirut: Dār al-aḍwā', 1986.

Reinhart, A. Kevin. *Before Revelation: The Boundaries of Muslim Moral Thought*. Albany: State University of New York Press, 1995.

Repp, R. C. *The Müfti of Istanbul: A Study in the Development of the Ottoman Learned Hierarchy*. London: Ithaca Press, 1986.

Rizvi, Saiyid Athar Abbas. *A Socio-Intellectual History of the Isnā 'Asharī Shī'īs in India*. 2 vols. Canberra, Australia: Ma'rifat Publishing House, 1986.

Sabari, Simha. *Mouvements populaires à Bagdad à l'époque 'Abbaside, IXe-XIe Siècles*. Paris: Maisonneuve, 1981.

Sachedina, Abdulaziz Abdulhussein. *Islamic Messianism: The Idea of the Mahdi in Twelver Shi'ism*. Albany: State University of New York Press, 1981.

———. *The Just Ruler in Shi'ite Islam: The Comprehensive Authority of the Jurist in Imamite Jurisprudence*. Oxford: Oxford University Press, 1988.

———. "Al-Khums: The Fifth in the Imāmī Shī'ī Legal System." *JNES* 39 (1980): 275–89.

al-Ṣafadī, Ṣalāḥ al-Dīn Khalil b. Aybak. *al-Wāfī bi'l-wafayāt*. 17 vols. Istanbul: Maṭba'at al-dawlah, 1931.

al-Sakhāwī, Muḥammad b. 'Abd al-Raḥmān. *al-Ḍaw' al-lāmi' li-ahl al-qarn al-tāsi'*. 12 vols. Cairo: Dār al-kitāb al-islāmī, n.d.

Salati, Marco. "Ricerche sulo sciismo nell'Impero ottomano: Il viaggio di Zayn al-Dīn al-Šahīd al-Ṯānī a Istanbul al tempo di Solimano il Magnifico (952/1545)." *Oriente Moderno* 9 (1990): 81–92.

Salibi, K. S. "The Banū Jamā'a: A dynasty of Shāfi'ī jurists in the Mamluk period." *Studia Islamica* 9 (1958): 97–109.

———. art. "Ibn Djamā'a." EI^2.

al-Ṣan'ānī, Muḥammad b. Ismā'īl al-Amīr. *Uṣūl al-fiqh al-musammā bi-Ijābat al-sā'il sharḥ Bughyat al-āmil*. Ed. Ḥusayn b. Aḥmad al-Sayāghī and Muḥammad Ḥasan Maqbūlī al-Ahdal. Beirut: Mu'assasat al-risālah, 1988.

Santillana, David. *Istituzioni di diritto musulmano malichito con riguardo anche al sistema sciafiita*. vol. 2. Rome: Istituto per l'oriente, 1938.

al-Sarakhsī, Abū Bakr Muḥammad. *Uṣūl al-Sarkhsī*. 2 vols. Ed. Abū 'l-Wafā' al-Afghānī. Beirut: Dār al-ma'rifah, n.d.

Scarcia, Gianroberto. "Intorno alle controversie tra Aḫbārī e Uṣūlī presso gli imamiti di Persia." *Rivista degli Studi Orientali* 33 (1958): 211–50.

Schacht, Joseph. *The Origins of Muhammadan Jurisprudence*. Oxford: Clarendon Press, 1950.

Schmidtke, Sabine. *The Theology of al-'Allāma al-Ḥillī (d. 726/1325).* Berlin: Klaus Schwarz Verlag, 1991.

Sezgin, Fuat. *GAS.* 9 vols. Leiden: E. J. Brill, 1967–84.

al-Shāfi'ī, Muḥammad b. Idrīs. *Islamic Jurisprudence: Shāfi'ī's Risāla.* Trans. Majid Khadduri. Baltimore, Maryland: The Johns Hopkins Press, 1961.

———. *Kitāb al-umm.* 7 vols. Bulaq, 1902–6.

———. *al-Risālah.* Ed. Aḥmad Muḥammad Shākir. 2d ed. Cairo: Dār al-turāth, 1979.

al-Shahīd al-Awwal. See al-Jizzīnī, Muḥammad b. Makkī.

al-Shahīd al-Thānī. See al-'Āmilī, Zayn al-Dīn.

al-Shahrastānī, Abū al-Fatḥ Muḥammad b. 'Abd al-Karīm. *al-Milal wa'l-niḥal.* 2 vols. Ed. Abū 'Abd Allāh al-Sa'īd al-Mandūh. Beirut: Mu'assasat al-kutub al-thaqāfiyah, 1994.

Shaltūt, Maḥmūd. "Fatwā." *Risālat al-islām* 11 (1959): 227–28.

Shams al-Dīn, Muḥammad Riḍā. *Ḥayāt al-imām al-Shahīd al-Awwal.* Najaf: Maṭba'at al-gharī al-ḥadīthah, 1957.

al-Sha'rānī, 'Abd al-Wahhāb. *al-Ṭabaqāt al-ṣughrā.* Cairo: Maktabat al-qāhirah, 1970.

al-Shāṭibī, Ibrāhīm b. Mūsā. *al-Muwāfaqāt fī uṣūl al-sharī'ah.* 4 vols. Beirut: Dār al-kutub al-'ilmīyah, 1991.

al-Shawkānī, Muḥammad b. 'Alī. *Irshād al-fuḥūl ilā taḥqīq 'ilm al-uṣūl.* Ed. Abū Muṣ'ab Muḥammad Sa'īd al-Badrī. Beirut: Mu'assasat al-kutub al-thaqāfiyah, 1993.

Shboul, A. *Al-Mas'ūdī and His World.* London: Ithaca Press, 1979.

al-Shīrāzī al-Fayrūzābādī, Abū Isḥāq. *Kitāb al-luma' fī uṣūl al-fiqh.* Ed. Muḥammad Badr-al-Dīn al-Na'sānī al-Ḥalabī. Beirut: Dār al-nadwah al-islāmīyah, 1987–88.

———. *Ṭabaqāt al-fuqahā'.* Ed. Iḥsān 'Abbās. Beirut: Dār al-rā'id al-'arabī, 1970.

———. *al-Tabṣirah fī uṣūl al-fiqh.* Damascus: Dār al-fikr, 1980.

Sourdel, Dominique. "L'Imamisme vu par le Cheikh al-Mufīd." *Revue des Ètudes Islamiques* 40 (1972): 217–96.

———. art. "Karak Nūḥ." *EI*².

Stewart, Devin J. "A Biographical Notice on Bahā' al-Dīn al-'Āmilī (d. 1030/1621)." *JAOS* 111 (1991): 563–71.

———. "The First *Shaykh al-Islām* of the Safavid Capital Qazvin." *JAOS* 116 (1996): 387–405.

———. "The Humor of the Scholars: The Autobiography of Ni'mat Allāh al-Jazā'irī." *Iranian Studies* 22 (1991): 47–81.

———. "Ḥusayn b. 'Abd al-Ṣamad al-'Āmilī's Treatise for Sultan Suleiman and the Shī'ī Shāfi'ī Legal Tradition." *Islamic Law and Society* 4 (1997): 156–99.

———. "Popular Shi'ism in Medieval Egypt: Vestiges of Islamic Sectarian Polemics in Egyptian Arabic." *Studia Islamica* 84 (1996): 35–66.

———. "Taqiyyah as Performance: the Travels of Bahā' al-Dīn al-'Āmilī in the Ottoman Empire (991–93/1583–85)." *Princeton Papers in Near Eastern Studies* 4 (1996): 1–70.

Strothmann, Rudolf. "Recht der Ismailiten." *Der Islam* 31 (1954): 131–46.

———. art. "Shī'a." *EI*¹.

———. art. "Takiyya." *EI*¹.

Ṣubḥī, Aḥmad Muḥammad. *al-Zaydīyah.* Alexandria: al-Zahrā' li'l-i'lām al-'arabī, 1984.

al-Subkī, Tāj al-Dīn. *Jam' al-jawāmi'.* 2 vols. Cairo: 'Īsā al-Bābī al-Ḥalabī, n.d.

———. *Ṭabaqāt al-shāfi'īyah al-kubrā.* 10 vols. Ed. 'Abd al-Fattāḥ al-Ḥilw and Maḥmūd Muḥammad al-Ṭanāḥī. Cairo: Hajr, 1992.

al-Suwaydī, 'Abd Allāh b. al-Ḥusayn. *Mu'tamar al-Najaf.* Cairo: al-Maṭba'ah al-salafiyah, 1973. First printed as *al-Ḥujaj al-qāṭi'ah l'ittifāq al-firaq al-islāmīyah.* Cairo: Maṭba'at al-sa'ādah, 1905.

al-Suyūrī al-Ḥillī, Miqdād b. ʿAbd Allāh. *Naḍd al-qawāʿid al-fiqhīyah ʿalā madhhab al-imāmīyah.* Ed. al-Sayyid ʿAbd al-Laṭīf al-Kūhkamarī. Qum: Maktabat al-Marʿashī, 1983.

al-Suyūṭī, Jalāl al-Dīn. *Bughyat al-wuʿāt fī ṭabaqāt al-lughawīyīn waʾl-nuḥāt.* Cairo: Maṭbaʿat al-saʿādah, 1908.

———. *Kitāb al-taḥadduth bi-niʿmat Allāh.* In *Jalāl al-Dīn al-Suyūṭī,* vol. 2. Ed. Elizabeth M. Sartain. Cambridge: Cambridge University Press, 1975.

———. *al-Radd ʿalā man akhlad ilā al-arḍ wa-jahil ann al-ijtihād fī kull ʿaṣr farḍ.* Ed. Khalīl al-Mays. Beirut: Dār al-kutub al-ʿilmīyah, 1983.

al-Ṭabarī, Muḥammad b. Jarīr. *Tafsīr al-Ṭabarī: Jāmiʿ al-bayān ʿan taʾwīl al-Qurʾān.* 14 vols. Ed. Maḥmūd Muḥammad Shākir. Cairo: Dār al-maʿārif, 1961–69.

Ṭabāṭabāʾī, Sayyid Muḥammad Ḥusayn. *Shiʾite Islam.* Trans. Seyyed Hossein Nasr. Albany: State University of New York Press, 1975.

al-Ṭabrisī, Abū ʿAlī al-Faḍl b. al-Ḥasan. *Majmaʿ al-bayān.* 10 vols. Beirut: Dār al-maʿrifah, 1986.

al-Thaʿālibī al-Nīsābūrī, Abū Manṣūr ʿAbd al-Malik. *Tatimmat al-yatīmah,* vol. 1. Tehran: Maṭbaʿat fardīn, 1934.

al-Ṭihrānī, Aghā Buzurg. *al-Dharīʿah ilā taṣānīf al-shīʿah.* 26 vols. Beirut: Dār al-aḍwāʾ, 1983.

———. *Ṭabaqāt aʿlām al-shīʿah. Iḥyāʾ al-dāthir min al-qarn al-ʿāshir.* Ed. ʿAlī Naqī Munzavī. Tehran: Dānishgāh-i Tihrān, 1987.

al-Ṭūfī, Sulaymān b. ʿAbd al-Qawī. *ʿAlam al-jadhal fī ʿilm al-jadal.* Ed. Wolfhart Heinrichs. Wiesbaden: Franz Steiner, 1987.

Tunkābunī, Mīrzā Muḥammad. *Qiṣaṣ al-ʿulamāʾ.* Shiraz: Intishārāt ʿilmīyah islāmīyah, 1964.

Turkī, Abdel-Magid. "L'Ijmāʿ Ummat al-Muʾminīn entre la Doctrine et l'Histoire." *Studia Islamica* 59 (1984): 4–78.

al-Ṭūsī, Muḥammad b. al-Ḥasan. *Fihrist kutub al-shīʿah.* Ed. Sayyid Muḥammad Ṣādiq Baḥr al-ʿUlūm. Najaf: al-Maṭbaʿah al-ḥaydarīyah, 1961.

———. *al-Khilāf.* 3 vols. Tehran: Dār al-maʿārif al-islāmīyah, n.d.

———. *Ikhtiyār maʿrifat al-rijāl.* 2 vols. [= *Rijāl al-Kashshī,* printed with the *Taʿlīqah* of Mīr-i Dāmād Muḥammad Bāqir al-Ḥusaynī]. Ed. Sayyid Mahdī al-Rajāʾī. Qum: Muʾassasat Āl al-bayt, 1983–84.

———. *al-Istibṣār fīmā ikhtalaf min al-akhbār.* 4 vols. Ed. Sayyid Ḥasan al-Kharsān. Beirut: Dār al-aḍwāʾ, 1985.

———. *al-Mabsūṭ fī fiqh al-imāmīyah.* 3 vols. Ed. Sayyid Muḥammad Taqī al-Kashfī Tehran: al-Maṭbaʿah al-ḥaydarīyah, 1967.

———. *al-Nihāyah fī mujarrad al-fiqh waʾl-fatāwā.* Tehran, 1963.

———. *Tahdhīb al-aḥkām.* 10 vols. Ed. Sayyid Ḥasan al-Mūsawī al-Kharsān. Beirut: Dār al-aḍwāʾ, 1985.

———. *Talkhīṣ al-shāfī.* 3 vols. Ed. Sayyid Ḥusayn Baḥr al-ʿUlūm. Najaf: Maṭbaʿat al-ādāb, 1963.

———. *al-Tibyān fī tafsīr al-qurʾān.* 10 vols. Beirut and Najaf, 1972.

———. *ʿUddat al-uṣūl.* Tehran, 1896–97.

al-Tustarī, Asad Allāh b. Ismāʿīl al-Kāẓimī. *Kashf al-qināʿ ʿan wujūh ḥujjīyat al-ijmāʿ.* Qum: Muʾassasat Āl al-bayt li-iḥyāʾ al-turāth, n.d. Reprint of Bombay, 1899 ed.

al-Udfuwī, Jaʿfar b. Thaʿlab. *al-Ṭāliʿ al-saʿīd al-jāmiʿ li-asmāʾ al-ruwāt bi-aʿlā al-Ṣaʿīd.* Cairo: Maṭbaʿat al-Jamālīyah, 1914.

Watt, W. Montgomery. "Conditions of Membership of the Islamic Community." *Studia Islamica* 21 (1964): 5–12.

———. *The Formative Period of Islamic Thought.* Edinburgh: Edinburgh University Press, 1973.

Weiss, Bernard G. "Al-Āmidī on the Basis of Authority of Consensus." In *Essays on Islamic Civilization Presented to Niyazi Berkes,* 342–56. Ed. Donald P. Little. Leiden: E. J. Brill, 1976.

———. "The Primacy of Revelation in Classical Islamic Legal Theory as Expounded by Sayf al-Dīn al-Āmidī." *Studia Islamica* 59 (1984): 79–109.

———. *The Search for God's Law: Islamic Jurisprudence in the Writings of Sayf al-Dīn al-Āmidī.* Salt Lake City: University of Utah Press, 1992.

Zayd, Muṣṭafā. *al-Maṣlaḥah fī al-tashrī' al-islāmī wa-Najm al-Dīn al-Ṭūfī.* Cairo: Dār al-fikr al-'arabī, 1964.

Zebiri, Kate. *Maḥmūd Shaltūt and Islamic Modernism.* Oxford: Clarendon Press, 1993.

Index